Personifying Prehistory

The Bronze Age is frequently framed in social evolutionary terms. Viewed as the period which saw the emergence of social differentiation, the development of long-distance trade, and the intensification of agricultural production, it is seen as the precursor and origin-point for significant aspects of the modern world. This book presents a very different image of Bronze Age Britain and Ireland.

Drawing on the wealth of material from recent excavations, as well as a long history of research, it explores the impact of the post-Enlightenment 'othering' of the non-human on our understanding of Bronze Age society. There is much to suggest that the conceptual boundary between the active human subject and the passive world of objects, so familiar from our own cultural context, was not drawn in this categorical way in the Bronze Age; the self was constructed in relational rather than individualistic terms, and aspects of the non-human world such as pots, houses, and mountains were considered animate entities with their own spirit or soul. In a series of thematic chapters on the human body, artefacts, settlements, and landscapes, this book considers the character of Bronze Age personhood, the relationship between individual and society, and ideas around agency and social power. The treatment and deposition of things such as querns, axes, and human remains provide insights into the meanings and values ascribed to objects and places, and the ways in which such items acted as social agents in the Bronze Age world.

Joanna Brück is Professor of Archaeology at University College Dublin and was previously Professor of Archaeology at University of Bristol. Her primary area of research is the archaeology of Bronze Age Britain and Ireland. She is particularly interested in the treatment of the human body and concepts of the self; depositional practices and what these reveal about the meanings and values ascribed to objects; and the relationship between space and society including domestic architecture and the changing organisation of landscape. She co-organises the Bronze Age Forum and is an editor of *Archaeological Dialogues*. She has also conducted research on the archaeology and material culture of the revolutionary period in early twentieth century Ireland.

Personifying Prehistory

Relational Ontologies in Bronze Age Britain and Ireland

Joanna Brück

Great Clarendon Street, Oxford, OX2 6DP,
United Kingdom

Oxford University Press is a department of the University of Oxford.
It furthers the University's objective of excellence in research, scholarship,
and education by publishing worldwide. Oxford is a registered trade mark of
Oxford University Press in the UK and in certain other countries

© Joanna Brück 2019

The moral rights of the author have been asserted

First published 2019
First published in paperback 2021

Impression: 2

All rights reserved. No part of this publication may be reproduced, stored in
a retrieval system, or transmitted, in any form or by any means, without the
prior permission in writing of Oxford University Press, or as expressly permitted
by law, by licence or under terms agreed with the appropriate reprographics
rights organization. Enquiries concerning reproduction outside the scope of the
above should be sent to the Rights Department, Oxford University Press, at the
address above

You must not circulate this work in any other form
and you must impose this same condition on any acquirer

Published in the United States of America by Oxford University Press
198 Madison Avenue, New York, NY 10016, United States of America

British Library Cataloguing in Publication Data
Data available

Library of Congress Cataloging in Publication Data
Data available

ISBN 978-0-19-876801-2 (Hbk.)
ISBN 978-0-19-285825-2 (Pbk.)

Printed and bound by
CPI Group (UK) Ltd, Croydon, CR0 4YY

Links to third party websites are provided by Oxford in good faith and
for information only. Oxford disclaims any responsibility for the materials
contained in any third party website referenced in this work.

Acknowledgements

Many people have helped to shape my ideas about the Bronze Age. I am grateful to my colleagues at University College Dublin and University of Bristol for creating such stimulating and supportive environments in which to work. I have benefited from discussions over the years with friends and colleagues working on the prehistory of Britain, Ireland, and north-west Europe, and in particular from my PhD students and the many people who have presented their research at meetings of the Bronze Age Forum since its inception in 1999. The image captions in this volume tell their own stories of enchainment, for more than half of these were kindly supplied by colleagues; particular thanks to Anne Leaver, who redrew and edited several of the images, and to John Sunderland for the wonderful cover photos. I am especially grateful to David Fontijn, Ann Woodward, and Andy Jones (Southampton), who read and commented on a draft of this book; of course, only I can be held responsible for its shortcomings. I dedicate this book to the memory of Barry Raftery; his combination of healthy scepticism, intellectual engagement, and personal kindness were exactly what I needed at the start of my own Bronze Age journey.

Contents

List of Figures ix

1. Introduction: Identity and alterity in Bronze Age Britain and Ireland 1
2. Fragmenting the body 16
3. Object biographies 69
4. The living house 115
5. Social landscapes 163
6. Conclusion: The flow of life in Bronze Age Britain and Ireland 224

Bibliography 243
Index 291

List of Figures

2.1 Grave of the Boscombe Bowmen, Wiltshire	18
2.2 Sequence of intercutting inhumation burials at South Dumpton Down, Kent	21
2.3 Bodily relations: burials in barrows C49 and C83, Riggs, East Yorkshire	22
2.4 Cist 2 at Dryburn Bridge, East Lothian	26
2.5 Central grave in the barrow at Sutton Veny, Wiltshire	28
2.6 Bone belt hook from Wilsford barrow G15, Wiltshire	31
2.7 Inhumation and cremation burials at Middle Barn Farm, Warminster, Wiltshire	37
2.8 Cremation burial, funeral pyre, and fence/screen at Snail Down, Wiltshire	41
2.9 Body of a girl deposited in a field boundary at Golf Crossing, Wiltshire	43
2.10 Ring-barrow cemetery at Ballintaggart, County Down	44
2.11 Early Bronze Age barrow at Butcher's Rise, Cambridgeshire	45
2.12 Deposits of cremated human bone and pottery at South Hornchurch, Essex	53
2.13 Shoreline location of the Sculptor's Cave, Covesea, Moray	55
2.14 Composite male mummy from house 1370, Cladh Hallan, South Uist	58
2.15 Burial pit at Cliffs End Farm, Kent	59
2.16 Bundle of bones from Cliffs End Farm, Kent	60
3.1 Inhumation burial, Garton Slack, East Yorkshire	70
3.2 Spacer plate necklace from Grindlow, Derbyshire	73
3.3 Primary inhumation grave and grave goods in barrow 1, Irthlingborough, Northamptonshire	78
3.4 Grave 203, Barrow Hills, Oxfordshire	80
3.5 Central cremation burial in barrow 1, Barrow Hills, Oxfordshire	82
3.6 The Amesbury Archer and his grave goods	84

List of Figures

3.7 Macehead from Bush Barrow, Wiltshire	90
3.8 Axe and leather sheath from Brockagh, County Kildare	91
3.9 Hoard from Bloody Pool, Devon	93
3.10 Hoard from Bradley Fen, Cambridgeshire	97
3.11 Broken items from the shipwreck at Langdon Bay, Kent	100
3.12 Hoard from Ockham, Surrey	106
3.13 Ceramic forms of Earliest Iron Age date from East Anglia	110
4.1 Early Bronze Age 'house' at Corcreeghy, County Down	119
4.2 Early Bronze Age pit cluster at Cloghabreedy, County Tipperary	122
4.3 House 1, Ridlington, Rutland	126
4.4 Late Bronze Age roundhouse at Ballylegan, County Tipperary	127
4.5 Middle Bronze Age settlement at Cloghabreedy, County Tipperary	129
4.6 Middle Bronze Age roundhouse at Navidale, Sutherland	130
4.7 Longhouse at Barleycroft Farm, Cambridgeshire	133
4.8 Ringwork at Oliver Close Estate, Leyton, London	135
4.9 Buildings and other features at Reading Business Park/Green Park, Berkshire	136
4.10 Restructuring the landscape at South Hornchurch, Essex	138
4.11 The 'village' at Corrstown, County Londonderry	140
4.12 Ringwork at Mucking North Ring, Essex	143
4.13 Selection of non-ceramic finds from Potterne, Wiltshire	150
4.14 Late Bronze Age rampart, hearths, pits, and other features at the Breiddin, Powys	156
5.1 Cross section through part of the barrow at Upton Pyne, Devon	166
5.2 Tregarrick Tor and cairn cemetery, Cornwall	173
5.3 Inverted tree trunk at the centre of the monument at Holme-next-the-Sea, Norfolk	174
5.4 Barrow cemetery, rivers, and modern routeways at Bromfield, Shropshire	176
5.5 Burnt mound with wooden trough and pipes at Charlesland, County Wicklow	179
5.6 Anthropomorphic figure from Cloncreen Bog, County Offaly	180
5.7 The Dover boat during installation in Dover Museum	181
5.8 Relationship between hillforts, lakes, and votive deposits at Navan, County Armagh	185
5.9 Aggregate field system at Big Moor, Derbyshire	189

List of Figures

5.10	Coaxial field system around Rippon Tor, Dartmoor, Devon	190
5.11	Landscape zoning at Bradley Fen, Cambridgeshire	193
5.12	Early Bronze Age barrows and Middle Bronze Age boundaries in the east of England	197
5.13	Animal and human burials around the pond barrow at Down Farm, Dorset	202
5.14	Grave 4969, Barrow Hills, Oxfordshire	205
5.15	Dog burials from house 401, Cladh Hallan, South Uist	210
5.16	Antlers deposited in pit 77, Westcroft Road, Surrey	212
5.17	Crowding alley and sheep race at Hamilton, Leicestershire	215
5.18	Part of a wooden block-wheel from Edercloon, County Longford	216
5.19	Ravens and waterbirds on the Dunaverny flesh-hook	218

1

Introduction

Identity and alterity in Bronze Age Britain and Ireland

In 2004, excavation in advance of the construction of a bypass around Mitchelstown in County Cork uncovered a number of pits on the banks of the Gradoge River (Kiely and Sutton 2007). On the bottom of one of these pits, three pottery vessels and a ceramic spoon had been laid on two flat stones. The pots had been deposited in a row: at the centre of the row was a small vessel that clearly models a human face with eyes, a protruding nose and ears, and, at the base of the pot, two feet (cover images). Oak charcoal from the pit returned a date of 1916–1696 cal BC. This find calls into question one of the basic conceptual building blocks that underpins our own contemporary understanding of the world—the distinction between people and objects—for it hints that some artefacts may have been imbued with human qualities and agentive capacities. This book is about the relationship between Bronze Age people and their material worlds. It explores the impact of the post-Enlightenment 'othering' of the non-human on our understanding of Bronze Age society. As we shall see, there is in fact considerable evidence to suggest that the categorical distinctions drawn in our own cultural context, for example between subject and object, self and other, and culture and nature, were not recognized or articulated in the same way during this period. So too contemporary forms of instrumental reason—encapsulated in a particular understanding of what constitutes logical, practical action and in the distinction we make between the ritual and the secular—have had a profound effect on how we view the Bronze Age world.

What does the Bronze Age mean?

Our understanding of the Bronze Age has undoubtedly changed dramatically since Christian Jürgensen Thomsen first popularized the term in his famous formulation of the three-age system in 1836 (Morris 1992). The very notion of a 'Bronze Age' foregrounds concepts of technical efficiency and advancement that doubtless chimed with the preoccupations and cultural values of Thomsen's audience in the industrializing world in the nineteenth century. This vision of the period persisted until relatively recently, for example in the identification of different 'industrial stages' (e.g. Burgess 1968, 17; 1980, 277), characterized by changes in artefact type, mould technology, and alloy recipes. Equally influential was Childe's argument a century later (1930) that the Bronze Age smith was a primary catalyst of socio-economic transformation. Smiths, he suggested, were a detribalized caste of full-time specialists who travelled from place to place to obtain raw materials and to sell their products. Thus, he argued, international trade and innovation flourished and the European entrepreneurial spirit was born: the dynamism, independence, and inventiveness of European Bronze Age society, he proposed, were what distinguished it from the despotism of the Near East. This vision of the Bronze Age as the origin-point of contemporary European ideology and identity continues to resonate today. In 1994, the Council of Europe memorably identified the period as 'the first golden age of Europe' (Hølleland 2010) and, in more recent years, research programmes exploring innovation, connectivity, and identity during the European Bronze Age have been particularly successful in securing major European Union funding (e.g. Suchowska-Ducke et al. 2015).

Few today would concur with this proto-capitalist vision of the European Bronze Age economy, but rationalist and individualistic undertones continue to pervade our interpretations. In recent decades, dominant narratives of the European Bronze Age have identified a series of key characteristics thought to differentiate the period from the preceding Neolithic. The use of bronze, of course, is one, and an increasing dependence on its constituent materials, copper and tin (the sources of which are restricted in their distribution), appears to have resulted in a significant growth in the scale and intensity of long-distance exchange over the period. Since Childe first discussed the status of the smith, increasing specialization is considered to have played a key role in the development of social complexity, while the circulation of metals is thought to have facilitated the differential accumulation of wealth and to have provided new ways of marking and maintaining social difference resulting in the appearance of chiefly hierarchies (Earle 2002; Kristiansen and Earle 2015).

Yet the significance of metals continues to be a subject of debate, and it is now widely accepted that at the beginning of the period metals were just one of a range of desirable materials acquired via long-distance exchange networks that had developed during the Late Neolithic (Roberts 2009; Roberts and Frieman 2012). There has been considerable debate around how metalworking was introduced to the British Isles. For much of the early- and mid-twentieth century, it was widely accepted that either large-scale population movement—the migration of the so-called 'Beaker folk'—or smaller-scale incursions by Beaker metal-prospectors from continental Europe were key factors (e.g. Childe 1925, 329–31; Case 1966; Clarke 1970). With the decline in popularity of culture-historical approaches in the 1970s and 1980s, however, long-distance trade came to be viewed as the primary mechanism of social and economic change, and it has been suggested that emerging indigenous elites in Britain and Ireland adopted novel material culture (including metalwork) and social practices in processes of competitive emulation that would allow them to display and increase their social standing (Burgess and Shennan 1976; Thorpe and Richards 1984): the distant, foreign, and 'other' were viewed as a source of cosmological and political power, so that novel and exotic materials such as copper provided new ways of marking elite status (Needham 2000a; Garwood 2012). Recently, isotope and aDNA evidence (Chenery and Evans 2011; Parker Pearson et al. 2016; Olalde et al. 2018) have again raised the possibility of significant population movement and even large-scale population replacement by metal-using groups from the Continent during the first few centuries of the period.

The extent to which metals resulted in dramatic social change remains open to question, however. In southern England, recent programmes of radiocarbon dating have demonstrated that some of the largest elements of Late Neolithic ceremonial complexes such as Stonehenge and Avebury were built around 2500 BC and in the subsequent two to three centuries, suggesting that, whatever the mechanism, processes of innovation and change did not always involve the wholesale or immediate replacement of one set of 'traditions' by another (Cleal and Pollard 2012). The social practices that characterized early metal-using communities on the Continent were not adopted wholesale in Britain and Ireland but adapted to local concerns and conditions: in Ireland, Beaker ceramics were deposited not with single inhumations in earth-cut graves but in pit deposits and with cremation burials in communal wedge tombs that can be seen as the reinvention of earlier traditions of megalithic burial (Carlin and Brück 2012).

Although exchange is now seen as socially embedded rather than motivated solely by economic imperatives, in fact the chiefs that populate recent accounts of the European Bronze Age are conjured as entrepreneurial individuals who accumulate wealth through trade to enhance their social position (Kristiansen 1998; Earle 2002; Kristiansen and Larsson 2005). Prestige is now considered the primary currency of Bronze Age exchange, but this model retains distinctly capitalist underpinnings, for it views competitive individualism as the key stimulus of social change (Brück and Fontijn 2013; Fowler 2013, 87–8). This understanding of the character and origins of power is problematic, for it depends on a categorical distinction between subject and object. The literature is peopled with active, powerful chiefs (usually figured as male) who have the capacity to manipulate, control, and dispose of objects in strategies of accumulation, aggrandizement, and display.

This vision of objects as passive and inert, and our continued tendency to view them as mere indices of wealth and status, is, however, a product of capitalist ideology. As we shall see, Bronze Age objects were not viewed solely as a source of economic and social capital. On the one hand, they embodied cultural values and moral imperatives. On the other, they too were conjured as active social agents. Bound into complex and often lengthy exchange histories, they formed inextricable components of the self. Anthropological studies describe how the objects that circulate in gift-exchange economies are viewed as inalienable (e.g. Mauss 1990 [1954]; Weiner 1992): they cannot ever be fully separated from the giver, and their circulation as part of core social transactions (for example as bridewealth) is essential to the creation of the human subject, for they generate key interpersonal relationships and they bring to those relationships particular qualities and values. Personal identity and worth are made evident by the gifts one is given; the attributes of these objects both reflect and constitute the self.

So too the vision of the Bronze Age chief is dependent on a formulation of personhood that is characteristic of the modern, Western world and that has, often unthinkingly, been imposed on the past. The widespread appearance of traditions of single burial is considered to indicate the development of increasingly competitive and hierarchical societies in which the status of the dead was directly reflected in the objects that accompanied them into the grave. Implicit within this view is a categorical distinction between individual and society. Traditions of single inhumation burial with grave goods have been taken to indicate the emergence of an ideology of the individual, stimulating interpersonal competition and resulting in the development of social hierarchies (Renfrew 1974; Shennan 1982). Yet the idea of the individual is a product of a particular historical context (Morris 1991): as a core element of post-Enlightenment rationalism and capitalist economics, the thinking individual subject (implicitly figured as male) is constructed in opposition to an irrational and objectified other that can be controlled and manipulated for economic and political gain.

As we will see in this volume, however, there is much to suggest that the Bronze Age self was not constructed in this way. Ethnographic studies of personhood in non-Western societies indicate that concepts of the self are often relational (Mauss 1985; Strathern 1988; Battaglia 1990): relationships with others are what constitute the person. In many cultural contexts, the self is viewed as an unbounded amalgamation of substances and elements brought together and reformulated at significant points in the lifecycle through the exchange of objects. As such, personhood is fluid and unstable. This means that it is rarely possible to wield absolute power: people are never autonomous but are subject to the demands of others. So too, configurations of power are contextually specific, for power is a property of the relationships enacted within specific events, practices, and performances.

In Bronze Age studies, the continued focus on the relative status of burials is reductionist, for this does not explain the inclusion and careful arrangement in the grave of small 'everyday' objects such as flint scrapers or bone awls or of 'non-functional' artefacts such as fossils. So too, existing narratives that foreground the emergence of social stratification dramatically underplay the wealth of evidence from the settlement record. The latter conjures an image of life in the Bronze Age that does not sit easily with ideas of chiefly hierarchies, but speaks instead of the negotiation of intimate familial, domestic, and neighbourly relations, and of the significance of community and inter-community identities. Focusing only on materials such as metals or finds such as 'high-status' grave goods strips the narrative of much of its richness and depth. Here, instead, we will explore the alterity of Bronze Age societies by attending to the most humble of objects—burnt flint, pieces of worked bone, fragments of pottery—from contexts that range from graves to waterholes and field boundaries. As we shall see, even sites such as hillforts, often viewed as the apex of a settlement hierarchy, can be interpreted in other ways. This is not to remove discussions of social and political power from the picture, of course (cf. Fowler 2013, 88–9). Rather, power should be viewed not as the property of a small and circumscribed group of chiefly individuals, but as immanent in the creative and shifting conjunctions of people and their material worlds.

The evolutionist narratives that dominate our understanding of the Bronze Age have other effects too. The gradual increase in the range of objects made from bronze over the course of the period is thought to have facilitated increased productivity and efficiency: new tool types such as sickles and chisels became common, particularly towards the end of the period, while the appearance of weapons such as swords are thought to indicate an improvement in martial functionality and effectiveness. There is evidence too for significant changes in the organization of agricultural production, notably in the appearance of field systems during the Middle Bronze Age. These are widely understood to signal the intensification of agriculture (Bradley 1980; Yates 2007). Such interpretations are, however, based on an understanding of the natural world as an object of exploitation—a source of raw materials that can be employed to maximize economic and social gain (e.g. Shennan 1999). According to this view, nature is opposed to culture: it is located outside of human society and beyond the jurisdiction of the cultural values and ethical considerations that govern interpersonal relationships (Kneisel et al. 2012). Such an implicit view of human-environment relations works to locate the origins of capitalism in the Bronze Age.

It is, however, problematic to assume that a distinct division between culture and nature was recognized in the past, for this too is a product of our own historical context. During the eighteenth and nineteenth centuries, the natural world was set apart as an object to be explored, exploited, and domesticated by the thinking man of reason (Ingold 1996; Olwig 2002). This served a political purpose, for it legitimated the seizure of land in the colonies as well as enclosure of common land in Europe. In contrast, anthropological studies of landscape indicate that nature is often considered part of the social universe. Mountains, rocks, plants, animals, and other components of the 'natural' world are not devoid of cultural meaning and may be considered to have their own spirit or soul (Descola 1994; Hirsh and O'Hanlon 1995). In such a context, the natural world cannot be an object of exploitation, for social and ancestral relations bind people and landscape together.

The relationship between people and things

This book will challenge the dualistic conceptual frameworks that underpin contemporary narratives of the Bronze Age. As we will see, the archaeological evidence suggests that dichotomies such as individual–society, self–other, subject–object, and culture–nature were not articulated or understood in the Bronze Age in the same way as they are today, and indeed they may not even have been recognized. That such conceptual categories are far from universal is a particular focus of interest across the social sciences, and in this I follow the extensive body of recent literature that locates agency not solely in the human subject but in the particular affordances that arise when things (in the broadest possible sense) enter into relationships with each other (e.g. Latour 1999; DeLanda 2006; Ingold 2011; Hodder 2012; Jones 2012). Things (such as pots, human bodies, bronze, soil, or stone), are not stable, bounded categories but amalgamations of elements, potentialities, and relations. They are definable only within particular moments of encounter, though these moments in turn have their own subsequent impact on object trajectories.

The argument that the properties of things emerge out of their relationships has important implications for archaeology, for it suggests that the boundaries between people and the material world are not defined and immutable. Things absorb and interpenetrate other things so that boundaries are broken down and redrawn. People and objects, for example, are caught up in mutually constitutive relationships (Boivin 2010; Fowler 2013; Knappett 2014): objects are so closely bound into our lives that to remove them would fundamentally alter—and perhaps even unravel—the subject (Hoskins 1998). Yet objects themselves are always emergent: the product of particular conjunctions of human desires and competences, material affordances, and social practices. Common-sense conceptual categories—such as culture and nature— are therefore the result of particular historical instantiations of the relations between people, animals, plants, earth, and stone, amongst other things (Cipolla 2018). Understanding how assemblages of objects and attributes are brought together, configured, and reconfigured can therefore provide insights into the creation and transformation of conceptual structures and systems of value. The relationship between people and things will therefore be a particular focus in this volume; as we shall see, there is evidence to indicate that in Bronze Age Britain the human self was not viewed as a bounded and stable entity set apart from the external world. Instead, concepts of personhood were profoundly relational, with significant elements of the material world forming core components of the self.

Post-humanist perspectives have sought to decentre the person by arguing that objects themselves have agency (Witmore 2007; Alberti and Bray 2009; Olsen 2010). Ethnographic accounts describe how people in many different cultural contexts consider certain objects to be living things—effective agents with their own personality, spirit, or soul that enter into social relationships with people (e.g. Mauss 1990;

Holbraad 2006; Santos Granero 2009). As we shall see, there is much to suggest that Bronze Age objects could sometimes be viewed in this way: structural similarities in the treatment of bodies and artefacts, for example, and the close relationship between human and object life-cycles hint that such diverse things as pots, houses, and daggers were thought to share some of the qualities and attributes of people. Others have argued that it is problematic to equate human and object agency in this way (Barrett 2014). Although objects have real effects in the world, they are not conscious beings, nor can they exercise intentionality, a distinction that Gell (1998, 36–8) sums up in his differentiation of primary and secondary agency. This view is not itself unproblematic, however, for it runs the risk of devaluing indigenous ontologies. Such debates raise other ethical issues too. In a world where climate change caused by human activities is having a devastating impact on the environment, decentring the human subject—and arguing that the agency of other things must be recognized and valued—is a tempting way to redress the balance. Yet this can also act as a means of spreading the blame and of obscuring the micropolitics of power (Sørensen 2013; Van Dyke 2015). Close analysis of the many components of particular actor-networks provides a valuable approach to understanding continuity and change, but treating human and non-human actors as equal rather than different can have troubling ethical implications: few would argue, for example, that helping the human victims of war should not take priority over saving archaeological sites threatened by conflict.

In this book I therefore take an unashamedly human-centred approach, for my focus of interest lies in understanding human relationships, identities, beliefs, and values and in exploring the conceptual structures that allowed Bronze Age people to navigate their world. As we shall see, however, the evidence itself requires us to call into question the boundaries between humans and things. It is evident that the sorts of categorical distinctions recognized today between, for example, people and elements of the natural world may not have been recognized or articulated in quite the same way in the Bronze Age. This does not mean that humans and other things were viewed as the same, however, and during the later part of the period in particular the creation of physical boundaries such as ditched enclosures around fields and settlements suggests an increasing concern over processes of categorization of one sort or another. In each of the following chapters, I will critically evaluate the dualistic conceptual frameworks that underpin accounts of the period by exploring different aspects of the relational construction of identity in Bronze Age Britain and Ireland. I will draw on recent work on materiality, the body, and human-environment relationships across the social sciences to consider how dualisms such as subject–object, culture–nature, and individual–society have impacted our understanding of the Bronze Age.

In order to understand how materials, objects, and persons were brought together, reordered, and dissolved in processes of assembly and categorization, my discussion will pay particular attention to contextual and spatial configurations; themes such as the arrangement of objects in graves and the creation and marking of boundaries and other special places in the landscape provide insights into personhood and identity. The treatment and deposition of things such as pots, bronze axes, and human remains cast light on the meanings and values ascribed both to objects and places, on the conceptual links and distinctions between different cultural categories, and on the ways in which such items acted as social agents. As we shall see, the boundary between the active human subject and the passive world of objects so familiar from our own cultural context was not drawn in this categorical way during the Bronze Age. Instead, the evidence suggests that the self was constructed in relational rather than individualistic terms—composed of an assemblage of elements incorporating objects, places, and people external to the body. Agency was not solely a property of bounded individuals such as the chiefs envisioned in many accounts of the Bronze Age but should instead be viewed as a product of the complex network of interactions between people and other components of the material world. This requires us to challenge common conceptions that impose anachronistic concepts of hierarchy and individualism onto the period and that view the 'natural' world as entirely distinct from human society. Yet, as we will discuss, there was an increasing interest in the creation of boundaries, particularly towards the end of the period: by the Late Bronze Age, the transgression of boundaries was viewed as a productive yet dangerous act.

The tyranny of categorization

One of the striking things about the archaeological evidence is that it so often fails to fit our own conceptual categories, as the pot from Mitchelstown described at the start of this chapter illustrates. It was the alterity of the material that fired the antiquarian and archaeological imagination, even in the early years of the discipline, and that requires us today to explore the otherness of the Bronze Age and to call into question the imposition of 'modernist fantasies' (Rowlands 1986) onto the past. It is all too simple to assume that this was a period in which familiar landscapes and social structures emerged. The fields and farmsteads of the Middle Bronze Age, for example, are easily conjured as the forerunners of the idealized English rural landscapes of the recent past (Brück 2000). So too Bronze Age roundhouses are usually viewed as the homes of small family groups. Yet this sense of familiarity breaks down when confronted with finds such as the mummies—discussed in Chapter 2—buried beneath the house floors at Cladh Hallan on South Uist (Parker Pearson et al. 2005; Booth et al. 2015). As we shall see in Chapter 5, Bronze Age field boundaries were concerned not merely with quantifiable aspects of landscape such as economic value: they did not subdivide space in a rational way, but took account of its cultural, symbolic, and qualitative attributes, as indicated by the relationship between boundaries and features such as barrows, bogs, and rocky outcrops. At the same time, objects—such as gold gorgets and bronze shields—that we might view as economically valuable forms of wealth were deposited in bogs and under boulders (Becker 2013). The evidence, then, conjures a very different image of the Bronze Age to that invoked in social evolutionist narratives which view the period as the origin-point of the forms of social difference and economic rationalism that characterize the modern, Western world.

Often, the particular interpretative labels that we apply to the material do not fit. This is nicely illustrated in the debates around the interpretation of post-built structures under Early Bronze Age round barrows. Piggott (1940) suggested that they can be interpreted as houses, and that funerary monuments were built over them when their occupants died: the small rectangular buildings under two barrows at Trelystan, Powys, for example, have been interpreted as domestic dwellings (Britnell 1982). Other authors have, however, interpreted such structures as ceremonial monuments constructed during the early phases of protracted mortuary rites (e.g. Ashbee 1960, 60–5). Pottery and struck flint found in and under barrows at sites such as Overton Hill and Snail Down in Wiltshire (Smith and Simpson 1966; Thomas 2005, 73–4) present similar problems. These can, on the one hand, be interpreted as the remains of feasting or other ritual activities carried out as part of the mortuary rite or during the construction of the barrow; on the other hand, they might equally be seen as refuse accidentally incorporated into the mound from an earlier settlement whose occupants were carrying out other activities in the vicinity, such as herding or hunting. In either case, the kinds of artefacts we might expect to find look little different. Such interpretative dilemmas arise because we feel the need to categorize sites, buildings and objects as ritual or secular when in fact the data suggests that Bronze Age people may not have employed the same systems of classification. In the contemporary Western world, a distinction is drawn between the sacred and the profane, with the mundane world of daily practice very firmly located in the latter (Brück 1999a; 1999c). Post-Enlightenment rationalism identifies ritual as non-functional and irrational action, but this serves a particular political purpose, for it allows certain types of people and practice to be valued over others: in this way, nineteenth-century ideology distinguished the rational male subject from the emotional 'other', a category into which women and colonized groups, for example, could be placed (Haraway 1991; Morris 1994; McClintock 1995).

This book attempts to break down such categories by taking a relational approach. The chapters that follow do not always map neatly on to conventional archaeological themes but instead address concepts of personhood and the relationship between people and the material world, focusing in turn on bodies, objects, houses, and landscapes. This means, for example, that round barrows and their contents are considered in a number of places throughout the volume. So too, because houses cannot be discussed without reference to their occupants, domestic inventories or relationships with place, topics such as the deposition of artefacts and fragments of human bone are addressed not solely in the chapters on objects and bodies. Employing a relational perspective requires us to take a flexible and open approach to assembling the evidence, and it highlights the limitations of any process of categorization.

In Chapter 2, we will begin by examining the treatment of the human body over the course of the period. In contrast to accounts that argue for the ideological significance of individual burial, our discussion will focus on practices that involved the fragmentation, manipulation, and curation of the body and consider what these might say about concepts of the self. Chapter 3 will address the varied relationships between people and objects. The treatment of objects in graves and hoards suggests both that certain artefacts were considered to have similar qualities to human agents and that they performed key roles in the creation of relational forms of identity: it is simplistic, in other words, for objects such as grave goods to be seen solely as reflections of individual status or as the possessions of the deceased. Chapter 4 will examine the relationship between people and houses. The character of domestic architecture and the organization of settlement space have much to tell us regarding ideas of place, community, and temporality, and suggest the existence of a close conceptual link between the lifecycles of houses and their inhabitants. Chapter 5 will examine the meanings ascribed to features of the 'natural' landscape such as mountains, caves, and rivers, as well as the place of animals in the social world. Some of the shortcomings of models that view Bronze Age field systems as evidence for the increasingly intensive exploitation of the landscape will be considered. Finally, Chapter 6 will explore how gift exchange and the circulation of bodies and objects facilitated the creation of particular ideas of personhood based on cyclical concepts of temporality and distributed notions of substance. This calls into question static models of hierarchy, for power was not a property of particular 'individuals' but was a product of the shifting and dynamic interactions between people, objects, and places.

Bronze Age Ireland and Britain, 2500–600 BC

The focus of this book is Bronze Age Britain and Ireland. Although these islands were well connected with the European mainland throughout the period—and, at points, south-east England seems to have had more in common in cultural terms with parts of north-west France and the Low Countries (Needham et al. 2006)—there are also significant differences in aspects of material culture, mortuary practice, and domestic architecture, amongst other things. Boundaries need to be drawn around any research topic, however, and as the pace of developer-funded archaeology has picked up, resulting in a substantial increase in the evidence available for the period, this book focuses solely on Ireland and Britain, although the significance of long-distance exchange with the European mainland will be addressed in the final chapter.

Of course, Britain and Ireland were not marginal places on the periphery of Bronze Age Europe: this is evident from the swift adoption from c.2500 BC of well-developed metal prospection and metalworking technologies (O'Brien 2004; 2012, 217–18) as well as the rapid take-up of tin-bronze from 2200 BC (Needham 1996)—as early as, if not earlier than, other parts of north-west Europe. The copper mines at Ross Island in County Kerry, for example, were in use from the very beginning of the period, and compositional analysis of Chalcolithic copper objects indicates that these were the main source of metal across Britain and Ireland during this period (Northover 2004). The Wessex area, with its 'wealthy' burials, is often figured as one of the core regions in the development of social complexity in Bronze Age Europe, although as we shall see in Chapter 3, interpreting grave goods solely as a reflection of status is problematic.

Just as communities in Britain and Ireland were connected with those on mainland Europe, so too the existence of distinctive regional traditions across the British Isles has long been recognized. Cyril Fox formulated this as long ago as 1932 when he noted that different artefact types and burial traditions are found in upland and lowland Britain. The character and extent of these regional differences continue to be a focus of interest. Recent research on the social context of Beaker pottery in Ireland, for example, has demonstrated that it is not found in graves containing single inhumations—as is the case in parts of southern and eastern England and Scotland—but was deposited in a range of other ceremonial, mortuary, and domestic contexts including middens and megalithic tombs (Carlin 2011). In the Middle and Late Bronze Age, there are considerable regional differences in domestic architecture, particularly between northern and southern Britain (Pope 2015). Likewise, Late Bronze Age ringworks—a distinctive type of substantial settlement enclosure—are found only in southern and eastern England, although very similar sites have also been identified in parts of north-west France (Bourgeois and Talon 2009; Marcigny and Talon 2009). However, a thematic book of this sort, the primary focus of which is relational concepts of the self, cannot do justice to the topic of regionality, and we will therefore not attempt to address this issue. Instead, we will explore themes common to the archaeology of Britain and Ireland (such as the construction of roundhouses or the deposition of metalwork in 'natural' places) through a variety of examples from different areas.

Nor, indeed, is the purpose of this book to provide a comprehensive account of the archaeology of Bronze Age Britain and Ireland. Instead, its main aim is to explore the relational construction of personhood, employing a series of thematic lenses. Detailed descriptions of, for example, the different object types or mortuary traditions identified over the course of the period will therefore not be provided, although general accounts of key trends will be set out, and many individual examples of sites and finds will be described and discussed. It would, of course, have been possible to write a whole book on either Britain or Ireland, but shared insular traditions as well as the wealth and diversity of the evidence from different regions mean that by considering both together we gain a richer image of Bronze Age personhood: the anthropomorphic pot from Mitchelstown is unique, for example, but discussing this alongside evidence from Scotland or southern England for the curation of heirlooms or the lifecycles of roundhouses significantly enhances our understanding of the relationship between people and things across these islands.

Our thematic discussions in the following chapters will attempt to follow broadly chronological lines, so that it is possible to chart changes to the treatment of the human body, for example, or the relationship between people and landscape, over the course of the period. We will employ the following broad chronological framework based on Needham's more detailed scheme (1996): Chalcolithic (2500–2200 BC), Early Bronze Age (2200–1550 BC), Middle Bronze Age (1550–1150 BC), Late Bronze Age (1150–800 BC), and Earliest Iron Age (800–600 BC). The Earliest Iron Age will be included here, as both bronze objects and key sites such as the monumental middens of southern England continued in use over this transitional period. Other chronological schemes exist, of course, notably Barrett and Bradley's distinction of an Earlier and Later Bronze Age (1980). We will retain the more traditional tripartite division into Early, Middle, and Late Bronze Age here, however, as it is evident that there are significant differences between the Middle and Late Bronze Age in material culture, mortuary practice, and settlement, amongst other things: certain types of settlements such as ringworks and middens are a feature of the Late Bronze Age and Earliest Iron Age, for example.

Barrett and Bradley's scheme does raise other interesting questions, however, for it divides later British prehistory into an earlier phase, encompassing the Neolithic and Earlier Bronze Age and characterized by the construction of ceremonial and funerary monuments, and a later phase including the Later Bronze Age and Iron Age in which the settlement evidence dominates the archaeological record. This has suggested to some that the Bronze Age itself might be a redundant category (Bradley 2001). Yet there is little doubt that the communities living in Britain and Ireland between 2500 and 600 BC experienced significant social and economic change and, as such, the term 'Bronze Age' continues to act as a useful means of bracketing this particular period of time. Of course, this is not to imply that the introduction of metals was the sole cause of these changes: as we shall see, the use of bronze to make items such as spearheads or cauldrons had a significant impact on the trajectory of Bronze Age communities, but it was just one component of their rich and complex lifeworlds.

Before turning to the evidence itself, a few final points need to be made. This book explores the relational construction of the Bronze Age self, but we too are relationally constituted in the present. By writing about the period, we as archaeologists and authors become part of the assemblage that, along with Food Vessels, postholes, and axes, together make the thing we call the Bronze Age (cf. Fowler 2013, 1–5)—imagined always in and for the present. In turn, the way in which we enter into and relate with the Bronze Age world forms an integral part of our own identity. The challenges around disentangling subject from object even

Introduction

in our own investigations were brought home to me some years ago at a conference on Bronze Age settlement and landscape when I and two female colleagues gave papers about roundhouses while our male contemporaries spoke about landscapes; until then, it had not occurred to me that my interest in domestic architecture might stem from my own gendered experiences in the present or that it might provide me with a means of addressing and problematizing contemporary assumptions about gender roles and relationships. For this reason, I realize that I cannot hope to write an objective account of the Bronze Age and that my own interests and concerns inevitably mean that what follows can only ever be a very partial description of the period. Certainly, I recognize that my focus on identity, personhood, and the body, on the definition and transgression of social and conceptual boundaries, and on the mediation of the self-other divide comes from a particular gendered vantage point and from a position of being something of an ethnic mongrel—not quite Irish enough but definitely not English and hardly very German—within a globalizing world. These are obvious and well-worn points, of course, but they go some way towards explaining the perspective I take in the following chapters.

2
Fragmenting the body

In 2002, the extraordinarily wealthy inhumation burial of a single adult male was discovered less than 5 kilometres from Stonehenge in Wiltshire. The Amesbury Archer, as he soon came to be known, was buried sometime between 2380 and 2290 BC (Fitzpatrick 2011), and he was accompanied by an array of grave goods including three copper knives, a pair of gold ornaments, five Beaker pots, seventeen barbed and tanged arrowheads, two stone bracers, a shale belt ring, and a possible cushion stone for the working of metal objects. The appearance of single burials with grave goods at the beginning of the Chalcolithic has long been interpreted as indicating the emergence of an ideology of the individual (e.g. Renfrew 1974; Shennan 1982). The objects buried with the Archer have been viewed as a direct reflection of his wealth and status, and the discovery seems to support established views of Bronze Age society as increasingly hierarchical—dominated by individuals who drew political power from success in long-distance exchange, control over specialist technologies such as metalworking, and prowess in hunting and warfare (Needham 2000a; Needham et al. 2010; Sheridan 2012).

It has frequently been recognized, however, that such evolutionist narratives in fact present a reductionist reading of the evidence (e.g. Petersen 1972; Petersen et al. 1975, 49; Brück 2004a; Gibson, A. 2004), and detailed evaluation of human remains from both mortuary contexts and elsewhere indicates considerable variability in the treatment and perception of the human body (Sofaer Derevenski 2002; Gibson, A. 2004; Brück 2006a; Fitzpatrick 2011, 201–2; Appleby 2013; Fowler 2013, ch. 4). We will return to consider the significance of grave goods in Chapter 3; here we will focus on the treatment of the body both in Bronze Age mortuary rites and in other forms of social and ritual practice. As we shall see, the bodies of the dead were manipulated in complex ways that indicate the existence of concepts of the self that differ profoundly from those familiar from our own cultural context. Social relationships and cultural values are lived through the body (e.g. Sofaer 2006; Robb and Harris 2013), and the treatment, circulation, and deposition of human bone played a significant and changing role in the construction of social categories over the course of the Bronze Age.

Inhumation burial—often under large round barrows or cairns—has long been viewed as the dominant mortuary rite during the first few centuries of the period. From *c.*2100 BC on, evidence for cremation is more common, and by the Middle Bronze Age inhumation burials are virtually unknown. During the Late Bronze Age, mortuary practices are archaeologically invisible in most regions. Instead, fragments of human bone were incorporated into a range of non-mortuary contexts, including settlements: now, there is evidence to suggest that human remains may not have been viewed as referencing known individuals, but were employed as one of a range of meaningful materials that located people and things in relational cosmographies. Throughout the period, the circulation of human bone outside of the mortuary context calls into question the distinction between body and objects, for human bones became elements of material culture that were displayed, curated, and ultimately deposited, sometimes with other heirlooms, but often alongside 'mundane' items and even materials that we might otherwise identify as refuse. This chapter will examine changes over time in the treatment of human remains in order to explore concepts of the body and the self and their relationship to broader narratives of social and community identity.

The unburnt body in the Chalcolithic and Early Bronze Age

The appearance of individual inhumation burials accompanied by Beaker ceramics and the earliest metal objects in the centuries after *c.*2500 BC has long been understood to indicate a moment of profound social transformation. The burial of complete bodies in individual graves has captured the archaeological imagination to the near exclusion of other forms of mortuary practice. Yet there was clearly significant variability: 'classic' Beaker burials are virtually absent from Ireland, for example (Carlin 2011). In fact, the treatment of the unburnt body in other burials of Chalcolithic and Early Bronze Age date provides interesting counterpoints to common narratives of individual power.

Less than 1 kilometre north of the Archer's grave, the near-contemporary burial of the Boscombe Bowmen hints at quite different concepts of the body and the self (Figure 2.1; Fitzpatrick 2011). This grave contained

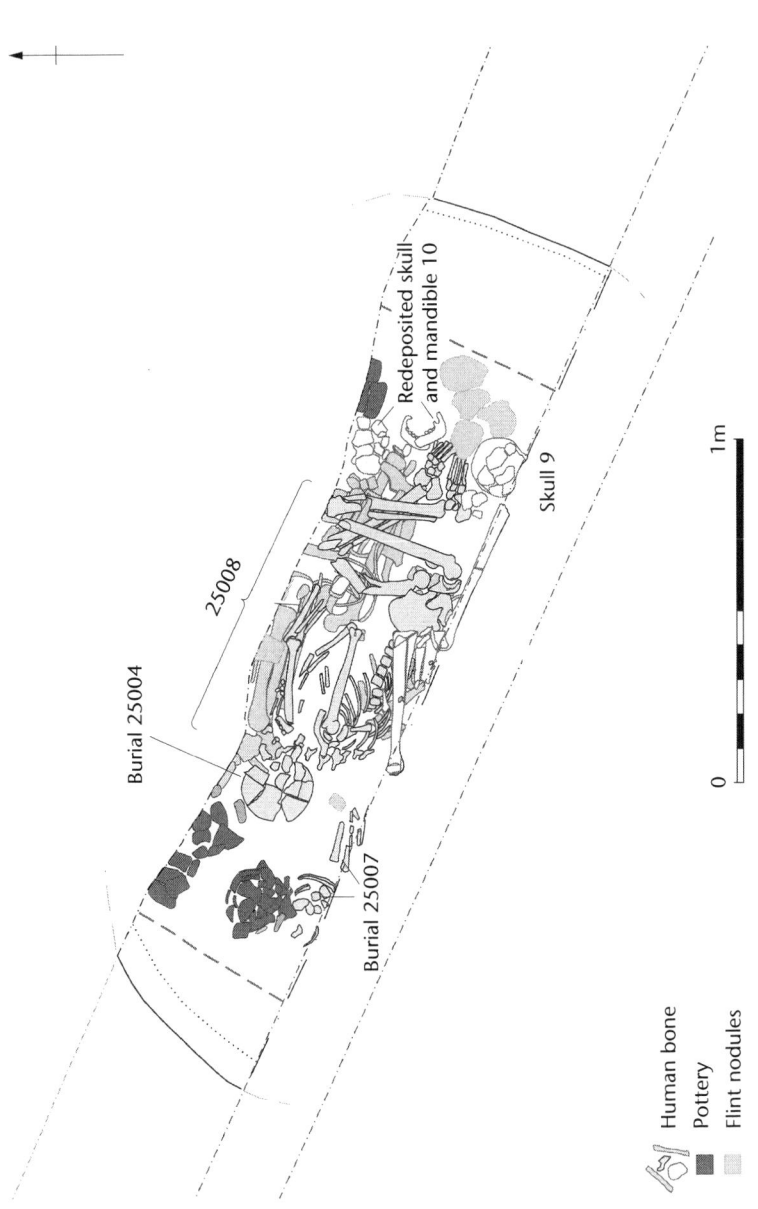

Figure 2.1. The grave of the Boscombe Bowmen, Wiltshire (© Wessex Archaeology, with slight alterations by Anne Leaver).

the incomplete remains of several adults and children (McKinley 2011, 28–31). These included the inhumation burials of an adult male (burial 25004; missing his left hand and forearm) and a 5–6-year-old child (25007) at the base of the grave. A bundle of disarticulated bone (25008) found under the body of the adult male comprised selected skeletal elements from four other individuals (two adult males, one subadult male, and a juvenile), predominantly long-bone fragments from the left side of the body. Radiocarbon dates indicate that these may have been as much as two centuries older than the two inhumation burials. Two crania (9 and 10) and part of a mandible lying at the feet of the adult male may have belonged to the two adults represented in the bone bundle. It is possible that these bodies had originally been placed complete in the grave but were disturbed and their bones rearranged during subsequent interments; if so, a significant proportion of their bones appear to have been removed for use or deposition elsewhere. Alternatively, the bone bundle and other elements may have been brought to the grave from another location, possibly a site or sites where bodies were stored either above or below ground. The upper layers of the grave produced a significant quantity of other disarticulated remains, as well as the inhumation and cremation burials of two further children.

Bodily relations

The presence of multiple burials in the same grave as well as incomplete and disarticulated bodies calls into question Renfrew's classic formulation of the 'individualising chiefdom' (1974), for it is evident that social identity was not solely based on the ability of individuals to acquire and display 'prestige goods' but on their relationships with others. Multiple burials are a well-recognized feature of the Early Bronze Age (Petersen 1972), and the implications of this form of mortuary rite for our understanding of social relationships during this period have been a focus of considerable interest (Barrett 1991; Garwood 1991; Mizoguchi 1993; Appleby 2013). In general, these are understood to indicate the reopening of an existing grave in order to insert a second or subsequent burial. The deep central grave in barrow 52, Aldro, East Yorkshire, contained a series of burials (Mortimer 1905, 62–3). At the base of the feature lay a crouched inhumation accompanied by a flint knife. Two further crouched inhumations, a near-complete articulated arm, and a neat pile of disarticulated bones (including a skull) were found in the upper levels of the grave; the latter may represent a burial disturbed when the grave was reopened, although, as we shall discuss later in this chapter, such deposits might also be the result of other processes.

Sometimes, the referencing of existing burials extends to the positioning of the body as well as the location of the grave. At South Dumpton Down in Kent, three intercutting pits at the centre of a ring-ditch contained the remains of seven crouched inhumations which seem to have been deposited in sequence (Figure 2.2; Perkins n.d.). All but one of these burials were placed so that they lay perpendicular to the body of the previous interment. In other words, the earliest burial, which lay on a roughly north-east to south-west alignment, was followed by a second burial on a roughly north-west to south-east alignment, and so on; this pattern of alternate alignment appears to have been followed throughout the sequence with just one exception. Grave 2 in barrow C49 at Riggs, East Yorkshire, contained two crouched inhumations, both lying on their left-hand side, one oriented north and the other oriented south (Figure 2.3 top; Mortimer 1905, fig. 431); they were positioned in the grave so that they were face-to-face, suggesting a particularly intimate relationship between these individuals. In the same cemetery, barrow C83 contained three inhumation burials in three distinct grave cuts (Figure 2.3 bottom; Mortimer 1905, fig. 461). Burials 4 and 5 were adult inhumations. Burial 4 lay on its right-hand side with its head to the north, facing west. Immediately east of this grave, burial 5 lay on its right-hand side with its head to the south, facing east. Perpendicular to these graves and cutting across both of them at a higher level in the barrow was burial 3, the inhumation of a child lying on its right-hand side with its head to the west. This burial formed a physical link between the two adults who, though buried in adjoining graves on the same alignment, are positioned facing away from each other. As such, the placement of these bodies worked to express powerful messages of connection and disjunction.

It has been long suggested that practices of multiple burial indicate the continued significance of interpersonal and familial relationships during the Early Bronze Age, and discussion during the 1990s in particular examined the range of ways in which the spatial relationships between individual burials may have been employed to give material form to the social and political links (whether actual or desired) between particular people (Barrett 1991; 1994, 109–31; Garwood 1991; Mizoguchi 1992; 1993; Last 1998). That research examined not only the significance of the relationships between individuals buried in the same grave, but also the placement of burials in individual barrows, as well as the relationship between different monuments in barrow cemeteries. Last's study (1998) of the series of Beaker graves in the barrow at Barnack in

Fragmenting the body

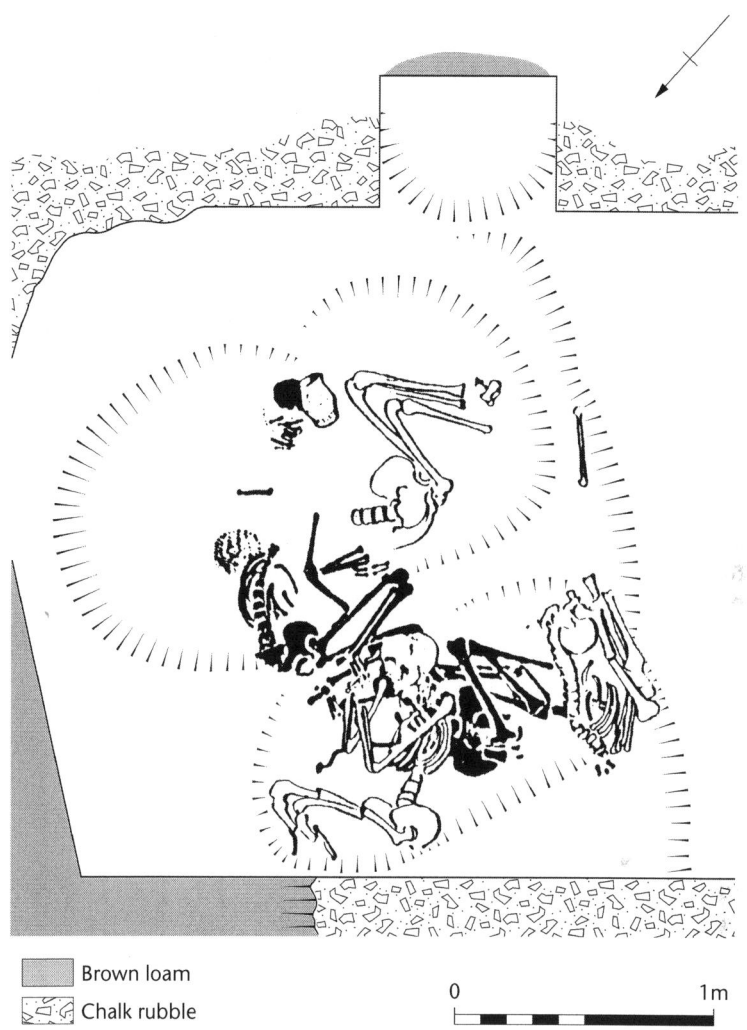

Figure 2.2. The sequence of intercutting inhumation burials at South Dumpton Down, Kent (redrawn by Anne Leaver after Perkins n.d., fig. 5; reproduced with permission of the Trust for Thanet Archaeology).

Cambridgeshire demonstrates that burials took careful account of the location and bodily positioning of previous interments. By referencing earlier mortuary rites, identities were created for the dead through processes of comparison and distinction that literally placed them relative to others.

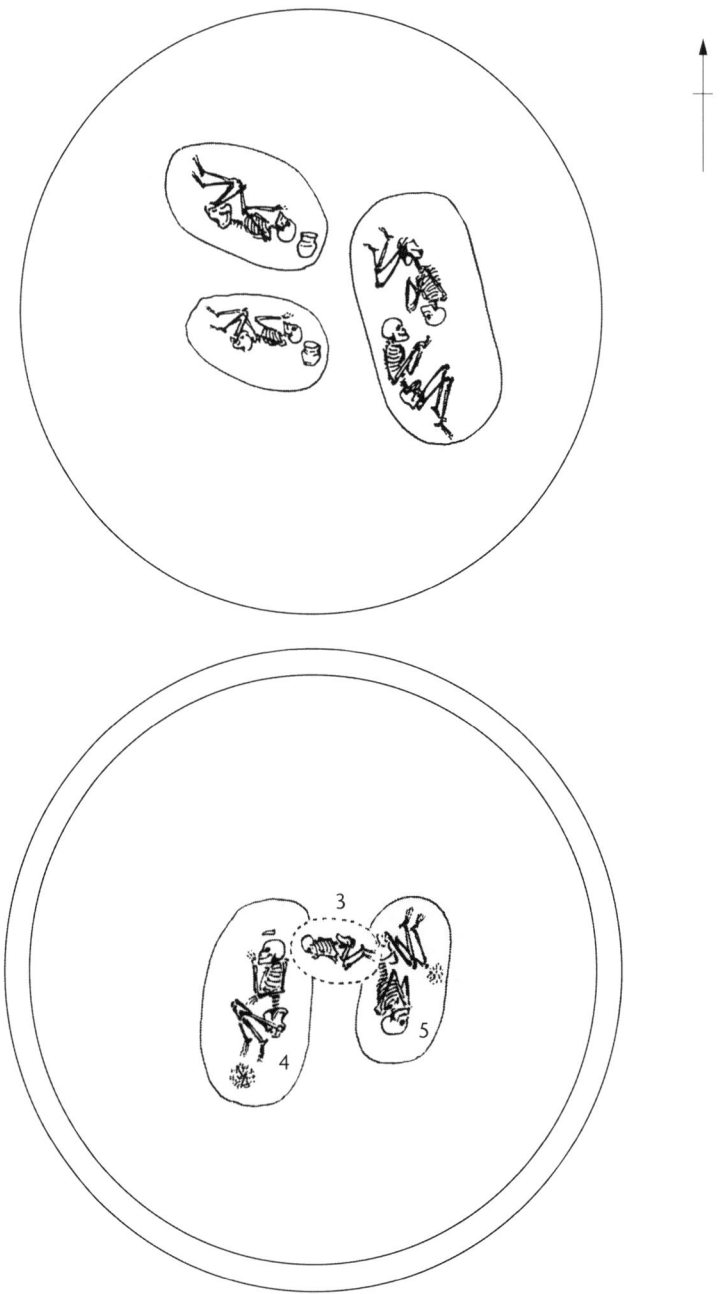

Figure 2.3. Bodily relations: burials in barrows C49 (top) and C83 (bottom), Riggs, East Yorkshire (after Mortimer 1905, figs 431 and 461, with slight alterations by Anne Leaver).

Sometimes it is evident that bodily positioning related to normative concepts of social identity. Shepherd's examination (2012) of the orientation of Beaker burials indicates that the position of the body in the grave was often employed to reference gendered identity. In north-east Scotland and East Yorkshire, for example, males were buried on their left-hand sides with their heads oriented east, whereas females were placed on their right-hand sides with their heads oriented west. Both males and females faced south, so that bodily positioning invoked points of similarity as well as difference. Mizoguchi (1993, 225–6) describes how the majority of primary Beaker inhumations in the barrows of the Yorkshire Wolds were adult males, with women and children usually placed in secondary or 'satellite' positions. This has been taken to indicate that men held positions of particular authority in Chalcolithic and Early Bronze Age communities. However, this model ignores change over time in mortuary practice. In eastern England, for example, men are better represented than women in the mortuary record of the Chalcolithic, while burials of women and children become frequent after c.2100 BC (Harding and Healy 2007, table 4.4). By this time, the practice of reusing existing barrows had become common (Garwood 2007, table 4.1), and it is therefore no surprise that the graves of women and children (along with men buried after 2100 BC) are most often found inserted into the 'margins' of older monuments. This does not mean they themselves were marginalized, however; instead, the reuse of barrows gave material form to perceived links between recently deceased members of the community and more distant ancestors. Indeed, there may be an element of regional variability to the pattern identified by Mizoguchi: Harding et al.'s study of mortuary practices in eastern England over the Chalcolithic and Early Bronze Age identified nineteen male primary burials and thirty-one male secondary burials, compared to fourteen female primary burials and twenty-six female secondary burials (2007, table 4.5). Here, in other words, 38 per cent of men were buried in primary locations compared to 35 per cent of women; these numbers are not dramatically different.

Beyond the individual barrow, Garwood (1991) discusses how the location of monuments in barrow cemeteries can be read as the materialization of fictive kinships, employed to negotiate the political position of the living and the dead: linear barrow cemeteries, for example, may give material form to ideals of genealogical succession. However, the chronological relationship between individual barrows remains poorly understood, although a recent programme of radiocarbon dating at an Early Bronze Age barrow cemetery at Over in Cambridgeshire provides interesting insights into the sequence of monument construction at this site (Garrow et al. 2014). The cemetery at Over comprised three turf mound barrows and two pond barrows, as well as a number of inhumation burials in flat graves. A detailed analysis of the radiocarbon dates from the site indicates that the thirty-five cremation burials from the five monuments were probably deposited over just one or two centuries—perhaps every five to six years. This provides an interesting insight into the temporal scale over which collective and personal memory functioned, and suggests that the occupants of barrows were not always distant and unidentifiable ancestors, but must often have been known individuals. It also indicates that the temporality of monument construction was influenced by sociopolitical imperatives rather than practical requirements: barrow 12, the earliest monument in the group, was constructed before the last of the flat graves was dug, while the first phase of barrow 13 was built shortly after the main turf mound of barrow 15, even though there was plenty of space for further burials in the latter. We can therefore suggest that the construction of the barrows and strategic location of burials within them functioned to map out relationships (or divisions) between both particular people and broader social groups.

Manipulating the body

The continued significance of interpersonal (and indeed genealogical) relationships indicates that it is problematic to draw too sharp a contrast between the communal burials of the Neolithic and the individual burials of the Early Bronze Age. As many researchers have noted, the presence of disarticulated bone in Early Bronze Age graves also calls this into question (Petersen 1972; Petersen et al. 1975; Gibson, A. 2004). This is, however, a topic that has only recently begun to attract detailed attention (Gibson, A. 2004; Brück 2004b; 2006a; Fitzpatrick 2011; Appleby 2013; Fowler 2013, ch. 4). Although it is easy to assume that the occurrence of disarticulated bone is the result of later disturbance, as graves were reopened for the addition of new burials, in fact the evidence suggests a complex range of processes involving the deliberate manipulation of human bone. This included practices of secondary burial (the deposition of human remains after multiple stages of mortuary treatment, classically the reburial or relocation of human bones from their original place of disposal: Metcalf and Huntingdon 1991), as well as the disaggregation and rearrangement of the body in the grave.

As we have already seen in the case of the Boscombe Bowmen, complete bodies were not always present in the grave. A Beaker burial at Manston in Kent, for example, was missing vertebrae, arms, teeth, mandible, and pelvis (Perkins and Gibson 1990, 13). At Babraham Road in Cambridge, a grave containing the partially articulated and incomplete remains of a young adult male dating to 2205–1895 cal BC was found (Hinman and Malim 1999). Less than half of the body was present, and it is evident that this was not the result of soil conditions alone. Articulated elements included the right arm, which was still attached to the right-hand side of the ribcage, although the hand was missing. The mandible had been placed on a pile of partially articulated foot bones just below the pelvis. A cut-mark 'visible where the jaw joined with the skull' is interpreted as possible evidence for decapitation, although this may also have been made when the mandible was detached; this suggests that the grave was reopened and the bones rearranged (and possibly removed) when the body was in a partially decomposed state. Elsewhere, processes of bodily disaggregation occurred prior to burial. At Horsbrugh Castle Farm in Peeblesshire, the inhumation burial of an adult male was placed in a cist (Petersen et al. 1975). The skull was missing, however, and several other bones had been moved from their correct anatomical positions; the right and left halves of the pelvis, for example, appear to have been transposed. The excavators argue that the cist was too substantial to have been reopened after construction. They suggest that the body was buried in a partly decomposed or skeletonized state and the bones arranged to simulate a crouched inhumation.

Elsewhere, incomplete and disarticulated remains were deposited together with other burials. At Dryburn Bridge, East Lothian, two cists were uncovered (Dunwell 2007). Cist 1 contained the well-preserved, crouched inhumation burial of an adult male. Lying over the pelvis and abdomen were the disarticulated remains of a second adult male. The crouched inhumation burial of another adult male was found in cist 2 (Figure 2.4). Partly overlying the feet and lower legs were the disarticulated remains of a 6–8-year-old child. Both disarticulated bodies were incomplete: although most of the larger bones were present, smaller bones were under-represented. The preservation of the bone was good, however, suggesting that this is not the result of post-depositional processes, and it seems likely that the cists never contained the complete bodies of the disarticulated individuals. Instead, it is possible that the larger skeletal elements such as long bones were deliberately selected for deposition in the grave. In contrast, none of the skeletal remains from the cist at Mill Road, Linlithgow, West Lothian, were articulated (Cook 2000). These included the partial, disarticulated, and mixed remains of at least one adult and four children (as well as a few burnt teeth from an infant). The adult was represented by a skull and a fragment of femur,

Figure 2.4. Cist 2 at Dryburn Bridge, East Lothian (reproduced with permission of Dave Pollock, Andrew Dunwell, and the Society of Antiquaries of Scotland, with slight alterations by Anne Leaver).

although it is not known if these belonged to the same individual. The children were represented by a much wider range of skeletal elements, although there were relatively few hand and foot remains. As at Dryburn Bridge, the lack of smaller bones and the generally good condition of the assemblage suggest that the bodies may already have been partial and/or disarticulated when they were deposited in the cist. Interestingly, three of the four sides of the cists comprised large slabs set on their edges, but the fourth side was made up of three smaller stones, and it is suggested that these could have been dismantled to allow the cist to be reopened for successive acts of deposition, retrieval, and manipulation.

At other sites, more care was taken to arrange the remains of bodies that may have been partly or completely disarticulated prior to burial. The cist at Allerwash in Northumberland contained only a few bones belonging to an adult, but these were arranged to resemble a flexed inhumation (Newman and Miket 1973). Parts of the pelvis and tibia were deposited in place of the skull and arms respectively, while portions of the left and right femurs were arranged to look like complete legs. The 'body' was accompanied by a bronze dagger. The central grave in a bell barrow at Sutton Veny in Wiltshire contained the complete but partially articulated crouched inhumation of a young adult in a lidded coffin (Figure 2.5; Johnston 1978). The right humerus was detached and displaced to behind the pelvis. The position of the articulated left humerus and ulna also suggest they had been separated from the body. The left radius lay parallel to the ulna but was orientated in the opposite direction, with the fingers at the wrong end of the arm. The skull and maxilla were placed at the head end of the body, but some 20 centimetres from the mandible, which remained in the correct anatomical position. The excavator suggests that the body was partially dismembered prior to burial, although no cut marks were noted on the bones themselves. Soil stains suggest that a wooden bier was originally placed beneath the coffin (Johnston 1978, fig. 5): if so, then the partially disarticulated remains of this individual may have been open to view for part of the mortuary rite.

Curating the dead

It is, of course, interesting to consider what happened to the missing bones from burials such as those at Horsbrugh Farm and Babraham Road. Single bones sometimes occur as 'grave goods' in other burials, suggesting that bones may have been curated or exhumed for deposition in later burials (Brück 2004b; 2006a). At Waterhall Farm in Cambridgeshire, the inhumation burial of a young adult male was accompanied by the skull of a child aged 6–7 (Martin and Denston 1976, 7), while grave 13 at Keenoge in County Meath contained the inhumation burial of a young adult female, along with three skull fragments belonging to a mature male (Buckley 1997, 54–5). An Early Bronze Age grave dug into

Personifying Prehistory

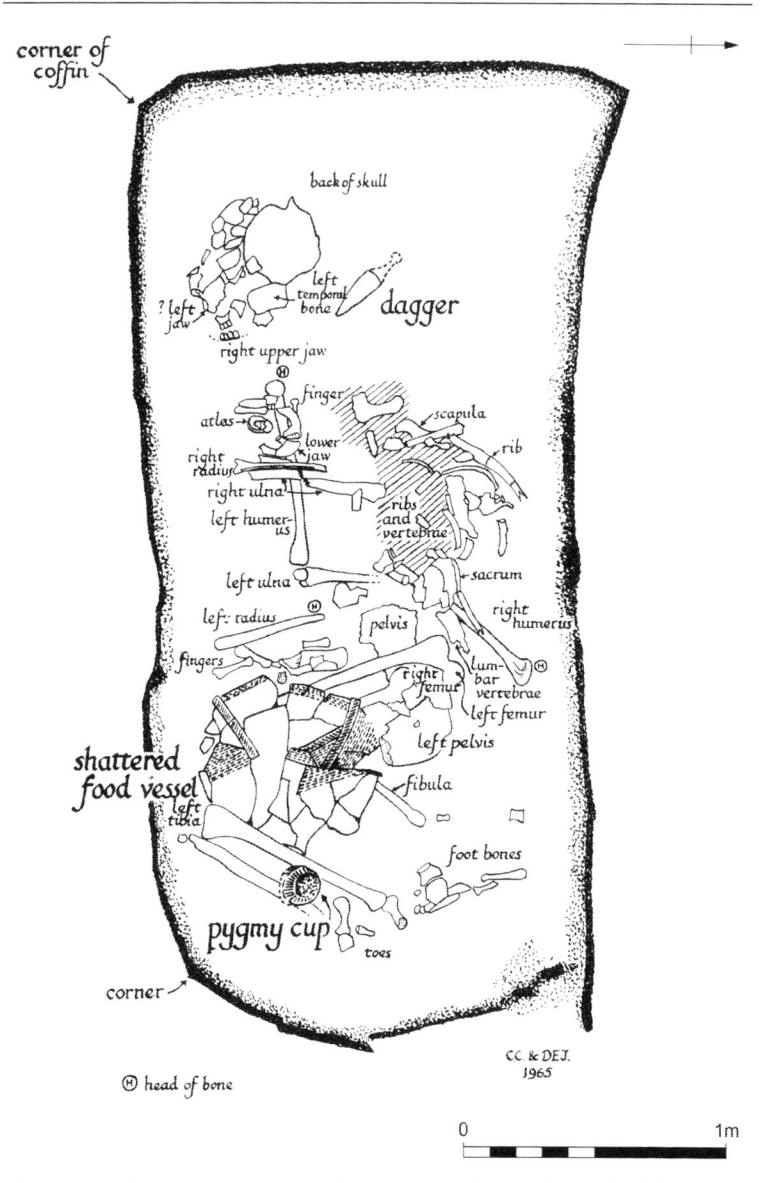

Figure 2.5. The central grave in the barrow at Sutton Veny, Wiltshire (after Johnston 1978, fig. 4, with slight alterations by Anne Leaver; reproduced with permission of the Wiltshire Archaeological and Natural History Society).

a long barrow at Redlands Farm, Irthlingborough, Northamptonshire (Bradley 2007, 167–9), contained the complete inhumation of an adult female. This was accompanied by two incisors, a skull fragment, and a possible pelvis fragment from a second adult and a humerus fragment from a subadult. The inhumation burial was dated to 1890–1630 cal BC (3450+/−45 BP; BM−2833), but the subadult humerus fragment was dated to 2290–1980 cal BC (3730+/−45 BP; OxA 5550). It is possible that these additional bones had been curated above ground. Alternatively, earlier burials may have been encountered (either accidentally or deliberately) when digging the grave, and 'ancestral' elements incorporated into the later burial. As Appleby (2013, 92–3) argues, the reopening of inhumation graves and the manipulation, curation, and redeposition of human bone hint that time was viewed as neither linear nor cyclical; instead, ancestral relics interjected into the world of the living so that the past remained an active element of the present.

The recent identification of evidence for possible mummification in the British Bronze Age illuminates some of the processes that may have been involved in the curation of human remains (Parker Pearson et al. 2005; Booth et al. 2015). We will discuss the famous mummies from Cladh Hallan, which date to the Late Bronze Age, later in this chapter, but a number of possible examples are now known from the earlier part of the period. Work by Booth et al. (2015) suggests that patterns of arrested bacterial attack demonstrated by unusually good histological preservation of human bone may result from cultural practices that prevent putrefaction such as mummification. Histological analysis has recognized patterning of this sort at several Early Bronze Age sites. The well-preserved bone microstructure of the primary inhumation burial in a ring-ditch at Canada Farm in Dorset indicates arrested bioerosion (Booth et al. 2015; Smith et al. 2016). The radiocarbon dating of this body suggests that it was at least a century older than the Beaker that accompanied it, and a number of the bones were slightly misplaced (notably the mandible, which was found separated from the body in the north-west corner of the grave), suggesting that the body was not fully fleshed when it was buried. Another possible mummy from Neat's Court in Kent displays discolouration and fissuring to the skull, teeth, and articular ends of the long bones (Booth et al. 2015, 1165, fig. 7). This suggests that the body was exposed to a degree of heat treatment, and it may have been preserved by smoking.

We have seen above that the cist at Mill Road Industrial Estate in East Lothian was constructed in such a way that it could be reopened. Wooden chambers or mortuary structures have been identified at many sites (Ashbee 1960, 52–4), and these may have provided other ways of accessing human bone. At Chilbolton in Hampshire, the area between the grave and the pit in which it was located was filled with tightly packed chalk rubble (Russel 1990, 156–7). The rubble had steep inner sides, suggesting that it had originally been shored up with planking. This, and the presence of a soil stain along the western side of the grave, suggests the original existence of a now-decayed mortuary structure. The primary inhumation burial had been disturbed when a secondary inhumation was deposited but that had occurred without the chalk rubble collapsing, suggesting that the mortuary structure was still standing when the later interment was inserted into the grave; some of the bones from the primary burial were missing. The stake-built rectangular mortuary house at Beaulieu Heath II in Hampshire also appears to have been free-standing for some time: it had begun to collapse by the time the barrow was constructed over it (Piggott 1943, 7–9). Such structures may have facilitated continued engagement with the body, allowing the addition, removal, and rearrangement of bones.

We have already suggested that some of the missing bones from particular graves may have been incorporated into later burials. However, it is evident that human remains circulated outside of the mortuary context also. Unburnt human bone has been identified in pit deposits and other contexts of Chalcolithic and Early Bronze Age date: as we shall see in Chapter 4, pit groups are frequently interpreted as evidence of settlement. At Rectory Road, Bluntisham, Cambridgeshire, the primary fill of a large oval pit produced a few flint flakes, cattle and sheep bone, an adult human tooth, charred hazelnut shells, and several grains of wheat and barley (Burrow and Mudd 2008, 2). Most of a single, large, rusticated Beaker were found in the secondary fill, along with charcoal including oak, ash, and mistletoe. The uppermost fill of the feature contained a sheep tibia and eighteen fragments of human bone comprising parts of the lower leg, foot, hand, and ribs of an adult. A fragment of hazelnut shell from the primary fill yielded a date of 2290–2030 cal BC. At Yarnton in Oxfordshire, a neonate was deposited in the top of pit 8782; other finds from this feature included coarse domestic pottery, worked flint, animal bone, charred plant remains (cereals and hazelnut shells), and a polished bone point (Hey et al. 2016, 90, table 7.4). The finds from Rectory Road and Yarnton exemplify the 'domestic' assemblages from Beaker pits more generally, although the presence of mistletoe at Rectory Road is interesting, given the supposed symbolic significance of mistletoe in the Iron Age as well as more recently (e.g. Ross 1986).

Occasionally, there is evidence that unburnt human bone was used to make particular objects, hinting at patterns of curation and circulation that are likely to have stretched beyond the mortuary context. Woodward and Hunter's recent study of Early Bronze Age grave goods

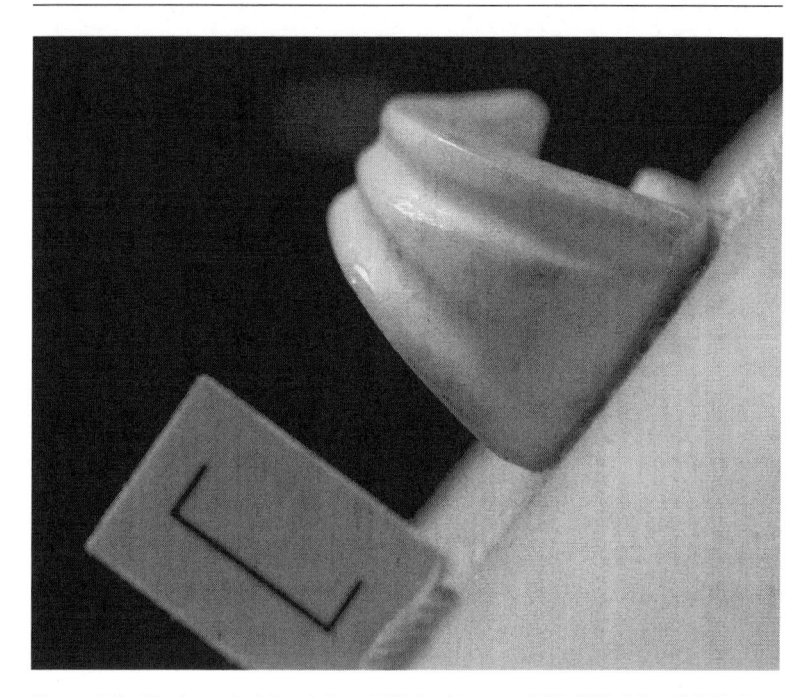

Figure 2.6. The bone belt hook from Wilsford barrow G15, Wiltshire (© Wiltshire Museum).

has identified three belt hooks made from human femurs (2015, 56). The primary cremation in Wilsford barrow G15 in Wiltshire, for example, was accompanied by a belt hook of human bone (Figure 2.6) and a dagger-shaped bone pendant (Woodward and Hunter 2015, table 3.3.1, 200). Although it is possible that the choice of human bone was not deliberate, there is evidence for selection of material for other Early Bronze Age bone items: as we will see in Chapter 5, cetacean bone was often chosen for the production of dagger pommels (O'Connor 2015), while bone points were usually manufactured from sheep limb bones (Woodward and Hunter 2015, 99). The use of human bone to make bone belt hooks is interesting, for these were items that were worn on the body and they are likely to have been visible elements of apparel. Such objects perhaps allowed links to be made between particular people and significant ancestors, or they may have invoked specific symbolic properties. It is possible, too, that the choice of human bone rendered them animate objects with their own particular potency. Even more interesting is the bone tube from Wilsford G58 made from a human femur (Woodward and Hunter 2015, 114; Woodward and

Needham 2012). The interior of this item has been scraped out and its outer surface polished. It is generally interpreted as a whistle: it originally had a side hole, although that part of the object has been damaged and the hole no longer survives. This item accompanied an inhumation burial, probably of an adult male, at the base of a large bell barrow. The whistle, along with a variety of other artefacts including a greenstone battle axe, bronze axe, bone handle, boar's tusk, and grooved stone block, appears to have been placed at the man's feet. It is not known whether the whistle was primarily employed in a social or ritual context, but in either case playing music on what may have been recognized as an ancestral relic would have been a powerful act.

Processing the body in Early Bronze Age cremation burials

From *c.*2100 BC on, practices of cremation burial come to dominate the archaeological record. As has long been recognized, the process of cremation differs in significant ways from the variety of practices involving unburnt human remains described above. Cremation is by its nature a spectacular event and is likely to have impacted the mourners and shaped memories of the funeral in a very different way to inhumation rites (Mizoguchi 1993, 232; Barrett 1994, 128; Downes 1999; Williams 2004). The transformation undergone by the body itself is dramatic and swift, and—unlike unburnt bone—once the burnt remains have been removed from the pyre and handled, most are reduced to indistinguishable fragments. Barrett (1991, 121–2) describes how the temporal and spatial character of cremation burial differs from inhumation: the display and burning of the body on the pyre was an event that may have been separated both in space and time from the final deposition of the bones. He suggests that cremation, unlike inhumation, allowed the natural process of decay to be socially controlled. However, in light of the evidence presented above for the manipulation of unburnt bone, we can perhaps suggest that this distinction is overdrawn, for unburnt bone was also subject to practices of secondary burial. Like cremation burials, disarticulated remains had their flesh removed and were deposited in a fragmentary state, potentially some distance from the location of earlier stages in the mortuary rite and perhaps also after a long period of post-mortem manipulation.

Like some of the deposits of unburnt bone described above, Early Bronze Age cremation burials frequently contain just a portion of the body of the deceased: the average weight of bone recoverable for an adult in a modern crematorium is about 2 kilograms (McKinley1993, 285), but Early Bronze Age cremation burials are usually much lighter in weight. Five of the six cremation deposits analysed from Keenoge, County Meath, comprised less than 600 grams of burnt bone: cist grave 3, for example, yielded a carefully placed discrete deposit of bone that weighed just 135 grams (Buckley 1997, table 1). It is tempting to suggest that this was the result of post-depositional factors, such as soil conditions, but this does not always appear to have been the case. The cremation burial of an adult female deposited in a pit under a small kerbed cairn at Stoneyburn Farm in Lanarkshire weighed just 538.7 grams (Banks 1995, 297). The presence of small bones, such as those from the hands and feet, suggests careful collection from the pyre, yet not all of the body was buried. This suggests either that only a portion of the body was recovered from the pyre, or that some of the cremated remains were removed for use or deposition elsewhere. A particularly evocative image of the retrieval and deposition of portions of the body from the pyre is evident at Carrig in County Wicklow. Here, one of the cists was filled with soil through which were dispersed 'small pockets of bone' (Grogan 1990, 14), suggesting that the mourners threw handfuls of burnt bone into the grave as it was being filled.

The regular identification of partial or 'token' cremation burials raises the question of whether there is evidence for deliberate selection of particular anatomical elements for burial. The fragmentary nature of cremated bone means that it is often difficult to identify specific skeletal elements, but some attempts have been made to estimate the representation of different body parts. The cremation burials from Dunure Road in Ayrshire included elements from all areas of the body (Duffy 2007, 90). This suggests careful collection of a representative sample rather than, for example, the simple deposition of a shovelful of bone from the pyre. Elsewhere, there is occasional evidence for selection: half of the fragments of cremated bone from cist grave 5 at Keenoge, County Meath, were from the skull (Buckley 1997, 25), while the cremation burials from cist graves 3 and 4 contained relatively few skull fragments, suggesting that these may have been removed for deposition elsewhere. A detailed study of Scottish urned cremation burials has demonstrated that skull fragments weighed proportionally more than other skeletal elements (Medina-Pettersson 2013, 172). This suggests that the skull may sometimes have been preferentially retrieved from the pyre site, although it is also possible that relatively dense anatomical elements such as skull fragments survived the cremation process better than other bones or were easier for the Bronze Age mourner or the contemporary osteoarchaeologist to identify. Scottish Early Bronze Age cremation burials predominantly comprise clean deposits of human bone, however, and Medina-Pettersson (2013, 176) argues that this indicates careful collection of individual fragments: although animals and artefacts accompanied the dead onto the pyre, the rarity of such finds suggests a focus on the retrieval of human bone rather than other materials.

Curation and temporality in cremation burials

Just as many cremation burials contain only part of the body, so too others comprise elements from more than one individual: twenty-four of Medina-Pettersson's sample of seventy-five urned burials from Scotland contained parts of more than one body (2013, 131). Similar patterns can be identified elsewhere: a cremation burial in a Collared Urn from a cairn on Birkside Fell, Northumberland, contained the cremated remains of an adult with a few cranial fragments from a second individual (Tolan-Smith 2005, 63–4). Cremation burial 6411 from barrow 3 at Irthlingborough comprised 1222 grams of burnt bone. Much of this belonged to a young adult female, but a distal right humerus fragment belonging to a second individual was also identified (Allan et al. 2007a, 151). It is possible that the inclusion of one or two fragments of bone from a second individual indicates deliberate curation, though this may also have been accidental—the result of reuse of a pyre site, for example (Fowler 2013, 166–7). Some finds are more strongly indicative of curation, however. A cremation burial deposited in a pit in a bowl barrow at Tynings South, Somerset, comprised the remains of two individuals (Taylor 1951, 115). These bodies appear to have had different histories, for the bones of one of the individuals had been gnawed by a small carnivore while still unburnt. Although the unburnt bodies may have been stored in different places and burnt together, it is possible that this deposit is the result of two cremation events, with the burnt bones of one individual retained or stored elsewhere for some time prior to deposition; alternatively, these bones may have been recovered from an earlier cremation grave.

Sometimes, substantial portions of the bodies of more than one individual were buried together. An inverted Collared Urn buried at the centre of barrow 5 at West Cotton, Northamptonshire, contained 2846 grams of cremated bone, comprising the remains of three adults (one female, one male, and one of indeterminate sex) (Allan et al. 2007c, 141); multiple replication of skeletal elements indicates that, in this case, significant portions of each of the three bodies were present (Mays 2007, 714). It is possible that these individuals died within a few days of each other and were cremated together, although the bone may also have been curated. Stable isotope analysis of Early Bronze Age inhumation burials indicates not only sporadic movement over very long distances, but also frequent episodes of mobility that may indicate journeys made on a seasonal or annual basis (Jay et al. 2012). In such a context, it is possible to imagine that cremated remains might have been curated until ancestral burial grounds were revisited at a particular point in the year. Alternatively, unburnt bodies may have been stored until there were enough bodies to warrant the work and resources required to build a pyre (Thomas 2005, 283–5). There is little indication of the regular storage of fleshed bodies, however. Analysis of Scottish Early Bronze Age cremation burials, for example, reveals little evidence in that region for the cremation of dry bone; the colour and surface texture of the cremated remains indicate that most bone was still fleshed when it was burnt (Medina-Pettersson 2013, 163). However, there are occasional indications of pre-cremation manipulation of the dead, suggesting potentially protracted mortuary rites prior to cremation. At West Heath, Harting, West Sussex, the cremation burial of an adult male was missing all of the bones of the skull (Drewett 1985, 40), suggesting that the body had been decapitated before it was placed on the pyre. At Seafield West, near Inverness, Highland, a skull fragment from the cremation burial of an adult displayed two parallel cut marks across its external surface (McKinley 2003, 71). It is not known if these were inflicted before or after death, although they appear to have been made on fleshed bone, before the body was cremated.

At some sites, it has been suggested that bodies were inhumed for a period prior to exhumation and cremation. At Weird Law in Peeblesshire, a large oval pit some 1.6 metres long and 0.8 metres wide lay at the centre of a ring cairn (MacLaren 1967). Over the pit, a layer of burnt material was interpreted as the remains of a pyre, and two cremation burials were recovered from features dug through that layer. It is suggested that the pit may originally have held the fleshed bodies of the two individuals who were later cremated. At Snail Down in Wiltshire, unburnt skull fragments from the ditches of barrows I and XX— monuments in which only cremation burials were found—hint that fleshed bodies may have been stored or exposed at this site before they were burnt (Thomas 2005, 284). A wooden structure under barrow XVII at the same site may have been used to display or expose a body (Thomas 2005, 96–101). After a while, the timber structure was dismantled and a pit was dug, into which the cremation burial of a probable young adult male was placed. The presence of pellets from large birds of prey suggests that that there may have been an interval of some time between the erection of the timber structure and the burial itself, for these birds are likely to have avoided the site when people were present. The pellets also indicate that the structure was standing during the summer or autumn: sometimes, there may have been an auspicious time for the bodies of the dead to be cremated and buried.

Whatever the complex processes involved in the creation of multiple cremation burials, we can suggest that they acted as a means of marking interpersonal relationships. Certainly, the types of person interred in this way suggest that this may have been the case: most multiple cremation burials comprise the remains of two or three people, often an adult and child, or two children (McKinley 1997, 142; Medina-Pettersson 2013, 139), although Petersen et al. (1975, 49–50) point out that adult/child associations may be over-represented, as it is easier to identify the remains of different individuals where there is a marked disparity in age. Four of the five multiple cremation burials from the barrow cemetery at Over in Cambridgeshire, for example, comprised an adult and child, while the fifth comprised two children (Garrow et al. 2014, table 2). It is often assumed that these deposits mark familial relationships. Yet this need not indicate that understandings of kinship were the same in the Early Bronze Age as they are today. Males were more likely than females to be included in multiple cremation burials in Scotland (Medina-Petterssen 2013, 138), and men were buried with children elsewhere also. Cremation burial 6400 from Barrow 1 at Raunds in Northamptonshire contained about 2.5 kilograms of burnt bone from two individuals, a probable adult male and a child aged 13–14 years (Allan et al. 2007d, 159–61).

Cremation and inhumation

So far we have treated the deposition of burnt and unburnt bone separately, but there was a long period (*c.*2100–1700 BC) during which both inhumation and cremation burial were practised (Sofaer Derevenski 2002; Garwood 2007; Harding et al. 2007, 237; Brück 2009; Appleby 2013). Although a broad trend from inhumation to cremation can be seen, in fact this is not always the case at individual sites: at Over in Cambridgeshire, for example, the cremation burials in barrow 12 predated the final flat inhumation graves (Garrow et al. 2014). Sometimes burnt and unburnt bone was deposited in the same grave, and this requires us to consider why people might have been treated in different ways. At the Mound of the Hostages, County Meath, an unburnt arm bone was found amongst a deposit of cremated bone in a stone cist (O'Sullivan 2005, 191). At Middle Barn Farm, near Warminster in Wiltshire, a grave contained the crouched inhumation burial of an adult male accompanied by the cremation burial of an adult female (Figure 2.7; McKinley 2008, 176–80). The cremation burial was located in front of the chest and overlying the arms of the adult male. The inhumation burial was dated to 1975–1760 BC.

Fragmenting the body

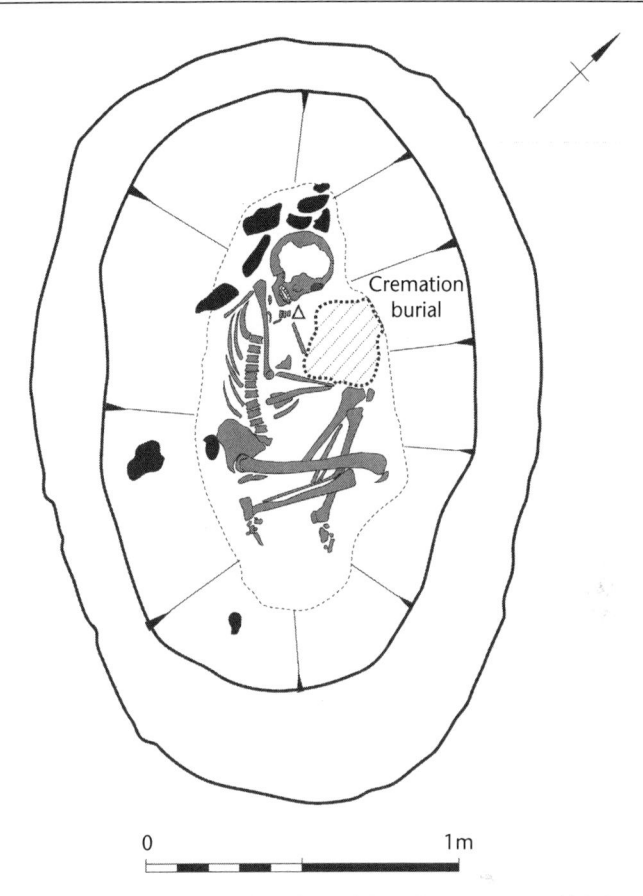

Figure 2.7. The inhumation burial of an adult male accompanied by the cremation burial of an adult female, Middle Barn Farm, Warminster, Wiltshire (© Wessex Archaeology, with slight alterations by the author).

There was no fill between the male and female individuals, suggesting that these had been deposited at the same time.

Antiquarian and early archaeological interpretations of such finds often drew on colonial accounts of the practice of suttee (or sati) in India, to suggest that the co-occurrence of inhumation and cremation was evidence for the sacrifice of a wife or servant (e.g. Mortimer 1905, lxxvi). There is nothing to indicate that this was the case in the Bronze Age, however, and this phenomenon can be interpreted in other ways. At Barns Farm in Fife, the coffin in grave 1 contained a crouched inhumation burial along with three cremation burials—one above the head, one in front of the chest, and one behind the hips (Watkins 1982, 71–2). As we shall see in

Chapter 3, these are exactly the locations in which one might expect to find ceramic vessels or objects such as copper knives or flint artefacts in other graves. Grave 3 at Keenoge in County Meath contained the crouched inhumation of an adult female; a Food Vessel and a cremation burial were placed behind her head (Mount 1997b, 9). Such practices constructed identity in a profoundly relational way. The positioning of cremation burials relative to particular points of the unburnt body employed the symbolic properties of the body to draw attention to certain forms of connection or articulation. It also worked to draw a link between people and objects, a topic we shall return to in the Chapter 3.

There is an interesting gendered dimension to the distinction between inhumation and cremation burial. It has often been noted that males outnumber females in Beaker inhumation graves, including in well-furnished examples (e.g. Clarke 1970, 264–5; Pierpoint 1980; Woodward and Hunter 2015, tables 11.14, 12.5). By *c*.2100 BC, however, when cremation began to dominate the mortuary record, women are well represented (Garwood 2007, 47; Harding et al. 2007, 230). In general, women were more likely to be cremated than men during the Early Bronze Age (Brück 2009; see also Harding et al. 2007, table 4.4). Gendered patterning in the distinction between cremation and inhumation is manifest in other ways: a study of burials from eastern England demonstrates that primary inhumation burials were more frequently male, whereas primary cremation burials were more frequently female (Harding et al. 2007, table 4.5). The prevalence of partial or token cremation burials hints that cremation—as a particular technology of the body—was designed to facilitate the fragmentation, curation, and circulation of ancestral relics outside of the mortuary context, and the tendency for women to be cremated may relate to their positioning at significant nodes in kinship systems (Harding et al. 2007): the circulation of curated fragments of bone perhaps maintained and symbolized intergroup relationships created through marriage. By contrast, bodily integrity (facilitated more easily by inhumation) may have been considered important for those located at other positions in genealogical networks: descent groups often wish to retain certain people and objects, although exchange with others may be viewed as both an economic and social imperative (cf. Weiner 1992). McKinley's observation (1997, 142) that cremation burials from primary positions in Bronze Age barrows produce much higher weights of bone than those from other locations may support the argument that there was a link between genealogical position and bodily integrity.

Appleby (2013, 92) argues that one of the differences between cremation and inhumation burials is that cremation graves were not often reopened. Although there has not yet been a detailed study of the frequency with which Early Bronze Age burials of any sort were reopened, there is certainly some evidence to suggest that bones could be added to and removed from cremation graves. Two cremation burials, each accompanied by a Food Vessel, were laid on the base of cist D at Carrig in County Wicklow (Grogan 1990). Sometime later, three successive pits were dug into the fill of the cist for the deposition of three further cremation burials, each in an inverted Cordoned Urn; this sequence of deposits is not dissimilar to the succession of inhumation burials found in grave pits in East Yorkshire, for example. A pit beneath barrow VI at West Heath, Harting, West Sussex, produced two Collared Urns, one containing the cremated remains of an adult male. Above this and in the same feature were located two further Collared Urns containing the cremated remains of an adult male and a few burnt bones from a child respectively (Drewett 1985, 40). At Snail Down in Wiltshire, the cremation burial of a child in a Collared Urn was deposited in a pit under a small flint cairn located on the berm between the mound and ditch of barrow III (Thomas 2005, 40). At some point after burial, however, the cairn was dismantled, the pot removed, and most of its contents emptied on the ground to the east. The urn was then replaced in the pit; here a grave was reopened not to deposit a new burial, but to encounter and manipulate the remains of the dead. Appleby's suggestion (2013, 92–3) that the introduction of cremation resulted in a dramatic change in the temporality of the mortuary rite can therefore be questioned. Instead, we can suggest that the addition, removal, and manipulation of cremated remains may have performed similar roles to some of the practices documented above for unburnt bone.

The materiality of Early Bronze Age cremation burials

The constituent elements of cremation deposits are interesting also, for they cast light on concepts of the body and the relationship between self and other. In many cases, cremation burials comprise deposits of clean cremated bone that must have been carefully picked piece by piece from the pyre. The bun-shaped deposit of clean cremated bone from cremation burial 8 at Easton Down, Allington, Wiltshire, may have been deposited in a cloth bag (Ride 2001, 167): a bronze awl that lay on top of the bone may have been used to secure the opening of the bag. Cremation 2 at Avebury G55 (Smith 1965, 31) formed an oblong mass of about 48 by 20 centimetres and may originally have been placed in a wooden box. Sometimes deposits of pyre debris were placed separately in the same pit or nearby (McKinley 1997, 137–9), so that the body was physically divided from the other burnt by-products of the cremation process. A pit beneath a barrow on Knighton Hill, Broad Chalke, Wiltshire, contained a deposit of clean cremated bone in a pot (Rahtz 1970, 78–9); beneath this, and lying on the base of the pit, was a deposit of pyre debris. At other sites, the pyre debris was buried at a distance from the body. The cremation burial of an adult female and infant at the centre of barrow 3, Guiting Power, Gloucestershire, had been carefully cleaned; a separate deposit of pyre debris was buried in a pit in the berm of the barrow (McKinley 1997, 139; Marshall 2004a, 11). The careful deposition of the pyre debris itself indicates that this too was considered a significant and powerful material that required disposal in the correct way.

Of course, the degree of spatial segregation between burial and pyre may have varied. Many more Early Bronze Age cremation burials are known than contemporary pyre sites, so for the most part we do not know where the act of cremation itself took place. This apparent spatial dislocation may suggest that there was at least sometimes a temporal hiatus between cremation and deposition. At some sites, however, pyres have been identified. An area 'some 5 ft. square, which had been reddened by fire' lay at the centre of barrow 7 at Barrow Hills, Radley, in Berkshire, and was interpreted as a pyre site. This appeared to have been swept clean and the pyre debris deposited in a small pit dug into the pyre floor (Atkinson 1954, 28, 30–1). At Snail Down in Wiltshire, the primary burial under barrow III comprised the cremated body of an adult female (Thomas 2005, 32–3). A few metres north of the burial, a group of burnt timbers forming an east–west oriented pile are probably the remains of an *in situ* funeral pyre (Figure 2.8); the old land surface on which they lay was also burnt. A fragment of hazelnut shell amongst these timbers suggests that the cremation may have taken place in the late summer or early autumn (Thomas 2005, 283). To the north-west of the pyre and burial pit was a line of stake-holes that may have screened off the activities of those involved in the cremation and subsequent burial.

Although the burnt bone and pyre debris were often separated, in other cases these materials remained commingled and were deposited together. A pit beneath barrow II at Snail Down in Wiltshire contained the cremated remains of a possible female mixed with sherds of pottery and pyre debris including wood ash and charcoal (Thomas 2005, 29). Just over one kilogram of bone was present, and an unburnt disc of human skull had been placed on the floor of the pit. A pit close to the centre of a ring-ditch at Ashville Trading Estate, Abingdon, Oxfordshire, had burnt and sooted sides and contained mixed deposits of pottery sherds, burnt human bone, and charcoal (Parrington 1978, 9). Elsewhere, it has been argued that burnt bone was just one of a range of meaningful

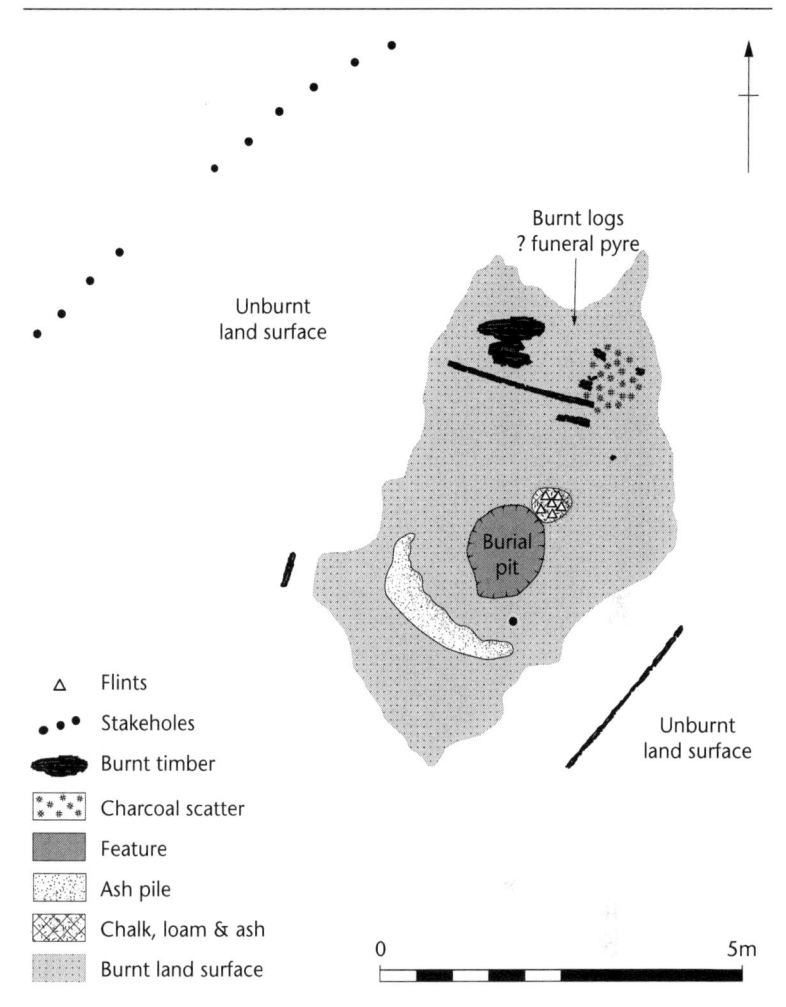

Figure 2.8. The cremation burial, funeral pyre, and fence/screen beneath barrow III at Snail Down, Wiltshire (redrawn by Anne Leaver after Thomas 2005, fig. 12; reproduced with permission of the Wiltshire Archaeological and Natural History Society).

materials deposited in barrows so that the distinction between human bone and other substances may not have been considered so great. Cornish barrows, for example, have produced few burials and they may not have functioned solely as repositories for the bodies of the dead. Instead, they were foci for the deposition of a variety of materials including ceramics, quartz, and charcoal, as well as—sometimes—small quantities of burnt bone (Jones 2005, 140, 205). Here the focus may have been on employing token deposits of human bone not as a means of memorializing the identity of a particular individual, but as a symbolic resource in significant ceremonial activities or to give meaning to particular places in the landscape. The key point here is that burnt human bone was just one of a range of substances used in similar depositional practices; this calls into question the division between persons and things.

Mortuary practice and identity in the Middle Bronze Age

Cremation was the most common mortuary practice during the Middle Bronze Age, but occasional inhumation burials are known, for example the five adolescents and children whose graves were cut into the edge of an existing Early Bronze Age round barrow at Canada Farm in Dorset (Smith et al. 2016). Several of these display evidence for complex practices involving the manipulation and possible curation of human remains. Two of the burials displayed drill marks to the epiphyseal and diaphyseal ends of several bones that must have been made after the bodies had decomposed (Bailey et al. 2013; Smith et al. 2016). Yet the bodies were laid in the grave with all of the bones in their correct anatomical position. It has therefore been suggested that the holes were made in order to allow the bones to be kept together or reassembled (for example with wooden pegs) after the flesh had begun to decay. Cut marks on one of these bodies and on another of the inhumation burials from the site hint that post-mortem practices may also have involved defleshing. None of the bodies were accompanied by grave goods.

Unburnt bodies and body fragments have also occasionally been found in non-mortuary contexts. At Golf Crossing, Battlesbury, near Warminster in Wiltshire, the body of a 16–18-year-old girl dating to 1520–1400 BC was found lying prone on the primary fill of a probable field boundary (Figure 2.9). The position of the body suggested that she had been thrown into the ditch (Ellis and Powell 2008, 184–5, fig. 12.2). Other Middle Bronze Age boundaries have also occasionally produced unburnt bone. At Clay Farm, Trumpington, Cambridgeshire (Phillips and Mortimer 2012, 21, 23, 25), unburnt bone fragments (predominantly portions of the skull) were recovered from five ditches forming part of a Middle Bronze Age field system and associated settlement. One skull fragment was recovered from the terminal of a ditch that enclosed an area of settlement; this displayed a distinct cut mark and was identified as probably male. Possible cut marks were also identified

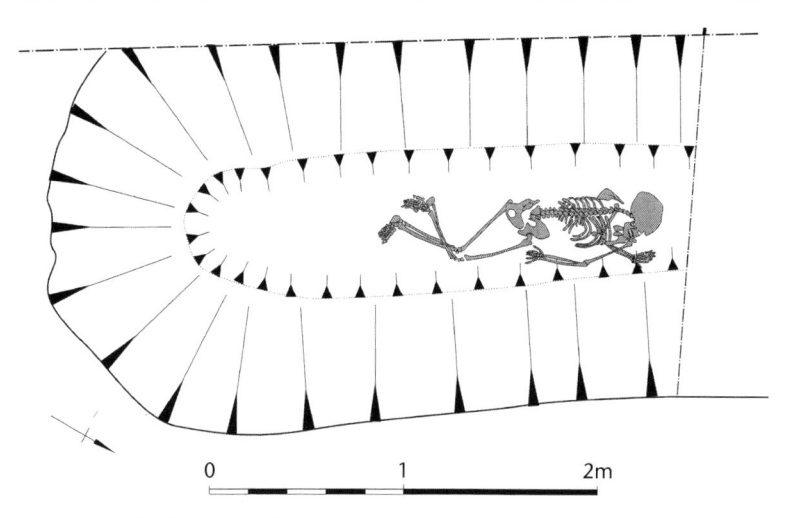

Figure 2.9. The body of a 16–18-year-old girl deposited in a field boundary at Golf Crossing, Battlesbury, near Warminster in Wiltshire (© Wessex Archaeology, with slight alterations by the author).

on a femur and fibula from a nearby Middle Bronze Age pit. Such finds cannot be interpreted as formal burials; instead, human bone appears to have been employed to mark out significant places in the landscape, a practice that became common in the Late Bronze Age, as we shall see later in this chapter.

Cremation was, however, the predominant mortuary rite during the Middle Bronze Age (Ellison 1980; Caswell and Roberts 2018). Flat cemeteries are common: at Daneshill, Basingstoke, Hampshire, fourteen cremation burials, twelve of them in urns, were deposited in a small cluster of pits (Millett and Schadla-Hall 1991). Although barrows were sometimes still constructed, these were usually smaller than their Early Bronze Age predecessors (Ellison 1980, 117), and tend to occur singly rather than in groups. Burials were deposited both in and around these monuments. The barrow at Watton in Norfolk was just 8.5 metres in diameter (Mason 2011). The cremation burial of an adult was located at the centre of the barrow, while five other burials (four of which were of adults) were deposited in pits outside of the monument. At West Cliff, Ramsgate, in Kent, a small cairn of flint and chalk was surrounded by a ring-ditch some 4 metres in diameter; four pits outside of the barrow produced small quantities of cremated bone (Moody et al. 2010).

Sometimes, more extensive barrow cemeteries are known. At Ballintaggart, County Down, a linear cemetery of eight small ring-barrows with internal diameters of about 1–3 metres was identified, each with a central cremation burial (Figure 2.10; Dunlop 2015, 74–6). At Brightlingsea in Essex, thirty-one small ring-ditches were identified (Clarke and Lavender 2008); here, most of the cremation burials were found between the monuments rather than inside them. Existing Early Bronze Age barrows were also reused (Robinson 2007, 36; Cooper 2016). A group of Middle Bronze Age cremation burials was placed in the southern half of Early Bronze Age bell barrow XV at Snail Down in Wiltshire (Thomas 2005, fig. 25), while at Butcher's Rise in Cambridgeshire thirty-one cremation burials were deposited in the edge of an Early Bronze Age barrow and in the fill of the outer ditch (Figure 2.11; Evans and Knight 1998). This suggests that relationships with the ancestral dead continued to be considered important. Further north, other classes of monument were

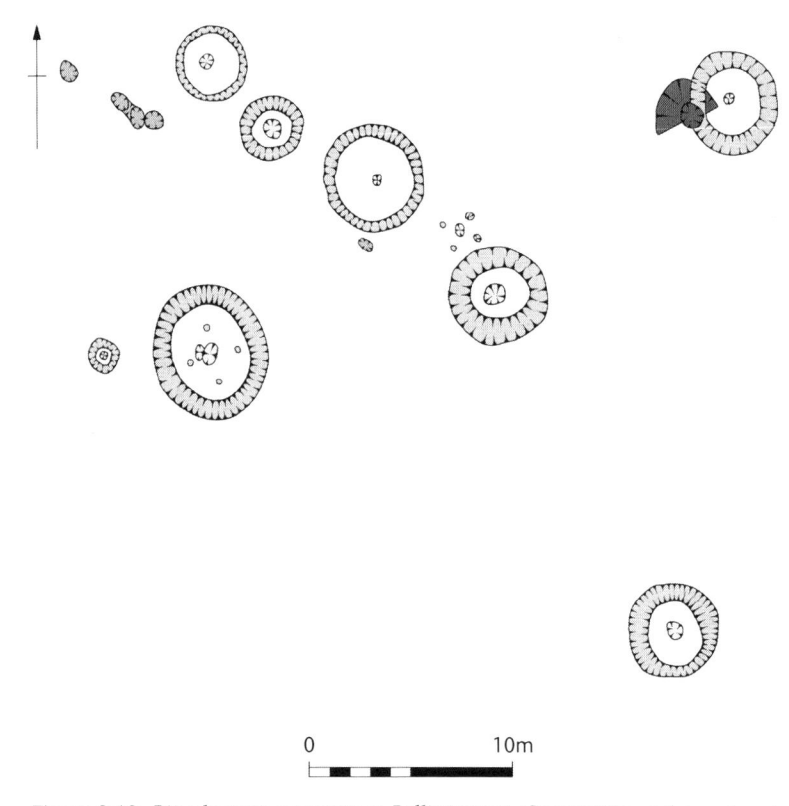

Figure 2.10. Ring-barrow cemetery at Ballintaggart, County Down (reproduced with permission of Colin Dunlop and Northern Archaeological Consultancy, with slight alterations by Anne Leaver).

Fragmenting the body

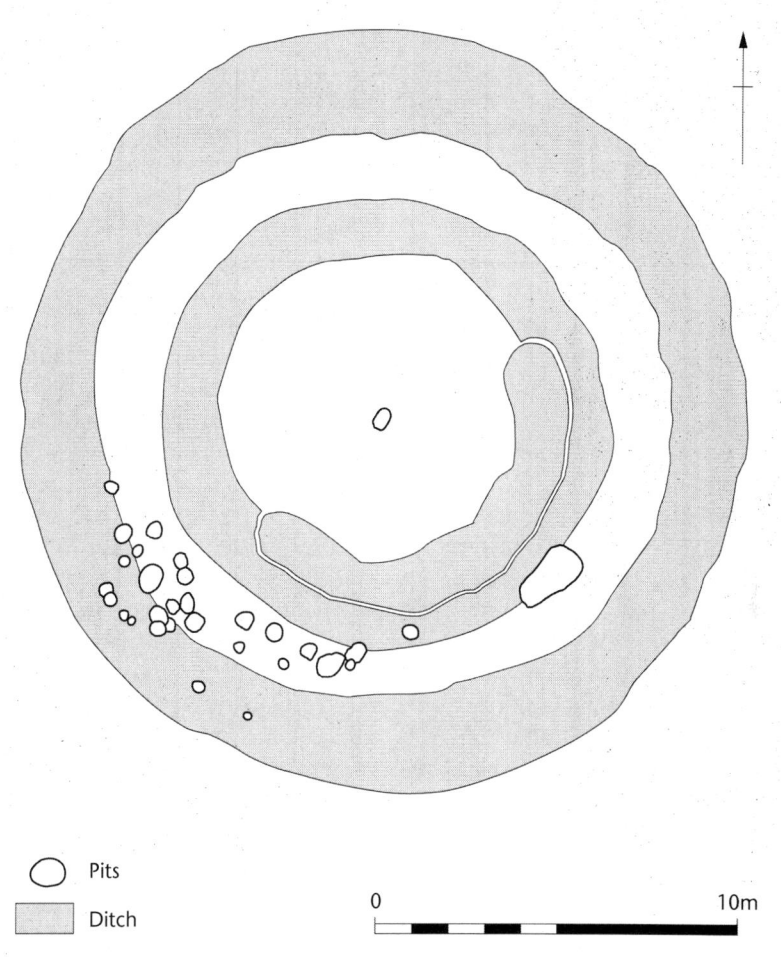

○ Pits

▓ Ditch

Figure 2.11. The Early Bronze Age barrow at Butcher's Rise, Cambridgeshire; the group of pits between and overlying the inner and outer ring-ditches on the south-western side of the monument contained Middle Bronze Age cremation burials and pyre sweepings (reproduced with permission of Cambridge Archaeological Unit; redrawn by Anne Leaver).

reused. At Cairnwell, Portlethen, Aberdeenshire (Rees 1997), a large cremation pyre of Middle Bronze Age date was lit inside a stone circle that may have been constructed a thousand years earlier. A circular timber enclosure about 5.7 metres in diameter and surrounding five pits that produced small quantities of cremated bone was then built in the centre of the circle. Finally, a ring-cairn was constructed directly on top of the earlier monument.

45

Ellison (1980) argues that, in contrast to the barrow cemeteries of the Early Bronze Age, which are likely to have been focal points for the gathering of large numbers of people, the scale of Middle Bronze Age cremation cemeteries suggests that these were the individual burial-places for smaller social groups. The presence of men, women, and children (Ellison 1980; Robinson 2007, table 4.1) and the spatial proximity of some cemeteries to contemporary settlements (Bradley 1981) suggest that Middle Bronze Age cemeteries were used by extended families (Ellison 1980). At Butcher's Rise in Cambridgeshire, for example, the cremation burials included four males and three females. There were eleven adults in total, alongside fifteen children (less than 13 years old) and four subadults/adults (Dodwell 1998). Caswell and Roberts (2018) challenge the extended family model, however. They demonstrate that 33 per cent of Middle Bronze Age burial sites comprise just a single cremation burial, with 56 per cent of sites producing fewer than five individual bodies. Relatively few Middle Bronze Age cemeteries have been recorded in comparison to the large number of contemporary settlements known, and the average distance between cemeteries and settlements is 1742 metres (Caswell and Roberts 2018). Moreover, radiocarbon dating suggests that at individual cemeteries burial may have been a relatively rare event. Caswell and Roberts therefore argue that only certain people were afforded formal burial in Middle Bronze Age cremation cemeteries.

We have seen that the spatial arrangement of Early Bronze Age burials demonstrates close attention to interpersonal relationships. Middle Bronze Age burials also show careful spatial structuring. Bradley (1998, 157) has noted that Middle Bronze Age burials often cluster in the south-east quadrant of earlier barrows, an orientation shared with contemporary roundhouses. At Latch Farm in Hampshire, for example, some ninety Middle Bronze Age cremation deposits were deposited around the southern edge of an Early Bronze Age barrow (Piggott 1938, fig. 1). As we shall see in Chapter 4, studies of domestic architecture of the period have argued that south-east may have been considered an auspicious direction, referencing ideas of light, life, and fertility—no doubt appropriate symbolism in a funerary context also. Elsewhere, there is an element of variation on this theme. At Westhampnett in West Sussex, the entrance to ring-ditch 6108, a small penannular enclosure of Middle Bronze Age date, was located to the south-east, but the associated cremation burials were deposited on the south-west of the monument, two in the ditch and the third just outside of it (Chadwick 2006, fig. 5). Similarly, the cremation burials at Butcher's Rise, Cambridgeshire, were located in the south-western margins of the monument (Figure 2.11; Evans and Knight 1998). Here, in contrast, the focus on the south-west—where the sun sets—may have conjured images of death and darkness.

Many other sites show clear evidence for the careful placement of burials. At Bromfield in Shropshire the cremation burials were arranged in an arc at the western end of an Early Bronze Age barrow cemetery (Stanford 1982, figs 3, 7), with the 'arms' of the arc pointing away from the earlier monuments. Lines of burials have been identified at many Middle Bronze Age cemeteries. At Chitts Hill, Colchester, Essex, a line of twelve cremation burials neatly bisected the space between two small neighbouring ring-ditches (Crummy 1977, fig. 3). This arrangement may have given material form to ideas of genealogical succession or other forms of interpersonal similarities and distinctions. The flat cremation cemetery at Templenoe in County Tipperary comprised seventy-four pits, of which fifty-seven contained cremated bone. The pits formed a series of roughly linear but intersecting arrangements running approximately east–west and north–south (McQuade et al. 2009, fig. 3.35). Here, although individual rows could represent different family groups, the tight clustering of the burials, most of which are located in an area of 4 x 4 metres, suggests a close-knit community. Robinson (2007, 69) has noted that, in East Anglia, lines of cremation burials at sites such as Eye Quarry in Cambridgeshire often share the alignment of nearby field systems of contemporary date; we will explore the significance of this relationship in Chapter 5.

Fragmenting and combining the Middle Bronze Age body

Middle Bronze Age burials were rarely accompanied by objects other than pots (Ellison 1980; Caswell and Roberts 2018), suggesting that the expression of social status was not a primary concern of funerary practices during this period; this and the small scale of most cemeteries of the period suggest that Middle Bronze Age mortuary practices 'embodied intimacy and simplicity' (Robinson 2007, 31). Yet it is evident that the human body was treated with care and that Middle Bronze Age cremation rites involved complex and highly structured practices. The human remains from the small cremation cemetery at Loughton, in Milton Keynes, Buckinghamshire, indicate the sophistication of the cremation technology. The bone from this site was well burnt, and the presence of cremation slag suggests that high temperatures were regularly reached and were maintained for long periods of time. This suggests careful tending of the pyre (Start 2003, 98).

Not all of the burnt bone appears to have been deposited in the ground, however, and Middle Bronze Age cremation burials tend to comprise even smaller quantities of bone than those of the preceding period. The mean weight of Middle Bronze Age cremation burials in Britain is 390.9 grams (Caswell and Roberts 2018), while Robinson's study of cremation burials in East Anglia demonstrates that 40 per cent of burials from this region weigh less than 100 grams (2007, 21). The average weight of the urned cremation burials (which we might expect to be relatively well preserved) from Coneygre Farm in Nottinghamshire was just 327 grams, for example (Allen et al. 1987, 211). At Westhampnett in West Sussex, the urned burials range in weight from 87 to 978 grams (McKinley 2006). The bone in these deposits is relatively well preserved and there is no evidence that they were truncated. The Irish evidence is similar, with a significant decrease in average weight from the Early Bronze Age (Lynch and O'Donnell 2007, table 5.6): at Templenoe in County Tipperary, for example, most of the fifty-seven pits containing cremated bone yielded less than 10 grams (Geber 2009, 213). Occasionally, there are tantalizing hints for the possible selection of particular body parts for deposition. Skull fragments are over-represented in all of the well-preserved urned burials from Birch's Pit near Colchester in Essex (Anderson 2005, 14), although these are, of course, easier to identity than other skeletal elements. Two of the cremation burials at Mitchelstowndown, County Limerick, also produced significantly higher quantities of skull fragments than might be expected, while long bones were over-represented in four other instances (Ó Donnabháin 1988, 193–4). Although there is little evidence for the deliberate crushing of bone in Britain (McKinley 1994, 340), the small size of the bone fragments from some Irish Middle Bronze Age burials suggests that in certain regions further processing of the remains took place after they were recovered from the pyre (Lynch and O'Donnell 2007, 112).

The 'token' character of many Middle Bronze Age cremation burials suggests that bone may have been distributed among the mourners for curation and redeposition outside of the mortuary context (Brück 2006b; McKinley 2006). There may have been a significant degree of variability in depositional practice, with certain bodies—or certain parts of those bodies—buried swiftly after they were burnt on the pyre, while others were curated for some time and deposited later. As in the Early Bronze Age, identifiable pyre sites are rare, hinting at possible spatial and temporal disjunctions between cremation and deposition. At Kimpton in Hampshire, two areas of burning immediately adjacent to the cremation burials were identified as pyre sites

(Dacre and Ellison 1981, fig. 6). Four large pits set slightly apart from the cluster of cremation burials at Templenoe in County Tipperary have been identified as possible pyre ventilation features, dug beneath the pyres to aid combustion (McQuade et al. 2009, 133); these yielded only small quantities of charcoal, although the species present were the same as those from the adjacent pits containing cremated bone.

Middle Bronze Age cremation burials tend to comprise the remains of single individuals (Caswell and Roberts 2018), and in Ireland there is a notable decrease in the number of multiple burials in comparison to the Early Bronze Age (Lynch and O'Donnell 2007, 123). Multiple burials do occasionally occur, however. At Westhampnett in West Sussex, the cremation burial of an older woman was deposited together with a single fragment of bone from a second individual (McKinley 2006). Another cremation burial from the same site comprised the fragmentary remains of two adults and a child. Three of the thirty-one cremation burials at Butcher's Rise in Cambridgeshire yielded the remains of several individuals—two including an adult and child and the third an adult and two children (Dodwell 1998). Multiple burials with more than two or three individuals are particularly rare: one extraordinary example is the multiple burial at Whitton Hill, Northumberland, which weighed just over 1.5 kilograms but comprised parts of at least twenty-four individuals (Miket 1985).

Although grave goods other than ceramics are rare in burials of Middle Bronze Age date, a structured series of choices often appears to have been made in how to treat the body on deposition. At Butcher's Rise in Cambridgeshire, twelve of the thirty-one cremation burials were deposited in pottery vessels, but the remainder were not (Evans and Knight 1998, 25). The pots in which some cremation burials were placed could be upright or inverted: at Chitts Hill, Colchester, Essex, eight of the urns were upright, while five were inverted (Crummy 1977, 7). Other cremation burials may have been deposited in organic containers. The compact rounded shape of the deposit of bone in pit F42 at Bromfield in Shropshire suggests that this was originally placed in the grave in a cloth or skin pouch—a container that could easily have facilitated curation (Stanford 1982, 301). Here, although these bodies were not complete, an attempt was made to define their edges and distinguish them from other materials.

Often, as in the Early Bronze Age, pyre debris and cremated bone were deposited separately. At Westhampnett in West Sussex, cremation burial 6003 was contained in an inverted urn. Pyre debris had been deposited in the urn after the bone (Chadwick 2006, 14). In other cases, bone, charcoal, and ash were not separated but remained

49

commingled and were deposited together—even within a 'second skin' such as a pot. At Bromfield in Shropshire (Stanford 1982), the contents of the pits varied significantly: some produced clean deposits of burnt bone, while others contained charcoal only, charcoal with distinct layers of bone, charcoal with fragments of bone mixed throughout, or layered combinations of different types of material. This suggests that there was not always a concern to maintain a distinct boundary between the human body and other materials. It also indicates that mixed materials remained powerful and had to be deposited with care.

Circulating the dead in the Late Bronze Age

In most parts of Britain, Late Bronze Age burials are virtually unknown. Inhumation burials are very rare: at Reading Business Park in Berkshire, for example, the unaccompanied inhumation burial of an adult female was found in one of a group of Late Bronze Age pits within a densely settled landscape (Moore and Jennings 1992, 11), while two crouched inhumations, one of which was radiocarbon-dated to the Late Bronze Age, were deposited in pits dug into an Early Bronze Age midden on Manish Strand on the island of Ensay in the Western Isles (Simpson et al. 2003, 182–5). An oak log coffin from a barrow at Rylstone in North Yorkshire has recently been radiocarbon-dated to the Late Bronze Age (Melton et al. 2016); although no human remains survived, the size and shape of the coffin suggest that it may originally have held an inhumation. Other unburnt bodies are more difficult to interpret as formal burials. The position of a fully articulated adult female from the basal silts of a well at Bradley Fen in Cambridgeshire indicated that she had been thrown head first into this feature (Gibson and Knight 2006, 35); her wrists were crossed as if bound, and the uppermost fill of this feature contained the articulated skeleton of a dog.

In some regions, there are hints that cremation was still practised. At Bolam Lake in Northumberland, a small, low cairn, just 4 metres in diameter, produced three cremation burials weighing 125 grams, 225 grams, and 700 grams respectively (Waddington 2002). In Essex, twenty-nine pits in two distinct clusters at Chelmsford Park and Ride produced small amounts of cremated human bone, averaging just under 80 grams per feature (Boghi 2007, 9); these were located immediately south-east of a possibly contemporary Late Bronze Age settlement. Five of the group of nine cremation deposits from Stone Hall, Essex, weighed less than 100 grams (Powell 2007, 31). The clustering of these deposits makes it possible to tentatively identify these as 'cemeteries', although the presence of such tiny quantities of bone raises the question of how the rest of the body was disposed of.

In Ireland, traditions of cremation appear to have continued, and recent developer-led archaeology has resulted in the identification of increasing numbers of Late Bronze Age cremation burials. At Kilmahuddrick in County Dublin, for example, two Late Bronze Age cremation burials were found at the centre of a small ring-barrow (Doyle 2005). At Chetwynd between Ballynora and Lehenaghmore, County Cork, six pits contained the cremated remains of eight people, including five adults, a juvenile aged 14–16 years, and a child aged 3–6 years. The bones of one of these individuals were eroded, suggesting that they may have been curated (Cleary 2015, 56). Cremated bone was recovered from a number of pits and spreads of burnt material in and around a ring-ditch at Dalystown, County Westmeath (Lynch and O'Donnell 2007, table 5.1). Most of the bones had the characteristic fissuring indicative of the cremation of fleshed bone (McKinley 2000, 405); however, the bone from two of the pits did not, and it can be suggested that this was cremated as dry bone (Lynch and O'Donnell 2007, 111).

Many of the deposits of human bone found in Late Bronze Age contexts are difficult to identify as formal burials, however. Instead, fragments of unburnt bone and 'token' deposits of cremated bone were commonly incorporated into a variety of features across the settled landscape (Brück 1995; Cleary 2005). For example, at Must Farm in Cambridgeshire a complete skull was found in a midden deposit adjacent to a roundhouse (M. Knight, pers. comm.). Given the wealth of finds from this extraordinary, waterlogged site, it is not clear just how 'typical' this site is, but the discovery of human bone from a 'domestic' context is not at all unusual (Brück 1995). Some fragments are found inside houses: an unburnt human toe bone was found in a short gully at the entrance to roundhouse 1 at Game Farm near Brandon, Suffolk (Gibson, C. 2004, 18), while two deposits of cremated human remains weighing just 35.9 grams and 121.5 grams respectively were recovered from neighbouring postholes of a roundhouse at Aird Quarry, Castle Kennedy, Dumfries and Galloway (Cook 2006, 13). Other features on Late Bronze Age settlements also frequently produce human bone. An open settlement at Striplands Farm, Cambridgeshire (Evans and Patton 2011, 10, 16), included a roundhouse, a possible longhouse, four-post structures, fence-lines, pits, and waterholes: two unburnt skull fragments were found in waterhole F13, while pit F63 produced 225 grams of burnt bone along with a near-complete pot, a fragment of saddle-quern and a loom weight. At Shorncote Quarry, Gloucestershire, part of an unburnt human skull was found in the basal fills of a waterhole that formed part of an extensive open settlement comprising densely packed roundhouses, four-posters, pits, and waterholes (Boyle 2002, 69).

Bodies and liminality

It is evident that human remains from non-mortuary contexts were often deposited in boundaries of one sort or another (Brück 1995). The inner ditch surrounding a Late Bronze Age settlement at Chancellorsland in County Tipperary produced four skull fragments belonging to a young adult; these were found in deposits of domestic refuse at the entrance to the site (Power 2008). A shallow pit dug into the lower silts of the terminal of a double linear ditch (a land boundary of Late Bronze Age date) at Sidbury in Wiltshire yielded a skull and a few other bone fragments (Bradley et al. 1994, 42). At South Hornchurch in Essex (Guttmann et al. 2000), 6 grams of cremated human bone was recovered from one of the postholes that formed part of the porched entranceway of roundhouse 8. Elsewhere at this site, the entrances to a large ringwork enclosure were marked in a similar way. A deposit of cremated bone was found in a pit just outside the southern entrance to the enclosure, while fragments of burnt bone were placed in the northern terminal of the ditch at the north-eastern entrance (Figure 2.12). A break on the south side of the phase 2 droveway just north of the ringwork was marked by two pits that may have formed part of a gateway structure; one of these produced 1 gram of cremated bone.

Just as fragments of bone from settlement contexts were often found in locations that can be described as liminal—spaces of transition such as boundaries, thresholds, and entrances—the same qualities can be ascribed to other places in which human remains were deposited during this period (Brück 1995). At Bradley Fen in Cambridgeshire, a hoard of damaged and incomplete spears, swords, ferrules, and chapes was deposited in waterlogged peat immediately next to a major junction at the edge of a field system (Figure 3.10; Gibson and Knight 2006, 26–8). This location also attracted the deposition of other objects, including three fragments of human skull found in the peat some 5 metres north of the hoard. In fact, skulls have frequently been recovered from wet places including rivers, lakes, and bogs. The skull of an adult male, for example, was found in the basal layers of peat deposits at Poulton-le-Fylde, Lancashire (Wells and Hodgkinson 2001); no other bones were recovered, and the lack of a mandible indicates that the skull was deposited after the soft tissues had decomposed. A number of skulls from the River Thames have been dated to the Late Bronze Age (Bradley and Gordon 1988; Schulting and Bradley 2013); like other rivers, the Thames was a particular

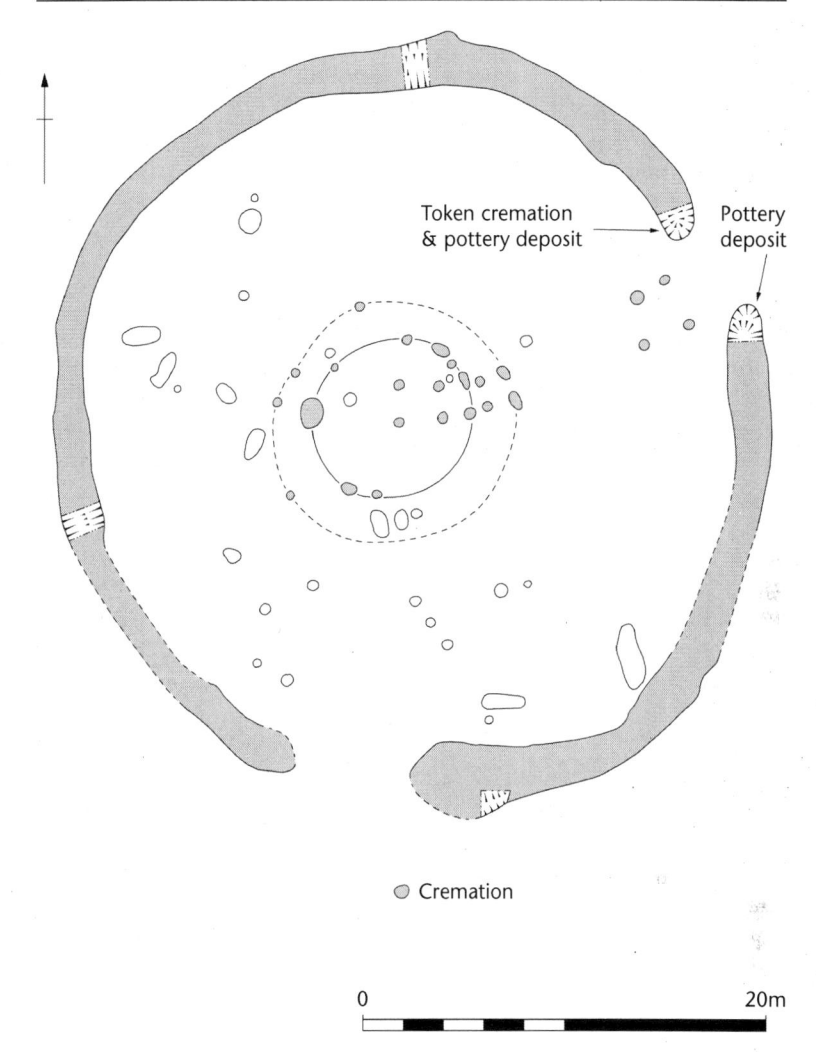

Figure 2.12. Deposits of cremated human bone and pottery at the entrances to the ringwork at South Hornchurch, Essex (redrawn by Anne Leaver after Guttmann et al. 2000, fig. 8; reproduced with permission of the Prehistoric Society).

focus for the deposition of metalwork, notably swords and spearheads, during this period (York 2002). A palaeochannel of the River Soar in Leicestershire produced several bones from an adult male (Ripper and Beamish 2012); slash marks to the vertebrae indicate that this individual had suffered a violent death.

In some cases, finds from wet places are associated with wooden structures, such as the causeway constructed in a creek on the Crouch estuary, Essex, which produced two skulls (Wilkinson and Murphy 1995). The well-known platform and causeway at Flag Fen, from which a significant quantity of disarticulated human bone was recovered (Halstead and Cameron 1992), represents another good example. Some of these structures may have been built specifically to facilitate votive deposition into the water: watery places, it has often been suggested, may have been associated with gods, spirits, or ancestors during this period—a conduit to the otherworld—and it is no surprise that both human remains and Late Bronze Age metalwork have been found in such locations (Torbrügge 1971; Bradley 1990; Hansen 1994; Schulting and Bradley 2013). It seems likely, too, that rivers and other wetlands may have demarcated social and political boundaries (Bradley 2017). Here, human remains were associated with landscapes of transition, places at the edges of the settled landscape that were hazardous in physical, social, and cosmological terms. Indeed, because metal objects were deposited in graves during the Early Bronze Age, but in wet places during the Late Bronze Age, it has been suggested that consigning the bodies of the dead (either burnt or unburnt) to water may have been the normal mode of mortuary treatment for this period (Bradley 1990, 107).

Human bone was also deposited in caves during this period, again often alongside metalwork. Mandibles found at the entrance to the Sculptor's Cave at Covesea, on the edge of the Moray Firth, suggest that fleshed heads may once have been displayed there from which the jaws eventually dropped. Some of these belonged to children (Shepherd 2007). The cave also produced Late Bronze Age metalwork, including some possible 'high-status' objects such as arm-rings and 'ring money' (Benton 1931). A recent programme of radiocarbon dating has shown that the deposition of human remains in the cave was practised sporadically from the Late Bronze Age through to the Late Iron Age (Armit et al. 2011) and that the skull was a particular focus of interest throughout this period. The cave is accessible only at low water and is potentially hazardous at other times (Figure 2.13; Armit et al. 2011): it seems possible that it may have been seen as an entrance to the underworld and thus as a suitable location for rites of passage—transforming children into adults or the dead into ancestors. The cave at Heathery Burn in County Durham produced significant quantities of human bone as well as Late Bronze Age metalwork (Greenwell 1894; Britton 1968); these were found during quarrying activities in the nineteenth century, so it is unclear if they were directly associated. Interestingly,

Fragmenting the body

Figure 2.13. The shoreline location of the Sculptor's Cave, Covesea, Moray (reproduced with permission of Lindsey Büster and Ian Armit).

a number of finds from the site can be linked to metal production: these include one side of a mould for casting socketed axes, a casting jet, an ingot fragment, and various broken bronze objects. Although it is unlikely that the casting of bronze objects was carried out *in situ* in this cave, ethnographic research (e.g. Herbert 1993) has shown that metalworking is often viewed as a hazardous and transformative process. At Heathery Burn, a range of transformative activities involving the processing of significant materials, including metals and bodies, was referenced. As such, the deposition of objects associated with bronze production together with human bone in a liminal place provides interesting insights into how the remains of the dead were perceived and valued—human bone, too, may have been viewed as a dangerous material because of its association with processes of physical decay and social disruption.

Elsewhere, human remains were deposited at ceremonial monuments of various types. The cremated remains of an adolescent deposited in a pot at the centre of the stone circle at Drombeg in County Cork yielded a Late Bronze Age radiocarbon date (Fahy 1959; O'Brien 1992, 33), although it is not clear if the monument itself was constructed at this time or earlier. At Dunure Road, Ayrshire (Duffy 2007, 87), a small pit next to a standing stone contained 227 grams of burnt bone belonging to an adult; this was dated to 1260–1010 BC. Some 20–30 centimetres east of the stone, another pit produced 12 grams of cremated bone of similar date; here, the remains were those of an infant. At Loanhead of Daviot, Aberdeenshire, a series of Late Bronze Age cremation burials were inserted into a ring-cairn constructed at the centre of a recumbent stone circle (Kilbride-Jones 1935; 1936); in Scotland, monuments of this class have been dated to the Early Bronze Age (Bradley 2005b; Welfare 2011). The presence of human bone at sites such as these can be interpreted in a number of ways. On the one hand, where pre-existing monuments were reused, this indicates an interest in referencing the past and locating the newly dead into a particular genealogy of landscape. On the other hand, monuments such as the standing stone at Dunure Road may themselves have been constructed in the Late Bronze Age. However, the presence of human remains need not indicate that they were created as mortuary monuments per se. Instead, the deposition of human bone at these sites may have imbued these places with particular cultural meanings, just as the symbolic significance of bone was drawn on in contemporary settlement contexts. The south-westerly orientation of Irish recumbent stone circles has long been recognized (Ó Nualláin 1975), suggesting that rites at these monuments took place at or near midwinter; human bone—a powerful material that referenced death and the afterlife—may therefore have been considered a particularly apposite means of marking the significance of these places. Moreover, if we interpret sites such as Drombeg or Dunure Road as ceremonial monuments at which communities gathered, it is not difficult to see how the politics of personal and community identity might draw on the symbolism of human bone—whether that belonged to a known individual or was representative of a more generalized ancestry.

Practices of post-mortem manipulation

The paucity of burial evidence for the Late Bronze Age and the fragmentary nature of the human bone found in settlements and other contexts has been argued to indicate that excarnation was the normal mode of mortuary treatment for much of the population (Brück 1995; but see Carr and Knüsel 1997). For example, much of the disarticulated material from the Late Bronze Age–early Middle Iron Age settlement outside of the hillfort at Battlesbury near Warminster in Wiltshire displays evidence for canid gnawing and weathering that suggests 'some level of exposure linked to deliberate human manipulation involving excarnation and possible "curation"' (McKinley 2008, 81–2).

Whatever the source of the human remains from non-mortuary contexts, there is clear evidence for selection and other forms of complex post-mortem manipulation of human bone. The upper silts of a ditch surrounding an Early Bronze Age round barrow at East Northdown, Margate, Kent, produced what is described as a 'bundle' of unburnt bones comprising four long bones and the lower jaw of a young adult (Smith 1987, 245). These lay directly below a deposit of Late Bronze Age pottery, struck flint, animal bone, and fragments of loom weight and quernstones. The majority of the cremated bone from the two Late Bronze Age pits at Dunure Road, Ayrshire (Duffy 2007, 87), comprised skull and long-bone fragments, suggesting an element of deliberate selection.

Unburnt bone from other sites of this date also tends to comprise disarticulated fragments, usually pieces of skull and long bone. The 139 fragments of human bone recovered from the midden at Potterne in Wiltshire included a significant proportion of skull fragments, while amongst the axial bones there was a clear preponderance of elements from the right-hand side (McKinley 2000, 99). At Cliffs End Farm in Kent, skull fragments and right femora dominate an assemblage that comprises the remains of at least twenty-four individuals (McKinley et al. 2014, 217). Although these are the elements that survive best, the recovery of fragments of skull from locations such as boundaries and entrances at many sites hints at patterns of deliberate selection. Occasionally, there is evidence for the deliberate working of bone in Late Bronze Age contexts. At Green Park in Berkshire, a fragment of human skull was recovered from a waterhole adjacent to two round-houses (Boyle 2003). This had originally formed part of a worked disc of bone with a drilled perforation at its centre. The perforation was worn, suggesting that it had been suspended—for some time—from a cord, perhaps to allow it to be worn on the body or displayed elsewhere in or around the home.

Perhaps the best-known example of complex practices of post-mortem manipulation dating to the Late Bronze Age are the 'bodies' from the settlement at Cladh Hallan on South Uist (Parker Pearson et al. 2005; Booth et al. 2015). A tightly flexed burial from a pit in house 1370 was found to comprise skeletal elements from three different adult males reconstituted as a single inhumation burial: the head and neck belonged to one individual, the mandible to a second, and the postcranial remains to a third (Figure 2.14). These men had died $c.$1500 BC but were not buried in this house until 400 years later. A second burial from

Personifying Prehistory

Figure 2.14. The composite male mummy from house 1370, Cladh Hallan, South Uist (reproduced with permission of Mike Parker Pearson).

the same building appears to have combined elements from a man and a woman—again some 300 years older than their final depositional context. Some of the bones from this 'body' had been removed prior to burial: these included the left knee joint, which was deposited separately in a pit outside the door of the building. The deposition of bodies that were at least partly intact so long after the deaths of these individuals suggests practices that involved deliberate preservation of corpses. Histological analysis of the first of these burials showed unusually little evidence for bacterial attack, suggesting that the soft tissues may have been preserved through mummification. Demineralization of the bone surfaces indicates that this may have been facilitated by temporary deposition in an acidic environment such as a bog.

At the opposite end of the country, the site at Cliffs End Farm in Kent has produced evidence for a diverse range of activities involving the

Fragmenting the body

manipulation of unburnt human bone (McKinley et al. 2014). These were focused around a large pit that yielded a number of complete and partial articulated bodies, as well as disarticulated fragments of bone (Figure 2.15). Finds included the complete inhumation burial of an elderly female (3675) lying flexed on her left-hand side close to the base of the feature. She had suffered a number of sword blows to the back of the head: the lack of evidence for self-defence and the careful deposition of her body suggest that her death may have been the result of sacrifice rather than combat. Next to her, a subadult female (3680), about 17–18 years old, lay flexed on her right-hand side, her head resting on a cattle skull. Other burials from the pit included the crouched and

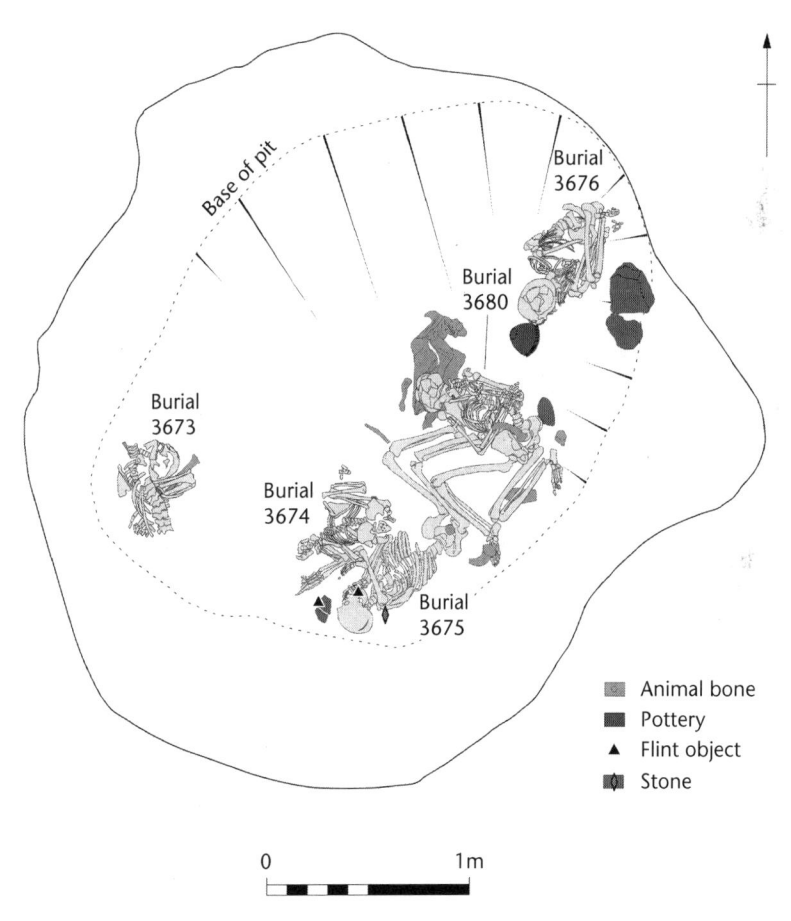

Figure 2.15. The burial pit at Cliffs End Farm, Kent (© Wessex Archaeology, with slight alterations by Anne Leaver).

prone body of a child (3674), about 10–11 years old; this individual was missing its right hand and most of its skull. The body of a second child (3676) of around the same age was laid in a tightly crouched position on its right-hand side; its skull had been twisted round to face half of a ceramic vessel deposited behind the head, probably once the body had partially decomposed. The articulated but incomplete body of an adult male (3673) was also found (Figure 2.16). This comprised the skull, spine, left half of the ribcage and upper left arm arranged as a bundle; the awkward relative positioning of the different elements suggested that the body must have been partially decomposed when it was deposited in the pit. Unusually—for grave goods are virtually unknown during this period—this body was associated with a composite copper and bone object, interpreted as a possible pendant. Radiocarbon dating, stratigraphic evidence, and the condition of the burials together indicate that the complete and partial skeletons may have been deposited within ten years of each other. There is no evidence for re-excavation of the pit between episodes of deposition, and this suggests that the feature may

Figure 2.16. A bundle of bones representing part of the body of an adult male (3673) from Cliffs End Farm, Kent, with numbered thoracic and lumbar vertebrae (© Wessex Archaeology).

have been left open with perhaps a temporary cover in place to protect the bodies from the elements.

Elsewhere in the fill of the pit, an articulated foot and substantial numbers of disarticulated bones were also found; the presence of clearly definable groups of bones, particularly skulls and long bones, suggests deliberate deposition rather than accidental inclusion. The radiocarbon dates from several of the disarticulated bones from the upper layers of the pit demonstrate that these are older than the elderly female who lay close to the base of the feature. This indicates either that these bones were curated or that they were disinterred and redeposited. If they represent the remains of disturbed earlier burials from the same feature, this raises the question of where the rest of those bodies have gone. Interestingly, there is no evidence that these 'heirloom' bones were subject to exposure. By contrast, some of the other disarticulated remains from the pit appear to have been exposed, at least for a short period, as indicated by the presence of evidence for canid gnawing, longitudinal fissures, bleaching, and loss of trabecular bone. A green precipitate noted on two juvenile skull fragments from the upper fill of the pit suggests that these had spent some time in a waterlogged environment prior to their deposition in this feature. It is possible that one of these might have belonged to the child burial with the missing skull described above. If so, the skull was removed, stored elsewhere, and finally redeposited in the same feature as the rest of the body. Isotopic analysis suggests that some of the bones deposited in the pit belonged to non-locals—perhaps from as far away as Scandinavia or the Mediterranean. Non-locals were identified both among the complete/near-complete bodies and the disarticulated skeletal elements, and Needham (2014, 221) suggests that, in some cases, it may have been curated bones rather than living individuals who travelled.

Conclusion

It is clear that the evidence presented in this chapter cannot fit a neat narrative of unilineal evolution. The argument that the bodies buried in Early Bronze Age graves can be construed as 'individuals' in the modern, Western sense of the word is problematic, for it underplays the complexity and variability of the mortuary evidence. As we have seen, bodies were deposited both complete and incomplete. This distinction warrants further discussion, for it is difficult to link this solely to status: contrary to Rowlands (1980, 51), who argues that cremation was reserved for those of lower status because it destroyed the body and negated individual identity, we can argue that the complex range of practices documented above indicates that the process of deliberate fragmentation in fact served other ideological purposes. Bones were selected and removed from graves and pyres for curation, display, and deposition elsewhere; occasionally, these were even made into objects that were worn on the bodies of the living (such as belt hooks) or used in significant social and ceremonial settings (such as the whistle from Wilsford G58: Woodward and Hunter 2015, 114). Practices such as excarnation or dismemberment may have been employed to fragment unburnt bodies, although burials were also reopened and bodies were disassembled and rearranged in the grave. Complete and partial bodies, as well as individual skeletal elements, were buried together with other bodies, and their relative positioning was often carefully choreographed. Together, this suggests that the fragmentation of the body worked to create ancestral relics that were employed in the construction of social and political identities both for the living and the dead. We have seen that unburnt bone was subject to complex forms of fragmentation, manipulation, and curation, and we can suggest that cremation became increasingly common precisely because it facilitated these processes. Those whose bodies were fragmented may therefore have been people of particular significance, however that was defined. Over the course of the Bronze Age, however, bodies become more and more fragmented, until they occur as scattered pieces that may have become entirely disconnected from their original identities.

The evidence therefore indicates that it was considered ideologically acceptable to fragment the human body. This is interesting, for it suggests that Bronze Age concepts of the self may have been quite different to our own. In the modern, Western world, there is a clear concern to maintain the integrity of the body; scandals over the unauthorized retention of human tissue by hospitals and debates around the use of animal organs for human transplants demonstrate just how emotive a topic this is in our own cultural context. For us, the body is often neatly mapped on to a particular understanding of the self: a model of the 'individual' that views the person as an independent and homogeneous whole with clearly definable boundaries (Morris 1991). Of course, the dominance of this model has been challenged both by those who argue for a more 'symmetrical' relationship between humans and other elements of the world (e.g. Latour 1999; DeLanda 2006; Olsen 2010), and by the pace of technological change, which has seen the distinction between bodies and objects increasingly eroded, for example in the creation of prosthetic limbs (Haraway 1991). Yet the fragmentation and commingling of bodies in the Bronze Age—perhaps most powerfully captured by the mummies from Cladh Hallan (Parker Pearson et al. 2005; Booth et al. 2015)—hint that Bronze Age concepts of the self did not prioritize an ideology of bodily integrity. Instead, bodies were disarticulated and their elements employed to create relational rather than individualistic forms of identity. The importance of interpersonal relationships in structuring Bronze Age mortuary practices has long been recognized, but discussion has tended to focus on the relative positioning of different graves in barrows and cemeteries, rather than on the treatment of the body itself. Here, we can build on these observations to argue that the fragmentation and intermixing of bodies suggest both that identity was viewed as relational, and that the person was considered to be composed of multiple elements (each itself the product of relationships with others) that could be disaggregated, rearranged, and combined in new ways with parts of significant others.

The relational character of Bronze Age personhood is demonstrated also by the occasional use of human bone to make objects. Here, the boundary between self and other—between persons and things—was not drawn as sharply as it is in our own cultural context. We have seen too that the deposits of cremated bone that sometimes accompany inhumation burials were placed in locations where grave goods were usually deposited. In these contexts the distinction between people and objects was elided. However, this need not indicate that the cremated remains were somehow subordinate to the inhumation burials, for that is to impose on the past our own view of objects as inferior to humans and at our disposal to do as we wish; as we shall argue in Chapter 3, Bronze Age objects were not seen in this way. The careful disposal of pyre debris (usually containing fragments of human bone) indicates that the process of cremation did not always require the strict separation of the human body from other materials; indeed, those mixed materials may have had their own particular power. Elsewhere, the deposition of structured sequences of pyre debris and clean cremated bone at sites such as Bromfield in Shropshire (Stanford 1982) indicates that the relationship between people and other materials was relatively flexible and could be defined and constructed in a variety of ways. In regions such as Cornwall, the treatment of cremated human bone in Bronze Age barrows indicates that it was considered just one of a range of powerful substances (including pottery, burnt bone, charcoal, and quartz) that were employed, usually in small quantities, in place-making practices and other ceremonial activities (Jones 2005, 140, 205).

In the Late Bronze Age, fragments of human bone—like quernstones, loom weights, pots, and other objects (as we shall see in Chapter 4)— were used to mark out significant points in settlement space. This suggests that the modern, Western distinction between active human subjects and passive objects was not recognized. Instead, the agency of persons and things was generated in sequences of fragmentation, mixing, and transformation that both defined and renewed the relationships between them. During this period, evidence for the practice of excarnation—a technology that resulted in the disaggregation and disappearance of much of the body—hints that the boundaries between culture and nature were not considered unbreachable: the exposure of the body to the elements and its consumption by animals allowed much of the body to be subsumed into the natural world. This suggests a very different understanding of the integrity of the body, the character of the person, and the relationship between culture and nature to that familiar from our own cultural context.

One interesting pattern that calls into question the permeable boundaries between self and other suggested above is the relative frequency of containers of various sorts in Early and Middle Bronze Age burials. We have seen that cremation burials were deposited in bags, boxes, and pots, and that inhumation burials could be placed in coffins and mortuary houses. Such containers may have been designed to maintain the integrity of the individual body in a context of relative bodily fluidity. This is not to say, of course, that containers could not be opened, or that only complete, single bodies were placed inside them: as we have seen, the partially disarticulated body from Sutton Veny in Wiltshire, for example, was deposited in a lidded coffin (Johnston 1978, 33), while at Fordington Farm in Dorset, two discrete piles of disarticulated bone, one belonging to a young adult male and the other to a child, were deposited in a coffin or timber-lined grave beneath a round barrow (Bellamy 1991, 108). Nonetheless, it does suggest that there was sometimes a concern to create a second 'skin' for the body (or bodies), and to define the boundaries between the remains of the dead and the world of the living. Acts of containment worked both to bring things together and to keep them apart and were therefore effective vehicles of categorization. They were also a means of hiding or controlling powerful or dangerous substances (Jones 2010)—and as we shall see below, human bone may sometimes have been viewed in this way. Set in the broader context, however, containment was just one of a range of transformative processes brought to bear on the human body on death, including burning, mixing, fragmenting, layering, and (un)veiling, each of which functioned to comment metaphorically not only on the social impact of death but also on the place of the deceased in the wider world. Such processes also revealed the composite character of the body, and hint at the productively permeable nature of bodily boundaries.

Garwood's argument that the presence of individual bodies in Chalcolithic burials suggests 'not so much a concern with lived individuality or biography, but rather the iconic status of individual bodies as a means of mediating undivided and exclusive kinds of identity in death' (2012, 301) is therefore only one part of a complex picture in which, over the Bronze Age as a whole, the bodies of certain persons were kept complete while others were fragmented. There is some evidence that particular categories of person may have been more subject to fragmentation than others; as we have seen, women were more likely to be cremated during the Early Bronze Age, for example (Brück 2009). As argued above, however, this need not indicate differences in status, but may relate to other aspects of social identity, such as relative positioning in kinship networks, or the ideological significance of specific types of interpersonal relationships. Certain deaths may have provoked particular concerns over inheritance, the definition of social categories or intercommunity relationships and bodies may therefore have been treated in quite varied ways. Moreover, Barrett's argument (1994, 115–19) that Early Bronze Age traditions of inhumation burial provided a means of fixing a particular image of the deceased in the memories of the mourners is arguably problematic, for at least some inhumation graves were reopened and the bones of their occupants manipulated and rearranged. As such, the integrity of individual bodies may not have been viewed as a fixed and immutable state.

A concern with boundaries is perhaps best illustrated by the deposition of human remains in the Late Bronze Age. During this period, fragments of human bone were deposited at boundaries and entrances, both in and around settlements and across the wider landscape. Here, the remains of the dead were used to draw attention to places and moments of transition—spaces that were socially sensitive, where it was important to draw a distinction between inside and outside, between those who belonged and those who did not. Human bone is found in other types of liminal space too, notably caves, bogs, and rivers: these were locations that may have been viewed as entrances to the underworld, the dwelling place of spirits or ancestors, where dangerous encounters took place between the familiar and the foreign. In this context, human bone symbolized the hazards of encounters between different worlds and of transformation from one state to another (Brück 1995). Death is, of course, the ultimate transition (Metcalf and Huntingdon 1991) and the remains of the dead thereforeprovided a potent means of symbolizing transformative processes. It is perhaps no surprise that disarticulated and fragmentary human bone rather than complete bodies were deposited in such contexts; the process of fragmentation speaks of moments of profound transformation, and the ontological fears provoked by bodily dissolution may have neatly symbolized the dangers that might be faced at points of social and spatial disjuncture.

Yet this is a rather one-sided reading of the evidence. The routine deposition of human bone in settlement contexts, even in the intimate space of the roundhouse itself, and often alongside objects that formed core elements of domestic life such as ceramics and quernstones, suggests that the remains of the dead were not always viewed as dangerous or problematic. Occasionally, objects made of human bone could even have been worn on the body, suggesting that attitudes to death and the dead are likely to have very different to our own. The horror and disgust provoked by the dead body in our own cultural context are the product of a specific set of historical circumstances (e.g. Mitford 1996; Jupp and Walter 1999) and are not universally shared (Barley 1997): the Berewan of Borneo, for example, often store the decomposing bodies of the dead in large ceramic jars in their houses for some months before final deposition in a mausoleum (Metcalf 1978). Certainly, the ubiquity of human bone in Late Bronze Age settlements hints that the distaste and fear provoked by the bodies of the dead in the contemporary Western world cannot be projected into the past.

There are in fact interesting hints that the remains of the dead were viewed in positive terms during the Late Bronze Age and earlier periods. We have seen, for example, that Middle Bronze Age cremation burials were often deposited on the south side of earlier barrows, so that the remains of the dead were linked with concepts of light, life, fertility, and rebirth. During the Late Bronze Age, human bone often formed a component of what we might identify as 'refuse' deposits alongside other broken domestic materials. Our identification of the contents of Late Bronze Age middens, pits, and ditches as 'rubbish' is, however, a value judgement based on contemporary ideas around obsolescence, dirt, and decay rooted in the social and economic conditions of capitalism. By contrast, as we will see in Chapter 3, broken objects (including fragments of human bodies) were positively valued in the Bronze Age because they gave material form to significant interpersonal relationships, including links between the living and the dead: objects were often deliberately broken to create 'heirlooms' or fragments that could be shared among multiple people. Moreover, there is evidence to suggest that Late Bronze Age 'refuse' was considered a productive and valuable substance: on Orkney and elsewhere, midden material was spread on the fields to enhance agricultural yield (Simpson et al. 1998), while as we will see in Chapter 4, the monumental middens found in parts of southern Britain during this period can be considered 'stores of fertility'—a means of making visible evidence of craft production, feasting, and the consumption of exotic materials such as gold and amber (McOmish 1996; Waddington 2010). In the Late Bronze Age, then, 'refuse' does not appear to have had solely negative connotations. As part of the matrix of materials central to the creation of objects and relationships, human bone—like other types of refuse—may have been valued as a source of new life: anthropological studies of mortuary rituals indicate that in many societies life and death are intrinsically linked as elements of a cyclical process of regeneration (Bloch and Parry 1982). This helps to explain the location of Middle Bronze Age cremation burials on the southern side of Early Bronze Age barrows.

Of course, practices involving intimate engagement with human remains in a domestic context indicate a level of familiarity and intimacy between the living and the dead, and we can therefore suggest that at least some of these bones may have belonged to members of those same communities—family members whose remains were employed to underpin ongoing links between people and place. Certainly, in the Early Bronze Age the reopening of graves and the removal and manipulation of bones from the mortuary context suggest that items such as the bone belt hook from Wilsford G15 (Figure 2.6; Woodward and Hunter 2015, table 3.3.1) were most likely made from the remains of venerated ancestors (or, at the very least, the bones of 'fictive' ancestors: cf. Garwood 1991). Whether these individuals were known or were viewed as members of a more generalized ancestry remains unclear, however. In some cases, the relatively short time frame between initial deposition of the body and later revisiting of the grave suggests that the identity and personal relationships of the deceased would have been known. The complete and incomplete inhumation burials from the mortuary pit at Cliffs End Farm in Kent (McKinley et al. 2014, 217) appear to have been deposited over a short period of time, possibly as little as ten years: as such, the missing skull and hand of the child from this feature may have been removed just a few years after that individual was buried. In contrast, the mummies from Cladh Hallan on South Uist were already several centuries old when they were buried, and indeed did not comprise the remains of single 'individuals' but composites of multiple bodies whose identity and origin may not have been known (Parker Pearson et al. 2005; Booth et al. 2015). Certainly, the practice of excarnation hints that the expression of individual identity may not have been central to Late Bronze Age mortuary rites: the potency of pieces of human bone deposited in houses or worn around the neck perhaps came not from their links with named individuals, but from association with death and the generalized ancestral dead.

By the Iron Age, however, it is evident that there was an interest in engaging not only with the remains of the familiar dead, but also in obtaining and manipulating the bodies of others. Armit (2012) has discussed evidence for headhunting and the display of trophy heads in Iron Age Europe. The discovery of skull fragments in and around the entrances to Late Bronze Age settlements could be read to suggest that these practices emerged during this earlier period. If so, items such as the roundel of skull from Green Park in Berkshire (Boyle 2003) may originally have belonged to a vanquished enemy rather than an esteemed ancestor. Unfortunately, the paucity of burials from Late Bronze Age contexts makes it difficult to identify 'non-kin' or 'foreigners' through isotope or aDNA analysis. Whatever the case, the recovery of human bone from liminal locations in the Late Bronze Age indicates that the relationship between the living and the dead was somewhat ambivalent: human bone helped to define the boundaries of social categories, yet it also expressed their inherent instability as well as the inescapable centrality of processes of transformation to social life. Like the refuse deposits of which they were so often a component, fragments of human bone may have spoken both of decay, disorder, and disruption, and of the creative potential of change. The deposition of human remains in contexts such as caves, rivers, and the entrances to settlements hints that they were viewed as dangerous yet productive agents of transformation. The implications of this for our understanding of social boundaries and processes of social categorization will be explored further in Chapter 6. It is already evident, however, that this sense of ambivalence towards the remains of the dead is more clearly visible in the Late Bronze Age than earlier periods, and this must be set in the context of wider social changes.

3
Object biographies

In September 1886, John and Richard Mortimer excavated a large barrow at Garton Slack, East Yorkshire (Mortimer 1905, 229). At the centre of the barrow lay the inhumation burial of a young adult male (Figure 3.1). A flint knife, a clay button, and two lumps of yellow ochre had been arranged behind his head; at his left hand were two quartz pebbles and fragments of two boar's tusks, while the scapula of a pig had been laid on top of his ribs. One detail of this burial seems particularly alien to contemporary eyes, however. When the body had begun to decompose, his mandible was removed and placed carefully on his chest, and a miniature Food Vessel inserted into his mouth. Here, a pot replaced an element of the human self and the physical boundary between person and object was elided: the open mouths of both pot and body worked as channels through which relationships flowed in processes of communication and commensality.

This chapter will explore the relationship between people and objects in the Bronze Age. The Bronze Age saw the introduction of new technologies, notably metalworking, which had a significant impact on concepts of personhood and identity. A greater diversity of materials was employed than in previous centuries, including visually striking substances such as amber and faience, while more 'mundane' materials such as bone were used to make a new and wider variety of objects, particularly during the later part of the period. Such objects were incorporated into new contexts too, notably settlements and burials, and our interpretation of these finds—especially those from burials and hoards—has had a significant impact on our understanding of the period. We will start by examining objects from Early Bronze Age contexts, focusing in particular on burials, before moving on to consider what technologies such as metalworking and cloth production can tell us about the construction of concepts of the self in the Middle and Late Bronze Age.

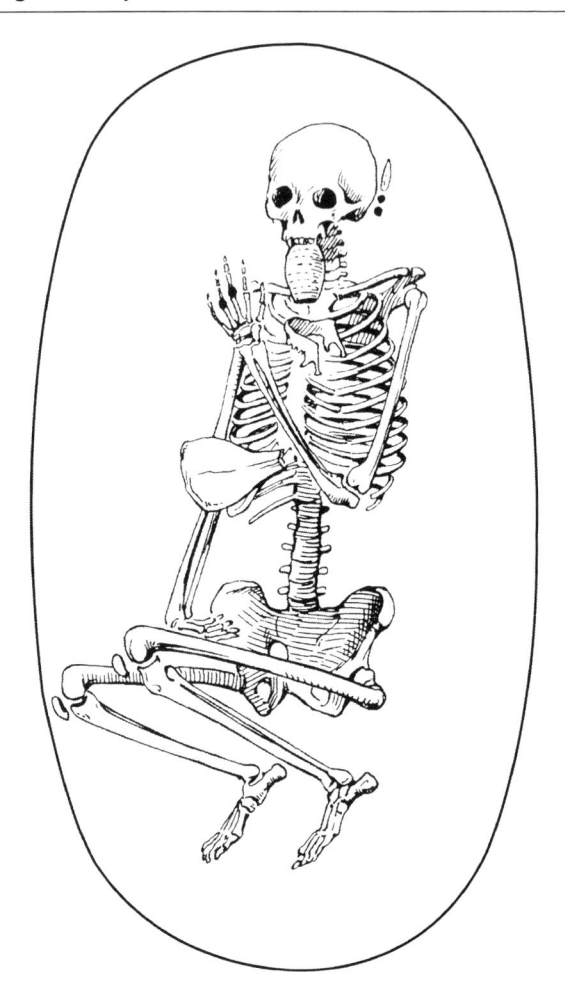

Figure 3.1. Inhumation burial, Garton Slack, East Yorkshire (after Mortimer 1905, fig. 585, with slight alterations by Anne Leaver).

During the early part of the period, artefacts such as copper-alloy daggers, bone pins, pottery vessels, and stone tools were buried with the dead. Other objects such as copper and bronze axes were deposited in hoards or as single finds, while pit groups (often interpreted as the remains of settlements, as we shall see in Chapter 4) yield artefacts such as struck flint and ceramics. From the beginning of the Middle Bronze Age, grave goods were rarely deposited with the dead. Instead, pottery, small decorative items such as shale bracelets, and tools of stone and bone are recovered from settlements, while bronze objects such as swords and axes were usually deposited singly or as components of hoards at other significant locations across the landscape. The categorical distinction between people and objects made in the contemporary Western world has had a profound impact on how artefacts from these different contexts have been approached in studies of the British Bronze Age. As grave goods in burials or as components of votive deposits, they have primarily been viewed as markers of ethnicity and status, and as passive objects to be manipulated by active human agents in the pursuit of particular social and political ends. In more 'everyday' contexts such as settlements, their practical role and economic significance have tended to be emphasized.

In recent years, the agency of objects such as decorated Early Bronze Age axes or of magical materials such as jet and amber (Woodward 2000, 109–10; Jones 2001; Sheridan and Davis 2002, 824; Sheridan and Shortland 2003) has begun to be explored. As we shall see in this chapter, there is much to suggest that there were close emotional ties between people and objects, and that objects were seen as powerful agents in their own right. Artefacts were bound up with personal, family, and community histories, so that they became core components of the self (Brück 2004a). In this way, the self extended beyond the confines of the human body. Moreover, similarities between Bronze Age technologies and the treatment of the human body on death hint that both objects and persons were understood as composite entities whose elements were brought together in a range of generative processes, notably exchange (Brück 2006a; 2006b). Although the relationship between people and objects was therefore fluid, an increasing concern with processes of categorization in the Late Bronze Age indicates that boundaries of one sort or another continued to be important. However, the character or configuration of these made them quite different to the physical and conceptual boundaries familiar from our own cultural context, a theme we will revisit in Chapter 6.

The relationship between people and things in Early Bronze Age burials

The metaphorical link between pots and people suggested by the burial at Garton Slack can be seen elsewhere too (cf. Jones 2001, 342). As we saw in Chapter 2, bodies could replace pots in the grave. We have already described how cremation burials were deposited above the head, in front of the chest, and beneath the hips of the crouched inhumation burial in grave 1 at Barns Farm in Fife (Watkins 1982, 71–2): these are locations in which Beakers and Food Vessels were placed in other Early Bronze Age inhumation graves. Elsewhere, Early Bronze Age cremation burials were deposited in urns, so that the ceramic vessel became a second skin for the body (Jones 2010, 107–8). Here, the processing, cooking, and storage of food may have been considered analogous to the activities that surrounded the treatment and deposition of the human body on death (Williams 2004). Other types of object could also become part of the body: a clay stud found with the cremated remains of a woman from Whitelow Cairn in Lancashire (Tyson 1995) may have been worn in the ear or lip. Studs of wood, clay jet, and shale often occur in pairs, and where they accompany inhumation burials, they tend to be found in the area of the head or neck (Woodward and Hunter 2015, 513). It is possible that such artefacts were gifted at significant points in the life of the individual, and they are therefore likely to have been considered an essential component of the person.

Elsewhere, it is clear that human and object biographies were closely interwoven. The deposition of heirlooms in Chalcolithic and Early Bronze Age burials has been well documented (Sheridan and Davis 2002; Woodward 2002a; Woodward and Hunter 2015). Dagger pommels were often deposited separately from the blades of these objects, and many display significant evidence for wear (Woodward and Hunter 2015, 51–3). In some cases, repolishing or bevelling of old breaks indicates that pommels were reworked to fit different daggers. It is therefore possible to suggest that dagger pommels, including those made of 'mundane' materials such as bone, may have been highly valued and socially significant objects. Most pommels accompany mature adult males over the age of 40 (Woodward and Hunter 2015, 523). These items may have been obtained early in life and curated and re-used over the life course, or they may have been heirlooms.

Other items also had lengthy histories. The wristguard fragment from the primary Beaker inhumation grave in barrow 1 at Irthlingborough Island, Northamptonshire, was reworked as a burnishing tool (Humble and Healy 2008, 252–3): one end of the object is smooth and rounded from use, and it displays microscopic striations that have been interpreted as suggesting it may have been employed for the processing of hide. Two tiny flakes located midway along each of the long sides of the object are worn, suggesting that the broken bracer was hafted for reuse as a tool (Woodward and Hunter 2015, 489). Sometimes objects appear to have been curated and reworked over very long periods so that it becomes difficult to imagine that they were associated with named ancestors. At Tubney Wood in Oxfordshire, for example, a gold sun disc that was already several centuries old was deposited with the cremation burial of an adult (Simmonds et al. 2011, 110). Gold items of this sort are characteristic of the Chalcolithic, c.2500–2200 BC, but the burial itself was radiocarbon-dated to 1780–1620 cal BC. Heirlooms such as this may have been considered particularly powerful and inalienable objects (cf. Weiner 1992).

Assembling and fragmenting the person in Early Bronze Age burials

Work by Alison Sheridan (Sheridan and Davis 1998; 2002; Sheridan 2015) has demonstrated that beads of jet and jet-like substances were also frequently curated. For example, variability in the raw materials, morphology, wear patterns, manufacturing techniques, and decoration of the different components of the spacer plate necklace that accompanied an inhumation burial from a barrow at Grindlow in Derbyshire suggests that these are likely to have derived from a number of different sources (Figure 3.2; Sheridan, Woodward and Hunter 2015, 313–19). The spacer plates, for example, include six decorated jet plates of similar size and shape, a smaller undecorated jet plate, and a much wider

Figure 3.2. The spacer plate necklace from Grindlow, Derbyshire (© Museums Sheffield).

decorated bone plate. Twenty of the fusiform beads were made of jet, but six were made of cannel coal, while the size of the boreholes and the shape of the thirty-six buttons differed significantly. Most of the components were worn, but the degree of wear varied, particularly amongst the buttons. This 'object', in other words, appears to have been assembled over a period of time, probably from the remains of several older necklaces and ornament sets.

We can suggest that the circulation, dissolution, and reassembly of such collections acted as a means of giving material form to interpersonal relationships that extended over time and space (Frieman 2012a; Jones 2012, ch. 6). Beads may have been curated as special objects gifted at important moments in the human life course, they may have been passed down from one generation to the next, and they may have circulated in exchange networks as symbols of significant social relations; in assembling collections of such items in the grave, the mourners evoked and reworked the web of relationships that together constituted the deceased. Such finds indicate that the lives of people and objects were inextricably intertwined (Brück 2004a). The treatment of items such as necklaces suggests that personhood was composite: both persons and things were composed of multiple elements—strands that could be woven together, unravelled, and recombined. Such acts of assembly and dissolution might have taken place in the context of life-cycle rites, including at the graveside, with objects such as bone pommels or jet spacer plates circulating as gifts amongst the living and between the living and the dead. It seems likely that the exchange history of objects contributed to their meaning and value (Barrett 1994, 121–2; Woodward 2000, 116–19; 2002; Jones 2002), and particular items may have featured in the stories used to create family and community identities.

Just as jet necklaces were unstrung, the deliberate destruction of objects was a significant element of Early Bronze Age mortuary rituals (Mortimer 1905, 1; Ashbee 1960, 96, 103; Shepherd 1982, 131; Brück 2004a, 319–21). We have already seen that dagger pommels could be deposited without their blades. Examination of the daggers themselves has identified bent tangs, damaged hilt plates, and twisting to the blades that suggest that the hilts of these items were often deliberately removed as part of the mortuary rite (Woodward and Hunter 2015, 38–44). For example, the hilt plate of the dagger that accompanied a cremation burial at Knook G1a in Wiltshire was badly damaged, and the blade itself had also been broken in two (Woodward and Hunter 2015, fig. 3.1.11). Other types of object were also deliberately fragmented. At Dunure Road in Ayrshire, sherds from the same two pots were recovered from the floor of cist 300, the old ground surface outside of the cist, and the overlying mound material. The cist had been backfilled and closed with a large capstone before the mound was built, and the excavator suggests that the vessels must have been smashed at the side of the cist before it was backfilled and sealed (Duffy 2007, 83–5). Similarly, a Collared Urn from barrow XVII at Snail Down in Wiltshire had been 'demolished by a series of sharp blows, sending sherds northeastwards for a distance of up to 6 feet' (Thomas 2005, 101), while one corner of the gold-studded stone bracer from the primary inhumation at Barnack in Cambridgeshire had been broken off (Donaldson 1977, 209); both parts were present in the grave, however.

Sometimes objects accompanied the body onto the pyre: the quartz pebble, bone pommel, and bone toggle found in the cremation deposit in cist 1 at Beech Hill House, Coupar Angus, Perth and Kinross, were all burnt, suggesting that they had been placed on the pyre alongside the deceased (Stevenson 1995, 204). Often such practices highlight the different histories of the objects found in the grave. A cremation burial cut into the south side of barrow 1 on Irthlingborough Island, Northamptonshire, was accompanied by a burnt antler pommel fragment, a burnt bone or antler pin, and an unburnt bronze dagger (Allan et al. 2008d, 159–61). Although it might be assumed that the pommel was originally part of the dagger handle, in fact it is too small to have ever formed an element of this object.

Of course, such acts of deliberate destruction allowed ontological concerns around temporality, change, and loss to be addressed: breaking or burning an object that was a core element of the identity of the deceased, or that may have been employed during the mortuary rite, spoke powerfully of the social impact of death (Mortimer 1905, l; Ashbee 1960, 96, 103; Shepherd 1982, 131; Needham 2000b, 44; Woodward 2000, 107; Brück 2004a). Often, these practices were overtly transformative, as when objects accompanied the body onto the pyre. Yet, in light of the evidence for the retention of heirlooms, it is also possible to interpret the practice of deliberate destruction as a means of creating fragments (cf. Chapman and Gaydarska 2007), some of which could be deposited in the grave, while others were kept by the mourners as tokens of the deceased: the deposition of dagger pommels without their blades, for example, suggests that different parts of an object could follow very different pathways. However, such practices were not confined to exotic materials like jet or to objects—such as daggers—that can be configured as 'high status'. Two large fragments of a Collared Urn were deposited in the upper fill of a pit at the edge of barrow XVII at Snail Down in Wiltshire. They are described as 'carefully and deliberately packed, each with the inside uppermost, the larger fragment overlying the smaller, with the collar on each facing the centre of the barrow' (Thomas 2005, 100); both were weathered, suggesting that they may have been curated, perhaps from an earlier burial. In this way, practices of fragmentation allowed relationships between the living and the dead to be expressed and reconfigured.

Collections and containment

Importantly, practices of deliberate fragmentation tell us that the objects deposited in the grave were not always employed to comment on intrinsic or circumscribed elements of individual identity but acted to create identities that were composite and relational (Jones 2001; 2012, ch. 6). This sense of relationality is expressed in a number of key ways. For example, Early Bronze Age mortuary assemblages brought together and ordered objects and materials with different histories and origins. The composite necklace that accompanied the cremation burial at Oxteddle Bottom, Mount Caburn, East Sussex, included beads of faience, amber, jet, shale, and possibly cannel coal (Woodward and Hunter 2015, 431–4). There was considerable variability in the wear displayed by individual components of this collection, and it is possible that the jet fusiform beads had originally formed part of an older necklace, while the jet and shale biconical beads were relatively new. Here, materials from different sources and with different histories were assembled—beads of red, blue, and black that spoke of transformative processes (the use of fire to make faience, for example) and places (such as the distant spaces between land and sea where pieces of amber or jet were collected). These beads may have been collected or gifted at certain points in the lifecourse of the deceased. Alternatively, they may have been given by the mourners to map the combination of relationships that linked the living and the dead and to speak of the symbolic qualities and cosmogenic origins of those connections.

The same points can be made for objects of more 'humble' origin. At Easton Down, Allington, Wiltshire, a bronze awl, two quoit-shaped beads of sandstone or fired clay, one shale barrel bead, and a segment of fossil belemnite were placed on top of the cremation burial of a child (Ride 2001). In contrast to 'exotic' materials such as amber, the beads in this assemblage are more difficult to label as simple indices of status. Instead, we can view them as gifts acquired during life or at the graveside—items that spoke of particular places or people, and of relationships of love and care: it has been suggested, for example, that the inclusion of fossils in Early Bronze Age graves may have been apotropaic (Sheridan and Shortland 2003; Brück and Jones 2018).

As at Easton Down, awls are often associated with composite necklaces and collections of beads in Early Bronze Age burials. While it is easy to view such objects as markers of female gendered identity, they can be read in other ways too. Woodward (2000, 115) suggests that they may have been used to tattoo or scarify the skin as part of the mortuary rite, or they may have been employed as fasteners for bags. Awls speak both of the rupturing or puncturing of skin (human or animal) and of the process of stitching or sewing: in this sense, it is particularly interesting that they are often associated with items such as beads that were themselves strung together. Links that extended beyond the microtopography of the grave can also be discerned in the deposition of skeuomorphs in Early Bronze Age burials. The extraordinary Encrusted Urns in which Irish Early Bronze Age cremations were often deposited mimic basketry (Manby 1995); flint daggers reference those made from copper (Frieman 2012b); and the visual similarity between segmented faience beads and beads made from fossil crinoids is striking (Sheridan and Shortland 2003). This process of referencing underlines the relational context in which identity was constituted through the use, display, and deposition of meaningful objects (Jones 2001, 340–7; 2012, ch. 6).

In some cases, the objects deposited in Early Bronze Age burials were brought together as distinct collections, for example by placing them in bags, boxes, or other containers (Brück 2004a). The beads, wooden studs, and flint flake from the Whitehorse Hill cist on Dartmoor, Devon (Jones 2016), were buried in a basket. The primary grave in barrow 1 on Irthlingborough Island, Northamptonshire, contained the crouched inhumation of an adult male in a plank-built oak chamber or coffin (Figure 3.3). A Beaker pot lay at his feet and beside this was a neat pile of other items: three bone spatulae, a boar's tusk, five jet buttons, an amber ring, a slate 'sponge finger', an elongated chalk object, a bracer, and a variety of flint objects including a dagger, an arrowhead, two knives, two scrapers, and several flakes (Allan et al. 2008d, 153, fig. 3.99). These are likely to have been originally deposited in a box, calling into question the frequent assumption that the grave goods in Early Bronze Age mortuary contexts functioned as items of display. Instead, the objects buried with this man were hidden, and they had a range of distinctive and interesting histories (Harding and Healy 2007, 245–55, table 4.9). We have already seen that the bracer fragment was subsequently reused as a burnishing tool. The jet buttons displayed varying degrees of wear, suggesting they had different origins, and they may have been given as gifts at different points in the life of the deceased. The boar's tusk was radiocarbon-dated and was

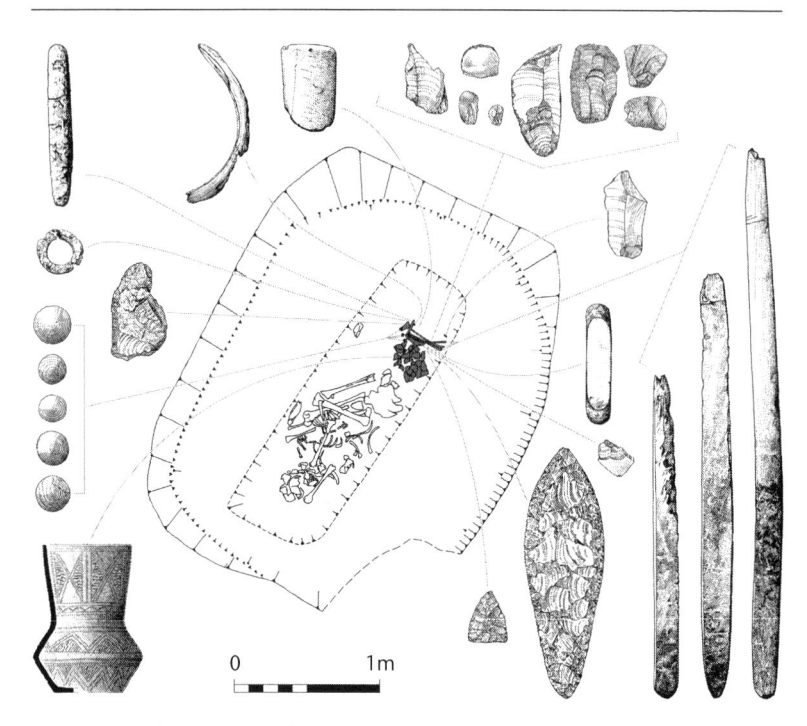

Figure 3.3. The primary inhumation grave and accompanying grave goods in barrow 1, Irthlingborough, Northamptonshire (© Historic England, with slight alterations by Anne Leaver).

shown to be have been at least 500 years older than the burial itself: this item may have been passed down over the generations as an heirloom, or it may have been encountered and recovered from an earlier grave. In contrast, the fresh condition of the flakes and scrapers indicates that they were made for the funeral rite, and microwear analysis suggests that they were employed for a variety of activities including butchery, and scraping and cutting wood, antler, and hide. These items commented not on activities that the deceased had carried out during life or on links with long-dead ancestors, but on relationships with the living: it seems likely that tasks undertaken as part of the mortuary rite, such as making the coffin or preparing food, would have been assigned to people who had particular connections with the deceased (Brück 2004a, 317).

The process of assembling or 'bundling' objects generated links between them that spoke of the complex relationships that together constituted the person (Jones 2012, ch. 6). These were links not only with other people but with other times and places; they were not static but had to be defined afresh in death. Practices such as wrapping objects or placing them in bags and boxes helped both to articulate interconnections but also to define distinctions (Jones 2010; cf. Fowler 2017). The dagger that accompanied the cremation burial of a possible adult female at Amesbury G58 in Wiltshire was deposited in its sheath and wrapped in layers of fabric and moss (Ashbee 1985, 43). This may have served to protect a valued item; alternatively, it may have been the mourners themselves who required protection from a powerful or polluted object. The act of wrapping objects often separated them from other items in the grave, but it nonetheless worked to define them in relational terms. The fabric in which the Amesbury dagger was wrapped must have been made (and perhaps worn) by a particular person, and may itself have had a significant history. The moss may have come from a specific location, and the task of collecting this material and wrapping the dagger may have been given to someone especially close to the dead woman. Indeed, the dagger itself was already a composite object: traces of its horn hilt were preserved, although its pommel had been removed, presumably to be retained or reused.

Geographies of the body

Just as processes of wrapping or containment created close spatial as well as conceptual links between objects, the relational character of identity is also indicated in the arrangement of objects in the grave. In particular, it is evident that grave goods were carefully placed not only relative to each other but also relative to the human body (Clarke 1970, 454–5; Lucas 1996; Brück 2004a; Woodward and Hunter 2015, 507–17). Grave 203 at Barrow Hills in Oxfordshire, for example, contained the crouched inhumation burial of an adult male, around which a variety of objects had been deposited (Figure 3.4; Barclay 1999, 136–41). These included a Beaker pot behind his head; a bone awl, bone spatula, and flint scraper at his waist; a collection of five barbed and tanged arrowheads behind his feet; and a bronze awl and a selection of other flint flakes and tools under his lower legs. Some of these items lay in tight groups, suggesting they may originally have been deposited in bags. Flat grave 4660 at the same site also contained the crouched inhumation of an adult male. A bone pin lay just above his head and a copper dagger in front of his face; a group of grave goods at his feet included a Beaker pot, an antler spatula, a barbed and tanged arrowhead, a flint flake, and a flint blade (Barclay 1999, 60–4, fig. 4.22).

The careful arranging of objects relative to the body can be seen in Early Bronze Age cremation burials also. For example, barrow G61a

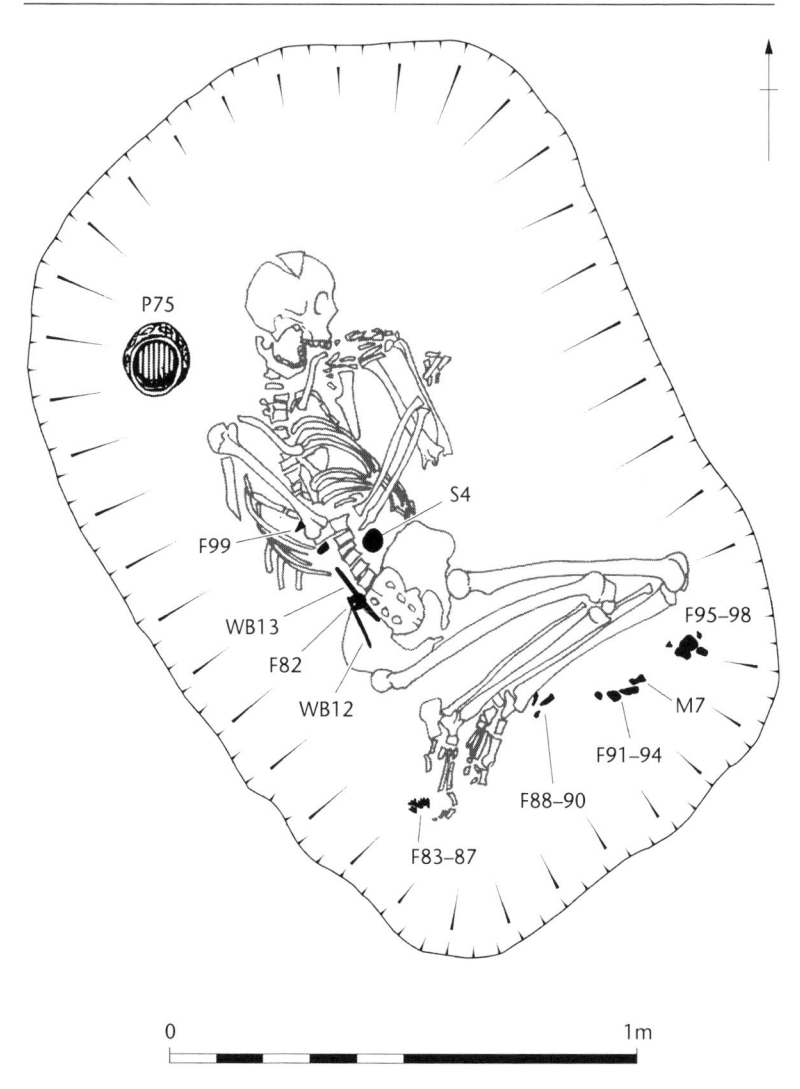

Figure 3.4. Grave 203, Barrow Hills, Oxfordshire: P75, Beaker pot; F99, barbed and tanged arrowhead; S4, fragment of iron pyrites; WB12–13, bone awl and bone spatula; F82, flint scraper; F83–7, barbed and tanged arrowheads; F88–90, flint flakes; F91–4, flint flakes, scraper, and piercer; M7, bronze awl; F95–8, flint piercer and flakes (after Barclay and Halpin 1999, fig. 4.76, with slight alterations by Anne Leaver; reproduced with permission of Oxford Archaeology).

at Amesbury in Wiltshire produced a number of burials, including a cremation burial of an adult in a rectangular grave (Ashbee 1985, fig. 39). This had been deposited in a clearly defined pear-shaped heap. A small ceramic vessel containing an amber bead, fossil crinoid, and two flint flakes was placed upright at the tapering end of this deposit. An amber-coloured beaver incisor was found standing against the pot. Under the pot there was a bronze awl, and seven additional beads of amber, faience, red steatite, and cowrie shell. The central grave in barrow 1 at Barrow Hills, Oxfordshire, contained a cremation burial, on top of which had been laid a bronze knife-dagger, bone tweezers, and a bone ring-headed pin (Figure 3.5; Barclay 1999, 141). The careful placement of grave goods suggests that this acted as a means of *locating* the person relative to the significant events, people, and places represented by these objects; identity was profoundly relational, and was constituted in a network of links expressed in the assembly and placement of objects in the grave.

For inhumation burials, it is evident that particular points of the body were emphasized (Lucas 1996): objects were most often placed above, behind, and in front of the head; in front of the chest; behind the hips; at the knees; and below the legs and feet. Woodward and Hunter (2015, 507–17) have identified patterning in the location of objects around the body: bronze daggers and battleaxes were deposited around the upper body, for example in front of the chest or behind the head; awls, spatulae, and sponge finger stones were placed at the feet or behind the back; and arrowheads were located at the feet or waist. It seems likely that different elements of the body were ascribed specific cultural meanings, so that the deposition of specific objects by the head or the feet, for example, may have spoken of the character or significance of particular interpersonal relationships. We can suggest, for instance, that different groups of kin may each have placed objects at different locations in the grave (Brück 2004a, 324): often points of articulation were emphasized, suggesting that concepts of interconnectivity were significant (Lucas 1996, 103; cf. Sørensen 1997, 104).

This requires us to reconsider some of the ways in which archaeologists have interpreted Early Bronze Age grave goods. It is often assumed that grave goods were the personal possessions of the deceased and can be read as a direct reflection of social identity. However, grave goods may not always have been owned by the deceased: some may have been used in the mortuary rite or have been given as gifts by the mourners (Barrett 1994, 116–18; Parker Pearson 1999, 85; Woodward 2000, 113–15). Thomas (1991, 38) distinguishes objects found inside and outside the coffin, and grave goods worn on the body from those

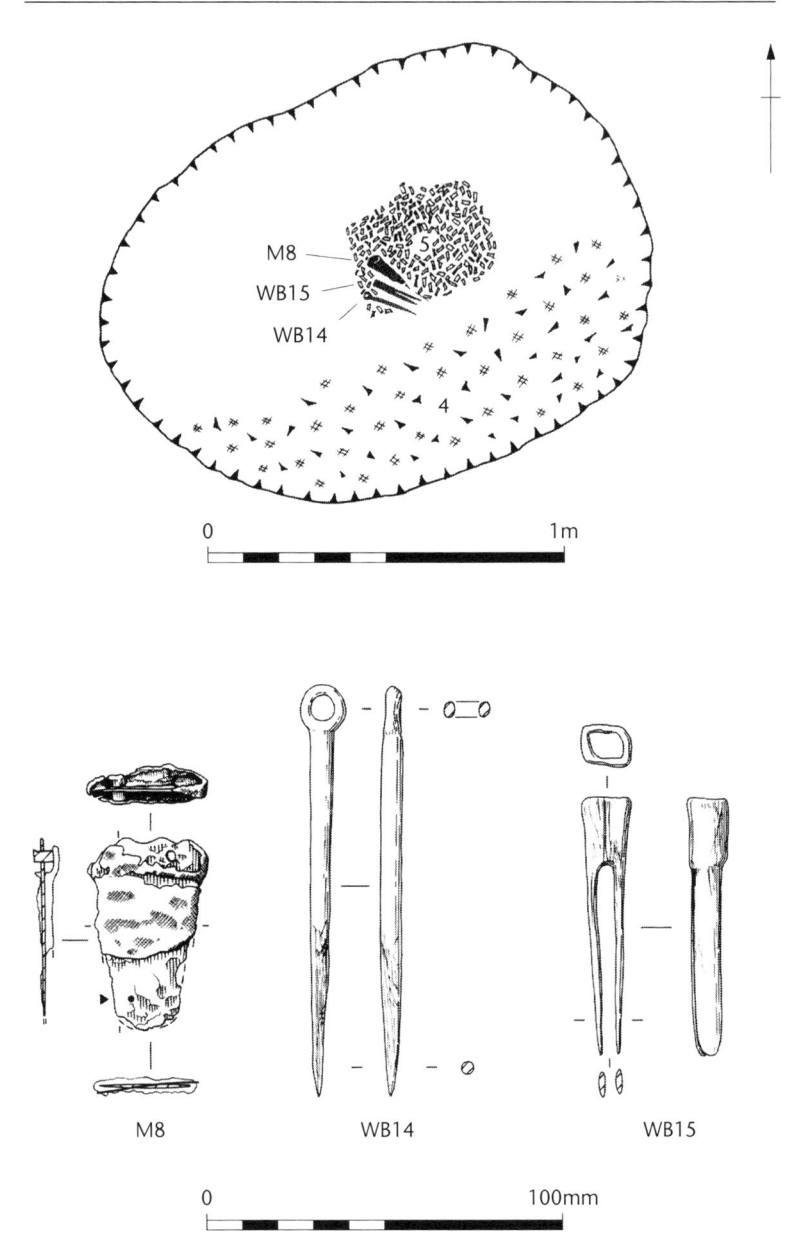

Figure 3.5. The central cremation burial in barrow 1, Barrow Hills, Oxfordshire: M8, bronze knife-dagger; WB14, bone tweezers; WB15 bone ring-headed pin (after Barclay 1999, fig. 4.82, with slight alterations by Anne Leaver; reproduced with permission of Oxford Archaeology).

placed next to it, suggesting that such choices allow us to differentiate, for example, items that marked out aspects of personal identity in life from objects used in the funeral rite. We will go further here, however, to argue that the deposition of objects in Early Bronze Age mortuary contexts always embodies a complex network of relationships and that it is problematic to assume that 'identity' or 'status' are intrinsic attributes of a bounded individual rather than properties of particular contexts or events.

Relational identity in the grave of the Amesbury Archer

We will explore this in more detail in relation to the well-known 'wealthy' burial of the Amesbury Archer in Wiltshire (Figure 3.6; Fitzpatrick 2011). This grave contained an extraordinary array of objects arranged around the flexed inhumation of an adult male. These included five Beaker pots placed at different locations around the body: two in front of the face, one behind the head, one below the pelvis, and one beneath the feet. A cache of flint artefacts, two boar's tusks, a copper knife, an antler spatula, an antler strip, a perforated oyster shell, and a piece of iron pyrites were deposited in front of the chest. A second copper dagger lay at the right shoulder, while a stone wristguard and antler pin were placed on the lower left arm. Behind the Archer's back was another cache of struck flints, two boar's tusks, and a cushion stone that may have been used for metalworking. A second wristguard, a shale belt ring, another copper knife, an antler strip, and two gold basket-shaped ornaments were found at his knees. A number of other flint objects were also found elsewhere in the grave, notably fourteen barbed and tanged arrowheads; most of these items were scattered in and around the lower half of the body.

The quantity of finds and the presence of gold and copper objects have been taken to indicate that this was a particularly high-status individual; similar items are known from many other Beaker graves, but the multiplication of objects such as pots and knives is much more unusual. The cushion stone and boar's tusks have been interpreted as possible metalworkers' tools—the cushion stone as a miniature anvil for goldworking and the boar's tusks as burnishing tools (Fitzpatrick 2011, 212–22; Needham 2011a). Stable isotope analysis suggests that the Archer may have spent his early life overseas, perhaps in the Alpine region (Chenery and Evans 2011), and it has been suggested that he was accorded a special status in death because he had brought esoteric knowledge of metalworking from the Continent (Fitzpatrick 2009). This model is not unproblematic, however. Analysis of the cushion

Personifying Prehistory

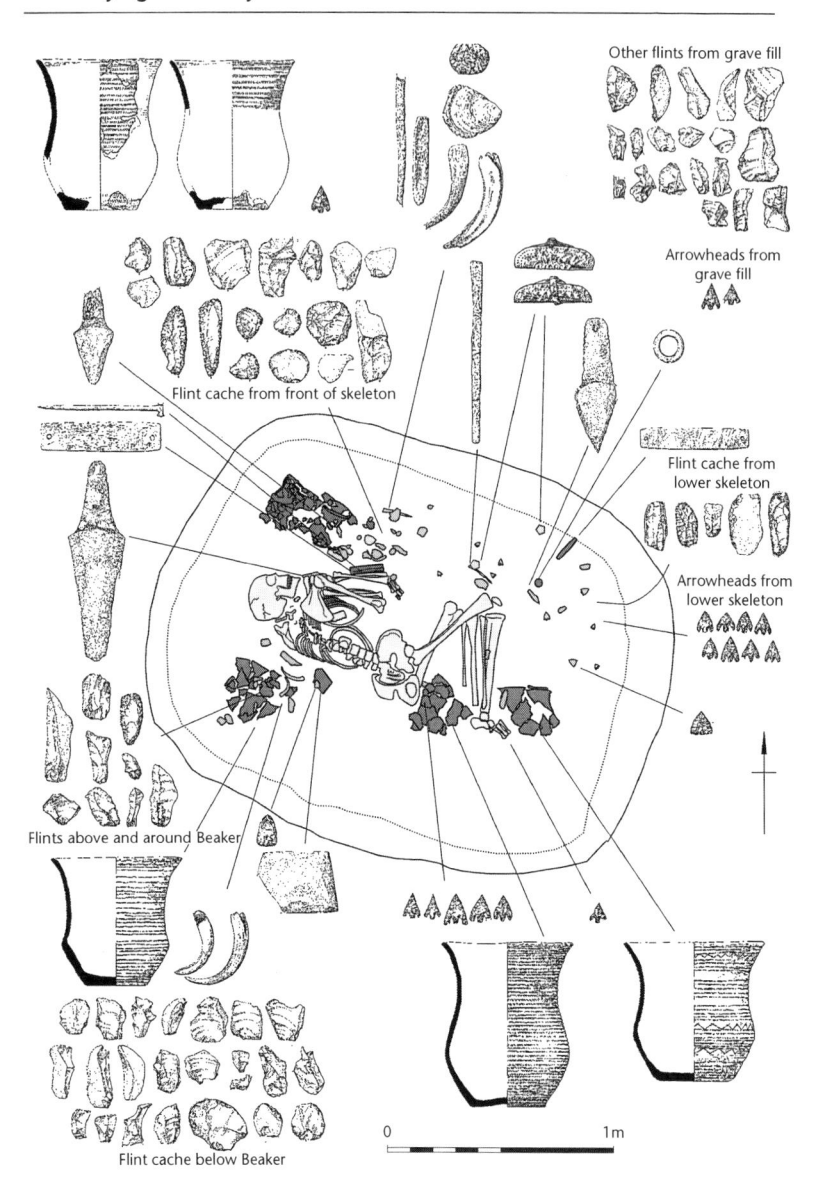

Figure 3.6. The Amesbury Archer and his grave goods (© Wessex Archaeology, with slight alterations by the author).

stone showed no traces of metal (Cowell and Middleton 2011), and the lack of use-wear on the boar's tusks suggests that they are more likely to have served as ornaments than tools (Woodward and Hunter 2015, 143). Even if we accept that these items were metalworking implements, this need not indicate that the Archer was a smith. As Kuijpers (2008, 57–8) puts it, the cushion stone and metal objects buried with the Amesbury Archer 'no more make him a metalworker than the beakers...make him a potter, the flints...make him a flintknapper or the arrowheads and wristguards...make him an archer'.

Instead, it is instructive to look at the arrangement and histories of different items in the grave, and to consider how the symbolism of the objects might have been employed in the mortuary rite. Each of the three main collections of objects—the assemblages in front of the chest, behind the back, and by the knee—may have been gifted by a different individual or group and might have spoken of events or places that evoked the particularities of those relationships. The objects themselves speak of different trajectories. Fabric analysis suggests that the ceramics were made locally (Cleal 2011). Three of the five Beakers were incomplete and displayed evidence of wear, hinting that these items had particular histories prior to deposition; some of the sherds from these objects may have been retained as heirlooms. In contrast, the two pots in front of the face were poorly fired and may have been produced specifically for the mortuary rite. Cleal suggests that two of the older vessels—the pot behind the head and that beneath the legs—may have been made by the same potter, and that this may also have been the case for the two Beakers made for use in the funerary rite. Other materials were obtained from further afield, notably stone, copper, and gold. The wristguards are contrasting colours, one red (possibly from Pembrokeshire), the other black (potentially from a source in continental Europe) (Roe 2011). Compositional analysis of the copper knives has identified two different sources of metal, at least one from as far as western France or Iberia, suggesting that these items had complex and different exchange histories (Needham 2011c). One of the copper knives is markedly less symmetrical than the others, indicating that it had been used and repeatedly resharpened over a long period of time. One corner of the cushion stone was missing (Needham 2011a), and the antler pin had also been damaged; the break on the latter was worn, suggesting that this happened some time prior to the burial (Fitzpatrick 2011, 157).

These items, then, were not simply markers of status but were bound up with personal and collective histories. Some objects may have been gifts from the mourners, signifying aspects of the relationship between the living and the dead: the Beakers, for instance, may have referenced the commensal ties between the archer and particular groups of kinsfolk or neighbours. The distribution of some of the arrowheads suggests that they were cast one by one into the grave; although the consistency in manufacturing technique indicates that they may have been made by a single knapper (Harding 2011), it is possible to imagine several mourners—different family members, perhaps—taking part in this act. The symbolic properties of particular objects may have been employed to comment on the character of those relationships or the circumstances or impact of death—the knives of flint or copper, for example, perhaps speaking of the cutting of ties (Fowler 2005, 125; recent use-wear and morphological studies of daggers from Early Bronze Age burials suggest that many were employed for cutting rather than stabbing: Woodward and Hunter 2015, 557). There are interesting similarities between the three main sets of objects—two of these, for example, produced pairs of boar's tusks, suggesting an element of iterability in the relationships between the living and the dead (cf. Jones 2001, 339–40). At the same time, the grave goods also evoke a series of contrasts: the red and the black of the wristguards are perhaps the most striking, but there are differences too between items that were freshly made for the grave and those that had use-lives prior to deposition; between objects that were local and those with more distant origins; between antler, bone, and tusk; between materials that were chipped, ground, and polished and those that were transformed through the medium of fire. Properties such as colour may have symbolized not only particular personal qualities but also certain types of relationship—affinal and agnatic kinsfolk, for example (see also Jones 2002).

Other objects, such as the flint flakes and scrapers, may have been used during the mortuary rite, defining the relationship between the deceased and particular mourners: the collection of flint objects in front of the chest included five scrapers (two of which were broken), a planoconvex knife/dagger, an edge-flaked knife/dagger, and several utilized flakes. By contrast, the cache of flints behind the Archer's back included a large number of unretouched flint flakes in pristine condition (Harding 2011, 89); the deposition of freshly knapped items into the grave was no doubt a powerful symbolic act, speaking of the social impact of death. If the cushion stone was indeed a goldworking tool, it may have been used during the mortuary rite to decommission one of the gold basket-shaped ornaments: this object had been carefully folded along the bottom of the 'basket' using a fine punch-like tool (Needham 2011b, 137). It is possible too that the ideals, values, and associations conjured by an object employed in the transformative act of metalworking could have been usefully drawn on to comment on the lives of particular people, their relationships with others, the transition between life and death, and their expectations of the afterlife. Alternatively, if this object was not connected with metalworking, it could have been used to prepare small quantities of substances of various sorts that might have been used (or ingested) as part of the mortuary rite (cf. Woodward 2000, 114).

The trajectories by which different items came to be deposited in the grave of the Amesbury Archer are therefore likely to have been varied. To assume that the quantity of grave goods is a direct reflection of wealth and status, or that items such as copper knives are indisputable indicators of rank, is problematic (Fowler 2013, 81–2); indeed, the significant percentage of Early Bronze Age burials that produce no grave goods (e.g. Harding and Healy 2007, tables 4.7–4.8) or just one or two objects—like flint flakes—that cannot be construed as 'prestige goods', reminds us that the communication of status is not the sole concern of mortuary rites (Tarlow 1992). Instead, we can suggest that the deposition of objects in the grave of the Archer allowed relationships between the living and the dead to be defined, and concerns around the ontological significance and social impact of death to be addressed. It may indeed be the case that the Amesbury Archer was particularly well connected, for many people appear to have contributed to his grave assemblage; social connections and social status are not quite the same thing, however, though they are often linked. Alternatively, it is possible that the death of the Archer provoked unusual concerns or anxieties, so that his identity and relationships with others required particularly careful definition (cf. Thomas 1991, 35).

Gender, status, and personhood

Our discussion of grave goods in preceding sections has implications for our understanding of gender during the Chalcolithic and Early Bronze Age, for it is evident that identity and status cannot be directly read from the objects that accompanied the dead. Nonetheless, many authors have commented on differences in the grave goods deposited with men and women. It has been argued that male burials tend to be richer than those of females and children (e.g. Clarke 1970, 264-5; Pierpoint 1980; for critique, see Woodward 2000, 105–7; Rogers 2013), and at first glance the Archer's grave appears to support this model. However, there is an element of both regional and chronological variability to this pattern. Harding and Healy's study of burials in eastern England demonstrates that, although a wider range of different grave goods were deposited with male than female inhumation burials in the Chalcolithic, the opposite is the case for Early Bronze Age cremation burials in that region (2007, tables 4.7 and 4.8). A study of well-furnished burials from East Yorkshire, the Peak District, and Wessex demonstrates similar trends (Woodward and Hunter 2015, tables 11.14 and 12.5, 517–27, 540–1): most well-furnished burials of Chalcolithic date are male, but there is a much more even number of 'wealthy' male and female burials after *c.*2100 BC. If we accept the argument presented above that grave goods do not solely function to indicate wealth and status but were employed to comment on various aspects of interpersonal relationships, we can suggest that the relationships in which men were enmeshed were of particular concern during the Chalcolithic, while the relational identities of women and children became a focus of significant interest in the Early Bronze Age. This may be the result of changing patterns of production, kinship, and inheritance outside the mortuary context.

Of course, objects such as knives and awls may have been employed in the mortuary rite (to prepare the funerary feast or to sew a shroud for the body) and may never have been owned or used by the deceased, so it is problematic to assume that grave goods relate directly to gendered identity. Nonetheless, the sorts of objects with which men and women were buried may give us further insights into varying concepts of personhood. For example, necklaces (which, as we have seen, frequently comprise beads of different origins and histories) were predominantly associated with women (Woodward and Hunter 2015, table 11.4), suggesting that female identities were viewed as composite and dividual, perhaps because of women's role in forging links between intermarrying groups. By contrast, men were buried with items such as daggers, battle-axes, and bone and antler spatulae (Woodward and Hunter 2015, tables 11.15, 11.21) that speak of the severing of links and technologies (like flint-knapping) that involve the subdivision of wholes into parts; male identities may have been more closely bound up with the definition and bounding of individual descent groups. It is interesting that the archaeological visibility of female burials increases when cremation is introduced *c.*2100 BC; the significance of this for changing concepts of the self has been discussed in Chapter 2. As such, we can suggest that it is overly simplistic to read the evidence as indicating that women were lower status than men during the period.

Animate objects in the Early Bronze Age

Finally, we may note that the close symbolic link between people and objects hints that objects themselves may sometimes have been thought of as animate (Jones 2001, 342; 2002, 164). However, objects did not merely gain their power from the way in which they were entangled in human social life, but from latent qualities that were recognized and drawn out in particular historical contexts. Woodward (2000, 109–10) and Sheridan (Sheridan and Davis 2002, 824; Sheridan and Shortland 2003) have argued that jet and amber may have been viewed as powerful and magical substances and that this may help to explain why beads made from these materials were curated as heirlooms during the Early Bronze Age. Unlike other materials of geological origin, they can float and be burnt, and they have electrostatic properties. They were sourced from the shoreline, a liminal zone between land and sea. The colour and lustre of such materials not only gave them a particular sensory attraction, but may have imbued them with agency (Jones 2002, 164). Light illuminates, dazzles, and transforms, and ethnographic research demonstrates that in other cultural contexts materials that are shiny or reflective are often viewed as alive (Saunders 2002). Colours that harness or negate such properties, or that reference significant substances such as blood or bone, may therefore also be considered sources of animacy.

Jones (2002, 170) suggests that technologies such as metalworking linked the colour and luminosity of materials such as bronze and gold with transformative powers. Symbolic links were sometimes drawn between metals and the sun in Britain and Ireland, for example in the sheet-gold 'sun-discs' of the Chalcolithic (Cahill 2015). By sharing some of the properties of the sun (such as luminosity, colour, and heat), metals and metalworking may have been viewed as sources of life and vitality (see also Helms 2012), so that objects such as axes and lunulae had their own life force. The appearance of copper and gold in the Early Bronze Age is accompanied by the use of a range of other coloured materials including not only jet and amber, but also bone, clay, faience, shell, and stone. Materials such as metals and amber often came from a distance, and their ability to cross boundaries may have contributed to their other-worldly character. These materials were brought together, for example in the composite necklaces of the first half of the second millennium which incorporated beads of different substances (Woodward and Hunter 2015, ch. 8). The contrast between colours may have been important in evoking ideas of opposition and complementarity, or different social categories and cultural values. So, for example, the sunburst motif on the base of an incense cup from the burial at Breach Farm, Llanblethian, Glamorgan (Grimes 1938, fig. 7), was originally filled with red ochre and white burnt bone. Substances that came from the earth or from other living things such as ochre, stone, and bone may have been equally potent. The macehead from Bush Barrow in Wiltshire, for instance, was made of a striking fossiliferous stone, the polished surface of the object enhancing the contrast in colour between the light-brown trace fossils and the darker matrix (Figure 3.7; Needham et al. 2015b, 248, fig. 6.2.6).

The decoration of certain categories of object also hints that they may have been considered to possess agency (Jones 2001; 2002; 2010). Although decoration may have functioned to mark out particular events and people (cf. Braithwaite 1982), not all decorated objects were visible: the decorated Early Bronze Age axe from Brockagh in County Kildare was found unhafted in a leather sheath that would have hidden it from onlookers (Figure 3.8; Rynne 1963). In other cultural contexts, decorating an object is considered a transformative act that imbues it with life and efficacy (Gell 1998), and it may have been the potency of the Brockagh axe that meant it needed to be shielded in this way (cf. Jones 2010). Other Irish Early Bronze Age decorated objects were also hidden. For example, the lunula from Crossdoney in County Cavan was deposited in a wooden box in a bog (Armstrong 1933, 10); this too may have been viewed as a powerful and dangerous object. Cahill (2006) has noted that some lunulae show evidence of having been repeatedly rolled and unrolled, and it is possible that this practice was associated with concealing these objects when they were not in use. Lunulae have often been interpreted as ceremonial regalia (Taylor 1999, 110), and are therefore likely to have been imbued with ritual potency.

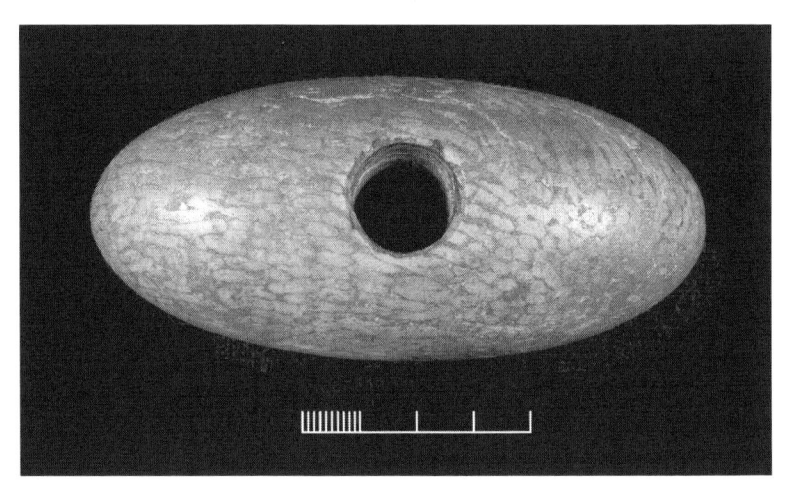

Figure 3.7. The macehead from Bush Barrow, Wiltshire (© Wiltshire Museum).

Object biographies

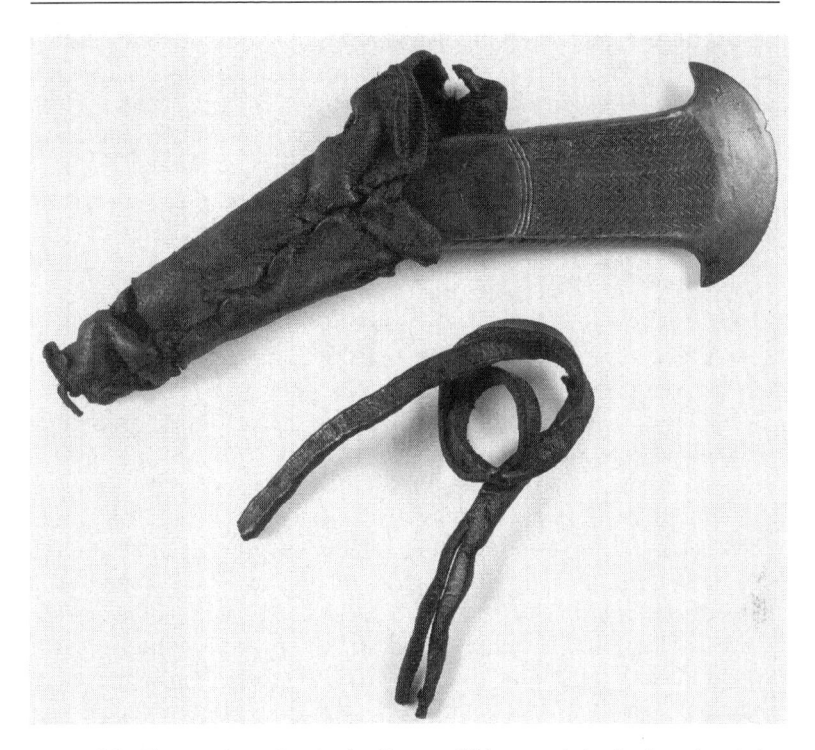

Figure 3.8. The axe from Brockagh, County Kildare, and the leather sheath in which it was found (© National Museum of Ireland).

Production, fragmentation, and exchange in the Middle and Late Bronze Age

Hoards and broken objects

It has often been observed that the types of object deposited in graves in the Early Bronze Age (for example, amber ornaments or bronze tools and weapons) tend to be recovered as single finds or from hoards in the Middle and Late Bronze Age (Torbrügge 1971; Bradley 1990, 99–100). Indeed, until the expansion of rescue and developer-funded archaeology in the 1980s and 1990s, single finds and hoards constituted the majority of archaeological evidence known from the Middle and Late Bronze Age. Although rarely considered together, the treatment of objects in Early Bronze Age graves in fact helps to cast interesting light on the interpretation of bronze hoards and other metal deposits in the later part of the period. We have argued above that the deliberate destruction of Early Bronze Age grave goods acted as a means of creating significant fragments that could be curated and circulated as ancestral relics and indices of interpersonal relationships (cf. Chapman 2000; Chapman and Gaydarska 2007). In the same way, the dissolution of composite objects such as daggers or necklaces and the combination and recombination of those fragments into new assemblages hint that people too were thought to be composed of multiple elements with different origins—their components brought together and reordered during mortuary rites and other forms of interpersonal interaction such as exchange and intermarriage. Broken objects, in other words, cannot simply be seen as 'rubbish' but played a significant and valued role in the creation and transformation of interpersonal links.

This point has significant implications for our interpretation of Middle and Late Bronze Age metalwork (Brück 2016), for this is often found in a broken and fragmentary state. It has long been argued that the deposition of metalwork in contexts such as rivers, lakes, and bogs can best be explained as the product of ritual practice (Torbrügge 1971; Levy 1982; Bradley 1990; Hansen 1994): finely crafted and doubtless valuable objects such as swords, shields, and spearheads have been recovered from such locations and have frequently been interpreted as votive offerings. Some of these objects are broken, and it has been suggested that the destruction of bronze and gold objects prior to depositing them in water acted as a means of ritually decommissioning these items at the end of their use-lives (York 2002).

The Late Bronze Age hoard from Bloody Pool in Devon, for example, comprises parts of a number of bronze spearheads and ferrules (metal caps to protect the butt-ends of spear shafts), and was recovered from an area of open water in a bog (Figure 3.9; Pearce 1983, plates 38–9). The spearheads have clearly been deliberately cut prior to deposition, and recent experimental work by Matt Knight (2018) indicates that they were probably heated before being broken, suggesting the involvement of someone with metalworking skills. Similar practices are well documented elsewhere. Research by York (2002, table 6) demonstrates that 48 per cent of spearheads and 59 per cent of swords recovered from the River Thames had been deliberately destroyed prior to deposition. Examples include the spearhead from Taplow Mills in Buckinghamshire which had been broken across the blade and both pieces deposited in the river (York 2002, 84, fig. 6); there was 'evidence of several blows on the wooden shaft' of this object. The weapons and weapon fragments from wetland hoards of the Wilburton phase (1150–1000 BC), for example one of the spearheads from the Blackmoor hoard in Hampshire, often display deep, regular, u-shaped notches to their blades very

Object biographies

Figure 3.9. The hoard from Bloody Pool, Devon (photograph by Matt Knight, with slight alterations by Anne Leaver; reproduced with permission of the Royal Albert Memorial Museum and Art Gallery, Exeter City Council).

different to the use-wear characteristic of combat damage, and it can be suggested that this acted as a means of deliberately decommissioning these objects prior to deposition (Mörtz 2010).

It is interesting, then, that broken bronzes from dryland contexts have so often been interpreted in functional terms. Broken metal objects found in settlement contexts are generally viewed as rubbish, while both in Britain and Ireland and further afield fragmented bronzes from dryland hoards have long been seen as scrap—items that no longer have a use value and are awaiting recycling (e.g. Evans 1881, 458–9; Falkenstein 1997; Huth 1997). Yet examples of what can be interpreted as ritual decommissioning of objects in dryland contexts are also known. The Late Bronze Age shield from Milsom's Corner near South Cadbury in Somerset had been deposited face down at the corner of a ditch dating to the Middle Bronze Age (Coles et al. 1999; Knight in press). It had been pierced three or four times by a blunt-ended tool (possibly a wooden stake) as it lay in the ditch: some fragments of bronze from the perforations were found beneath the shield. The terminals of the gold gorget from Gorteenreagh, County Clare, were torn from it prior to deposition; this item formed part of a hoard of six gold objects including two lock-rings, two bracelets, and a dress fastener found beneath a large stone slab (Raftery 1967). The gorget from Gleninsheen in the same county was folded in half before it was hidden in a rock fissure (Cahill 1995, 70). Such acts of destruction may have served to curb the potency of particular objects (for example, items that were considered polluted), or may have acted as a means of symbolically marking the death of their owners. Moreover, they also suggest that agency was attributed to such objects, and given the dazzling technical skills required to make them, this is perhaps no surprise (cf. Gell 1998).

Yet simpler objects such as small tools and axes appear to have been treated in similar ways. The overtly ritualized character of the destructive performances described above hints that we should consider similar interpretations for the objects from smiths' and founders' hoards— collections of broken bronzes and metalworking waste from dryland contexts that have traditionally been viewed as scrap awaiting recycling. It has been observed by a number of authors that the treatment of objects in scrap hoards cannot always be explained in functional terms. Turner (2010) has noted that the mouths of axes from Carp's Tongue hoards in south-eastern England were often crushed or filled with fragments of other broken objects, as if to render them unusable (cf. Hansen 1996–1998, 22–3). Similar practices can be identified elsewhere: the small dryland hoard from Booltiaghadine in County Clare, for example, comprised a razor and broken chisel packed into the socket of an axe (Eogan 1966), while a socketed axe containing four fragments of at least two gold bracelets (of probable Irish origin) was found at Rossett, near Wrexham in Clwyd (Gwilt et al. 2005).

Others have identified patterns of artefact selection that indicate particular rules regarding what could or could not be included in such assemblages (see also Bradley 2005a, ch. 5). The composition of dryland hoards in the Irish Late Bronze Age, for example, appears to have been carefully controlled (Becker 2006; 2013). Certain categories of object, such as horns and shields, were usually excluded from such contexts. Dryland hoards comprising tools and weapons tend to contain only single examples of swords alongside larger numbers of other artefacts; in almost every case, only one sword fragment is included. In southern England, mixed hoards containing broken axes usually include either the blade-end or the butt-end of individual axes but not both (Maraszek 2000, 214). Such rules indicate that the histories and meanings of objects such as swords and axes continued to matter even after they were broken. Other hoards include broken objects alongside artefacts that were still usable. The Ewart Park hoard from Long Bredy in Dorset, for example, comprised three sword fragments alongside three complete objects—a bifid razor, a pegged spearhead, and a socketed gouge. Fragments of the wooden hafts of the gouge and spearhead were still preserved inside their sockets, suggesting that they were deposited as complete composite objects. This makes it difficult to read these artefacts as scrap (Knight 2016).

Such assemblages cannot therefore be interpreted in purely functional terms, and a number of authors have sought alternative explanations. It has been suggested, for example, that scrap hoards may represent *pars pro toto* offerings (Nebelsick 2000, 169; Hansen 2016), with portions of objects that were destined for recycling being consigned to the ground as sacrifices to ensure success for the smith. Some may result from acts of ritual decommissioning. However, the breaking of objects may also have functioned to create fragments that could be curated or circulated to give material form to significant interpersonal relationships (Bradley 2005a, 162–3). This is a compelling argument given the other evidence for curation in Late Bronze Age contexts, particularly of fragments of human bone, as we have seen in Chapter 2.

Of course, it is usually impossible to trace the subsequent histories of missing fragments of objects, although occasional examples have been identified. Two joining fragments of a single sword from Staffordshire were deposited as isolated finds on two nearby hilltops; the hilltops themselves were intervisible and lay some 3 kilometres apart on either side of the River Trent (Bradley and Ford 2004). One of these pieces was more heavily worn than the other, suggesting different histories of use. Nonetheless, their depositional contexts were so similar that we can suggest that the history and original relationships of the pieces were known—and considered important—even at the end of their lives. This suggests that, contrary to Bradley's argument that the destruction of objects served to strip them of their cultural meaning (1985), in fact this process may have worked to produce fragments of important objects with known origins that could be shared between those bound together in significant relationships. Fontijn (2002, 230; 2005) argues that the deposition of metalwork in wet places played a significant role in the transformation of social identity; rites of passage involving the deconstruction of particular identities and the creation of new ones may have required the decommissioning of objects bound up with particular but transient concepts of personhood. It is useful to consider how this may illuminate the fragmentation of objects in dryland contexts also; we can suggest that the deposition of broken artefacts facilitated the reformulation of relational identities both through the (sometimes ritualized) destruction of the objects themselves and the curation, circulation, and remelting of those fragments that were not deposited in the ground

(Brück 2016). Acts of ritual destruction marked and mediated the crossing of boundaries when socially significant objects were recycled from one form to another. Moreover, the process of breaking metal objects can be interpreted as a means of removing their individuality and accentuating instead their substance and malleability—qualities that may have been viewed as essential attributes of personhood, at least in particular contexts.

The relational or sociocentric character of Bronze Age identities is underlined by other aspects of the metalwork evidence. The size of many bronze hoards, particularly during the Late Bronze Age, suggests that they may have been assembled by a number of people (cf. Needham 1988, 246). Furthermore, objects such as bronze swords or gold gorgets were not deposited in graves but were detached from the bodily identities of individual persons. Some items may have already been old on deposition: a fragment of animal bone found immediately beneath the shield from Milsom's Corner in Somerset returned a radiocarbon date as much as a century younger than the accepted date range for this type of artefact (Needham et al. 2012, table 2), suggesting that the shield was deposited several generations after it was originally manufactured. Artefacts such as this may have been heirlooms, and it is therefore possible that they were not tied to particular individuals but were inalienable objects that symbolized the collective identities of family or lineage groups (Fontijn 2002, 27, 226).

The depositional context of metalworking residues in the Middle and Late Bronze Age

The argument that the destruction of bronze objects facilitated the transformation of social identities is supported by details of the contexts from which 'scrap' hoards have been recovered. At Bogshole Lane, Broomfield, Kent, a pit cut into the upper fill of a Late Bronze Age ditch produced a hoard of twenty-seven bronze objects, including parts of eleven axes and two spearheads, as well as twelve amorphous lumps of bronze (Allen 1999; Helm 2001, 23). The hoard from Bradley Fen in Cambridgeshire included fragments of swords and spearheads and was deposited in a low earthen mound in the watery fen edge immediately adjacent to the junction between two field boundaries (Figure 3.10; Gibson and Knight 2006, 26–7). A hoard of bronze objects was deposited in a pit in the porched entrance to house 1 at Tower Hill, Ashbury in Oxfordshire (Coombs et al. 2003). The assemblage comprised both complete and fragmentary objects, including Sompting axes (one unfinished), bracelets, rings, casting jets, scrap metal, and

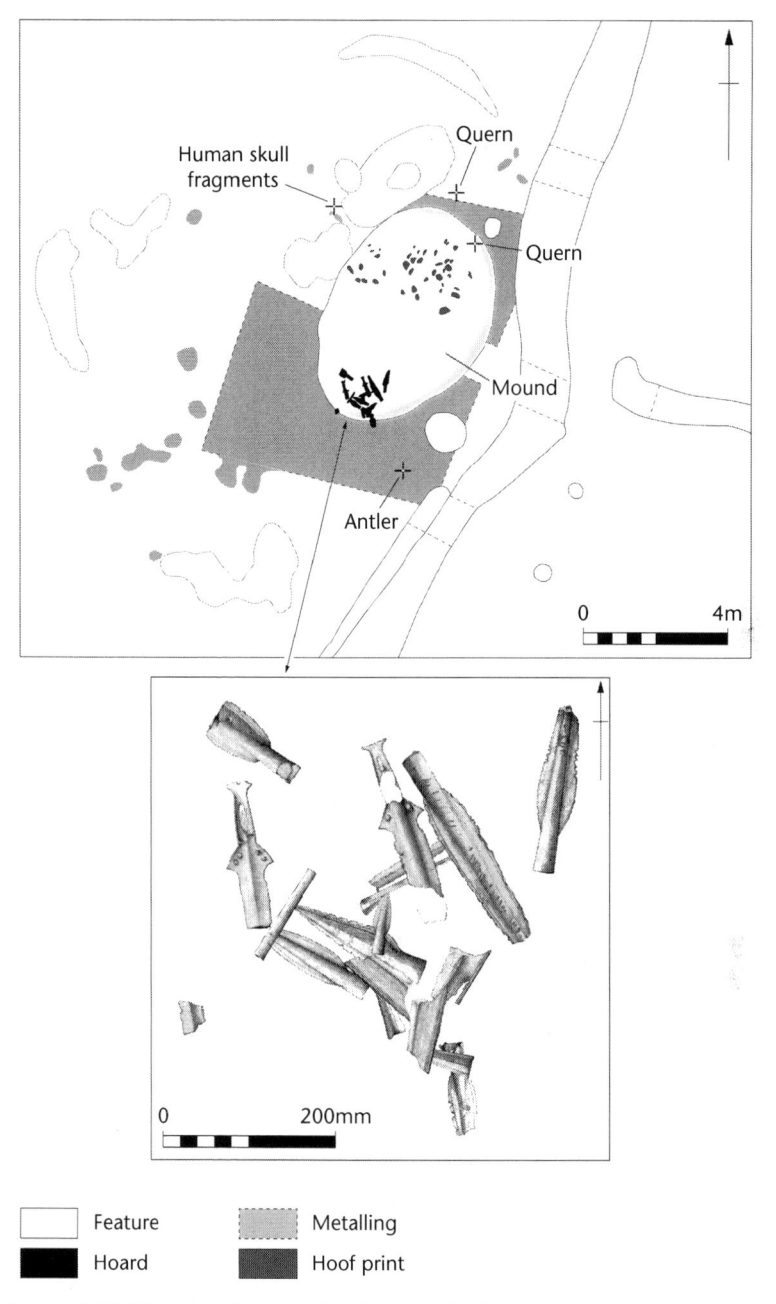

Figure 3.10. The hoard from Bradley Fen, Cambridgeshire, in its excavated context (reproduced with permission of Cambridge Archaeological Unit, with slight alterations by Anne Leaver).

one piece of slag. Here, we can suggest that the combination of objects in a state of transition—some new, some old, and all the product of a magical, dangerous activity—were viewed as particularly suitable items to mark out the entranceway, a space of encounter and transformation.

Indeed, it is interesting that other types of metalworking evidence have also been recovered from liminal contexts. Seventy clay mould fragments, probably from the casting of a single bronze sword, were found in a pit that may have functioned as the socket for a gatepost at the entrance to a hilltop enclosure at Norton Fitzwarren in Somerset (Ellis 1989, 10; Needham 1989). Two crucible fragments and parts of three stone moulds for the production of pins were found in peat deposits adjacent to a timber platform at the edge of the River Witham at Washingborough in Lincolnshire (Allen 2009). Sites of this sort are widely interpreted as locations of ritual significance where bronzes, human remains, and other special objects were consigned to the waters, and dredging of this stretch of the river during the eighteenth and nineteenth centuries produced a number of bronze artefacts. At Cranford Lane, Harlington, London, fragments of a crucible and several clay moulds (probably for the production of swords) were deposited in the lower fills of one of a pair of wells flanking the entrance through one of the boundaries of a Late Bronze Age field system (Elsden 1996, D-15). The deposition of human bone in wells and waterholes of this date elsewhere, as we shall see in Chapter 4, suggests that such features may have shared some of the properties of 'natural' locations such as rivers and lakes. Other wet places may have been created specifically as venues for deposition. At the King's Stables near Navan, County Armagh, an artificial pond some 25 metres in diameter and surrounded by a bank was dug in the Late Bronze Age (Lynn 1977). This produced antler, animal bone, part of a human skull, and eighteen mould fragments for the production of swords.

Such finds suggest that the transformative potential of metalworking (cf. Hingley 1997; Haaland 2004; Goldhahn and Østigård 2007; Helms 2012) rendered the residues of this process equally powerful; materials such as fragments of moulds or crucibles not only had to be disposed of in a particular way, but could also be employed to draw attention to places or processes of transition, including rites of passage or significant moments in the lifecycle of a site and its occupants, and we can suggest that the deposition of scrap hoards may have served similar purposes. The recovery of human bone from similar contexts hints that the process of transformation could be seen as dangerous as well as productive. The recycling of bronze artefacts suggests that social identity was viewed as fluid and mutable during this period. Yet the process of melting and recasting such items was inherently disruptive, for it involved the destruction and transformation of objects that played a significant role in upholding particular social categories (cf. Bradley 1985). As such, the deposition of metalworking residues in liminal contexts highlighted the dangers involved in transgressing social and spatial boundaries. The power of such materials is occasionally made evident in other ways: the fragment of stone palstave mould found in a posthole just next to a roundhouse at Corrstown, County Londonderry, had been drilled through in several places, suggesting that it may have been reused as an amulet (Ginn and Rathbone 2011, 248-9).

It is interesting to note that many of the bronze objects from the well-known shipwreck sites at Langdon Bay in Kent and Salcombe in Devon had been fragmented (Needham et al. 2013). In part, this may have been to facilitate packing for transport, but it may also have formed one step in the important and ritualized process of transforming these objects for use in a new cultural context. The assemblage from Langdon Bay, for example, was found by divers on the seabed in what was probably originally a small inlet in the estuary of the River Dour and dates to the thirteenth century BC. It comprised 360 objects including axes, palstaves, chisels, hammers, swords, rapiers, spearheads, pins, and bracelets; the morphology of these artefacts indicates that most originated in northern France. Although many were broken, one rapier had been bent into a pronounced curved shape (Needham et al. 2013, fig. 3.18, no. 334)—a striking act that cannot have been carried out purely for the purpose of recycling this object—while the mouth of a socketed axe (Needham et al. 2013, fig. 3.11, no. 119) had been blocked by the insertion of a number of bronze fragments (Figure 3.11); this, and their wet location, has suggested to some that these assemblages are not shipwrecks but votive deposits (Samson 2006; Brandherm 2014), an interpretation that Needham et al. (2013, 149) accept for other metal finds of insular type from the coastal and intertidal zones.

Whatever the case, it is interesting that so few 'foreign' objects are found in Britain, despite metallurgical evidence that continental Europe was the main source of bronze during most of the Middle and Late Bronze Age. Examples include a Hunze-Ems-style axe from the wooden platform at Shinewater in the Willingdon Levels, East Sussex (Needham et al. 2013, 145): here, an exotic object was deposited at a wetland location of probable ceremonial significance. The rarity of such finds indicates that most continental bronzes were recast to produce objects of insular style, and this is supported by metallurgical analysis, which indicates extensive recycling in the Late Bronze Age (Northover 1982; 2013, 102). However, we can suggest that the fragmentation of the bronzes from Langdon Bay and

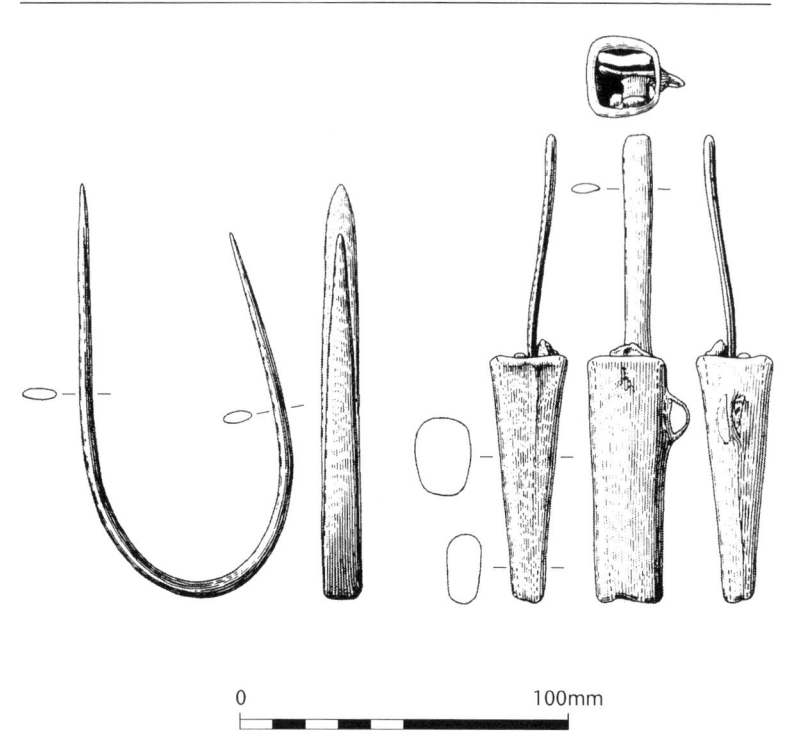

Figure 3.11. Two of the items from the shipwreck at Langdon Bay, Kent: bent rapier (left) and socketed axe with blocked mouth (right) (© The Trustees of the British Museum; after Needham et al. 2013, fig. 3.18 no. 334 and fig. 3.11 no. 119, with slight alterations by Anne Leaver).

Salcombe does not simply represent the scrapping of objects that had lost their cultural significance and were viewed as 'refuse', but formed part of the ritualized transformation of objects with particular power and significance. Given the intensity of interaction between southern England and northern France during this period (Bourgeois and Talon 2009; Marcigny and Talon 2009), the origins and histories of at least some of these objects may have been considered important; indeed, as we shall argue in the next section, the recycling of objects into new forms need not mean that this history was irrevocably lost.

Fragmentation, fertility, and regeneration

The preceding discussion suggests that destruction was a socially significant act. On the one hand, it acted to mark and maintain particular relationships through the exchange, mixing, and deposition of fragments of meaningful objects, at least some of which may have had known histories (Brück 2006a; 2016; Hansen 2016). On the other hand, it also facilitated processes of transformation that involved the dissolution of object form and the transgression of cultural categories. By the Late Bronze Age there appears to have been an element of ambivalence around the practice of deliberate fragmentation, as indicated by the deposition of items such as broken bronzes in locations that may have been viewed as dangerous or liminal, such as boundaries, bogs, and rivers (Bradley 1990; 2017). The crossing of boundaries—whether physical or social—was considered hazardous, yet it was also essential to the maintenance of life: exchange and intermarriage, for example, cannot happen without it. As such, it is perhaps no surprise that the practice of fragmentation and the subsequent mixing and amalgamation of broken objects were also linked with more positive concepts of fertility and regeneration (Brück 2006b).

The technology of bronze production demonstrates this well. Copper ore had to be crushed and cleaned before it could be smelted (Tylecote 1987; O'Brien 1994). Once smelted, it was mixed with other metals such as tin and lead and then cast to create bronze objects. At the end of their lives, broken bronzes could be remelted and recast to create new objects with new use-lives. Heat-mediated transformations involving fragmentation, mixing, and amalgamation were core elements of other generative processes also, notably food production and ceramic technology (Williams 2003). The production of pottery, for example, required the grinding and mixing of clay before the pot could be fired in the kiln. Materials such as stone and burnt flint (which we might view as 'rubbish') were crushed and added as temper. Burnt flint may have derived from cooking activities so that the residues of previous acts of commensality were already incorporated into the object, while the frequency of sandstone and granite inclusions hints that socially significant objects such as quernstones may have been deliberately broken for reuse in pottery production (Woodward 2002b, 110–11). Sometimes grog (fragments of broken pottery) was employed as a tempering agent, providing an explicit 'ancestry' for particular vessels (Brown 1995, 127). The frequent recovery of incomplete ceramic vessels from cremation burials suggests that pieces of pottery may have been deliberately removed and retained from the mortuary context (Woodward 2002b, 109). Bone-tempered ceramics are also known (Barclay and Doherty 1998), although as yet it has not been possible to demonstrate whether the bone is human or animal in origin. As we shall see in Chapter 4, although refuse was often deposited in the ditches around settlements, marking the boundary between clean and unclean, insiders and outsiders, it was also spread on fields as manure (Gingell 1992, 155; Simpson et al. 1998), so that it was at once viewed as dangerous and productive.

We have discussed the treatment of the human body on death in Chapter 2, but we can note here the significant structural similarities between technologies such as metalworking and pottery production and contemporary cremation practices (Brück 2006b). Like bronze objects, the dead were subject to burning and breaking as a core component of the funerary rite. Fragments of their bodies were curated, circulated, and mixed with other bodies and materials. This suggests that objects, like people, were considered to have lifecycles and that these were closely interlinked: as we will see in Chapter 4, objects such as quernstones and ceramic vessels were often broken and buried on the abandonment of a settlement (Seager Thomas 1999, 41; Watts 2014)—a moment that may have coincided with the death of a significant member of the household. Such similarities in the treatment of bodies and objects indicate that the production of objects and the construction of the self were considered analogous processes involving cycles of burning, breaking, combination, and regeneration mediated by technological and ritual acts (Brück 2006b). Like objects, people were viewed not as bounded and homogeneous wholes but as fluid, composite entities whose constituent elements were brought together, dispersed, and reordered in the context of exchange, intermarriage, and other rites of passage.

Technologies of the self: weaving and cloth production

The technologies we have discussed above involved the fragmentation, mixing, and amalgamation of different elements, but other productive processes worked in different ways. The increase in evidence for the weaving of cloth in the Middle Bronze Age is particularly striking. Loom weights and spindle whorls are common from this period onwards, particularly from settlement sites in southern and eastern Britain, although they are virtually unknown before, despite evidence for the use of cloth to wrap grave goods and bodies in Early Bronze Age burials. This suggests that ideas regarding the construction and presentation of the self changed at this time. The social significance of cloth production is evident in the often careful deposition of objects such as loom weights and spindle whorls in the Middle and Late Bronze Age. At Westhampnett, West Sussex, for example, a near-complete burnt loom weight was carefully placed on the base of a ceramic vessel in pit 8298 (Chadwick 2006, 18). This pit also contained a number of other sherds,

Object biographies

burnt flint, and a large deposit of charred grain. Four spindle whorls were arranged around a complete pot laid at the base of a pit at Horcott Pit in Gloucestershire (Lamdin-Whymark et al. 2009, 62). This feature was part of a group of pits and postholes close to four roundhouses. At Kemerton in Worcestershire, the upper fill of a large Late Bronze Age waterhole (CG4) produced an interesting range of finds including parts of at least six loom weights, large quantities of pottery, part of a shale armlet, the lower section of a bone pin, a fragment of human vertebra, and several clay mould fragments (Jackson 2015, table 10); deposits like this can be interpreted as evidence for the deliberate closing or decommissioning of what are likely to have been economically and socially significant features.

The occasional decoration of spindle whorls may also attest to the significance of textile production. A biconical spindle whorl found in a Late Bronze Age midden on an island in the Thames at Wallingford, Oxfordshire, had a neat series of fingernail impressions around the carination (Thomas et al. 1986, 191, fig. 5). At Killemly, County Tipperary, a mudstone spindle whorl found in a pit close to the hearth in a Late Bronze Age roundhouse was decorated on one face with a series of three engraved concentric circles (McQuade et al. 2009, 67). The decoration of objects is likely to have drawn attention to the activities in which they were employed and the people who used them (cf. Braithwaite 1982), and the presence of decorated spindle whorls suggests that spinning was a significant element of the identities of those who practised this craft.

There is evidence to suggest that cloth production was an important component of the household economy during the Middle and Late Bronze Age, and new fabric types such as linen were introduced during this period. The waterholes at Kemerton in Worcestershire may have provided water for the processing of wool or flax (Jackson 2015, 104, 108). Parts of thirteen clay loom weights were recovered from waterhole CG7, indicating that cloth production may have taken place in this area of the site. An adjacent pit may have been used to store water. Large quantities of burnt limestone were recovered from both the pit and the waterhole, suggesting that water may have been heated. Water is, of course, essential for processes such as retting flax (this involves the soaking of flax stems in water in order to break down the fibres), and fulling, dyeing, and felting wool. Flax pollen was identified at Kemerton and is present at other Late Bronze Age sites in southern England. At Reading Business Park in Berkshire, a row of waterlogged pits produced large numbers of flax seeds and capsule fragments and was interpreted as an area where flax retting was carried out (Moore and Jennings 1992, 110).

Flax and nettle seeds were also recovered from the Late Bronze Age midden at Potterne in Wiltshire (Carruthers 2000, 83). Seeds of blackberry and elderberry from the same site may suggest use of dyes for cloth. Spindle whorls from the earlier levels of the midden tend to be made from fired clay, while those from later layers were increasingly made from reworked potsherds, suggesting the production of finer textiles (Hall 2000). Textiles of the period are rarely preserved, but fragments of very fine linen have been recovered from beneath the timber platform at Must Farm in Cambridgeshire (http://www.mustfarm.com/progress/site-diary-6-textiles/), alongside pieces of cloth that appear to have been folded multiple times and may therefore originally have been very large. The discovery of bundles of plant fibres, balls of thread, and spindle whorls indicates that the manufacture of textiles took place at this site, and the quantity of material suggests that these were not made solely for household consumption. In contrast to earlier periods, bone tools of various sorts are a very common find at Late Bronze Age settlements (Brück 2007, 26), and it seems likely that at least some of these (notably awls and points) may have been employed in the production of cloth and clothing. The exchange of cloth wealth is a key component of social transactions such as marriage and funerary prestations in many parts of the world today (Schneider and Weiner 1989), and the production of cloth in large quantities during the Middle and Late Bronze Age hints that it may have fulfilled similar roles in that cultural context.

The evidence therefore suggests that cloth production was a significant element of the Bronze Age economy, particularly towards the end of the period. It was carried out not only at 'ordinary' open settlements like Kemerton but at places like Potterne that have been interpreted as high-status sites where people congregated for feasting and ceremonial activities (see Chapter 4). Cloth, then, is likely to have played a significant role in the construction of social identity both at the intimate level of day-to-day interaction and on special occasions when different communities came together. The lack of evidence for loom weights in the Early Bronze Age suggests that cloth may generally have been woven on small, handheld looms, in contrast to the larger, upright, warp-weighted looms of the Middle and Late Bronze Age (Henshall 1950). The latter would have allowed their users to make larger pieces of cloth; this may have been important if cloth became a significant item of exchange during this period.

Cloth production is, of course, a very different technology to metalworking, for it involves processes of weaving and binding that contrast quite dramatically with the fragmentation of objects and materials required in the production of bronze. We have suggested above that the increasing archaeological visibility of cloth production in the Middle and Late Bronze Age indicates that it became an important object of exchange during this period, and it is possible that the symbolic potential of weaving as a metaphor for human relationships (Schneider and Weiner 1989; Hoskins 1989) was recognized and valued: woven cloth binds different strands together just as exchange creates ties between communities. Cloth is not static, however: it can be woven and unravelled, sewn together and cut, just like the social relations generated through exchange. Those involved in the production and exchange of cloth may therefore have played an important role in creating, maintaining, and transforming intergroup links.

The significance of social transactions

We do not know who was involved in weaving cloth, and it may in fact have been multiple members of the household (Sørensen 1991, 124). Cloth may well have been one of the major 'bulk' items of exchange alongside bronze during this period, and the contrast between cloth and bronze both in terms of their material properties and the techniques required to produce them is interesting, for it suggests that different groups of people are likely to have been involved in the manufacture of these materials. Anthropological studies of exchange have often noted that specific categories of objects are considered appropriate gifts in particular types of transaction (Bohannan 1955; Weiner 1983). In marriage settlements, gifts often travel in opposite directions between the groom's kin and the bride's kin, and these usually have quite different properties. On the island of Seram in Indonesia, for example, large quantities of porcelain plates and shell armlets are given on marriage transactions by wife-takers and wife-givers respectively (Valeri 1980). These categories of object stand for the particular qualities brought to the marriage by husband and wife—body and blood, form and substance. Amongst the Kodi of Sumba, also in Indonesia but some 1200 kilometres to the south-west, gold ornaments were given by the groom's kin to the bride's kin, while gifts of cloth travelled in the opposite direction (Hoskins 1989). In this cultural context, cloth is associated with ideas of fertility and regeneration: just as in our own cultural context we talk about the 'thread of life' and the 'social fabric', here too the acts of spinning, weaving, and unravelling form potent metaphors of life and death. When a wife dies, her husband's group give further gifts to her natal kinsfolk to compensate them for their loss. In turn, these gifts will be used to arrange new marriages, ensuring the continuous flow of life (Hoskins 1989).

In the British Bronze Age, materials such as cloth and bronze may have been employed in such transactions, particularly if there was a gendered dimension to the production of these materials. In the absence of evidence for the gendered division of labour, it is, of course, problematic to assume that men worked metals while women wove cloth, but if that were the case, it is possible to imagine that cloth travelled from the bride's kin to the groom's, and bronze in the opposite direction. If so, the properties of cloth and bronze may have been employed to comment on what each partner brought to the union—substance versus form, for example. Bronze has a history that embodies an ideal of ancestry through the practice of recycling, while the process of cloth production encapsulates the creation of horizontal ties. Bronze and cloth may therefore have stood for agnatic and affinal relationships respectively.

There are other finds that may represent the residues of marriage transactions. The hoards of the Middle Bronze Age 'ornament horizon' in southern and eastern England (Smith 1959; Roberts 2007; Wilkin 2017) are particularly interesting, for they often include combinations of ornaments and palstaves. The hoard from Ockham in Surrey (Figure 3.12), for example, comprised six palstaves, two spiral finger rings and two bracelets of a distinctive type known as Sussex loops (PAS SUR-B41DB6). At West Buckland in Somerset, a bronze spiral-twisted

Figure 3.12. The hoard from Ockham, Surrey (© David Williams).

torc was found with two palstaves some 35 metres from the bank of the River Tone (Roberts 2007, cat. no. 9). Larger assemblages are also known, for example the hoard of seventy-nine objects found in a ceramic vessel near Lewes in East Sussex in 2011 (PAS SUSS-C5D042). This included three palstaves, four torcs, five 'Sussex loop' bracelets, eight finger rings, four tutuli, four sheet gold discs, a lozenge-headed pin, nineteen amber beads, and fragments of various other ornaments. The pairing or multiplication of objects in some of these hoards gives the impression that they may have comprised sets of objects belonging to one or more people (Wilkin 2017, 18).

Although artefacts such as bracelets and palstaves are rarely found in burials during this period (Roberts 2007; and where they do, the sex of the interments remains unknown), they occur in contemporary mortuary contexts elsewhere in Europe: in many regions, items such as neck rings and pins are associated with women, while axes were deposited in the graves of men (Kubach-Richter and Kubach 1989, 86; Bergerbrandt 2007, 8). If we assume similar gendered associations for such objects in Britain, the combination of palstaves and ornaments might symbolize marriage partnerships. Some of these assemblages might therefore be the product of marriage transactions—items that were given as gifts by the families of the bride and groom and that might have been displayed during the marriage ceremony. Indeed, the choice of artefacts in such hoards is interesting. Ornaments such as neck rings and finger rings are circular in form, expressing concepts of continuity and connection, while pins allow things to be joined; Wilkin (2017, 30–2) has noted how the arrangement of ornament hoards in the ground often involves nesting, stacking, and looping objects together. By contrast, axes sever connections. This symbolic evocation of cleaving and binding may have spoken of the different way in which men and women were articulated into kinship networks, and the tension between the desire to maintain the integrity of the descent group and the necessity of relationships with others.

It is notable that objects in ornament horizon hoards were often deposited in a fragmentary state, and some show evidence of repair (Roberts 2007, 148). Both of the Sussex loops and one of the finger rings from the Ockham hoard, for example, had been broken; in addition, one of the palstaves had been cut into two pieces. This suggests that such hoards may not have been deposited at the start of a marriage, but after its end—perhaps on the death of one of the partners. By contrast, Wilkin (2017, 32) describes how the stack of bracelets from Church Farm, Ripple, Kent, were graded by weight and size, with the largest and heaviest item at the bottom; these items reference different life stages, female growth and productivity, and the acquisition of new relationships and identities over the life course. Hoards from other periods may also have been the product of marriage prestations. The Late Bronze Age hoard from St Andrews in Fife, for example, contained bronze spearheads, axes, and tools, alongside shale armlets, amber beads, and a variety of bronze ornaments (Cowie et al. 1991); some of the objects were stacked or bound together with cord, while the presence of fragments of textile and leather hints that other groups of items may have been wrapped. The presence of cloth as well as tools, weapons, and ornaments of various materials is interesting, for it may speak of the productive and political endeavours of different kin and gender groups.

If ornaments were core components of transactions between kin groups, it is perhaps no surprise that the deposition of such objects was sometimes used to mark out social boundaries. At Kingsmead Quarry, Horton, Berkshire, for example, a complete quoit-headed pin just over 33 centimetres long was found in the upper fill of a ditched field boundary (https://www.wessexarch.co.uk/our-work/kingsmead-quarry-horton); the pointed end of this object had been bent into a curve, perhaps to render it unusable prior to deposition. The size of this pin and the challenges it must have posed to bodily movement when worn remind us that ornaments do not merely symbolize identity but have a profound effect on embodied experience and the practicalities of engagement with the world (Sørensen 1997). As González-Ruibal et al. (2011, 12) argue, objects 'are not a displacement of the self, but an intimate part of the self. The relationship is ontological, not analogical'. Certainly, the Middle Bronze Age ornament horizon—a period during which a variety of often large and heavy metal ornaments were worn—indicates the emergence of new technologies of the self during this period. This coincides with other social changes, including the disappearance of burials with grave goods, the introduction of monumental domestic architecture, and the creation of field systems (Barrett 1994)—developments that may relate in part to changes in inheritance patterns and the concepts of personhood and substance that these entail.

Categorization and difference

Objects, in other words, make people—but this is true not only for items worn on the body. The tools associated with particular crafts, for example, were no doubt bound up with the personal identity and self-worth of those who used them (Costin and Wright 1998; Edmonds 1999; Bender Jørgensen et al. 2016), so that craft activities involved the production of both objects and people. It is interesting to note the diversification of tools in the Late Bronze Age in particular: settlements of this period produce a much wider range of tool types (Brück 2007, 26), for example bronze gouges, chisels, and knives, and bone scoops and points, than earlier sites, and it is possible that this indicates a desire to more closely control, define, and distinguish not only the activities themselves but those who carried them out. This is part of a more general trend towards the proliferation of material culture at Late Bronze Age settlements (Brück 2007); this suggests not only that such sites were themselves a key social arena but also that the boundaries between different categories of person became more clearly marked out. Whether such social differences also indicate increasing social complexity or hierarchization is something we will return to later in this chapter, however.

We have already noted that the decoration of items such as spindle whorls may have served to draw attention to particular activities and people, and allows us to comment on the changing significance of particular elements of social practice. Middle Bronze Age pottery, for example, was rarely decorated, but the use of decoration became more frequent over the course of the Late Bronze Age, particularly after 800 BC (Figure 3.13; Barrett 1980b; Brudenell 2012). Rows of finger-tip impressions and incised linear and geometric motifs, particularly on the neck and shoulder, are common. In addition, some bowls and jars were coated with haematite (iron ore) and fired to create a burnished red finish (Cunliffe 1991, 92–3; Middleton 1987), so that colour symbolism was drawn into moments of social interaction. The increased use of decoration coincides with the introduction of a variety of new ceramic forms, notably serving vessels such as bowls and cups. The assemblage from Kemerton in Worcestershire, for example, included larger coarse-ware vessels containing burnt food residues alongside smaller fine-ware vessels with no residues, indicating clear differences between the pottery used to cook and serve food (Woodward and Jackson 2015, 52).

Both the decoration of Late Bronze Age pottery and the diversification of ceramic types suggest that the consumption of food became a key arena for the performance of social difference (Barrett 1989a). The social significance of objects such as cups and bowls helps to explain why these were decorated, for these were items that were required to be visible; they were not merely objects of display, but marked and made identities—differentiating residents from guests, or distinguishing particular age and gender categories. Although the biographies of objects and people may often have been inextricably linked, other artefacts were not associated with particular individuals but nonetheless played significant roles in the production of personhood. Objects such as Late

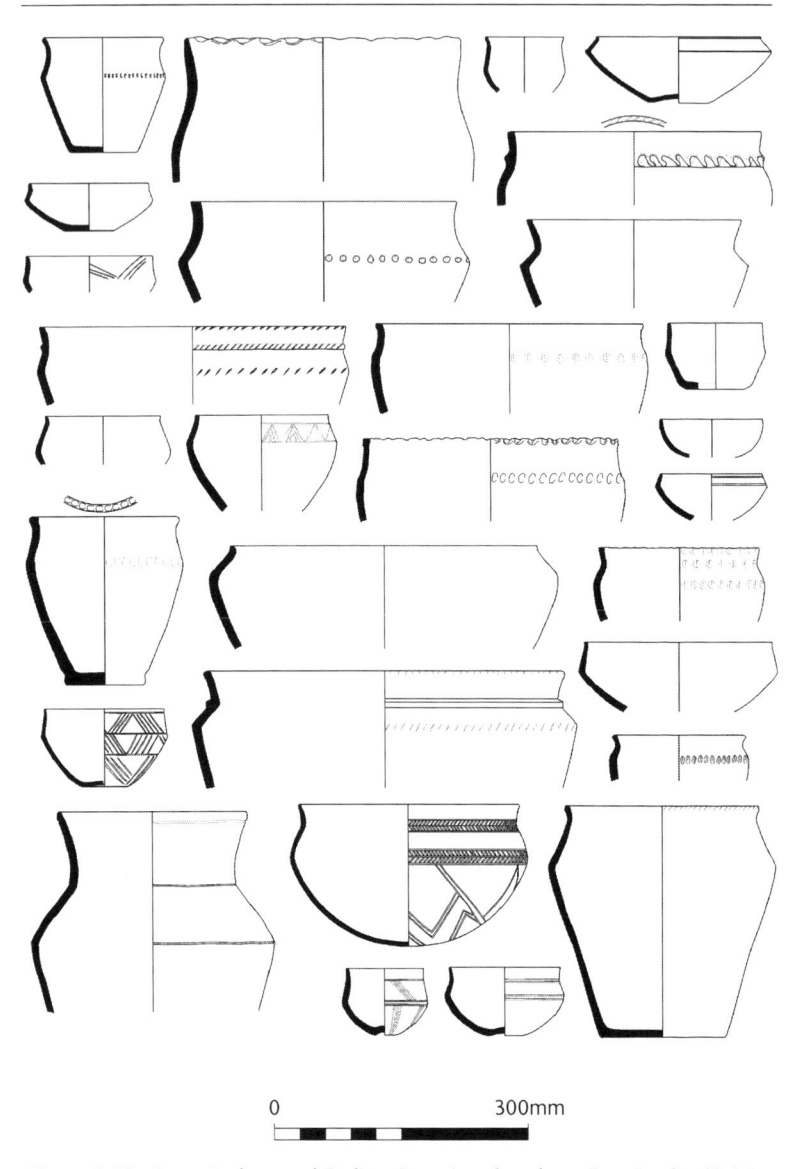

Figure 3.13. Ceramic forms of Earliest Iron Age date from East Anglia (© Matt Brudenell, with slight alterations by Anne Leaver).

Bronze Age cauldrons (Gerloff 2010), for example, forged social cohesion through the act of eating together. Yet, they may also have marked distinctions, for example in the order of preference in which people were served, or between those who cooked, those who served, and those who ate (cf. Joy 2014). As such, they made persons in a profoundly relational way—at least for the duration of particular ceremonial events. As we will see in Chapter 4, evidence for feasting events at Late Bronze Age midden sites suggests that these may have been one of the key locations in which identities were constructed and social boundaries defined through the consumption of food (Waddington 2010; Madgwick and Mulville 2015). Interestingly, these produce not only large assemblages of decorated ceramics as well as—more occasionally—fragments of cauldrons, but also diverse assemblages of tools, ornaments, and other items (e.g. Needham 1991; Needham and Spence 1996; Lawson 2000). Middens were places where visually distinctive materials from different sources, including amber, shale, bone, bronze, stone, and pottery, were combined and ordered; glass is rare but, where it is found, it is often a striking blue colour (e.g. Needham and Bimson 1988). Differences in the colour of items worn or used in feasts, ceremonies, and other activities at middens gave material form to social distinctions, just as the juxtaposition of such objects allowed the performance of cosmologies. Yet the diverse artefact assemblages from these and other Late Bronze Age sites were not simply a means of expressing wealth or status, and the communication of other forms of identity and belonging may have been equally important. Most of the shale armlets from the Late Bronze Age midden at Potterne in Wiltshire, for example, were small in size, with the majority in the region of 5–7 centimetres in diameter (Brück and Davies 2018). These would fit an older child but not an adult. Many had been broken into half- or quarter-sections, and it can be suggested that this was a deliberate act. We can perhaps suggest that the gatherings at middens were considered appropriate contexts in which to carry out rites of passage such as initiation into adulthood. The breaking of such items might have acted as a means of commemorating the end of a particular stage in the life course and of marking significant interpersonal relationships through the distribution of fragments to others.

Conclusion

Our discussion in this chapter calls into question the assumptions about objects that underpin core elements of social evolutionary narratives of the Bronze Age. Objects cannot be reduced to their function or economic value, for that places them too easily outside the sphere of human culture and society. Nor, on the other hand, should they be seen as passive markers of status or identity caught up in the social and political strategizing of human actors. Rather, objects were a core component of the self. As we have seen, the biographies of objects and people were often closely intertwined. They were bound into personal, family, and community histories, for they were acquired at significant points in the human life course and passed down from generation to generation. Items such as pots could become part of the human body while, as we have seen in Chapter 2, human bone could sometimes be made into objects. Like bodies, objects were subject to processes of assembly and dissolution. The destruction of objects was a significant element of Bronze Age social and ritual practice: this was designed not only to allow ontological conceptions of temporality, change, and loss to be addressed, but to create fragments which circulated to sustain relational forms of personhood. The arrangement of objects in the grave—as elements of assemblages placed around the body of the deceased—suggests the relational construction of the self. Mortuary practice involved the construction of narratives of identity that located the dead relative to significant places, people, and events. Yet the deposition of objects did not act solely as a means of fixing the self, but facilitated the relinquishing and refashioning of transitory forms of identity. Identities were not static or homogeneous, for grave goods were themselves constituted in relational terms (Fowler 2017) so that the memories and meanings evoked doubtless varied from mourner to mourner.

Similarities in the treatment of bodies and objects suggest that human and object life courses were viewed as analogous. The burning and breaking of objects such as pots, axes, or bone pins indicate that they were thought to have 'lives' that paralleled those of the people who used them—people whose bodies were also fragmented and cremated on death. Analogies between cremation and technologies such as potting and metallurgy suggest that the production of objects and the production of the human self were considered similar processes (Brück 2006b): in each case, the activities of burning, breaking, and amalgamation were a central component of transformative practices that facilitated the regeneration of life, so that both human and object lives were understood to involve a series of cycles of fragmentation, mixing, and renewal. Like objects, persons were viewed as comprising multiple components that were brought together, divided, and reordered at important moments in the human lifecycle. Practices that involved the breaking of objects and bodies were designed to facilitate the maintenance and regeneration of interpersonal relationships through the circulation of meaningful fragments. Such processes of circulation and exchange were essential to the maintenance of social and biological life so that the flow of objects made people.

Yet the destruction and reassembly of objects and materials was a process that was viewed with some ambivalence, particularly in the Late Bronze Age, for it involved the dissolution of social categories and the transgression of boundaries. This tension between processes of connection and division was given material form in Bronze Age technologies and in assemblages such as hoards that may themselves have been the product of particular histories of exchange. The apparent ambivalence around the social role of broken objects in the Middle and Late Bronze Age can be linked to contemporary social, political, and ontological processes, notably an increasing concern to mark spatial boundaries at various scales. It is therefore perhaps unsurprising that the residues of technologies such as metalworking—itself a transformative process—were employed to mark out other significant points of social and spatial transition: the generative yet destructive potential of this technology meant that even the residues of metalworking could be powerful (Helms 2012). Craftwork often involves the re-enactment of creation myths (Dieterlen 1957; Blier 1987), so that the production of objects facilitates the making of the social universe. The production, exchange, and deposition of objects were therefore generative acts that worked to construct both self and society. Bronze Age objects facilitated social categorization: they did so, however, not only through processes of distinction but by making relational networks of belonging.

We have seen that the biographies of people and objects were often intimately interconnected, and it is evident that certain objects were imbued with human qualities and agentive capacities. The intimate links between people and objects and similarities in their treatment, particularly on death, suggest that some artefacts were considered to possess their own life force. The agency of objects may have derived from the particular properties of the materials from which they were made (the luminosity of gold, for example), from the way in which they were bound into human lives, or from the significant social roles that they played. Animate objects did not simply mark identity but made the human self (Hoskins 1998). I have suggested elsewhere (2009), for example, that the introduction of metalworking resulted in profound changes to concepts of personhood, indicated by the increasing prevalence of cremation burial a few centuries after the appearance of the first metal objects. Metalworking involved new concepts of materiality and substance, with objects (and persons) composed of an amalgamation of other things—each with their own particular histories and meanings—which could be reordered through the performance of specific ritual and technological acts: both cremation and bronzeworking were heat-mediated, transformative processes that facilitated the regeneration of life through acts of destruction. The agency of objects such as bronze swords or jet beads of course meant that the disposal or transformation of such items was often a focus of ritual practice. Sometimes this indicates that objects themselves could be viewed as ambivalent: the deliberate decommissioning of items such as the shield from Milsom's corner (Coles et al. 1999) or the swords and spearheads from the River Thames (Yates 2007) hints that they may have been viewed as possessing dangerous powers.

Finally, our discussion in this chapter indicates that the boundary between people and objects may not have been drawn as categorically as it is in the modern, Western world. As we shall see in Chapter 6, this has significant implications for our understanding of social and political power. Moreover, this requires us to re-evaluate our understanding of the changing character of Bronze Age 'society'. It was not solely human agency that resulted in transformations over the course of the period in settlement, ritual, or agricultural practice. Rather, as we will discuss in Chapter 6, the material properties of bronze generated changing concepts of substance that had a profound impact on ideas of self, kinship, community, and landscape, so that metals had an historical agency beyond their ability to form more effective tools or more striking ornaments.

4

The living house

In the winter of 1995–6, a Late Bronze Age house was excavated at Callestick in Cornwall (Jones 1998). This showed an interesting sequence of activities on its abandonment. First, the timber posts that had supported its roof were removed and the sockets of those at the centre of the building were filled with materials that included charcoal, pottery, quartz, and fragments of rubbing stones. The low stone wall that originally surrounded the structure was pushed into the interior of the building, and a series of quartz blocks were placed across the doorway, as if to prevent access. The roundhouse was then filled with a deposit of clay containing stone, charcoal, quartz, pottery, flint, and an inverted saddle quern. Parts of a large decorated jar were placed just left of the doorway. Finally, a ring of quartz stones was arranged around the edge of the building, inviting visual comparison with the funerary cairns of earlier centuries.

This sequence of activities in many ways seems quite alien to us, for we have quite different experiences and understandings of house and home. The past two centuries have seen mass movements of people on an extraordinary scale as a result of war, urbanization, global differences in the distribution of wealth and opportunity, and a range of other factors. At the same time, dramatic social and political change has resulted in the perceived fragmentation of communities. All this has had a significant impact both on our relationship with the houses we live in, and on the concept of home itself (Allan and Crow 1989; Spain 1992; Birdwell-Pheasant and Lawrence-Zuniga 1999). Home may now be a transitory place, a state of mind evoked by the judicious arrangement of a few meaningful objects, but at the same time the idea of home remains highly emotive. High house prices in contemporary Britain and Ireland reflect the significance of the home in the cultivation of self-worth, emotional security, and social position. The materiality of the home evokes an aura of permanence in a world of change, acting as a *lieu de mémoire* in which ideas of personal and family history can be created. The significance of the boundary between the world of the home and the external world, as well as the internal subdivision of space, reflects the importance of privacy to modern, Western concepts of the self. The way we chose to furnish and decorate our homes speaks both of this aspiration for individualism and of concepts of taste that locate us firmly within a broader social milieu, creating a specific set of links between style and class, for example (Miller 2001a). In the same way, the practices of domestic life embody core social values, particularly relating to aspects of age and gender identity.

It is inevitable, then, that we approach Bronze Age settlements with a particular set of preconceptions. Of course, ethnographic accounts of houses and households in other cultural contexts demonstrate the highly variable character not only of domestic architecture but also of the people, relationships, and activities associated with the home (Netting, Wilk and Arnould 1984; Waterson 1990; Freeman 2013); nor, indeed, does the idea of 'home' evoke the same set of meanings as it does in contemporary Britain or Ireland. It has been all too easy, however, to project onto the past normative aspects of contemporary ideologies of the home, notably gender relationships. Likewise, Bronze Age houses are often seen as embodying a timeless rural idyll (Brück 2000), but this perhaps primarily reflects the fears and concerns of contemporary archaeologists at a time of significant social and economic change. On the one hand, there is an understandable urge to explicate Bronze Age houses in a way that we can identify with: the ceramic repertoire found at the Late Bronze Age settlement at Must Farm in Cambridgeshire, for example, has been described as 'the full Habitat range for Bronze Age Britain' (*Daily Mail*, 12 January 2016). Yet there is also a recognition that Bronze Age houses embodied a very different set of cultural values to those familiar to archaeologists today; as we saw in Chapter 2, a near-complete human skull was found in a midden next to one of the houses at this site (M. Knight, pers. comm.).

Moreover, the character and organization of settlement did not remain static over the period. The settlement evidence suggests that peoples' relationships with each other, their concepts of temporality, and their understanding of their place in the world changed dramatically from the beginning to the end of the Bronze Age. During the earlier part of the period, houses are archaeologically invisible, suggesting that personal identity and relationships with place were articulated quite differently to subsequent centuries (Brück 2000). In particular, the challenge of distinguishing domestic from ritual practice hints at very different ideas surrounding the home to those familiar from our own cultural context (Brück 1999a). Around 1500 BC or a little earlier, however, substantial roundhouses begin to appear in the archaeological record: this 'monumentalization' of the home suggests that the domestic domain was now one of the key contexts in which social identities were constructed, and it is perhaps no surprise that by the Late Bronze Age houses and settlements produce evidence for elaborate rituals of food consumption (for example in the form of decorated ceramics) that doubtless facilitated the construction of both intra- and inter-household social relationships (Barrett 1989a). This, of course, has interesting implications for our understanding of gender relations during this period, amongst other things. This chapter will therefore examine how the changing character of Bronze Age settlement can explicate ideas of the self, the boundary between self and other, and the variety of conceptual categories that were (or were not) employed to position both 'individuals' and 'communities' in relation to the broader social universe.

The lifecycles of Bronze Age houses will form a particular focus of interest, for it is evident that these related to the lifecycles of their inhabitants in a number of ways. Middle Bronze Age settlements seem to have been single-generational (Brück 1999b): here, changes in the use of space can be linked to the changing social and material needs of the household as it expanded and contracted over a few decades, and houses appear to have been abandoned on the death of their owners. Late Bronze Age settlements, on the other hand, were often longer lived: patterns of repair and rebuilding can be linked to moments of intergenerational transmission, and the spatial relationships between different houses (many of which were built directly on top of their predecessors) have much to tell us regarding ideas of temporality, place, and community. Practices involving the deposition of significant objects (small bronze items, pots, quernstones, animal bone, and the like) marked important moments in the histories of both houses and households during the Middle and Late Bronze Age, including foundation and abandonment, so that there was both a symbolic and a practical link between the life of the house and its inhabitants. The use of settlement space will also be explored here, in particular the tension between social practices that emphasized the links between communities, and those—such as the deposition of human remains in the ditches surrounding settlements—that underscored social difference and division.

Mobility and the domestic domain in the Chalcolithic and Early Bronze Age

With a small number of exceptions, few possible houses of Early Bronze Age date are known. At Northton on the island of Harris in the Western Isles, at least two and possibly three stone-built structures were identified (Simpson et al. 2006). Structure 1 was the best preserved of these. It formed an oval 8.7 × 4.7 metres in size and was oriented north-east to south-west. A possible entrance was located at its south-western end. Inside the building were a hearth, a scatter of peat ash, and a pit that produced a red deer antler and complete badger skull: the presence of the badger's mandible suggests this had been deposited in the pit in a fleshed state. A range of other artefacts were recovered from deposits in this building, including Beaker pottery, worked flint, quartz, and bone, a piece of bronze waste, and a fragment of human maxilla. Animal bone from the site produced a radiocarbon date of 2140–1740 cal BC. Elsewhere, only a tiny number of Early Bronze Age houses have been identified, and these are often small, light-weight structures built of timber. The suboval structure at Corcreeghy, County Down, was 6 metres long and 3 metres wide and was defined by thirty-nine stake-holes (Figure 4.1; Dunlop 2015, 54). Charcoal from one of the stake-holes yielded a date of 2308–2194 BC. A hearth and a number of pits, some of which produced struck flint, lay within the house. An oval stake-built structure at Sennen in Cornwall was constructed over a hollow of approximately 4 metres by 3 metres. An area of burning in the south-western part of the structure may indicate the original location of a hearth. The structure produced Beaker pottery, struck flint, and worked stone and has been radiocarbon-dated to 2300–2130 cal BC (Jones et al. 2012, 10–11). Outside of the structure were a number of pits and postholes, some in linear settings, as well as a hearth.

Evidence of this sort is very rare, however, in comparison with the many excavated houses of Middle and Late Bronze Age date. I have suggested elsewhere (Brück 1999a) that this is in part because of the expectations we bring to the data. Because of the socially significant role of the 'home' in modern, Western society, it is easy to assume that substantial, identifiable houses are a feature common to all human societies. If instead we view houses as fulfilling particular ideological roles, we need not reach the same conclusion. If we consider other forms of evidence for the occupation of Early Bronze Age landscapes—occupation that was more expansive, less place-bound, and that did not involve the construction of substantial houses—then it becomes

The living house

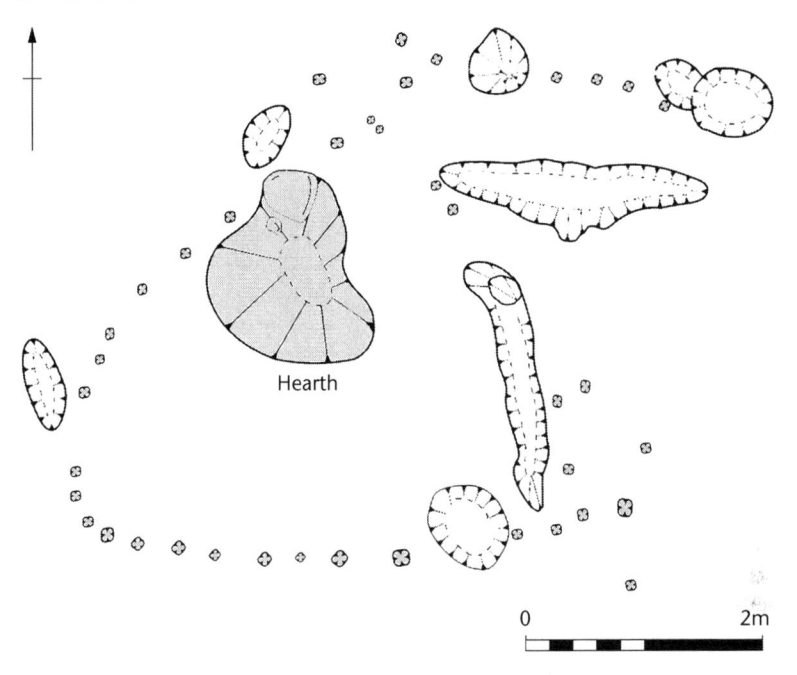

Hearth

0   2m

Figure 4.1. An Early Bronze Age 'house' at Corcreeghy, County Down (reproduced with permission of Colin Dunlop and Northern Archaeological Consultancy, with slight alterations by Anne Leaver).

easier to examine the character and organization of settlement during this period.

Large-scale field-walking surveys have recorded extensive Early Bronze Age flint scatters, and these hint at ways of engaging with place very different to our own 'homemaking' practices in the present. Although it can be difficult to distinguish a specifically Early Bronze Age component to such assemblages, objects diagnostic of this period can often be identified: the South Dorset Ridgeway Project, for example, recorded large numbers of items such as thumbnail scrapers, plano-convex knives and barbed and tanged arrowheads (Woodward 1991). Flint scatters are often located in particular parts of the landscape: in the Kennet Valley, tool clusters of Late Neolithic/Early Bronze Age date were frequently recorded on the floodplain terrace at the junction between the gravels and the heavier soils of the valley sides (Lobb and Rose 1996, 63), while others were in prominent locations overlooking the valley, close to streams and springs.

There is clear evidence for topographical and regional variation in the presence and percentage of artefact types, as Gardiner's study (1988) of assemblages from several different areas of southern England demonstrates. On Cranborne Chase in Dorset, Late Neolithic/Early Bronze Age flint scatters were ubiquitous across the clay with flints and adjacent chalk. These assemblages were highly varied in their composition, often with a wide range of different tool types, although scrapers predominated. On the North Hampshire Downs, flint scatters were again concentrated on the clay with flints, with only a thin scatter of artefacts of this period identified on the greensands. Scatters in this region produced a relatively high percentage of fabricators and chisels but fewer scrapers than those on Cranborne Chase. Scrapers, fabricators, and piercers dominated the assemblages from field walking north of Brighton, while large numbers of arrowheads were identified on the heavier soils of the Sussex High Weald. The scale of flint scatters also varied, with substantial flint assemblages recovered from the gravels around Christchurch Harbour but small scatters elsewhere, for instance at the head of drowned valleys in the Chichester region (Gardiner 1988). Overall, variability in the composition of flint scatters, as well as the extensive distribution of flint artefacts across a variety of topographical contexts, suggest a relatively mobile settlement pattern and use of a wide range of resources across the landscape.

The idea that Early Bronze Age people may not have lived in the same place year-round is supported by recent stable isotope analysis of Beaker inhumation burials, which provides significant evidence for human mobility during the first few centuries of the period. Some individuals appear to have moved very considerable distances, perhaps most famously the Amesbury Archer, who is thought to have spent his early life in central Europe and to have travelled to Wiltshire as an adult (Chenery and Evans 2011). More local patterns of movement are also evident. Sulphur isotope analysis of Beaker burials from the Yorkshire Wolds indicates that many of these individuals moved in and out of this area over the course of their lives: the foods they consumed appear to have originated both inside and outside the Wolds (Jay et al. 2012). The scale, frequency, and periodicity of this movement remain unknown, but a degree of residential mobility might suggest relationships with place that did not require the construction of substantial houses.

Pits, scatters, and place-making

However, it would not be true to say that particular locations were not significant, though these seem to have been marked by rather different practices. In recent years, developer-funded excavations have resulted in the recognition of numerous groups of Chalcolithic and Early Bronze Age pits. These vary greatly in scale and content. At Stirling Way, near Witchford, Cambridgeshire, two isolated pits lay 14 metres apart on the edge of a knoll overlooking a valley (Atkins 2011, 47–51). One of these produced Beaker ceramics, but as they were of a similar shape and size, they may have been dug as part of the same event. At Cloghabreedy in County Tipperary, four charcoal-rich pits, two of which were fire-reddened and may have been hearths, produced fragments of bipartite vase and vase urn as well as large quantities of burnt hazelnut shells (Figure 4.2; McQuade et al. 2009, 30–1). A fence-line some 3 metres to the south may represent a windbreak. In regions that may have been particularly rich in resources, for example the Fen edge in eastern England, larger complexes of pits have been identified, often forming multiple distinct groups of features. Four clusters of five to eight pits at Baston Quarry, Langtoft, Lincolnshire, produced Collared Urn, Biconical Urn and Food Vessel ceramics as well as animal bone, charcoal, and small quantities of struck flint (Webley 2004, 7–11). Their lower fills contained silt and gravel fills, often sterile and sometimes waterlogged; the larger features may have served as waterholes for livestock. By contrast, the upper fills of many of these pits contained artefact-rich layers, suggesting the deliberate 'closing' of these features when they fell out of use. The largest assemblage of ceramics from the site was recovered from the uppermost layer of pit F10000. Here, charcoal, burnt stone, worked flint (including a planoconvex knife), and 20 grams of well-burnt animal bone were found alongside significant portions of three Food Vessels and a single sherd of a fourth pot. The presence of the plano-convex knife, Food Vessel ceramics, and the 'cremated' animal bone perhaps referenced contemporary human mortuary practices.

At Feltwell Quarry in Norfolk, excavations revealed an even larger group of seventy-seven pits on the eastern edge of the Fens (Beadsmoore 2007). Finds included Beaker pottery, flint scrapers and knives, flintworking waste, a fragment of a shaft-hole implement, burnt stone, and charcoal. A possible hearth and thirteen scattered postholes were also identified, although the postholes could not be resolved into a building of any sort. Parts of thirty-two Beaker vessels were recovered from nine of the pits, including roughly equal numbers of fine- and coarsewares (Knight 2007). Sherds from the same pots were sometimes deposited in different pits, suggesting that these were open and receiving material at the same time. However, vessels were represented by no more than a few sherds each and none of the sherds could be refitted, indicating

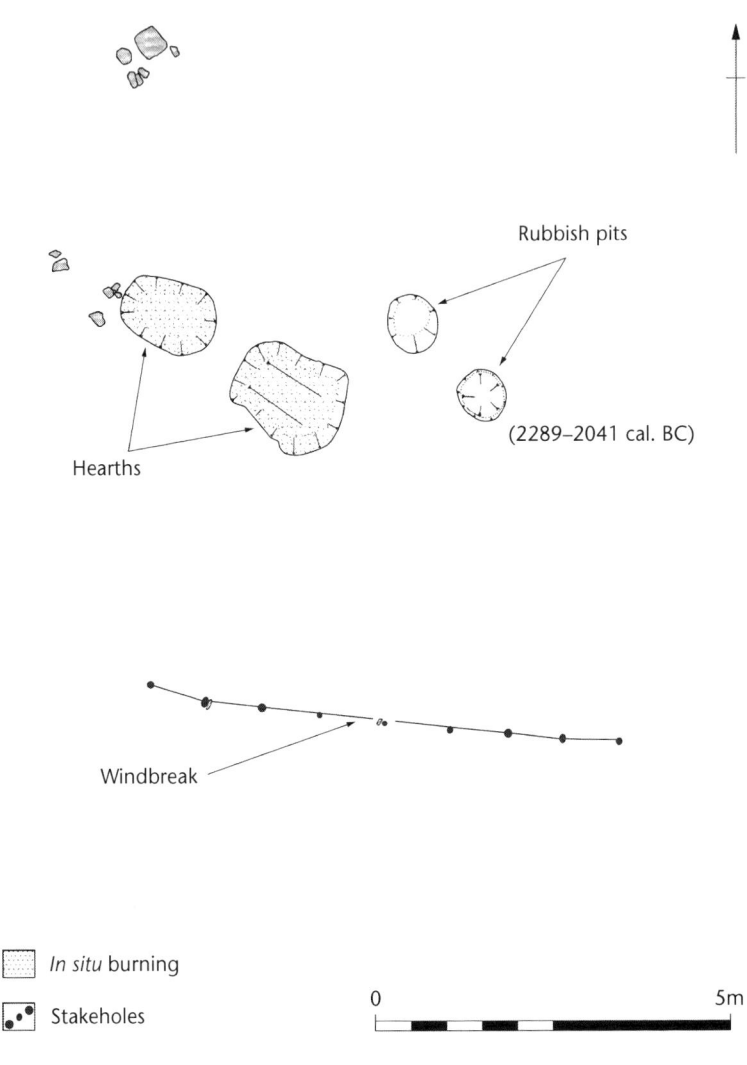

Figure 4.2. An Early Bronze Age pit cluster at Cloghabreedy, County Tipperary (reproduced with permission of Transport Infrastructure Ireland, with slight alterations by Anne Leaver).

that broken vessels were not immediately placed in the pits but may have spent some time in another depositional context, such as a surface midden. The variable condition of individual sherds also suggests complex depositional histories: fresh, weathered, and burnt sherds were found in the same pits, indicating that a period of time often passed between the breaking of a vessel and final deposition. Wild resources dominated the plant remains, notably hazelnut, sloe, and elder; no cultivated crop remains were recovered.

Early Bronze Age pit groups raise a variety of questions regarding the scale and temporality of occupation during this period. The many isolated pits and groups of just a few such features suggest small-scale and possibly short-term occupation, as indeed does the lack of evident structures at most sites. Sites such as Baston or Feltwell Quarries, on the other hand, may represent periodic gatherings of larger numbers of people, hinting at changes to the composition of the social group over the course of the annual cycle. Alternatively, large pit groups may be the product of repeated revisiting of the same site by individual groups and may indicate long-term attachment to place (cf. Pollard 1999). Recent discussion of similar pit deposits of Late Neolithic date has suggested that they may have functioned to mark particular places and events (Thomas 1999; Garrow et al. 2006; Carver 2012). It has been argued that at least some of these features were dug to receive the remains of specific episodes of occupation, forming 'closing' deposits to commemorate the ending of socially significant activities. It seems likely that a similar interpretation can be applied to pit deposits of the Chalcolithic and Early Bronze Age.

As we have seen, midden material appears to have been buried in at least some Early Bronze Age pits. This provides additional insights into the character of occupation practices during this period. Surface middens are, however, rarely preserved, although a number have been identified, particularly in western Britain and Ireland. At Manish Strand on the island of Ensay in the Western Isles, a midden deposit eroding out of the sand dunes produced limpet shells, sherds of Food Vessels, a perforated bone point and bone spatula, a flint scraper, animal bone, and charcoal (Simpson et al. 2003). In Ireland, recent analysis of Beaker-related sites indicates that Beaker occupation spreads are common, and some of these may represent the eroded remains of middens: one such example is an extensive charcoal-rich occupation spread at Kilgobbin, County Dublin, which produced pottery and lithics and covered an area of 26 metres by 9 metres (Carlin and Brück 2012, 196). The presence of middens suggests long-term relationships with particular locations, although it is less clear whether these sites were permanently occupied for a period of years or were sporadically inhabited for shorter periods of time, but perhaps on a seasonal or annual basis. In either case, middens provided visible evidence of attachment to place in the absence of occupation practices that involved the construction of substantial 'houses'.

Sometimes assemblages that in other contexts might be interpreted as 'domestic' or productive in nature occur at mortuary and ceremonial monuments. At Fordington Farm in Dorset, an area of *in situ* flint-working was identified on and to the west of the phase 1 round barrow (Bellamy 1991, 111). This activity did not occur during or immediately after the construction of the barrow but a short time later: some of the flint-knapping waste was located above a thin silty stabilization layer in the ditch of the monument. It might be tempting to suggest that the barrow was no longer viewed as 'sacred' when the flint-knapping took place, but this is clearly not the case, for three further phases of barrow construction also occurred at the site (Copson 1989). Pottery and struck flint were found in and under barrows on Overton Hill and Snail Down in Wiltshire (Smith and Simpson 1966; Thomas 2005, 73–4). On the one hand, such material might represent the residues of cooking or feasting generated by those gathered for the funeral rite; alternatively, it can be interpreted as refuse produced by people carrying out other, more 'mundane' activities in the vicinity, such as herding or hunting.

Overall, the evidence suggests that Early Bronze Age settlement was relatively mobile, and that people undertook a range of activities that might—in our terms—be defined as 'domestic', such as preparing food, mending clothes, and knapping flint, at a variety of places across the landscape. In general, they did not build substantial houses but employed different practices to engage with place, enshrine collective memory, and negotiate interpersonal relationships. These included the creation of middens and the digging and filling of pits. We do not yet have a clear understanding of the scale or periodicity of mobility, but it is possible that this incorporated not only regular movements within the local area to bring animals to new pastures, dig for flint, collect wild resources, or attend intercommunity gatherings, but also periodic travels to more distant locations: the scale of Late Neolithic and Early Bronze Age monument complexes such as those in the Kilmartin Glen or the Stonehenge area suggests that people may have journeyed to these places from considerable distances (Parker Pearson et al. 2013, 169–70). Together, this suggests a very different and more expansive relationship with landscape to the place-centred experience common in our own cultural context. Any attempt to understand Early Bronze Age settlement must consider the variety of ways in which people dwelt in the landscape: evidence as diverse as pit groups, scatters of flint artefacts, and ceramics from the upper ditch fills of barrows or earlier henge monuments each have something to contribute to our understanding of 'settlement' during this period.

The domestic architecture of the Middle and Late Bronze Age

What is extraordinary, then, is that from *c.*1550 BC on, recognizable houses became common across Britain and Ireland; I use the term 'house' advisedly, for we cannot assume that the social values or relationships given material form in these structures were in any way similar to our own experience of such buildings today. As we shall see in the next section, Middle and Late Bronze Age houses occur mostly as single buildings or as part of small clusters of two or three structures, although some larger groupings of houses are also known. They produce a wide variety of objects, including pottery; quernstones; worked flint; small bronze tools such as knives, chisels and gouges; loom weights; worked bone and antler; and decorative items such as pins, beads, and bracelets of bronze, gold, shale, and amber (Ellison 1981; Brück 1999b). They were predominantly circular or subcircular in shape, and most were built of timber, although there was some variability in the construction techniques employed.

Structure 1 at Ridlington, Rutland (Figure 4.3; Beamish 2005, 3–7), dates to the Late Bronze Age and is typical of many roundhouses in southern and eastern Britain. It comprised a ring of eight postholes representing the remains of internal timber roof-support posts. This post-ring was about 5.3 metres in diameter, although the house would originally have been larger: buildings of this construction are thought to have had light outer walls of wattle and daub, evidence for which does not always survive (Guilbert 1981). A well-defined porched entrance is formed by two pairs of postholes about 1.1 metre to the south-east of the post-ring. A single posthole lies on the inferred line of the original external wall directly opposite the entrance. This and the location of the porch suggest that the building would have been some 7.5 metres in diameter.

Sometimes elements of the outer, non-load-bearing structure survive. The Late Bronze Age roundhouse at Ballylegan in County Tipperary comprised an inner ring of substantial postholes that are likely to have formed the load-bearing component of the structure (Figure 4.4; McQuade et al. 2009, 69–72). Roughly concentric with this, an outer circuit of much smaller post- and stake-holes probably acted as a framework for wattle-and-daub walling. The building was some 8.5 metres in diameter and had an east-facing porch that projected beyond the line of the outer wall. At other sites, particularly in northern and western Britain and Ireland, the outer walls of roundhouses are defined by penannular ring-grooves which may originally have held upright

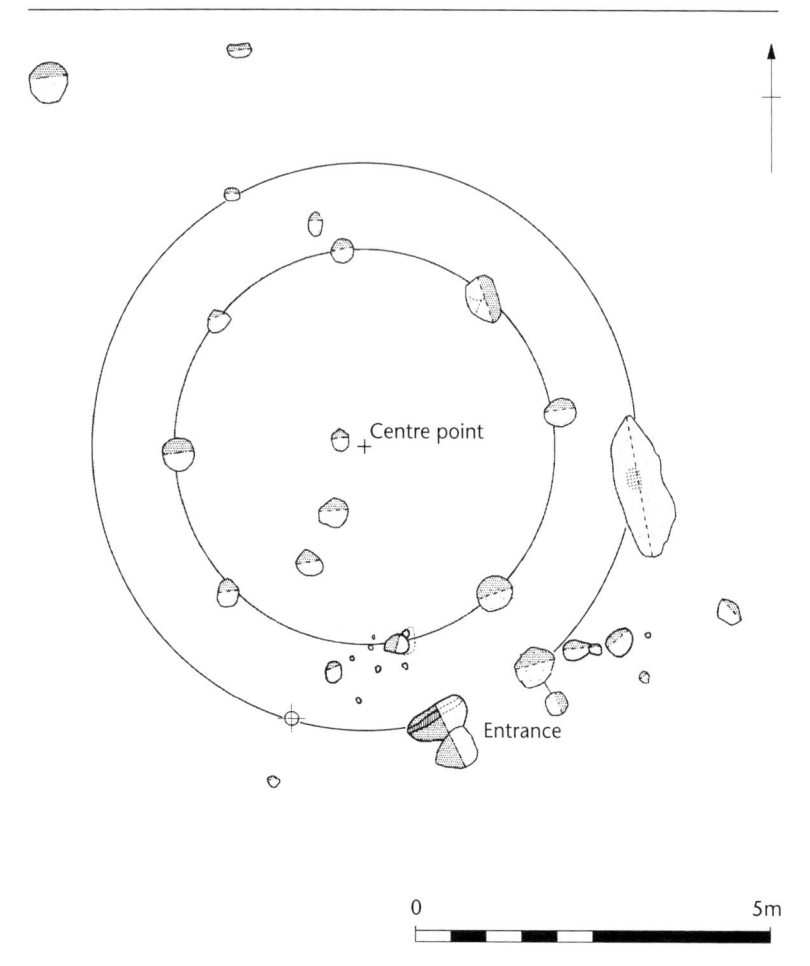

Figure 4.3. House 1, Ridlington, Rutland (reproduced with permission of Matt Beamish and University of Leicester Archaeological Services, with slight alterations by Anne Leaver).

timber planking or wattlework panels. The outer wall of structure A at Cloghabreedy in County Tipperary (Fig. 4.5; McQuade et al. 2009, 35), for example, was defined by a ring-groove with a series of stake-holes at its base. Much of the charcoal from the ring-groove was hazel, suggesting the original existence of a wattle wall structure. In upland areas such as parts of Wales and Scotland, the outer walls of roundhouses were often stone-built: for example, the Late Bronze Age roundhouse at Halls Hill near East Woodburn in Northumberland comprised an inner timber post-ring with an outer ring-bank of sandstone boulders, on which

The living house

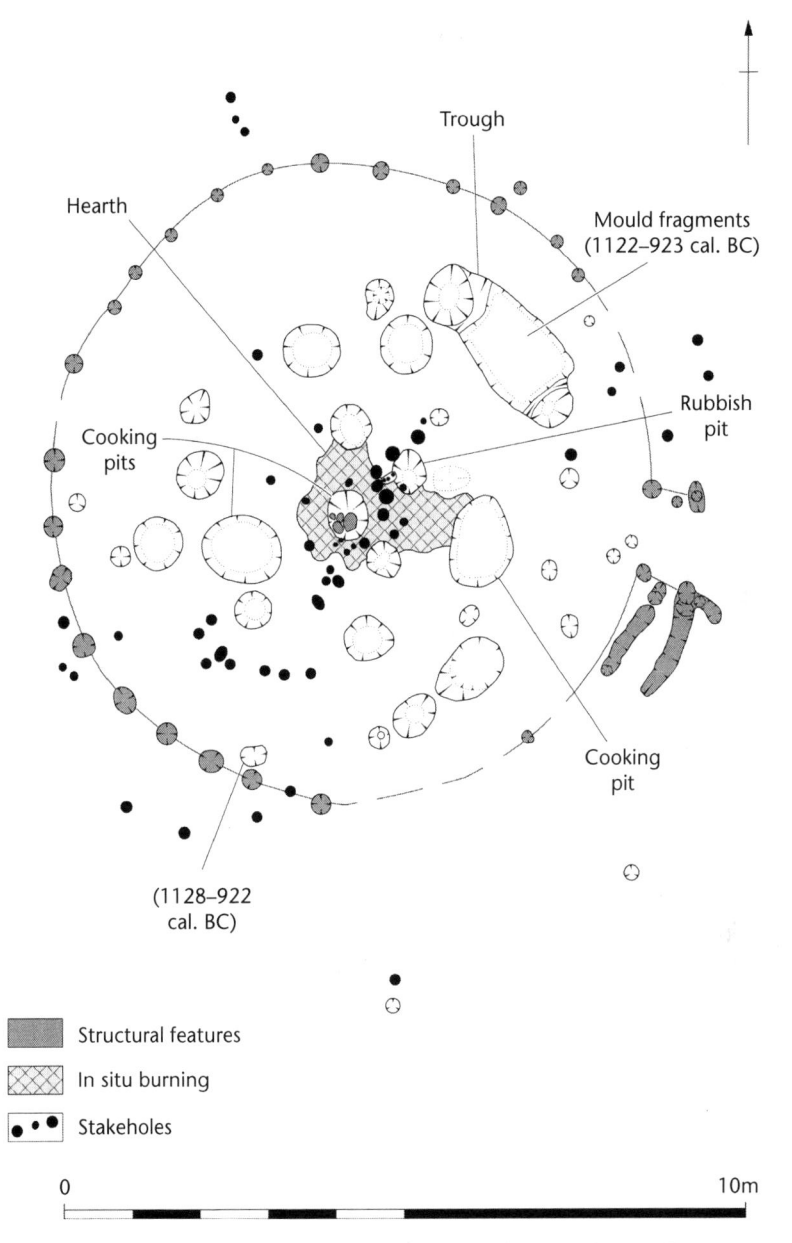

Figure 4.4. The Late Bronze Age roundhouse at Ballylegan, County Tipperary (reproduced with permission of Transport Infrastructure Ireland, redrawn by Anne Leaver).

127

there may originally have been a turf or cob wall (Gates 2009, 48, 57). No evidence of coursing or of the existence of wall-facing could be identified in the ring-bank, although this is not the case elsewhere: on Shaugh Moor in Devon, the walls of the roundhouses had rubble cores with regular stone facings formed by large upright slabs or smaller coursed stones (Wainwright and Smith 1980).

As we have seen in some of the examples above, Middle and Late Bronze Age houses often have porched entrances. These could be substantial and eye-catching structures. At Tober in County Offaly, a set of four particularly large postholes marks the location of the porch (Walsh 2014, fig. 3), suggesting that this was a significant and indeed monumental element of the structure. A hollow across the outer edge of the doorway may indicate the original location of a door saddle, while stake-holes just in front of the outer pair of porch postholes may have formed part of a door or door frame. The entrances to two of the Late Bronze Age houses at Hog Cliff Hill in Dorset (Ellison and Rahtz 1987, fig. 24) were marked by substantial postholes at either end of the penannular ring-grooves that defined these buildings, while at Cloghabreedy in County Tipperary, roundhouses B and D had long funnel-shaped entrances that would have projected beyond the line of the outer walls of these buildings (Figure 4.5; McQuade et al. 2009, fig. 3.8).

Most house entrances faced east or south-east: the entrance to the Middle Bronze Age roundhouse at Navidale in Sutherland, for example, was oriented south-east (Figure 4.6; Dunbar 2007). A cobbled surface laid in the entranceway extended outside of the structure through the doorway, creating a 'forecourt'. Two rubbing stones, a possible mortar, and a cup-marked stone (the latter positioned face down) had been reused as cobbles in this surface. As we shall discuss later in this chapter, roundhouse entrances were often marked by the deliberate deposition of important objects, and the reuse of these items may have been prompted by more than their utility as convenient pieces of stone. The architectural elaboration of roundhouse entranceways suggests that these were socially sensitive spaces (Brück 1999b); porches and other entrance features drew attention to the significance and potential danger of acts of social and spatial transition, for the boundary of the house was the meeting point between insiders and outsiders, between the familiar sphere of the household and the external world. Iron Age houses share a similar orientation, and it has been suggested that the east and south-east were viewed as auspicious directions, referencing the rising sun and associated with ideas of light, life, and fertility (Parker Pearson 1996).

The living house

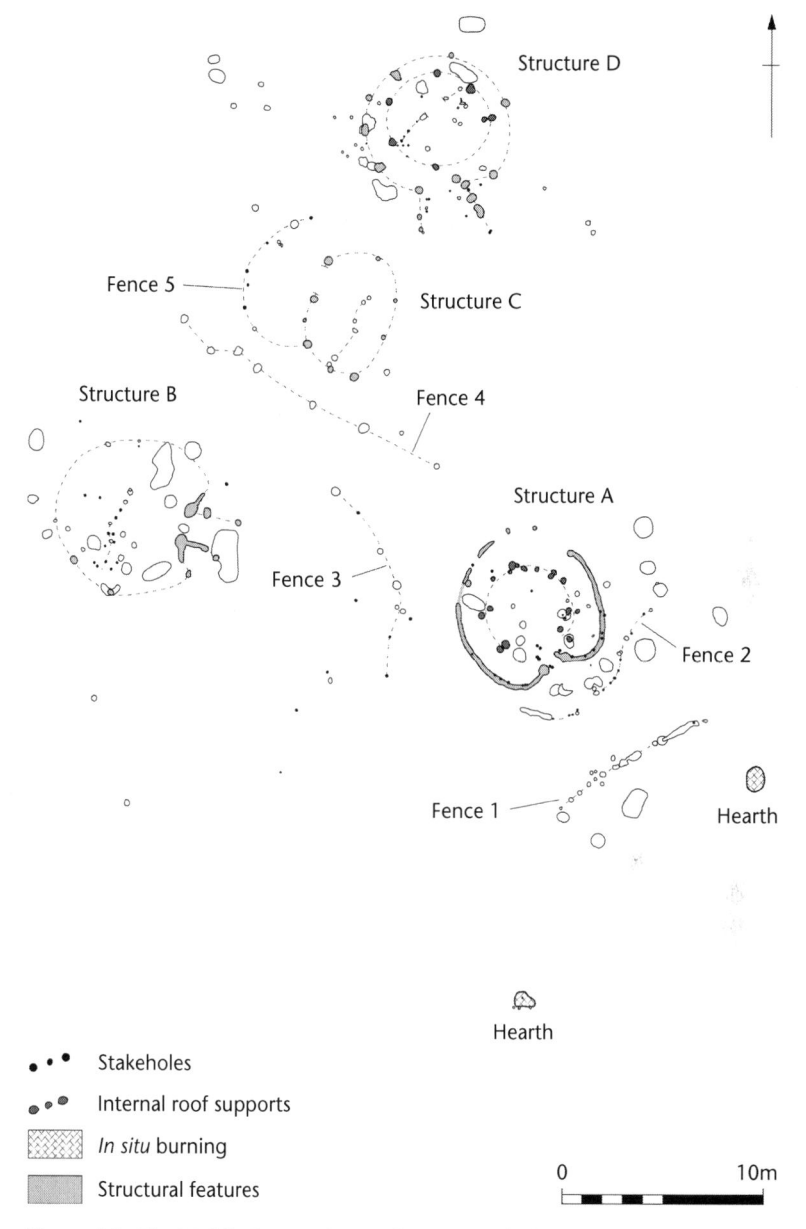

Figure 4.5. The Middle Bronze Age settlement at Cloghabreedy, County Tipperary (reproduced with permission of Transport Infrastructure Ireland, redrawn by Anne Leaver).

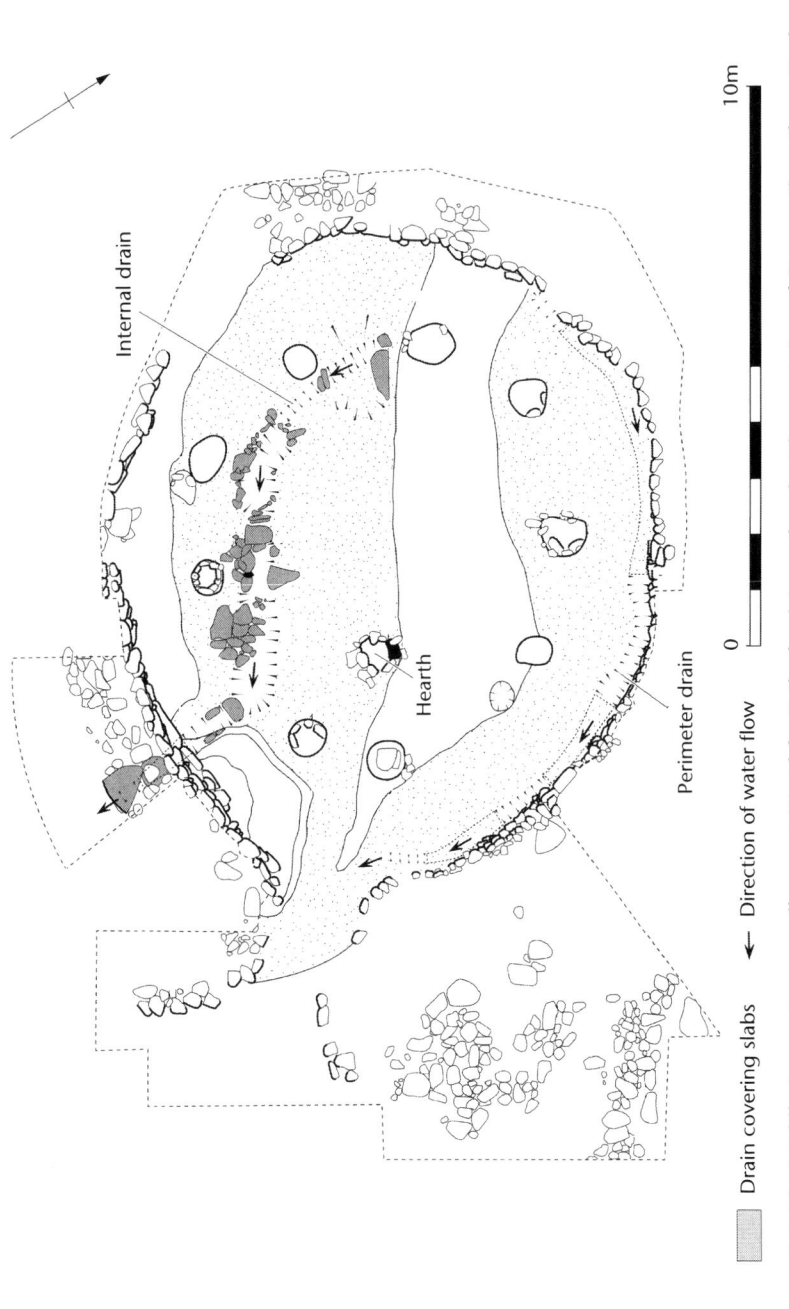

Figure 4.6. The Middle Bronze Age roundhouse at Navidale, Sutherland (reproduced with permission of Graeme Carruthers, Lindsay Dunbar, and the Society of Antiquaries of Scotland, with slight alterations by Anne Leaver).

The circular shape of most Bronze Age houses suggests that household space was relatively undifferentiated, but there is in fact copious evidence for the structured use of space in these buildings (Brück 1999b). Hearths are often located in the centre of the house or just inside the doorway. A stone-lined hearth lay just inside the entrance of the Middle Bronze Age roundhouse at Navidale in Sutherland (Figure 4.6; Dunbar 2007, 144). There was a central hearth in the Late Bronze Age roundhouse at Ballylegan in County Tipperary, and this was associated with numerous post- and stake-holes, suggesting the existence of various items of hearth furniture (Figure 4.4; McQuade et al. 2009, 69–72). Internal hearths are more common in the Late Bronze Age, and many Middle Bronze Age roundhouses do not have hearths. Instead, such features were often located outside of their associated buildings. At Knockdomny in County Westmeath (Hull et al. 2006), an external heath was identified some 8 metres north-west of a contemporary Middle Bronze Age roundhouse, while at Bestwall in Dorset there was an activity area comprising a series of pits and scoops centred around a hearth some 8 metres south of house 2 (Ladle and Woodward 2009, 74); in neither case was there a hearth in the house itself.

Despite its apparent simplicity, the architecture of the roundhouse encouraged particular ways of differentiating internal spaces. The presence of a porch, for example, facilitated the creation of a conceptual distinction between the front and the back of the house, and this is visible in other aspects of the evidence. For example, flat granite slabs were used to create a level flagged surface just inside the entrance of a stone-built roundhouse at Bellever Tor on Dartmoor, Devon (Hughes 2009, 4). Screens dividing the front and back of the house can sometimes be identified: lines of stake-holes that may originally have supported light wooden screens run across the centre of structure 7 at Corrstown in County Londonderry (Ginn and Rathbone 2011, 35) and structures B and D at Cloghabreedy in County Tipperary (Figure 4.5; McQuade et al. 2009, fig. 3.9), obscuring visual access from the entrance to the rear of these buildings.

The circular space of the roundhouse may also have been conceptually divided into a left-hand and right-hand side (Guilbert 1982). House 1 at Ridlington in Rutland (Figure 4.3; Beamish 205, 3–7), for example, displays a clear line of axial symmetry: the postholes of the internal post-ring were symmetrically arranged on either side of an imaginary line running through the entranceway to a posthole diametrically opposite at the back of the structure. In some buildings, this is reflected in the use of space: phosphate and magnetic susceptibility readings were higher to the east of the central hearth in the roundhouse at Tober in County

Offaly, suggesting that more activities may have been carried out here and that the hearth may have been cleaned out from this side (Walsh 2014, 26).

The space within the inner post-ring often appears to have been used in a different way to the area between the post-ring and the outer wall. Most of the pits and other features identified in the roundhouse at Ballylegan, County Tipperary, were clustered in the central area of the structure. Between the post-ring and the outer wall of the building, however, was a large rectilinear trough. Impressions on the sides of this feature indicate that it may have been lined with timber planks, and the excavator suggests it may originally have held water (Figure 4.4; McQuade et al. 2009, fig. 3.18). The floor inside the central post-ring of house 3 at Lairg in Sutherland showed a considerable degree of erosion in contrast to the area between the post-ring and the outer wall, and O'Sullivan (1998, 104–5) suggests that the latter may have been protected by matting.

Perhaps some of the best insights into the use of household space come from the well-preserved floor deposits of three houses at Cladh Hallan on the island of South Uist (Parker Pearson et al. 2004; 2005). These stone-built roundhouses faced east and had central fireplaces. The southern halves of the houses (to the left of the doorways) were the main focus of activity: considerable quantities of cooking wares and tools that may relate to food preparation were found in their south-eastern quadrants, while a range of other stone and bone tools were recovered from the south-western areas of these structures. The presence of turf platforms and the relative paucity of artefacts from the northern halves of these buildings (to the right of the doorways) suggest that these may have been sleeping areas. A number of human and animal burials were also found in the north-eastern quadrants of the houses; these included two dogs (one of which had been decapitated) deposited in a pit beneath the floor of house 401, and an infant buried in the top of a posthole prior to the renovation of house 1370. It has been suggested that the organization of space within the houses at Cladh Hallan was shaped by cosmological concerns. The orientation of these structures towards the rising sun hints that the southern and eastern areas of these buildings may have been associated with ideas of life, light, and fertility, and may therefore have been considered the most suitable locations for daily tasks such as cooking and craft activities. By contrast, the northern and western parts of the houses may have been associated with ideas of darkness and death, so that the architecture of round-houses embodied the cosmological schemes that structured the Bronze Age universe (cf. Fitzpatrick 1994). Such conceptual distinctions are

The living house

likely to have had significant social implications: in other cultural contexts, it has long been recognized that the subdivision of household space, and the meanings and values ascribed to different parts of the house, work to maintain social roles and relationships (Cunningham 1973; Humphrey 1974). This may have extended to aspects of power relations so that those members of the household most closely associated with the south-easterly quadrant might have been considered to possess positive qualities or powers relating to the cyclical regeneration of life.

Although circular or subcircular structures are by far the most common type of building found on Middle and Late Bronze Age settlements, rectangular buildings are also occasionally documented. At Barleycroft Farm in Cambridgeshire, a substantial four-aisled timber longhouse, some 16 × 5.5 metres in size, was set within a ditched enclosure that formed part of a coaxial field system (Figure 4.7; Evans and Knight

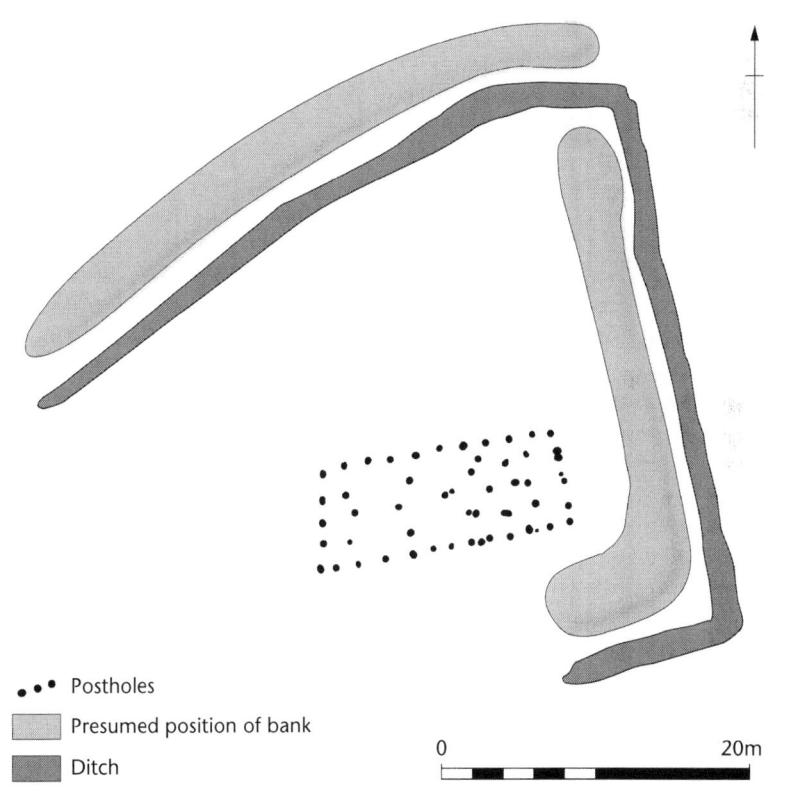

Figure 4.7. The longhouse at Barleycroft Farm, Cambridgeshire (reproduced with permission of Cambridge Archaeological Unit, redrawn by Anne Leaver).

1996). At Runnymede in Surrey, a rectangular building was constructed just behind and parallel to the wooden palisade or waterfront structure that defined the north-eastern edge of the site (Needham 1991, fig. 51). This was about 4 metres wide and at least 7 metres long; inside were found large quantities of burnt flint, a burnt clay spread, and a hearth that produced some tiny crumbs of bronze as well as charred cereals. Together, these suggest that metalworking, crop-processing, or some other form of heat-mediated, transformative activity may have been carried out in this structure, although Needham (1991, 382) also suggests that its upper levels may have functioned as a raised platform or tower. The ideological significance of the roundhouse may be one reason why rectangular buildings are rare: it has been suggested that the cosmological principles given material form in the circular monuments of the Late Neolithic and Early Bronze Age were subsequently manifested in the domestic architecture of the Middle and Late Bronze Age (Bradley 2012). If roundhouses embodied core principles of religious belief, as well as facilitating the reproduction of key elements of age and gender relationships, their domination of the settlement record is perhaps unsurprising.

Beyond the house: Middle and Late Bronze Age settlements

Most Middle and Late Bronze Age houses are associated with small clusters of other structures and features. For example, the Late Bronze Age open settlement at Bloodmoor Hill, Carlton Colville, Suffolk, comprised two roundhouses, one with a central hearth, along with several small four-post and six-post structures, a number of pits, and an external working hollow that produced large quantities of burnt flint and fired clay (Heard 2013). It is not known what purpose the four-post and six-post structures served, but it is generally thought that they were storage buildings of some sort, possibly raised granaries (Gent 1983). Other finds from the site include pottery (plainware jars, bowls, and cups), worked flint, animal bone, two fragmentary loom weights and a complete spindle whorl. The Middle Bronze Age settlement at Cloghabreedy in County Tipperary comprised a row of three buildings (Figure 4.5; McQuade et al. 2009, fig. 3.8). Two of these were roundhouses. Between them lay an oval structure (structure C) with an adjoining fenced yard; it is possible that this building housed animals. A third roundhouse lay just to the south. All three roundhouses faced roughly south-east, but the entrance to the oval structure was oriented west. Although there is no evidence that the site was enclosed, screens and fences in front of and between the buildings indicate a concern to divide particular areas of settlement space. Two hearths and several roasting pits were identified outside of the structures, and a range of other pits were found both inside and outside the buildings.

Other settlements were enclosed. At Tober in County Offaly (Walsh 2014), a Late Bronze Age roundhouse, two four-post structures and several pits were surrounded by a fenced enclosure, probably originally some 27 metres in diameter. The Late Bronze Age settlement at Oliver Close Estate in Leyton, London, comprised a substantial circular, ditched enclosure some 35 metres in diameter (Figure 4.8; Bishop and Boyer 2014). An entrance with a four-post gateway structure lay on the western edge of the site; the eastern segment of the ditch was not excavated but it seems likely from comparison with similar enclosures elsewhere that a second entrance would have been located there. Inside, a substantial roundhouse lay in the southern half of the enclosure; an internal fence or palisade appears to have divided the northern and southern parts of the site and to have screened the roundhouse from the entrance to the settlement. Another, much smaller roundhouse was located in the northern half of the site. A second fence or palisade outside of the western entrance funnelled movement towards the gateway and

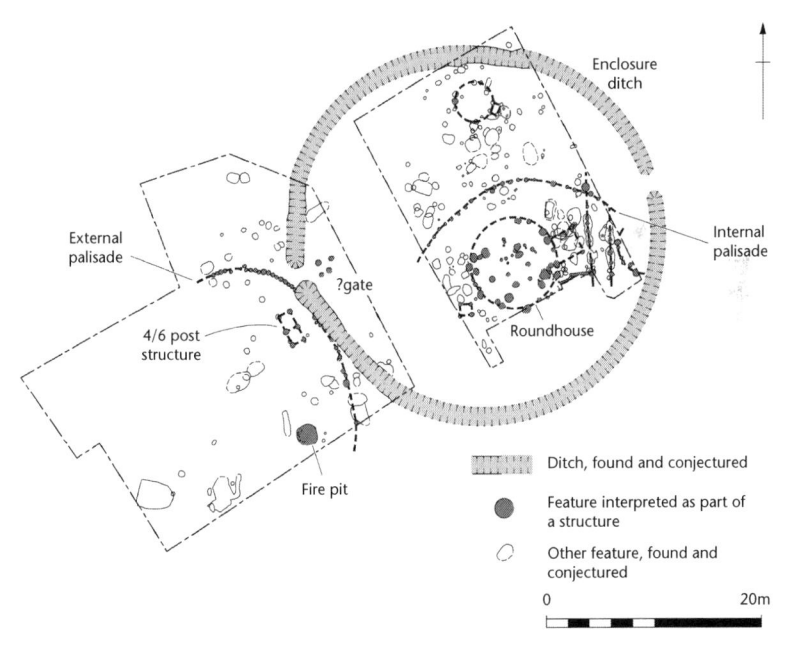

Figure 4.8. The ringwork at Oliver Close Estate, Leyton, London (© Pre-Construct Archaeology Ltd, with slight alterations by Anne Leaver).

divided the entrance from an area immediately to the south, where a four- or possibly six-post structure and a pit containing large amounts of pottery, burnt flint, burnt clay, and four conjoining crucible fragments were located. The ditch had been recut or cleared out at least once. Finds recovered include Late Bronze Age plainwares, burnt flint, fired clay, loom-weight fragments, and briquetage for the production of salt.

These were not isolated settlements, however, but were part of densely settled landscapes with lengthy histories and clear evidence for the structuring of settlement space and the zoning of different activities. Clusters of roundhouses were identified in several of the areas excavated at Reading Business Park/Green Park in Berkshire (Moore and Jennings 1992; Brossler et al. 2003). In areas 3100 and 3000B, for example, a group of twelve roundhouses was identified, although the ground plans of some overlapped and others were so close together that it is clear that these were not all contemporary (Figure 4.9). A number of

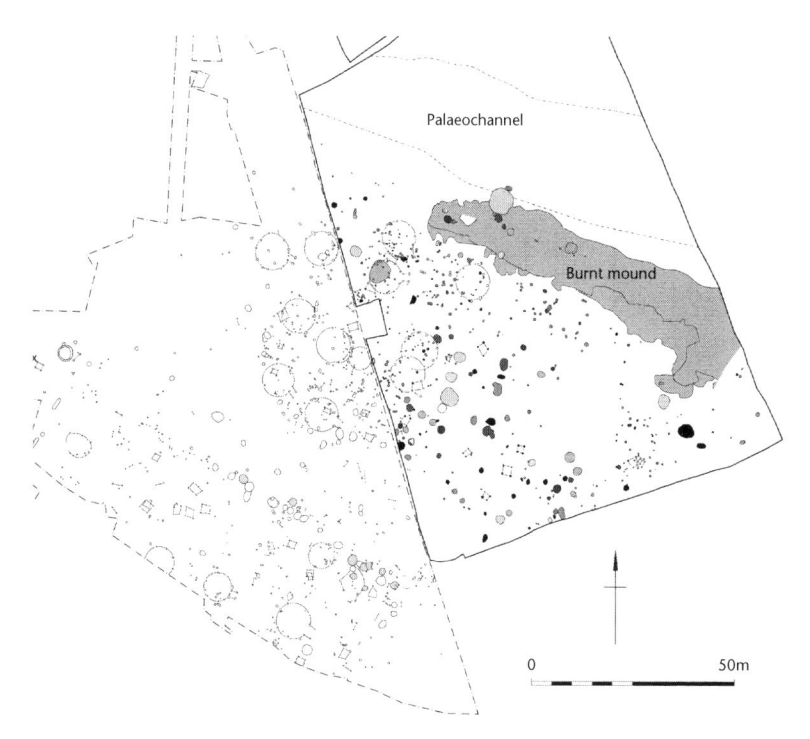

Figure 4.9. Buildings and other features at Reading Business Park/Green Park areas 3100 and 3000B, Berkshire (reproduced with permission of Oxford Archaeology, with slight alterations by the author).

four-post structures were located to the south-east of these buildings. The north-eastern edge of the settlement was demarcated by a palaeochannel, along which ran a substantial burnt mound, some 85 metres in length. To the south-west of the houses, and parallel to the palaeochannel and burnt mound, lay a line of pits and waterholes and a fence. South of this were two clusters of four-post structures and another four roundhouses. Finds from the site included pottery, worked wood including part of a possible cheese press, loom-weight fragments, part of a shale bracelet, a fragment of possible oven plate, and a complete saddle quern; in addition, the presence of worked flint and bone points suggests activities such as leatherworking or basketmaking.

The multiphase Late Bronze Age landscape at South Hornchurch in Essex illustrates equally interesting structuring of settlement space (Guttman et al. 2000). Here, a circular ditched enclosure some 36 metres in diameter and with a central roundhouse was associated with a substantial droveway and field system (Figure 4.10 [A]). The enclosure had two entrances, one to the south and one to the north-east. A possible four-post gateway structure lay just inside the north-eastern entrance. To the south and east of the enclosure lay groups of pits and postholes, some of which formed structures such as fence-lines. Two further roundhouses associated with pits and four-post structures lay in a field to the north of the enclosure. Sometime later, a new field system incorporating a possible sheep run for sorting livestock was laid out (Figure 4.10 [B]). The ditched enclosure continued in use, but immediately to the west a second subcircular fenced enclosure some 27–30 metres in diameter was also constructed. To the north of the sheep run, a loose row of six roundhouses was built, though these may not all have been standing at the same time. Although the ditched enclosure is the most striking feature in this landscape, producing a higher quantity of fineware than other parts of the site, evidence for craft activities including metalworking, cloth and salt production was not focused on this enclosure alone but was widely distributed across the excavated area: a sword mould fragment, for example, was found in a pit associated with one of the unenclosed roundhouses.

Most Middle and Late Bronze Age settlements (or settlement foci within more densely populated landscapes) comprise between two and five roundhouses. Within individual settlements there is often evidence for pairing of roundhouses (Ellison 1981). At Chalton in Hampshire, for example, two post-built roundhouses were identified (Cunliffe 1970). The larger of these structures produced pottery, animal bone, a loom weight, whetstone, bronze knife, bronze awl, and bronze palstave; in contrast, no finds were recovered from the smaller building. At Reading

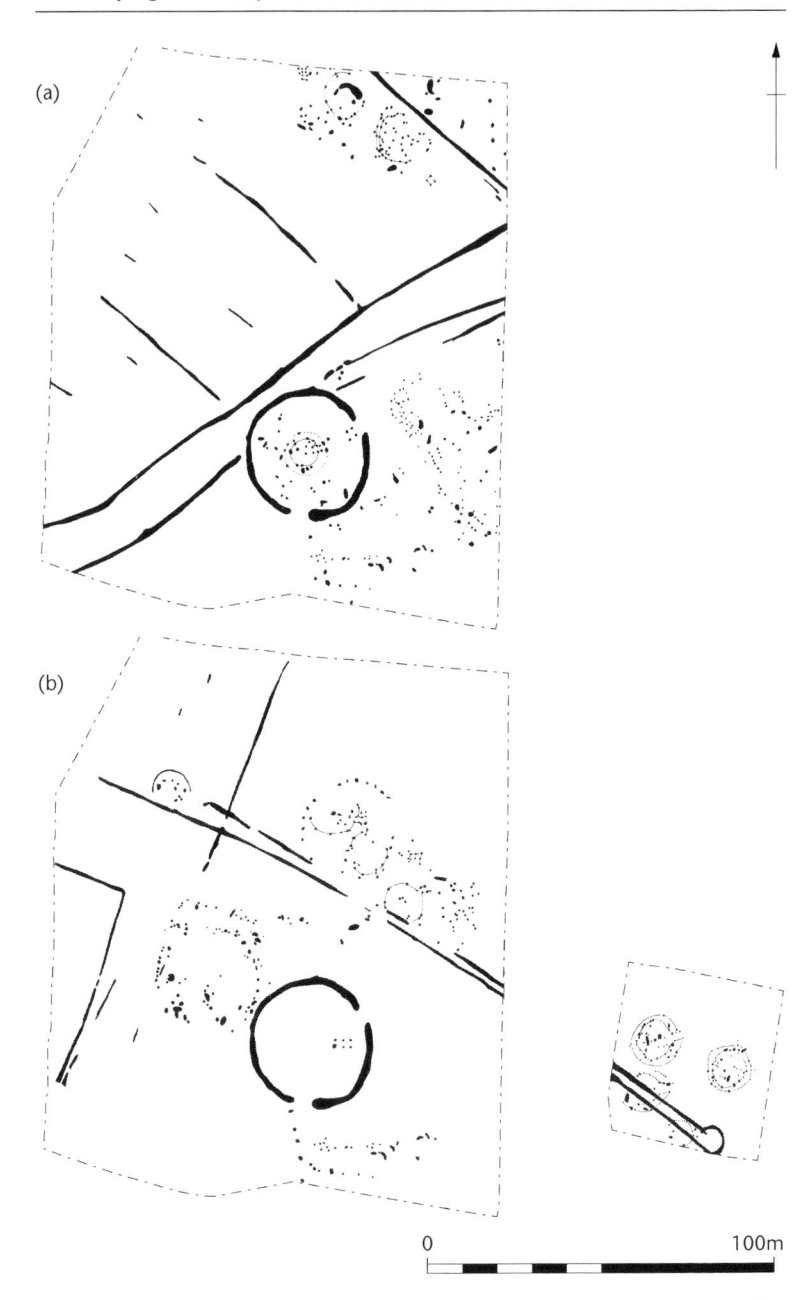

Figure 4.10. Restructuring the landscape at South Hornchurch, Essex: A earlier phase; B later phase (after Guttman et al. 2000, figs 7 and 11, with slight alterations by Anne Leaver; reproduced with permission of the Prehistoric Society).

Business Park, houses with a central post were often paired with another that did not have such a feature (Moore and Jennings 1992, 14), suggesting that there may have been a relationship between structure and function. Ellison (1981) argues that differences between paired roundhouses in size, architecture, and finds suggest that one building may have served as the main residence while the other functioned as an ancillary structure, perhaps for housing animals or for particular craft activities. Finds indicative of food consumption and craft production such as fineware ceramics, flint tools, whetstones, and loom weights, as well as 'high-status' objects such as items of bronze and shale, are usually recovered from the 'residential' structures. By contrast, ancillary buildings may produce items indicative of food preparation such as coarseware pottery, quernstones, and animal bone or sometimes no finds. However, single roundhouses associated with other structures and features are also known, particularly in the Late Bronze Age; these are frequently set within enclosures, as at Lofts Farm in Essex (Brown 1988). Although it is easy to assume that such small settlements comprising one or two roundhouses were occupied by single family groups, in fact the composition of individual households and families is highly variable cross-culturally (Netting, Wilk and Arnould 1984; Carsten 2012), and we must avoid projecting assumptions drawn from our own experience of the home into the past.

Where settlements comprise more than two roundhouses, these were often not contemporary but may have been built and used consecutively. In Area 5 at Reading Business Park in Berkshire (Moore and Jennings 1992, fig. 9), twenty roundhouses of Late Bronze Age date were identified, although the ground plans of many of these overlapped and others were so close together that it is clear that these were not all contemporary. Instead, what we may be seeing here is repeated rebuilding of a small group of three or four roundhouses on roughly the same location over several generations. This phenomenon is virtually unknown in the Middle Bronze Age but becomes more common during the Late Bronze Age. Of course, the addition of houses may have occurred over shorter time frames also, for example as the household group expanded or new buildings were required to house cattle or for other special-purpose activities. The number of roundhouses constructed may therefore reflect the social, reproductive, and economic success of the household over the course of its lifecycle (Brück 1999b).

Large nucleated settlements have rarely been identified. Corrstown in County Londonderry is particularly unusual in its size, with over seventy-four roundhouses packed tightly together in a series of roughly eight rows oriented approximately east–west/northeast–southwest

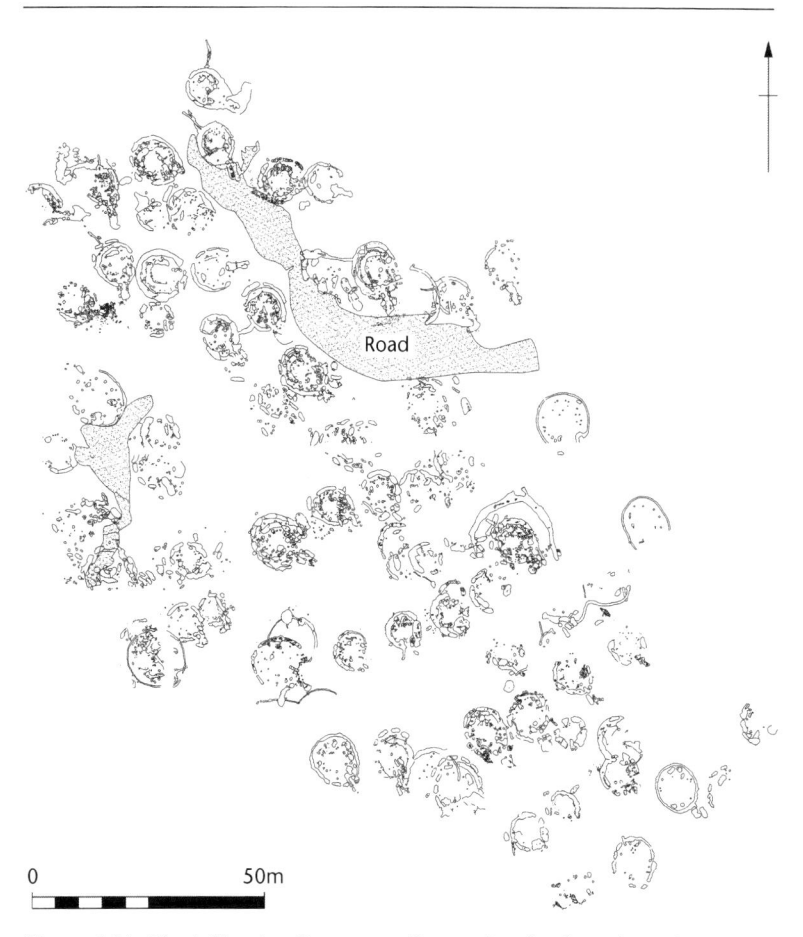

Figure 4.11. The 'village' at Corrstown, County Londonderry (reproduced with permission of Archaeological Consultancy Services Unit, with slight alterations by Anne Leaver).

(Figure 4.11; Ginn and Rathbone 2011). Very few of these buildings overlap, and it can be suggested that many were standing at the same time. With one exception, they are all oriented between east and south. Towards the north-eastern edge of the settlement there was a cobbled roadway some 10 metres wide and 95 metres long running in a north-west–south-easterly direction. The roundhouses have cobbled entranceways; cobbled pathways connect some of the houses, while others link houses to the roadway. The settlement was occupied from c.1500–1300 BC, and Ginn and Rathbone (2011, 223–4) suggest a population of 200–300 people at any one time.

The presence of distinct rows of houses may express ideas of lineal descent or relative genealogical seniority, and it is possible to interpret this layout in terms of the expansion and intergenerational succession of particular family groups over the lifespan of the settlement; likewise, the pathways between individual houses may have given material form to close social ties. Certainly, the scale and layout of this 'village' and the presence of shared features such as the roadway hint at a significant degree of community organization and integration. There is little to suggest marked social differences between houses, however. Most produced very similar assemblages of artefacts, predominantly flint and pottery, although more unusual objects were recovered from a small number of buildings, for example the Early Bronze Age macehead deposited in a posthole in the outer ring of structure 1, and a stone mould fragment for the production of a bronze chisel from the outer ditch segment of structure 8.

Gender, space, and social models of the Bronze Age household

A number of models of Middle and Late Bronze Age household structure have been proposed on the basis of the settlement evidence. Drewett's interpretation (1982) of the Middle Bronze Age settlement at Black Patch in East Sussex has been particularly influential. Five roundhouses were excavated at this site. Drewett viewed these as contemporaneous and, drawing on ethnographic parallels with Tiv and Hausa residential compounds in Nigeria, argued that they originally housed an extended family group comprising a 'headman', his wife, and dependent family members such as elderly parents or younger siblings. The central structure, hut 3, produced the greatest variety of finds, including pottery, a bronze razor, loom weights, a bronze knife, two bronze awls, struck flint, and large quantities of charred barley; Drewett saw this as the headman's hut. He interpreted hut 1 as the wife's cooking hut, as it produced pottery, quern fragments, flint flakes, animal bone, and two bronze finger rings. Huts 1 and 3 each had their own water source, a pond located in the fenced yard in front of the building. The finds from hut 4 indicated that it combined the functions of huts 1 and 3 in a single structure; this, and the fact that it lacked a pond, prompted Drewett to suggest that this may have been the home of a dependent relative. In contrast, huts 2 and 5 produced few finds, and may been used to stall animals.

This is an appealing model, but it is problematic for several reasons. To begin with, it is clear that the roundhouses cannot all have been standing at the same time. Each roundhouse was built on a platform cut into the hillside. However, the platforms on which huts 1 and 3 were built truncate the platform belonging to hut 2, cutting through the location of the original outer wall of this building. In the same way, the platform on which hut 4 was built truncates the platform belonging to hut 5. Russell (1996) and Seager Thomas (1999) have therefore suggested that there were at least two phases of occupation at the site, with just two or three buildings in use at any one time, although they differ in their sequencing of individual structures. If so, then the organization of this and similar multi-roundhouse settlements in Sussex and elsewhere in southern England can be reconciled much more easily with Ellison's model (1981), which, as we have seen, proposes that most settlements comprised a major residential structure plus one or two ancillary buildings.

A second problem with Drewett's interpretation is his assumption that the finds represent de facto refuse, dropped where they were used when the inhabitants abandoned the site. As Seager Thomas (1999, 46) points out, however, the finds from Black Patch may not have been used where they were deposited: the quern fragments from hut 1, for example, were found in layers of refuse that are likely to have been dumped after the building went out of use. The same can be suggested for the very large amounts of pottery (parts of at least 264 vessels) found in this building: both the ceramics and quern fragments may in fact have originated from elsewhere, so that their deposition relates to activities that occurred around or after the abandonment of this structure rather than during its lifetime. Moreover, at least some of the small metal finds from the site are likely to represent special deposits of one sort or another (Barrett and Needham 1988; Brück 1999b): the awl from the left-hand porch posthole of hut 3 may be a foundation deposit, for example, and may not directly indicate the sorts of activities that were carried out in this building.

Of course, the implicit assumptions in Drewett's gendering of space are also problematic. Hut 3 is interpreted as the headman's hut because it appears to have been the best-provided and hence the most 'important' structure: it produced more bronze finds than the other huts, for example, and these included a razor—an object that Drewett implicitly assumes to have belonged to a man. Yet, as we have seen, hut 3 also produced awls and loom weights—objects that might in other contexts be associated with women (awls generally appear to have accompanied female burials in the Early Bronze Age, for example: Woodward et al. 2015, 519–21). However, we do not in fact know who used objects such as loom weights or quernstones in the Middle Bronze Age. As such, it is surely equally problematic to assume that the presence of finger rings and cooking pots indicates that hut 1 was used by a woman.

The living house

A related set of assumptions regarding the gendering of settlement space underpins Parker Pearson and Richards's interpretation of the Late Bronze Age site at Mucking North Ring in Essex (1994, 50–2). Here, a substantial ditched, circular enclosure with an east-facing entrance contained three roundhouses (Figure 4.12). These three buildings were

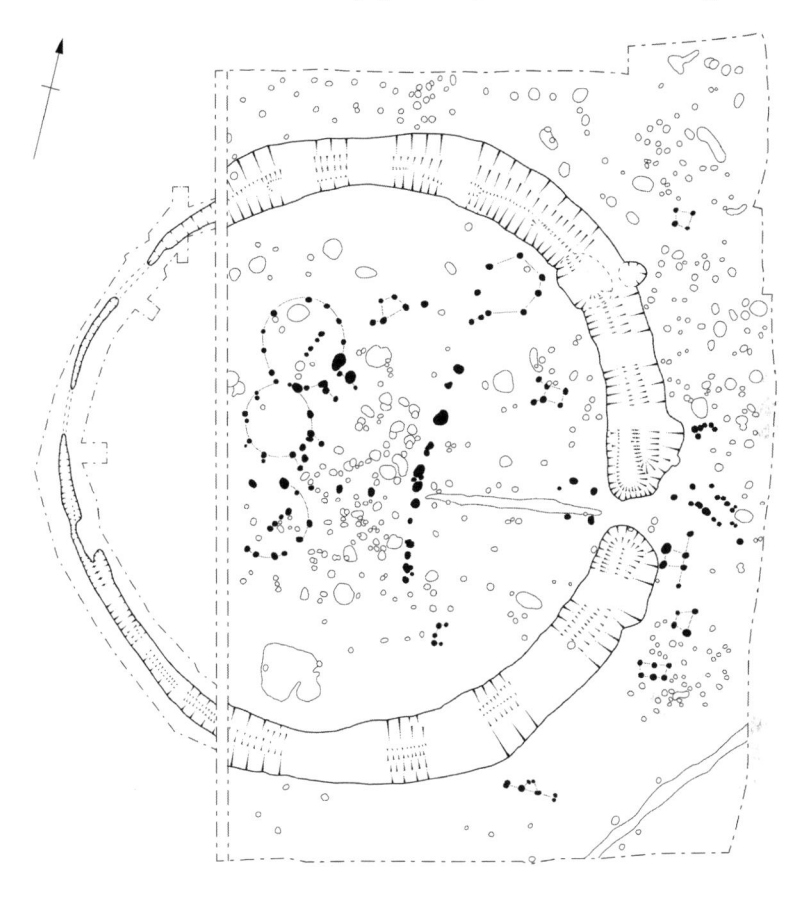

Figure 4.12. The ringwork at Mucking North Ring, Essex (redrawn by Anne Leaver after Bond 1988, fig. 3).

143

ranged in a row running roughly north–south across the centre of the enclosure, and the doorways of at least two of these structures faced the entrance to the enclosure. A line of posts, also running north–south, lay between the houses and the enclosure entrance, creating a fence or screen that may have restricted physical and visual access to the houses. There was a substantial gateway structure at the entrance to the site, as well as a number of fence-lines immediately outside the entrance that may have channelled movement in and out of the settlement. Parker Pearson and Richards argue that the architecture of the site worked to create a conceptual distinction between front and back, outside and inside. The presence of the screen and gateway structures, they suggest, indicates a division between public and private space, while the refuse associated with the houses and the lack of finds from the front half of the enclosure hint that the rear of the settlement may have been viewed as dirty, profane, and low-status, while the front was regarded as clean, sacred, and high-status. They argue that women may have been associated with the domestic activities carried out in and around the roundhouses, while interaction with the world beyond the confines of the settlement may have been primarily controlled by men, so that the values ascribed to settlement space helped to define gendered identities as well as the relative social position of men and women.

This is an interesting model, but it too presents some problems. We do not know, for example, that roundhouse space or domestic activities were viewed primarily as the domain of women during the Late Bronze Age. The interpretation of the finds from the roundhouses as 'refuse' and the negative value ascribed to this material are also not justified. As we have seen in Chapter 3, broken objects were not necessarily seen as 'rubbish'—at least in our sense of the term. Moreover, there is much to suggest that domestic refuse was valued in a positive way during this period: midden material appears to have been spread on fields as manure, and middens were themselves cultivated (Gingell 1992, 155; Simpson et al. 1998). Ethnographic analysis of the use of domestic space in other cultural contexts indicates that even where a distinction is drawn between public and private or between front and back, in fact the private, rear areas of a house or settlement may be the parts that are ascribed the higher cultural value (e.g. Waterson 1990, 178–9). In addition, Parker Pearson and Richards's interpretation presupposes that dualisms are necessarily oppositional (front versus back, clean versus dirty, male versus female, etc.), but this may not have been the case: the circular shape of the surrounding ditched enclosure suggests that the two zones within

Mucking North Ring may have been valued instead as complementary and inseparable elements of a single whole. It is therefore possible to suggest that this model is influenced too deeply by the meanings ascribed to domestic space in contemporary society as well as by nineteenth- and early twentieth-century formulations of the relationship between women and the home.

Event-marking deposits and the social life of the house

Multiphase sites such as Black Patch (Drewett 1982) suggest that Middle and Late Bronze Age settlements could be used over a relatively lengthy period of time. Although some roundhouses were single-phase structures, others show evidence for renovation or even complete rebuilding. Around half of the roundhouses at the Middle Bronze Age 'village' at Corrstown in County Londonderry show evidence for multiple phases of construction (Ginn and Rathbone 2011, 220). Rebuilding is even more common in the Late Bronze Age. Roundhouse CG55 at Kemerton in Worcestershire, for example, was rebuilt once and may also have replaced (or been replaced by) roundhouse C54, which partly overlapped it (Jackson and Napthan 2015, 39), while buildings 7 and 8 at Reading Business Park in Berkshire were reconstructed on almost exactly the same location (Moore and Jennings 1992, 22). Such events are likely to have been tied into broader rhythms of life on the settlement: houses may have been repaired, rebuilt, or replaced at important points in the lifecycle of the household, for example for an event such as a marriage or when a house passed from one generation to the next (Brück 1999b). Shorter cycles, such as the periodic reuse of particular parts of the landscape (grazing cattle on the floodplain in the summer, for example), may also have been marked by the renovation of buildings at seasonally occupied sites.

Certainly, there is much to suggest that important points in the lifecycles of the roundhouse were marked out, and this is particularly evident at the end of the life of the house. Buildings seem to have been treated in a variety of ways when they were abandoned. The lack of post-pipes in the postholes of the roundhouse at Middle Farm near Dorchester in Dorset suggests that the structure was dismantled (Smith et al. 1997, 80). Similarly, there were no post-pipes in the postholes of the Middle Bronze Age roundhouse at Weir Bank Stud Farm in Berkshire (Barnes et al. 1995, 11). However, fired clay, some bearing the imprint of wattling, was found in a ditch immediately adjacent to the building, so it is possible that the house was dismantled and its remains burnt nearby—just as the bodies of people were cremated during the same period (Brück 2006b). Other houses appear to have been burnt *in situ*, although it is, of course, very difficult to demonstrate that this was deliberate. At Corrstown in County Londonderry, the remains of burnt wooden planks and uprights were found in the ring-ditch surrounding structure 7 (Ginn and Rathbone 2011, 33), suggesting that this structure had been set alight. A substantial mound of burnt stone and earth, charcoal, carbonized plant remains, and large pieces of burnt wood sealed the roundhouse at Halls Hill near East Woodburn in Northumberland (Gates 2009, 50–1), and the excavator suggests that the house was burnt down at the end of its life. It seems possible that this was a deliberate act of ritual destruction. The postholes contained charcoal and burnt stone, but too little to indicate that the posts were burnt *in situ*; instead, the posts may have been removed and then burnt on the site of the house.

The remains of other roundhouses may have had more complex histories away from their original location. The timber posts deposited in one of the waterholes at Huntsman's Quarry, Kemerton in Worcestershire, may represent the remains of a dismantled roundhouse (Jackson and Napthan 2015, 113). Waterholes would, of course, have been crucial elements of a living landscape, and decommissioning this feature by depositing elements of a 'dead' house in it would doubtless have been a highly evocative act. Recent studies of charcoal from Bronze Age sites indicate that oak was the timber of choice for the construction of roundhouses. It is also the dominant species present in the remains of funeral pyres (O'Donnell 2016), and it is not impossible to suggest that pyres may have been built from the structural elements of dismantled dwellings; if so, the death of the roundhouse was inextricably intertwined with the death of its owner, so that a profound symbolic link was drawn between people and houses.

Not all houses were dismantled, however. There were well-preserved post-pipes in several of the postholes of roundhouse 1 at Blairhall Burn, Amisfield, Dumfriesshire, suggesting that this building had decayed *in situ* (Strachan et al. 1998, 60); here, the house was left standing as a visible monument to its occupants. Houses could be monumentalized in other ways also. Stone-built roundhouses on Dartmoor were frequently converted into cairns (Butler 1997, 137): a small stone cairn was built inside the collapsed walls of the roundhouse at Bellever Tor, for example, probably soon after it had been abandoned (Hughes 2009, 4). A whetstone was incorporated into this feature, perhaps referencing the cutting of ties occasioned by the death of the house. Similar practices can be identified elsewhere in south-west England: at Scarcewater in Cornwall, for example, a stone ring-cairn was built around an abandoned Middle Bronze Age roundhouse, while a low earthen mound was raised over another building at the same site after it was dismantled (Jones 2015). Sometimes houses referenced funerary monuments even while they were in use. The ring-bank of sandstone boulders that defined the outer edge of the Late Bronze Age roundhouse at Halls Hill near East Woodburn in Northumberland (Gates 2009, 48, 57) is strikingly similar to contemporary funerary monuments in the same region (see also Johnston 2001, 158–60). Here, the relationship between the roundhouse and its occupants was based on long-term genealogies of place in which structural similarities between the houses of the living and the houses of the dead played a significant role.

There is a variety of other evidence to suggest that the abandonment of Bronze Age houses was often accompanied by ritual acts (Nowakowski 2001; Brück 2006b; Jones 2015). After house 1 at Bestwall Quarry near Wareham in Dorset went out of use, a burnt mound (comprising heat-shattered stone that was probably a by-product of cooking activities) accumulated to the east of the doorway (Ladle and Woodward 2009, 70–1). The burnt mound developed around a pit that contained large amounts of pottery and a complete copper-alloy bracelet. It can be suggested that these features were the product of feasting activities marking the end of the life of the house. House 9 at the same site was dismantled, a small pit was dug in the centre of the former doorway, and a bronze gouge was deposited in this feature (Ladle and Woodward 2009, 118). Here, the longevity of such practices is evident, for house 1 has been dated to the Middle Bronze Age, while house 9 belonged to the subsequent Late Bronze Age phase. A polished stone axe was found in the upper fill of the slot trench that defined the Middle Bronze Age roundhouse at Lookout Plantation, Northumberland (Monaghan 1994, 36). Its stratigraphic position suggests that it may have been deposited late in the life of this building. It was found just east of the entrance and may have been ritually decommissioned: flakes of stone had been removed from the cutting-edge, the product of 'repeated, hammer-like blows'. The axe itself was already old and may have been curated, so that the abandonment of the house was marked by the deposition and destruction of what may have been viewed as an ancestral object.

Roundhouses were not the only focus for rituals of abandonment. Dumps of burnt flint in the upper silts of the northern terminal of the enclosure ditch at Down Farm in Dorset may represent the remains of a feast to mark the end of the life of this settlement (Green et al. 1991, 190). The upper fill of one of the waterholes at Huntsman's Quarry at Kemerton in Worcestershire produced a range of interesting objects, including loom weights, clay mould fragments, part of a shale armlet, the lower section of a decorated bone pin, and a fragment of human vertebra, and the excavators suggest that these layers represent deliberate and ritualized closing of this feature (Jackson and Naptham 2015, 110) with objects that, in some cases at least, may have conjured ideas of death, rebirth, and transformation.

It seems likely that other significant moments in the lives of Bronze Age settlements were also marked out through the deposition of special objects in pits, postholes, ditches, and other features. Foundation deposits can be identified, but other finds may relate to the refurbishment of a structure or to important points in the lifecycle of its inhabitants—the birth of a child, for example, or a successful harvest. A coarseware bowl was recovered from the first cut of each of the ditch terminals at the north-eastern entrance to the substantial circular enclosure at South Hornchurch in Essex, and these can be interpreted as a foundation deposit (Figure 2.12; Guttmann et al. 2000, 327). A bronze razor and awl were found on the base of the enclosure ditch at South Lodge Camp, indicating that these items were placed in the ditch immediately after it had been dug (Barrett et al. 1991, 161). Whole pots or large parts of pots are frequent finds: one of the possible flax retting pits in Area 3100 at Reading Business Park produced a fine burnished bowl (Moore and Jennings 1992, 42), while two small cups at the base of stratigraphic units H and I in Area 16 East, Runnymede, may have formed part of an event-marking rite recognizing a change in use of this area of the site (Needham and Spence 1996, 239). Guttman et al. (2000, 356) suggest that such deposits can be seen as residues of special meals or feasts associated with significant events in the life of a site: we might envisage reciprocal labour arrangements between households, for example, with neighbours and kinsfolk who helped in the construction of a house or the digging of a ditch being repaid in ritualized acts of commensality.

Other deposits marked important points in space, particularly boundaries and entrances. A large polished macehead was used as a packing stone in one of the postholes in the outer post-ring of structure 1 at Corrstown, County Londonderry (Ginn and Rathbone 2011, 22). Two complete quernstones were found just to the west of the doorway in the upper fill of the ring-gully surrounding the Middle Bronze Age roundhouse at Glanfeinion in Powys (Britnell et al. 1997, 193). The paving immediately outside the entrance to the Late Bronze Age roundhouse at Halls Hill near East Woodburn in Northumberland included half of a well-worn saddle quern; a conjoining fragment was found in a pit just next to the hearth that lay at the centre of the building (Gates 2009, 50). Peck marks to the surface of the latter suggest it was reused after its role as part of a quern had come to an end. Here, fragments that were already old—and that had different but interconnected histories—were deposited in key locations in roundhouse space: on the one hand, just outside the entrance, where inhabitants and guests would have to walk in the course of daily activities as well as for more special events, and on the other, right by the hearth—the social centre of the roundhouse.

The deposition of quernstones is interesting, for such practices may have referenced ideas of cyclical and intergenerational continuity, commensality, and the productivity of the household (Watts 2014). Such items, too, may have been associated with particular gender groups, so that gendered identity was folded into daily encounters with household space. Seager Thomas (1999, 41) has noted the deliberate burning and breaking of quernstones at several Middle Bronze Age settlements in Sussex, and similar practices can be seen elsewhere. At Bestwall Quarry in Dorset, for example, a complete but broken quernstone was deposited in two pieces on the base of a pit in house 7 (Ladle and Woodward 2009, 84). House 1 at Gardom's Edge in Derbyshire was left standing after abandonment. An inverted saddle quern was placed in the doorway, while three broken quernstones and a rubber were laid on cobbling just outside the entrance. A stone bank then was built around the southern side of the building, blocking the entrance and sealing these abandonment deposits (Barnatt et al. 2017, 99, 120). The emotive power of such acts of destruction is not difficult to imagine. By contrast, at Shaugh Moor in Devon quernstones were built into the walls of several of the roundhouses (Wainwright and Smith 1980; Watts 2014, 79), linking the act of construction with ideas of growth and fertility.

Community gathering-places in the Late Bronze Age

We have noted above that the majority of Bronze Age settlements comprised a small number of roundhouses and are likely to have been occupied by single household groups, although we have also discussed how these individual foci of activity formed part of larger settled landscapes, with often just a few hundred metres between adjacent (though not necessarily contemporary) settlements. In the Late Bronze Age, however, there is evidence for much larger agglomerations of people, notably at the so-called midden sites of southern and eastern Britain. Such sites have produced not only huge quantities of refuse but also evidence for a wide range of productive activities, as well as finds that have been interpreted as high-status items (Figure 4.13). Much of

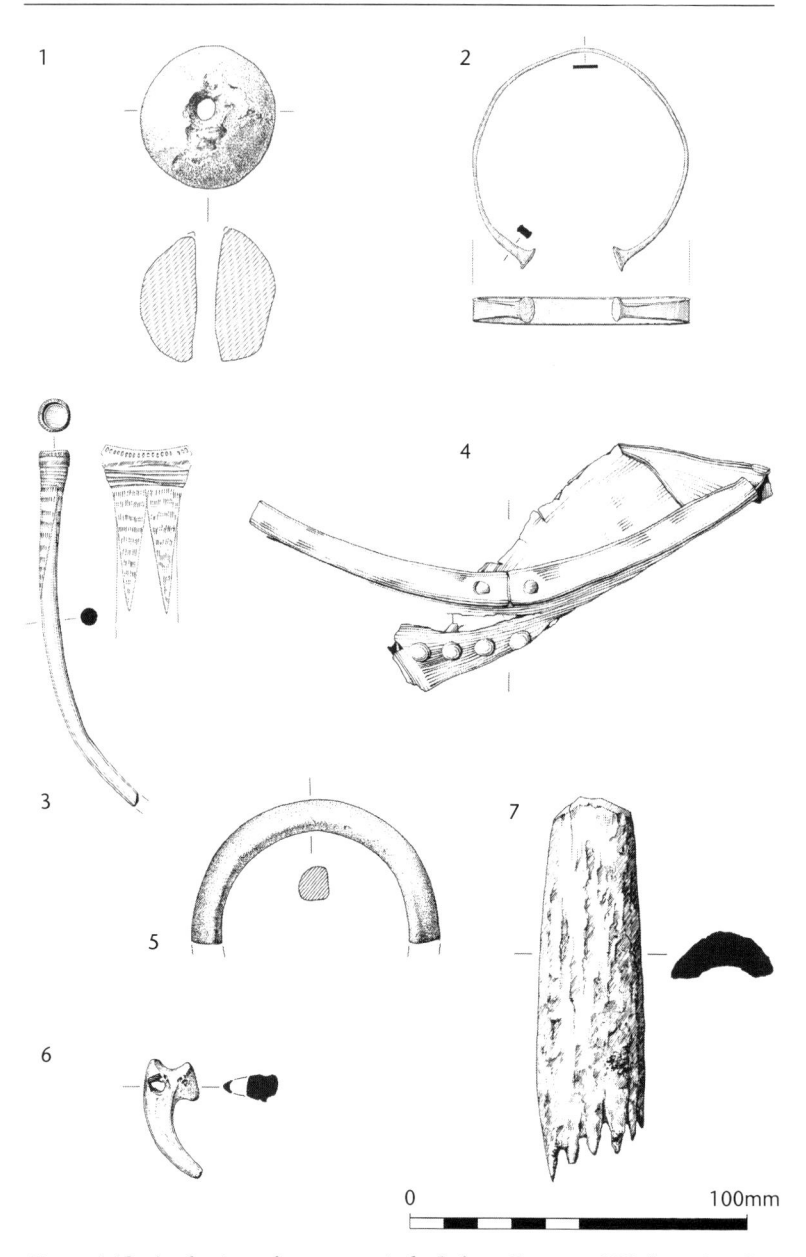

Figure 4.13. A selection of non-ceramic finds from Potterne, Wiltshire: 1 amber bead; 2 gold bracelet; 3 copper-alloy pin; 4 copper-alloy vessel fragment; 5 shale armlet; 6 pierced dog tooth; 7 bone weaving comb (after Lawson 2000, figs 67, 71, 72, 80, 86, 92, and 93, © Wessex Archaeology, with slight alterations by Anne Leaver).

the mound at Potterne in Wiltshire was made up of manure, stabling waste, and animal fodder (Lawson 2000). The site also yielded substantial quantities of debris from domestic and craft activities, including human coprolites, charcoal, ash, animal bone, and crop-processing waste, as well as very large numbers of artefacts, notably pottery.

The sizeable assemblages of animal bone found at this and other midden sites suggests large-scale butchery and consumption, probably the result of feasting, although the species involved appears to have varied. The majority (about 70 per cent) of the animals recovered from the midden at Llanmaes in South Glamorgan were pigs. Amongst the pig remains, 87 per cent of the limb fragments were forelimbs and 70 per cent of the elements that could be assigned to a particular side of the body were from the right-hand side; Madgwick and Mulville (2015) therefore suggest that individual households congregating at this site each contributed a standard portion—the right forequarter—to feasting events. By contrast, an estimate of the meat weight produced by different species at Runnymede suggests that most of the meat consumed at this site was from cattle (58 per cent), although pig (23 per cent) was also significant (Done 1991, 340). Less than 3 per cent of the bone fragments displayed butchery marks, suggesting that meat was cooked and consumed in large joints. At Wallingford in Oxfordshire, the presence of large quantities of burnt stone (Roe and Barclay 2006, 71) alongside daub that may derive from ovens (Barclay 2006a, 102–3) suggests large-scale cooking activities. Fineware pottery used for the consumption of food forms a significant element of the ceramic repertoire from these sites. A substantial assemblage of bowls, finewares and decorated ceramics as well as part of a wooden ladle were recovered from the river channel at Runnymede (Needham 1991, 381); the ceramics from this context included large portions of particular pots, suggesting the swift and possibly formal disposal of feasting debris. Of course, the preparation, display, and consumption of food plays a significant role in the construction of age and gender relationships, and it is no surprise that the objects employed in these activities were sometimes ostentatious. Several bronze cauldron fragments have been found at Llanmaes (Lodwick and Gwilt 2004): feasting, as a particular form of conspicuous consumption, doubtless worked to mark social position as well as to generate social networks (Lawson 2000, 268).

Although it is clear that midden sites such as Potterne and Llanmaes were places where large numbers of people came together, it is more difficult to say whether they were occupied year-round. Certainly, the feasting evidence suggests periodic rather than permanent occupation of these locations by large numbers of people. At East Chisenbury, sheep were the most common animal and there was a disproportionately high percentage of neonatal and/or foetal lambs (Brown et al. 1994, 48; Serjeantson et al. 2010, 63–4), hinting that this site may have been occupied during the springtime. The presence of large amounts of cattle dung and stabling refuse at Potterne suggests that at this site dispersed communities may have come together in the autumn or winter to cull, breed, or exchange animals, or to overwinter them in byres and stables (Lawson 2000, 270); as we shall see in Chapter 5, cattle may have been considered a significant form of wealth during this period. The landscape setting of many of these sites made them accessible to different communities. Potterne, for example, lies in an elevated position overlooking the River Avon. A track or roadway identified during the excavations was flanked by fence-lines and a line of boulders, suggesting that the approach to the site and patterns of movement through it may have been relatively formalized (Lawson 2000, 27). Although the presence of items of 'exotic' materials such as gold, amber, and shale at this site suggests that it was well connected to regional and supraregional exchange networks, this may also indicate significant movement of people into and out of the site, both from the local area and from further afield. Most of the pottery fabrics were from local sources, but some had more distant origins, including one fabric which contained fragments of biotite granite most likely from south-west England (Morris 2000, 146); over time, the proportion of non-local fabric types increased.

East Chisenbury too acted as a focal point within the landscape: seven linear ditches, a double-ditched avenue, and a pit alignment all converge on the site (McOmish 1996, 70). Some middens occur in locations that are likely to have been special in other ways. Both Runnymede and Wallingford were located on islands in the Thames, and Runnymede was located at the junction of the Thames and Colne Brook. It has been suggested that this was to facilitate control over trade from the Continent, although other factors are also likely to have been important (Needham 1991, 383): the deposition of fine metalwork and human skulls in the Thames (Bradley and Gordon 1988; Schulting and Bradley 2013) indicates that, like other rivers, it was viewed as a liminal location—a boundary between social groups or between this world and the next—and such places may have been viewed as appropriate locations for different communities to congregate. At Wallingford, a timber revetment ran along the western edge of the island on which the site was located and piles for two possible jetties extended out into a palaeochannel (Cromarty et al. 2006, 16). It is possible that these jetties provided highly visible locations from which special objects could be thrown into the waters during intercommunity gatherings: a variety of bronze objects were recovered during river-dredging carried out at Wallingford during the nineteenth and twentieth centuries (Thomas 1984).

There is other evidence for the performance of ritual activities at these sites. A total of 139 fragments of human bone were recovered from the midden at Potterne (McKinley 2000, 99): the preponderance of skull fragments suggests an element of selection and curation to the practices that resulted in their deposition at this site. Occasionally such 'objects' appear to have been carefully arranged on deposition: at East Chisenbury, for example, a fragment of human skull was laid vault-upwards on a prepared surface. Around this were placed several sherds from the same vessel and a fragment of sarsen (Brown et al. 1994, 48). We have already suggested that the presence of a large number of broken shale armlets at Potterne—items that would have fitted older children—hints that age-grade ceremonies were conducted at this site (Brück and Davies 2018). At least some rites may have required particular ways of communicating with the world of the spirits or ancestors: large numbers of opium-poppy seeds were recovered at Wallingford (Robinson 2006, 112), although it is not possible to tell if these were employed as narcotics.

Middens, then, appear to have been locations where people congregated for a range of purposes, including feasting, exchange, and ritual activities. It has long been noted that these sites produce relatively large numbers of decorative objects including items of gold, bronze, amber, shale, and glass. It is possible, on the one hand, to view these as evidence that middens were 'high-status' sites occupied by chiefs and located at the top of a settlement hierarchy. However, if we see these sites instead as places where communities gathered for socially significant activities, it is perhaps no surprise that particular attention was paid to the costumes that were worn. Bodies and clothing were decorated with visually appealing materials of various sorts. At Potterne, for example, a wide variety of ornaments were found, including a gold bracelet; bronze rings and pins; shale pendants and armlets; and beads of amber, glass, and shale (Figure 4.13; Lawson 2000). Rings, toggles, buttons, and sliders of bone and antler were also recovered. The presence of guillemot bones and the perforated claw of a white-tailed sea eagle at this site (Locker 2000, 119) is interesting, for the site is some 50 kilometres from the sea. It is tempting to imagine that these might have formed an element of the regional costumes (and perhaps even the ceremonial regalia) of visitors coming to Potterne from coastal areas. Bones of beaver, wildcat, polecat, and fox were also identified, perhaps hinting at similar use for skins. Perforated dog, horse, and deer teeth, a perforated fox mandible, and a perforated antler tine may also have formed elements of specific costumes.

The positioning of middens at locations that may have been viewed as liminal, and the performance of ritual activities at these sites, suggest that they may have been considered suitable places for transformative activities; this may be one reason why such a wide range of crafts were carried out at middens. Both the practice and products of craft activities are likely to have been closely bound up with particular aspects of social identity. At Potterne (Lawson 2000), metalworking evidence includes thirteen crucible fragments, three or four mould fragments, fuel ash slag bearing traces of copper, a casting runner, and several lumps of bronze; some of the stone rubbers or burnishers found at the site may also have been used in metalworking. Fifty-nine complete or fragmentary spindle whorls as well as several loom weights indicate that the production of cloth also took place here. Some of the bone artefacts found also played a role in cloth production and clothing manufacture, for example weaving combs, shuttle tips, awls, and needles, while bone points and awls may have been employed in leatherworking or decorating ceramics. Bronze tools from Potterne include knives, awls, a needle, and a graver/tracer. A variety of other bone tools were also identified, including 'rib knives' and gouges; bone-working debris suggests that at least some of these objects were made on site. Hammerstones, mullers, and rubbers may indicate the production of quernstones.

One of the most remarkable features of middens is their size: the deposits at Potterne, for example, were 2 metres thick and extended over some 3.5 hectares (Lawson 2000). These were conspicuous sites that provided visible evidence of the wealth and productivity of their communities. McOmish (1996, 68) describes such sites as 'deliberately curated accumulations of feasting debris', and as such they can perhaps be viewed as monuments to particular events, activities, and groups. These were places in which a range of transformative practices were carried out, and where particular forms of social identity were defined through ritual, productive activities, and the consumption of food and other substances (Waddington 2008; 2010). The wide range of different materials that are found at middens is especially unusual in comparison to other contemporary sites: here stone, bone, metal, clay, and other materials were brought together, worked, used, and deposited in activities that sought to order the world and create meaningful relationships between its different components. These were locations in which both people and objects were made and unmade in practices that defined their place and significance in the order of things.

Settlements and status in the Late Bronze Age

We have already seen that settlements of Middle and Late Bronze Age date were often enclosed, although open settlements were also very common. In the Late Bronze Age in particular, the enclosures surrounding some settlements could be substantial. The so-called 'ringworks' are one such category of site, and we have already discussed a number of these, including the enclosures at Mucking North Ring, Oliver Close Estate, and South Hornchurch—the latter set within a landscape that also included several areas of contemporary open settlement. Ringworks were circular enclosures surrounded by a substantial bank and ditch, and usually containing between one and four roundhouses. Some have a single entrance, while others have two diametrically opposing entranceways on either side of the enclosure; occasionally, more than two entrances are present. Their monumental banks and ditches have been taken to indicate that they were high-status sites, yet they often lie within a kilometre or so of other similar sites, and produce relatively few finds that might be identified as indicative of the presence of wealthy inhabitants (Needham 1992; Brück 2007). With the exception of a large deposit of mould fragments for the production of bronze swords, the finds from Springfield Lyons in Essex, for example, are not dissimilar in character or quantity to other contemporary sites, including open settlements: ceramics, perforated clay plates, struck flint, loom weights, and spindle whorls attest to a range of productive and domestic activities (Brown and Medlycott 2013). Deposits of sword moulds, although unusual, have also been found at open settlements (Webley et al. 2020). There are nonetheless hints that ringworks were settings for significant communal acts of food consumption: many have produced particularly large assemblages of perforated clay plates, thought to have been used for the baking of bread (a new technology in the Late Bronze Age: Champion 2004), and their pottery assemblages are dominated by fineware bowls and large jars (Brudenell 2012, 259–98). The creation of ringworks may therefore have played a role in social distinction but might also have functioned to define an element of the social landscape that was set apart for particular purposes or events.

Similar questions are raised by the earliest hillforts, which appear during this time. At the Breiddin in Powys (Figure 4.14; Musson 1991), charcoal from a timber-revetted rampart of stone and earth produced dates in the tenth and ninth centuries BC. It is not clear, however, if the samples can be directly linked with the construction of this feature; moreover, they were bulked samples, at least some including oak, so a date around 800 BC may be more realistic. The area enclosed by the

Personifying Prehistory

Figure 4.14. The Late Bronze Age rampart, hearths, pits, and other features at the Breiddin, Powys (bottom) and their relationship with the subsequent Iron Age hillfort (top) (redrawn by Anne Leaver after Musson 1991, figs 5, 8, 10, 13, and 15; reproduced with permission of Chris Musson).

156

rampart is unknown, although if it followed the line of the later Iron Age hillfort, it may have been as large as 28 hectares. Inside the rampart, a series of hearths, postholes, pits, and possible metalworking furnaces was identified. These features produced coarseware ceramics, clay moulds and crucibles, quern fragments, and a variety of stone tools. Bronze objects were also found, including a hammer, axe, knife, spearhead, portions of a sword, several pins, and part of a bracelet. Artefacts from within the body of the rampart may represent the remains of an earlier unenclosed phase of occupation. At Beeston Castle in Cheshire, groups of features including a linear arrangement of postholes and a possible slot trench may indicate the existence of an early palisaded enclosure prior to the construction of the rampart (Ellis 1993, 21–5). The rampart itself produced material of Late Bronze Age date, including ceramics and two Ewart Park axes (*c*.1000–800 BC). Both axes were complete, and one was unfinished, suggesting that they were not residual finds of earlier date, so the rampart too may have been built at this time. Late Bronze Age occupation layers, postholes, and stake-holes were found to the rear of the rampart. At Mam Tor in Derbyshire, a ditch and earthen rampart with stone retaining walls enclosed an area of 5 hectares (Coombs and Thompson 1979). The dating of these features is not clear, but some of the many hut platforms inside the hillfort produced Late Bronze Age plainware pottery as well as flint artefacts, whetstones, shale bracelet fragments, and part of a Late Bronze Age bronze axe.

Although sites such as the Breiddin have yielded a variety of finds, early hillforts in Britain generally produce fewer 'high-status' finds and less evidence for craft production than either middens or ringworks (Brück 2007, tables 1 and 2), and despite the labour required for the building of features such as palisades and ramparts, it may be simplistic to view these as the apex of a settlement hierarchy. Current interpretations of Iron Age hillforts view these as gathering places for dispersed communities (Hamilton and Manley 1997; 2001; Sharples 2010, 116–24), with the collective act of rampart-building helping to create a sense of shared identity, and this may have been the case for their Late Bronze Age predecessors also. It is interesting to note that hillforts are—by their very nature—located on particularly striking elements of the landscape. Mam Tor, for example, is one of a series of prominent gritstone hills in the Peak District, and the presence of two Early Bronze Age barrows indicates that this was already a significant location in preceding centuries (Coombs and Thompson 1979). The Breiddin forms part of a distinctive isolated volcanic ridge above the Severn valley. It is therefore possible that hillforts were constructed to mark out natural features that were already core elements of the social and sacred geographies of

Bronze Age communities (see also Gosden and Lock 1998; Hamilton and Manley 2001; Waddington 2013, 100). The occasional recovery of particularly 'rich' artefact assemblages from Late Bronze Age hillforts need not counter this interpretation: we have suggested above that the diverse range of finds from middens does not necessarily indicate that these were high-status sites in the traditional sense of the term, and hillforts can perhaps be interpreted in a similar way as locations in which community gatherings involved activities in which material culture was employed to underscore the social and cosmological order.

One hillfort that has produced finds as 'rich' if not 'richer' than the midden sites of southern and eastern Britain is the site at Rathgall in County Wicklow. Here, three concentric ramparts enclosed an area of about 7.3 hectares. Although the ramparts themselves have not been conclusively dated, the substantial roundhouse that lay at the centre of a ditched enclosure inside the innermost rampart was constructed during the Late Bronze Age: a pit near the centre of this building contained a deposit of burnt human bone and a gold hair ring. A 'workshop' area to the north-east of this enclosure produced an extraordinary range of finds, including hundreds of clay mould fragments for the production of swords, spearheads, axes, pins, and other objects; lumps of bronze waste; tools including a gouge, tanged punch, and whetstones; eighty-eight glass beads; shale armlet fragments; pieces of amber; a gold biconical bead; a bronze hair ring covered with gold foil; and a glass pendant with a gold inset (Raftery 1976; 2004; Raftery and Becker in press). These finds suggest that the site was a focus for the production of a wide range of weaponry, ornaments, and other objects. Yet other Irish hillforts of the same date, for example the substantial trivallate hillfort at Mooghaun in County Clare, have produced far fewer finds (Grogan 1999).

Elsewhere in Ireland, Late Bronze Age timber platforms (or crannógs) constructed in wetland areas or at the edge of lakes have often been interpreted as high-status settlements because of their finds assemblages. The site at Ballinderry in County Offaly (Hencken 1942), for example, produced a bronze flesh hook; such items are usually interpreted as feasting equipment. Finds from the Late Bronze Age platform at Moynagh Lough in County Meath include eight bronze pins; a bronze hair ring; thirty-two amber beads; an antler cheek piece that probably formed part of the bridle for a horse; parts of five bracelets, two rings and six beads of shale or lignite; a bone comb; spindle whorls; and quernstones (Bradley 2004). However, no buildings were identified, and Bradley suggests that this was not in fact a settlement, but a location where votive deposition into the waters of the lake took place. Certainly, the considerable number of objects that relate to the care and presentation of the self hints that this was a place where the articulation of identity was a matter of concern; if we interpret the site as a gathering-place where ritual activities were performed, this is perhaps no surprise. Similar timber-platform sites in Britain, for example Flag Fen in Cambridgeshire (Pryor 2001; 2005), have often been interpreted as locations that served as foci for ritual activities, notably the deposition of metalwork. By contrast, current interpretation of the extraordinary site at Must Farm in Cambridgeshire suggests that this was a settlement. Although this site has yielded an extensive assemblage of metalwork and other 'high-status' artefacts such as beads of glass and amber (Knight et al. 2016), the unusual circumstances of its abandonment make it difficult to compare the finds from this site with those from other contemporary settlements: it was destroyed by fire so that complete household inventories were left where they were used, and the excavators argue that less well-preserved settlements elsewhere might originally have had equally rich and diverse assemblages of artefacts.

Conclusion

The Bronze Age settlement record speaks of profound transformations in the way interpersonal relationships were constructed and mediated over the course of the period. The Early Bronze Age is characterized by a relatively fluid relationship with place, but one that was nonetheless marked through practices such as the deposition of pottery, struck flint, and other objects in pits. Later, structures such as roundhouses, fences, and enclosure ditches allowed differences to be drawn between spaces and the people associated with them, creating new settings in which cultural values could be enacted through the performance of activities central to social, material, and biological reproduction; yet spatial movement was still an important component of the settlement pattern. Although banks and ditches were indeed used to define community, particularly in the later part of the period, this occurred at a range of different scales and often involved a considerable element of permeability.

It is evident that the sorts of conceptual categories that structure our own engagement with domestic space were not always part of the Bronze Age experience of settlement. There is nothing to suggest, for example, that Bronze Age domestic architecture facilitated the production of gender relationships in any way similar to those of the modern, Western world; even Bronze Age burials tell us little about the gendering of activities such as grinding grain, cooking food, or knapping flint. Settlements were locations in which ritual practice such as the deposition of human bone (a substance that is rarely encountered in our own homes) could take place. Evidence for the performance of a variety of productive and other activities in the open air suggests that concepts of privacy were not articulated in the same way as in our own cultural context. The residues of feasting events indicate that settlements were a key arena for the creation of intergroup alliances and for the negotiation of social and political relations both at the micro- and macro-scale. In such contexts, people's relationship with the detritus of daily activities was also quite different, for 'refuse' seems to have been valued as a material which spoke of identity and memory, and which helped to locate people in a particular genealogy of landscape. Together, these points suggest that the sorts of binary dualisms that govern our own relationship with the home (public–private, for example, or ritual–secular) were not articulated in the same way (or indeed recognized at all) in the Bronze Age. Bronze Age houses were foci for a range of productive, political, and ritual activities; they were not solely the locations in which daily maintenance activities were carried out. This hints that the gendered identities and other social relations constructed in and through the 'domestic domain' are likely to have differed radically from those generated in our own homes today.

Like the households or family groups that occupied them, settlements expanded and contracted over time as roundhouses were added, repurposed, and demolished. There is evidence to suggest that important moments in the lifecycles of Middle and Late Bronze Age roundhouses, including construction, rebuilding, and abandonment, were marked by the deposition of significant objects and—as described also in Chapters 2 and 5—complete and fragmentary human and animal bodies. The deposition of objects such as quernstones referenced the generative potential of the household group (Watts 2014), but other items may have spoken of the intimate relationship between the house and particular occupants. It has been noted that most of the copper-alloy objects deposited in roundhouses were small personal items such as finger rings, pins, awls, and razors (Jones et al. 2015, 186-7); during the Early Bronze Age, these are exactly the sorts of artefacts that were deposited as grave goods with the dead. So too, roundhouses were often monumentalized after their abandonment, covered with mounds of earth and stone so that they resembled barrows or cairns (Nowakowski 1991; Jones 2015); others were burnt down just as human bodies were cremated (Brück 2006b). Similar life-cycle rites were performed for houses and their human occupants: the well-being of the house was intimately connected with the well-being of the household, so that the lifecycles of houses and people were linked in both practical and metaphorical terms. This suggests that roundhouses may have been viewed as living things with their own spirit or soul, and some of the small votive deposits made in and around these structures may have been propitiatory offerings to the house itself.

These points provide some insights into concepts of personhood, for they suggest that things other than humans could be viewed as 'persons', with lives, needs, and powers of their own. Human and roundhouse lives were intertwined (Brück 1999b)—each defined in relation to the other so that people's sense of self and their understanding of their place in the world was bound up with the well-being of the roundhouse and its positioning within the social universe. This reminds us too that concepts of the self were not fixed, for just as roundhouses were constructed, rebuilt, and abandoned, so too the identities of their occupants were transformed over the lifecourse. The rituals carried out in and around the house and the orientation of house entrances to the east or south-east suggest that the human lifecourse too may have been thought of as a series of cycles of growth, death, and renewal marked by rites of passage (Brück 2006b). Personhood was constituted in the gifting of objects like finger rings or awls that spoke of intimate relationships, and in daily engagement with items such as querns or pots that conjured familial ties as well as intergroup links. The deposition of such objects at significant moments in the life of the house and the household therefore worked to create and commemorate relational forms of personhood. Such items formed core elements of personal and community identity, so that their incorporation into the 'body' of the roundhouse sedimented human stories into household space and memory. In this way, the histories of people and houses became intimately interconnected. Houses were not merely passive settings for human action but were active elements of the constitution of the self, suggesting a rather different relationship between subject and object than that figured in our own cultural context.

Although identity was relationally constituted, it is evident that the creation of boundaries and the definition of particular conceptual categories became an increasing focus of concern over the course of the period. Residential mobility meant that people's relationship with place may have been relatively fluid during the Early Bronze Age, but in later centuries there was an emerging concern to define and bound different spaces. This is evident in the construction of roundhouses and in the ditches, banks, and fences used to delimit and differentiate settlement space. As we have seen, boundaries and entrances were marked by the deposition of objects. Although the architecture of the roundhouse appears to create a relatively undifferentiated circular space, in fact different parts of the house were used in different ways. This interest in spatial categorization no doubt mirrors contemporary processes of social distinction, but this need not indicate the emergence of dualistic conceptual frameworks, nor does it imply that such categories were fixed: there is considerable inter-site variability in the use of household space, for example (Brück 1999b). This is a topic we shall return to in Chapter 6. We have seen too that possible evidence for the emergence of social hierarchies, particularly in the Late Bronze Age, can be read in other ways. The settlement evidence for the period as a whole predominantly presents us with a picture of intimate relationships made on a local scale. Some places, for example the hillforts and middens of the Late Bronze Age, indicate larger intercommunity gatherings during which people may have worn regional costumes or objects such as shale bracelets or bronze pins that marked aspects of age or gender identity. Unusual items such as gold bracelets or glass beads may have been worn by persons of particular status, but there is little to indicate the existence of chiefs or other institutionalized positions of rank.

5

Social landscapes

In 1960 a rock climber found a small Middle Bronze Age pot wedged in a cleft in the rock halfway down the eastern face of Crow's Buttress, a granite outcrop on the southern edge of Dartmoor in Devon (Pettit 1974, 92). The Middle Bronze Age was a period during which extensive field systems were constructed on Dartmoor (Fleming 1988). As we shall see later in this chapter, these have often been thought to indicate the intensification of agriculture and an increasing concern to define land ownership in response to population pressure (e.g. Barrett 1980a; 1994, 148–9; Bradley 1984, 9; Yates 2007, 120–1; English 2013, 139–40). Such models imply the commodification of the natural world: the landscape is viewed primarily as a resource for economic exploitation. Yet this small pot calls such assumptions into question, for it can surely be best interpreted as an offering to spirit guardians or ancestors associated with a striking natural rock formation. This hints at a quite different way of engaging with and understanding the landscape.

In this chapter we will explore the links between people and landscape, beginning with the monumental landscapes of the Chalcolithic and Early Bronze Age, moving then to consider what the appearance of field systems during the Middle and Late Bronze Age tells us about human–environment relationships during the later part of the period, and finally considering some of the ways in which animals were incorporated into the social worlds of Bronze Age communities. Funerary and ceremonial monuments of various sorts are the most eye-catching feature of the Early Bronze Age landscape and have dominated our interpretations of the period. By contrast, as we have seen in Chapter 4, settlement evidence of this date is relatively sparse. This, and recent isotope analyses of Chalcolithic and Early Bronze Age inhumation burials (Jay et al. 2012; Parker Pearson et al. 2016), suggest a significant degree of residential mobility. The high-protein diet of many of these burials (Parker Pearson et al. 2016) hints that pastoralism was an important element of the economy, and this is supported by palaeoenvironmental analyses from many regions, which indicate that woodland had been cleared in many areas to create extensive areas of open grassland (e.g. Greig and Colledge 1988; Murphy 1994; Allen 1997; 2004; Stevens and Fuller 2012). The plant macrofossils recovered from pit clusters of this period often include a significant proportion of wild plants (e.g. Beadsmoore 2007, 8), though cereals (primarily emmer wheat and naked barley) were also consumed, at least in small quantities.

The landscapes of the Middle and Late Bronze Age, on the other hand, were dominated by monumental domestic architecture and features such as field systems, waterholes, and droveways that seem to speak of practical, economic concerns. The field systems of the period appear to have been designed primarily to facilitate stock-handling (Pryor 1996), although there was also a significant increase in cereal production from c.1500 BC (Stevens and Fuller 2012, fig. 3), with crops such as hulled barley and spelt wheat becoming common (e.g. Murphy 1988); occasional cereal-drying kilns dating to this period have been identified (Ellis 2013). The highly visible character of the settlements and field systems of the Middle and Late Bronze Age has meant that our interpretations of the period have often been framed in functionalist terms (Brück 2000). Yet it has long been recognized that features such as rivers, lakes, and bogs assumed particular social and cultural significance during the Middle and Late Bronze Age, for they were foci for the votive deposition of bronze weapons as well as ceremonial objects such as cauldrons and horns. Only recently, however, with the increase in large-scale developer-funded work, has it begun to be possible to understand how such finds relate to the settled landscape of farmsteads and field systems. At the same time, increasing recognition of votive deposits of various sorts in settlement contexts has called into question the assumption that everyday domestic activities were predicated on the 'rationalist' understanding of the world familiar from our own cultural context (Brück 2000). Many such deposits include quernstones, animal burials, or deposits of grain, and speak of ways of interacting with the 'natural' world that did not view it as outside of human culture and society.

The modern, Western distinction between culture and nature, of course, has its origins in particular political and historical conditions (e.g. Foucault 1970; Jordanova 1980; Pickles 2003; Descola 2013). By viewing the natural world as outside of human society, it was possible to legitimate the appropriation of land during the colonial expansions of recent centuries (Phillips 1997; Harley 2009). Landscape became objectified; it was mapped, measured, explored, and exploited in strategies that stripped it of cultural value. The distinction between culture and nature also served other political purposes: by drawing analogies between aspects of the natural world and certain categories of person (such as indigenous groups and women), the colonialist discourses of the eighteenth and nineteenth centuries defined these too as objects requiring social control (Plumwood 1993; Jahoda 1999). By recognizing the particular historical context in which a distinction between culture and nature emerged, it becomes easier to recognize and question the influence this has had on our understanding of Bronze Age landscapes.

Barrow cosmographies

We shall begin with the barrows and cairns of the Chalcolithic and Early Bronze Age, for these indicate that components of the 'natural' world such as stone or soil were not devoid of cultural meaning. These monuments frequently comprise interesting amalgamations of materials, including soil, stone, sand, chalk, clay, turf, wood, and charcoal, amongst others. These were often arranged in particular ways, notably in layers (Jones 2010, 108), but also in spreads that emphasize specific parts of the monument. The core of the barrow at Upton Pyne in Devon was composed of sand (Figure 5.1; Pollard and Russell 1969). This was then covered with a turf stack, followed by a layer of leached sand that was very pale—indeed almost white—in colour. After some time, a final capping of clay was added to the monument. This varied in colour from light buff through to yellow, orange, and red, suggesting it was brought from a number of different sources. The excavators noted that the different coloured clays could be seen as separate deposits, each around a basketload in volume. A small low mound of orange sand and cobbles covered the central burial at Quernhow, North Yorkshire, and acted as a focus for subsequent interments (Waterman 1951). This was enclosed by a penannular spread of cobbles. Over both the mound and cobble spread, a larger barrow of sand and loam was constructed. This was overlain by a cairn surrounded by an earthen bank and external boulder kerb including both local sandstones and a variety of erratics. Further burials were inserted into the cairn and bank, after which the whole monument was covered with a final layer of loamy sand.

Sometimes coloured materials appear to have been deliberately employed in the construction of barrows (Owoc 2002; Jones 2012, 164). Barrow 44 on Wyke Down in Dorset comprised a turf core capped by a layer of bright white chalk (Boulden 2011). Barrows 84 and 85 at

West   East

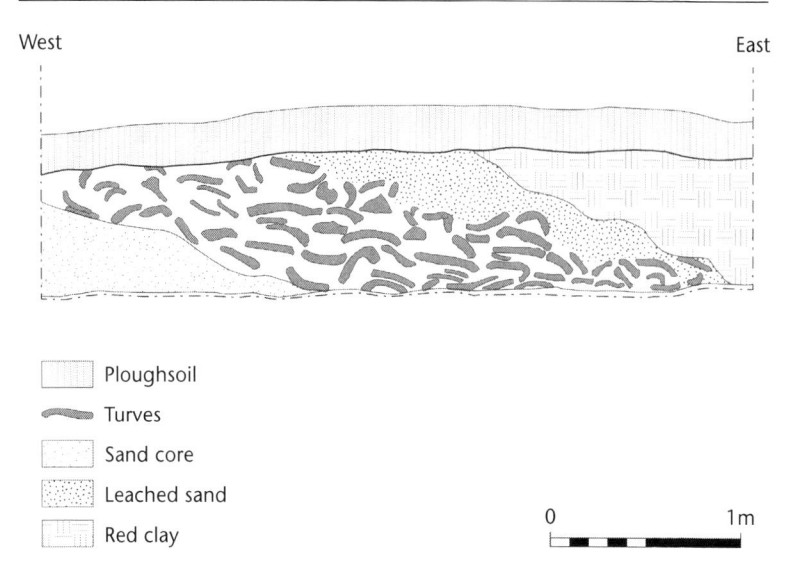

- Ploughsoil
- Turves
- Sand core
- Leached sand
- Red clay

0   1m

Figure 5.1. Cross section through part of the barrow at Upton Pyne, Devon (redrawn by Anne Leaver after Pollard and Russell 1969, fig. 4; reproduced with permission of the Devon Archaeological Society).

Painsthorpe Wold, East Yorkshire, included deposits of whitish loamy earth probably obtained from one of the springs at the foot of the chalk hills on which the monuments were constructed (Mortimer 1905, 119); springs—where water issued forth from the earth—may have been viewed as magical places. The structured use of clays and soils of different colours has been observed in Cornwall (Owoc 2002), where the choice of yellow clay in particular has been linked with an interest in marking solstitial events in barrow architecture: symbolically referencing the sunrise perhaps provided an appropriate metaphor of regeneration for mourners coping with the ontological challenge of death. This may be the case in other regions also: the turf stacked around the eastern edge of the barrow at Bedd Branwen on Anglesey, for example, came from an area with a distinctive yellow subsoil (Lynch 1971, 20). Ethnographic studies of colour indicate that it can be employed to give material form to social identities and cultural values, to mark the passage of time, and to symbolize significant elements of cosmological schemes (e.g. Turner 1967; Coote 1992; Taussig 2009), and funerary rites are exactly the kind of social context in which such concerns are foregrounded.

The materials employed to construct Early Bronze Age barrows were generally from the immediate locality, but that was not always the case.

The barrow at Treiorwerth on Anglesey was composed of a cairn of boulders capped by yellow clay that was not local (Lynch 1971, 42). At Towthorpe, East Yorkshire, barrow C37 covered the inhumation burial of an adult male accompanied by a bronze dagger and flint knife (Mortimer 1905, 6). The mound itself was built of materials from three distinct sources: first, soil from the immediate vicinity of the barrow; second, clay from the area around Burdale, less than 2 kilometres to the west; and third, clay from the vicinity of Duggleby, less than 3 kilometres to the north. The mound was composed of layers of these clays, alternating with layers of soil from the immediate vicinity of the barrow, and Mortimer describes how each kind of clay predominated at the side of the mound nearest the place from which it had been brought. Such practices were not unusual in this region: for example, barrow 86 on Calais Wold included spreads of dark soil on the northern and western side of the monument sourced from the bottom of Bradeham Dale just to the north (Mortimer 1905, 168). The choice of materials from particular places may have given material form to familial relationships, or referenced locations that were especially significant to the deceased during life.

The grave as mappa mundi

Like the components of the mounds themselves, the array of natural materials (both worked and unworked) deposited in Early Bronze Age graves evoked particular landscapes and places. A recent study of bracers has shown that certain types of stone were favoured for the production of these objects, notably tuff from Great Langdale in Cumbria and amphibolite, probably from south Wales or Cornwall (Woodward and Hunter 2011, ch. 3). These were visually appealing materials: it is possible that they were chosen for their distinctive light-green or blue-grey colour, but the source of the stone may also itself have been significant. The use of Langdale tuff for Neolithic polished axes has been discussed in detail (Bradley and Edmonds 1993, 134). Like other Neolithic axe quarries, the quarries on Great Langdale were located in an inaccessible but visually striking location that may have been considered a special place in Neolithic and Early Bronze Age cosmographies (Cooney 1998). Stone was, of course, chosen for its technical properties, but it may also have allowed the power of special places to be incorporated into the mortuary context.

The deposition of objects made from other materials, for example amber, jet, wood, or bone, may likewise have brought the wider landscape into the microtopography of the grave. Amber came from the beaches of north-east England and the Baltic, for example (Beck and Shennan 1991, 29–37), while jet objects are known to derive from particular geological deposits on the Yorkshire coast (Sheridan and Davis 2002). Objects made from bone or wood may have referenced more local landscape settings, calling to mind particular people, activities, and relationships. The cremation burial from Whitehorse Hill, Dartmoor, Devon, was wrapped in a bear skin and accompanied by an array of organic and non-organic materials, all laid on a bed of purple moor grass (Jones 2016). The grave goods included a composite object—possibly a belt—of finely woven nettle fibre and calf-skin, an armband of woven cow-hair decorated with tin rivets, a copper alloy pin, and a basket made from lime bast containing a flint flake, amber, shale, tin and clay beads, and four ear studs of spindle wood. Some of these materials seem quite mundane, yet we should not lose sight of their potential social significance, for they would have evoked particular locations in the social landscape as well as the activities of certain age or gender groups in those places. As such, the materials incorporated into Early Bronze Age mortuary assemblages spoke of different landscape contexts and material properties—the familiar and the foreign, fire and water, land and sea, above ground and below—as well as specific social practices and the relations these sustained (Goldhahn 2012). These were collections of objects that evoked particular cosmographies, and it is therefore no surprise that they were incorporated into narratives of the social world in the grave.

Barrows and the temporality of landscape

The incorporation of different materials into Early Bronze Age barrows illustrates how these monuments were bound into temporal rhythms that relate to broader patterns in the use of the landscape. A fragment of hazelnut shell found among the burnt remains of a pyre beneath barrow III on Snail Down in Wiltshire indicates activity in late summer or early autumn, while bird pellets from in and around the wooden mortuary structure under barrow XVII suggest that this was standing in summer or autumn (Thomas 2005, 283, 101). Charcoal from the old land surface under barrow VI at West Heath, Harting, West Sussex, included bell and ling heathers, indicating that the ground was made ready for the construction of the barrow during the summer months (Drewett 1985, 37). This hints that elements of barrow rituals may have been performed at particular times of year—times that may have had as much to do with the temporality of land use and patterns of movement through the landscape as with the times of death of those buried at these locations.

Such rhythms of engagement with the landscape would have been deeply bound up with personal and community identities (Edmonds 1999), for they may have involved the participation of particular age and gender groups or the meeting of neighbours in places that were already significant elements of collective memory.

The choice and placement of different types of stone in Clava cairns—a regionally distinctive form of Early Bronze Age mortuary monument found in north-east Scotland—suggest that the rituals carried out at these monuments also formed a particular element of the annual cycle linked to broader concepts of landscape and cosmology. At Balnuaran of Clava, the entrance passages in two of the cairns were aligned on the midwinter sunset. Red stones that absorb the light were most prevalent around the south-west of the cairns, while grey and white stones that reflect the light were concentrated on the north-east (Bradley 2000a, 126–7), suggesting that the use of coloured stones in particular parts of these monuments may relate to a desire to mark key points in the solar calendar. In this way, a contrastive symbolism of life and death, light and darkness, became embedded in the monuments themselves, linking mortuary practices to idioms of fertility and regeneration. As at Snail Down, the ceremonies carried out at Clava cairns were linked into temporal rhythms that operated at a landscape scale, and that folded the landscape into the monument through the inclusion of stone (and other materials) that had particular symbolic significance.

Nature and culture in Early Bronze Age barrows

Sometimes the process of barrow-making blurred the boundaries between nature and culture. At Minstead in West Sussex, a natural knoll was enhanced by the construction of a barrow (Drewett 1975). Elsewhere, Early Bronze Age burials were inserted directly into natural mounds, for example at Waterhall Farm, Cambridgeshire (Martin and Denston 1976). At Dunure Road, Ayrshire, a series of Early Bronze Age cists was constructed on a small sandy knoll; after some time, these were capped by a low earthen mound (Duffy 2007). Mullin (2001) suggests that such features were inadvertently mistaken for barrows, but, alternatively, we can suggest that no distinction was drawn between barrows and visually similar 'natural' landforms thought to have been created by ancestors in the distant past (see also Bradley 2000b, 109).

This extended also to materials that formed part of the grave assemblages themselves. A variety of natural objects were included as components of Early Bronze Age burials, often as grave goods alongside other artefacts. Quartz pebbles, for example, have been found in graves in

Scotland and Ireland. At Edmondstown in County Dublin, pit burial 12 comprised an area of dark soil within a stone setting. This contained an upright Cordoned Urn in which was found a small amount of burnt bone and several quartz pebbles (Mount and Harnett 1993, 47). Eight large quartz pebbles were arranged around the head and upper body of the inhumation burial at Forteviot, Perth and Kinross (Brophy and Noble 2009, 16). By contrast, quartz formed part of the grave structure itself at Mains of Scotstown, Aberdeen. Here, a cist containing the inhumation burial of an adult male had been provided with a floor of water-rolled pebbles of quartzite, gneiss, and granite (Ralston 1996, 124). The attractive visual qualities of quartz (which is shiny and reflective) and its unusual physical properties (it emits a greenish spark—triboluminescence—when struck) suggest that it may have been considered to possess other-worldly powers (Darvill 2002; Bradley 2005b).

Fossils too are sometimes included in Early Bronze Age grave assemblages (Brück and Jones 2018). We have already described the cremation burial from barrow G61a at Amesbury in Wiltshire (Ashbee 1985, 51–2) in Chapter 2. This was accompanied by a variety of objects including a fossil crinoid and beads of amber, faience, red steatite, and cowrie shell. There are, in fact, remarkable formal similarities between fossil crinoid stems, segmented faience fusiform beads (Sheridan and Shortland 2003), and shale and jet disc-beads, and it is no surprise that crinoids are often found with beads of other materials that look strikingly similar, as for example at Preshute G1a in Wiltshire (Cunnington 1907, 8–9). Such items may have been seen as beads fashioned by the ancestors, and they call into question any categorical distinction between the 'natural' and the 'cultural'. Elsewhere, fossils form components of mixed assemblages of 'natural' and 'cultural' objects that have been interpreted as the toolkits of ritual specialists. At Langton, North Yorkshire (Greenwell 1877, 138–9), for example, a small group of objects was found at the waist of an elderly female. This included three copper-alloy awls, a worked boar's tusk, a worked beaver's tooth, a pierced animal tooth fragment, a pierced nerita shell, three cowrie shells, a fragment of dentalium shell, a fish vertebra, a jet bead, and a fragment of fossil belemnite: these objects too may have been imbued with supernatural powers.

The construction of barrows and cairns was therefore a process that brought together substances from a variety of sources and contexts, an act of cosmogenesis that ordered the world and its constituent elements (Owoc 2002; 2004; Brittain 2004; Lewis 2007). Often, the aesthetics of the monuments appears to have mattered: aesthetics, of course, give material form to systems of value. The materials from which barrows were composed may have had particular meanings, or may have reminded those constructing the monument of specific places, people, and activities. As such, barrows were composite monuments that embodied relational identities. Their structure and constituent parts created an idealized landscape in miniature—a landscape in which both organic and inorganic elements were meaningful components of the social universe. The layered character of barrow monuments in some regions, for example Wiltshire and East Anglia, is interesting, for this mirrors the practices of wrapping and containment that we have noted in graves of this period (Jones 2010). Barrow-building mapped the deceased and their relationships with places and people, and analogies may have been drawn between the barrow itself and the human body. The construction of the monument therefore helped to transform living relative to dead ancestor: it has been noted, for example, that the outer capping of barrows is often harder and whiter than their inner layers (Owoc 2002, 133). However, human bone was often only one of a variety of substances manipulated and deposited at these monuments, and in regions such as south-west England and Wales the deposition of materials such as quartz, charcoal, and clay (both baked and unbaked) may have been equally important (Jones 2005, 140). Together, stone, wood, earth, clay, and bone were subject to sequences of fragmentation, transformation, and mixing that allowed the participants in barrow rituals to mark the passage of time and understand their place in the world.

Barrows and special places

The location of Early Bronze Age barrows and cairns in the landscape has also been a long-standing area of interest. This varies from region to region. Cornish barrow cemeteries, for example, are often found on elevated locations such as hilltops, plateaus, and ridges (Jones 2005). Most have views of prominent hills, tors, and the sea: Rough Tor, a distinctive and highly visible granite outcrop and the second highest hill in Cornwall, forms the focus of a group of barrow cemeteries on Bodmin Moor, and it seems possible that this feature had a special place in the origin myths of local communities. Interestingly, however, the barrows themselves were not always placed so that they were visible from neighbouring lowlands. In the counties surrounding the border between England and Wales, barrows often cluster on spurs, ridges, and hilltops where there are good views of the surrounding landscape (Johnson 2015). The roughly linear group of monuments at Moel Tŷ-Uchaf in Denbighshire is located on a knoll with views over the Dee valley. The monuments in this region are rarely placed on the highest points of these landscapes, however: the cairns and ring-cairns on the spur and ridge at Cefn Panagored, Clwyd, for example, were built in the lee of higher ground (Johnson 2015, 152).

In some regions, distinctive natural features were incorporated into barrows and cairns. Two of the barrows on Treen Common in Cornwall were built over rock outcrops that would have formed prominent elements of the natural landscape before the barrow cemetery was built (Jones 2005, 69–70). The base of the tor at Tregarrick in the same county is surrounded by a cairn of small stones (Jones 2005, 45); this composite monument forms the southern end of a linear barrow cemetery (Figure 5.2), and it defies categorization within a scheme that divides nature and culture. Other Early Bronze Age barrows also had non-human foci. Harding and Healy (2007, 213–15) identify a number of barrows where trees may have formed the central feature. There were tree holes at the centre of barrows 1 and 9 at Raunds in Northamptonshire, and in both cases the primary graves were cut into these features. At Holme-next-the-Sea in Norfolk, the inverted base of a fallen tree trunk was placed at the centre of a subcircular timber palisade (Figure 5.3; Brennand and Taylor 2003). The bark had been removed and the trunk carefully trimmed before it was laid in this position: the signatures of fifty-one different axes could be identified, suggesting the involvement of a significant number of people. Rituals often involve phases in which the natural order of things is challenged, and the deliberate inversion of the tree trunk may have been part of this process (Brennand and Taylor 2003 70–1; Evans 2015, 1117). The tree trunk was an oak, and it seems possible that the particular qualities of this tree—longevity and durability, for example—were of metaphoric value in the rituals carried out at this location.

Elsewhere, barrows were built on or near other kinds of interesting natural features, such as dolines or sinkholes. Tilley (1999, ch. 6) has discussed the possible link between the concentration of barrows and sinkholes on Bronkham Hill in Dorset, but such relationships have been identified elsewhere too. Several barrows constructed directly over sinkholes have been noted in the Yorkshire Wolds, for example barrow 41 at Riggs and barrow 219 on Huggate Wold (Mortimer 1905, 182, 310). Indeed, the similarity between Early Bronze Age pond barrows and features such as dolines is perhaps no coincidence: the latter may represent a response to natural features of this kind, a ritual re-enactment of an act of world-creation in the ancestral past.

Both dolines and pond barrows often retain water, and an interest in water sources is evident in the siting of other Early Bronze Age barrows. At Ladywell, Imber, Wiltshire, a number of barrows are clustered around

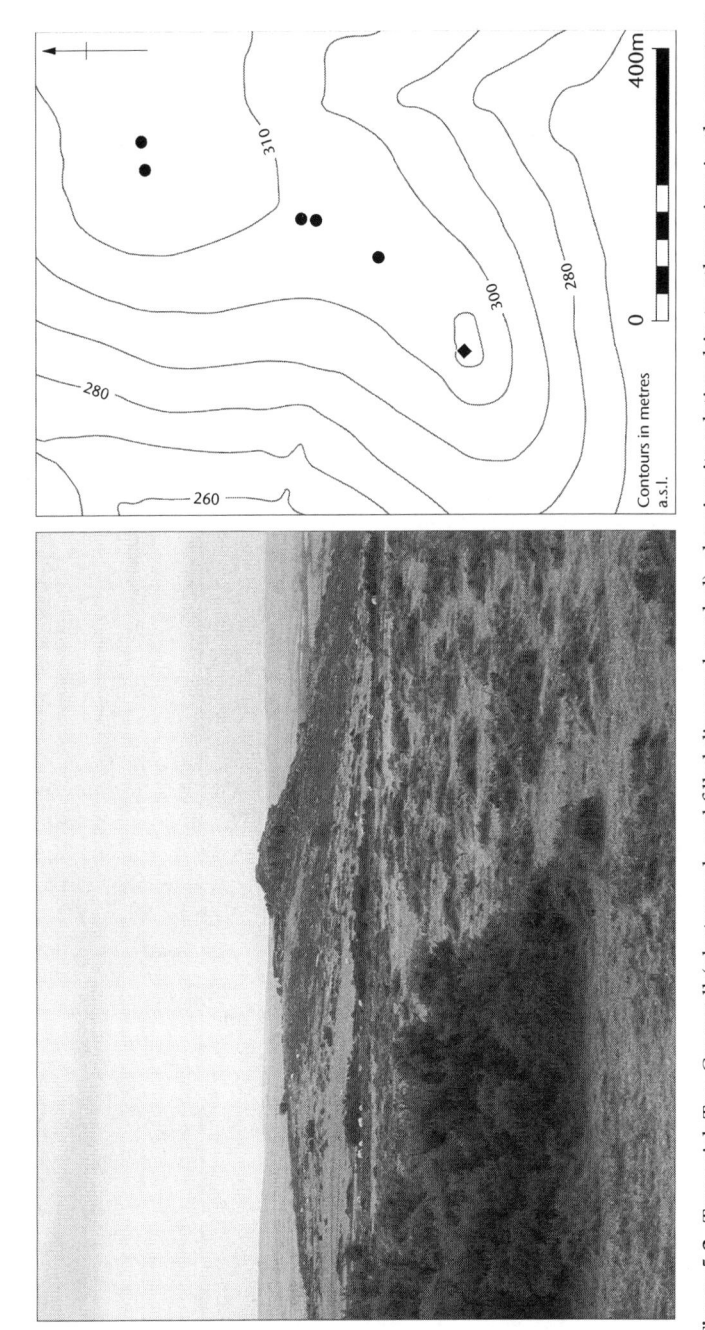

Figure 5.2. Tregarrick Tor, Cornwall (photograph and filled-diamond symbol), showing its relationship to other cairns in the cemetery (reproduced with permission of Andy Jones; redrawn by Anne Leaver).

Figure 5.3. The inverted tree trunk at the centre of the monument at Holme-next-the-Sea, Norfolk (© Historic England).

a spring (McOmish et al. 2002, 46–8), and many of the other barrow cemeteries on Salisbury Plain are located at the heads of valleys on the spring line. Similar relationships are evident in many other regions: the barrows on Banc Gorddwr in Powys, for example, lie immediately adjacent to the sources of several rivers that rise on this hill (Johnson 2015, 193). The construction of barrows at such locations—close to sources of life-sustaining water—may have had particular metaphoric value in the context of funerary rites, allowing ideas regarding the renewal of life in the face of death (or rebirth into the world of the ancestors) to be communicated and explored. Springs may also have been viewed as entrances to the underworld; the sudden appearance of sinkholes may have been seen in a similar way.

The location of Early Bronze Age barrow cemeteries in river valleys has also long been noted (e.g. Grinsell 1941, 75). The barrows at Irthlingborough, Northamptonshire, were built on the floodplain of the River Nene (Harding and Healy 2007), some near channels of this anastomosing river, others on islands. The small barrow cemetery at Over in Cambridgeshire was constructed on an island amidst several channels of the River Great Ouse (Garrow et al. 2014). The many barrows located elsewhere on the floodplain of the Great Ouse would themselves have become islands in winter as the floodwaters rose (Woodward 2000, 59). These were landscapes of transformation, liminal spaces in which the flow of water brought life but could also herald destruction, and it is perhaps no surprise that they were viewed as suitable places in which to build mortuary monuments. A similar set of ideas may explain the unusual location of the barrows on the seashore at Holme-next-the-Sea in Norfolk (Brennand and Taylor 2003; Robertson 2016).

It has often been observed that barrows located in river valleys tend to be arranged in linear groupings parallel to the river itself. Such linear cemeteries perhaps echoed patterns of movement along the river valleys: the dispersed groupings of barrows that follow the Summergil and Knobley Brooks in the Walton Basin, for example, lie along a natural routeway linking the lowlands of Herefordshire to the uplands of Powys (Johnson 2015, 220), while modern roads and a railway run alongside the linear groupings of barrows at Bromfield in Shropshire, which lies at the confluence of the Rivers Teme and Corve (Figure 5.4; Stanford 1982, figs 2 and 3). An association with routeways hints that death was seen as a journey, with water acting as a powerful medium of transformation (Fowler 2013, 193). Linear barrow cemeteries in other parts of the landscape may have encapsulated similar ideas, and the relationship between barrows and ancient routeways at much higher elevations in the landscape, such as the Dorset Ridgeway and the Icknield Way, has long been noted (e.g. Fleming 1971, 162). The barrows on Huggate Wold in East Yorkshire, for example, follow a routeway towards the coast (Mortimer 1905, 299), while those on Lansdown near Bath in Somerset are located on a ridge along which a busy modern road also runs. Travel, of course, involves processes of transformation; travellers confront the dangers of the unknown and the foreign and these landscapes may therefore have been viewed as liminal spaces appropriate for the construction of mortuary monuments, for the dead must also journey through time and space. The linear arrangement of barrows may also reference the idea that journeying to distant, other-worldly places was a particular source of cosmological power (Garwood 2012, 312).

Landscape and cosmology in the Early Bronze Age

Elsewhere in north-west Europe barrow landscapes have been viewed as a core element of Bronze Age belief systems which divided the cosmos into sky, earth, and underworld (Kristiansen and Larsson 2005, fig. 167; Bradley 2006; 2009, 150–75). In Scandinavia, for example, barrows are

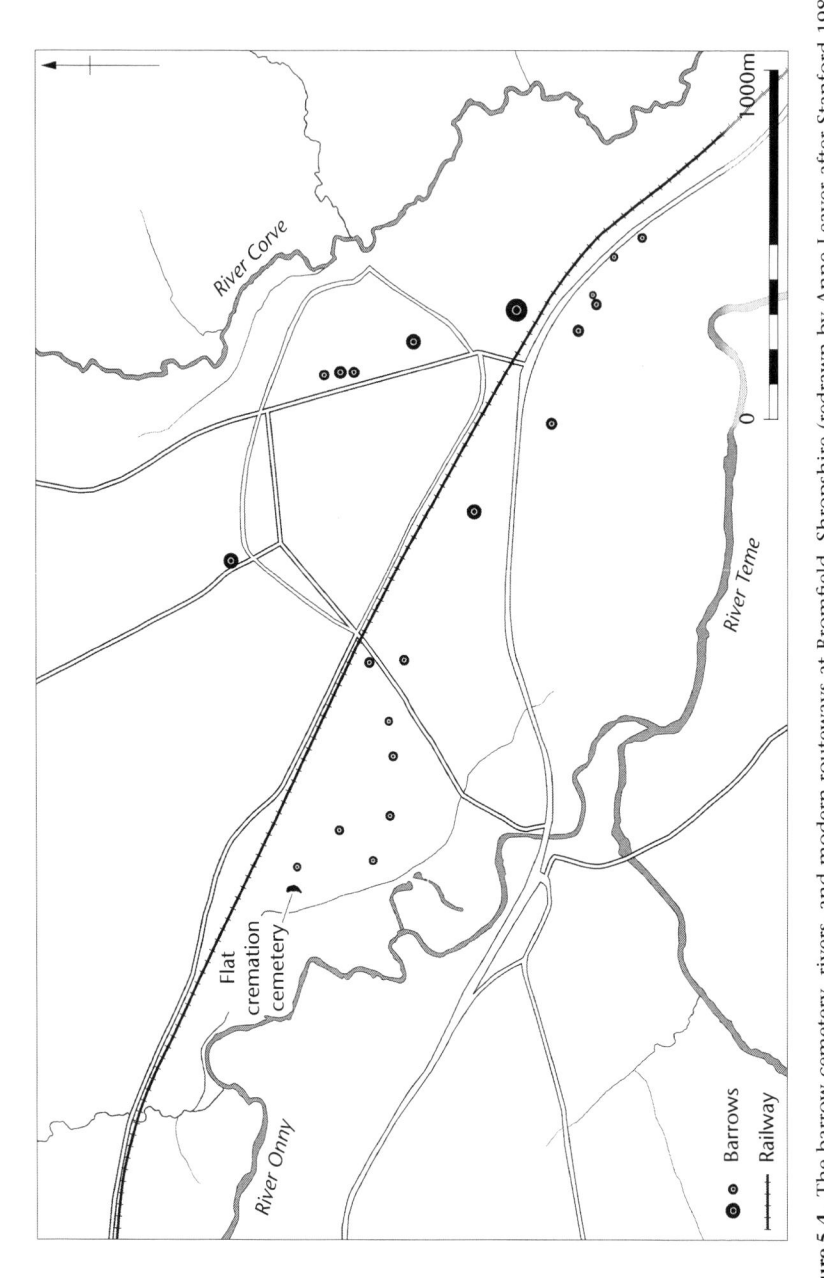

Figure 5.4. The barrow cemetery, rivers, and modern routeways at Bromfield, Shropshire (redrawn by Anne Leaver after Stanford 1982, fig. 3; reproduced with permission of the Prehistoric Society).

Social landscapes

found on hilltops and in other elevated positions. Metalwork was deposited beneath the waters in bogs and rivers, while settlements occupy the 'middle ground'—a land of the living sandwiched between the realms of gods, spirits, and ancestors. The landscape context of barrow cemeteries in Britain and Ireland may hint at similar cosmologies, although here, as we have seen, barrows are found not only on ridges, spurs and hilltops, but also on valley bottoms and close to water. Of course, it would be overly simplistic to assume that neither the uplands nor places such as bogs were part of the lived landscapes of Early Bronze Age communities, for it is evident that these were locations where activities such as hunting and fowling, the grazing of cattle, and the collection of materials such as reeds and stone were carried out (e.g. Coles and Coles 1986), yet it is clear that different meanings were ascribed to different parts of the landscape. Here we will discuss the meanings ascribed to watery places of various sorts, and in particular the act of journeying across the waters, as this will allow us begin to assess the relationship between people and landscape not only in the early part of the period, but also in the Middle and Late Bronze Age.

In Scandinavia it has been suggested that Bronze Age cosmologies centred around the daily travels of the sun; the movement of the celestial bodies is, of course, a matter of concern in all agricultural societies. Studies of rock art and of the iconography engraved on bronze objects such as razors suggest that by day the sun was thought to have travelled through the sky in a horse-drawn chariot, and by night to have been transported by boat through a watery underworld (Gelling and Davidson 1969; Kaul 1998). A symbolic connection between death and travel by water has been proposed (Bradley 2006) that may also be visible in Britain and Ireland. We have already seen that barrow cemeteries are often arranged along river valleys. Other barrows overlook the sea: an Early Bronze Age barrow located just behind the beach at Dunure Road, Ayrshire, had extensive views not of the land but of the Firth of Clyde (Duffy 2007). One of the stone cists beneath the barrow was boat-shaped, with a stone 'prow' pointing towards the island of Arran, while stones with rippled surfaces were chosen as covers for several other cists.

There are a number of other Early Bronze Age burials that were placed in containers that resemble boats or, in a few cases, may actually have been reused boats. At Seafield West, near Inverness, Highland, a boat-shaped log coffin with a pointed 'prow' and a squared-off 'stern' was found in a grave placed off-centre within a ring-ditch (Cressey and Sheridan 2003). Only a few fragments of human bone had survived, but the coffin is likely to have originally contained a crouched inhumation. Two boat-shaped coffins (one with a lid that also resembled a boat) were found beneath the barrow at Loose Howe in Yorkshire (Elgee and Elgee 1949). Although the excavators suggested that one of these was a reused dugout canoe, others have argued that this is unlikely (Heal 1986). At Barns Farm, Dalgety, Fife (Watkins 1982), an inhumation burial and a deposit of cremated bone were laid in what may have been a coracle: a thin soil stain indicates that these bodies were originally deposited in an organic container that was U-shaped in cross section, squared at one end and gently shelving at the other. Chemical analysis suggests that the container may have been leather, and the excavator proposes that it may have been a coracle with a wicker frame and hide cover. Such finds suggest that passage to the afterlife may have been thought to involve a journey by water.

Enduring metaphors: water, travel, and transformation from the Early to the Late Bronze Age

There are other interesting contexts in which parts of boats—or objects that resemble boats—have been found both in the Early Bronze Age and in later parts of the period. Hollowed-out tree trunks were used as troughs at burnt mound sites, for example at Greatisland, County Wexford (Hull 2015), and Killoran, County Tipperary (Gregory 2005), and it is possible that these referenced dugout canoes; these sites date to the Early and Middle Bronze Age respectively. At Nant Farm, Porth Neigwl, Gwynedd, a timber from a sewn-plank boat formed the base of an Early Bronze Age plank-built timber trough beneath a burnt mound (Smith et al. 2017). Burnt mounds comprise kidney-shaped deposits of burnt stone with a trough at the centre. It is thought that the trough was filled with water which was heated by the addition of hot stone. Various functions have been proposed for burnt mounds, including cooking, brewing, and bathing (Barfield and Hodder 1987; Quinn and Moore 2008; Ó Néill 2009), although recent palaeoenvironmental and multielement analysis at a number of Irish sites suggests that they may have been used for the washing, fulling, felting, and dyeing of cloth (Brown et al. 2016); the presence of a wooden launder at Nant Farm and of loom-weight fragments and sheep bone from the burnt mound at Green Park in Berkshire (Barclay 2003, table 4.23) hints that they may have performed similar roles in Britain.

Whatever the case, burnt mounds were sites where a range of heat-mediated transformative technologies were carried out. With their requirement for water, they were generally located next to streams or other water sources, often at the margins of the settled landscape.

The burnt mound at Green Park, for example, lay along one side of a palaeochannel at the northern edge of a Late Bronze Age settlement (Brossler et al. 2003, fig. 3.7), while Irish burnt mounds tend to be at a distance from other contemporary sites (Ó Néill 2009). It is no surprise that, located in liminal spaces and associated with transformative activities, burnt mounds should sometimes incorporate references to travel (in the form of boat fragments or boat-like troughs) or death: the trough at Tomies East, County Kerry, has been interpreted as a reused log coffin (Dunne and Doolin 2001, 23), while at Inchagreenoge, County Limerick, the skull of a young adult male was found at a spring that fed a trough dated to the Middle Bronze Age (Taylor 2004). As such, it is likely that the activities at burnt mounds were accompanied by rituals of various sorts: a set of graduated yew pipes was placed on the base of an Early Bronze Age wood-lined trough at Charlesland, County Wicklow (Figure 5.5; Holmes and Molloy 2006), suggesting that music accompanied the activities that took place at this site.

Fragments of sewn-plank boats have also occasionally been reused in timber structures such as bridges (van de Noort 2009). At Testwood Lakes in Hampshire, a boat cleat was found close to the remains of three

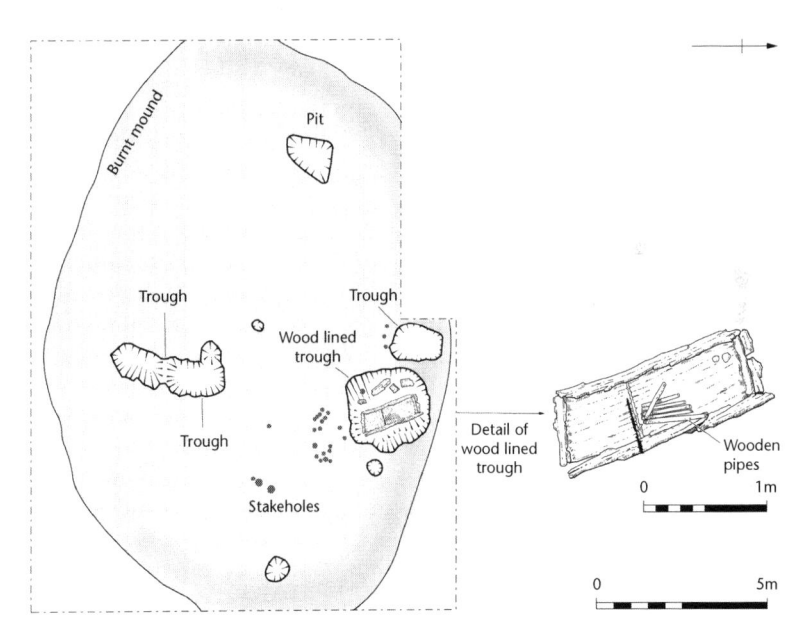

Figure 5.5. The burnt mound with wooden trough and pipes at Charlesland, County Wicklow (reproduced with permission of Margaret Gowen and Bernice Molloy; redrawn by Anne Leaver).

Early–Middle Bronze Age bridges built to cross the River Blackwater. It had been removed from a boat plank, suggesting that parts of boats may have been reused in the construction of the bridges. At Goldcliff in Gwent, two boat planks were reused in a Late Bronze Age timber structure that has been interpreted as a trackway crossing a channel in the intertidal zone of the Severn estuary. At both sites, it is evident that travel—and in particular the act of crossing liminal places such as rivers—was accompanied by ritual acts: two skulls were found at Goldcliff (Bell et al. 2000), while a Middle Bronze Age rapier was deposited in the river at Testwood Lakes (https://www.wessexarch.co.uk/our-work/testwood-lakes).

This is corroborated by evidence from other sites. At Vauxhall in London, a wooden structure consisting of a row of paired vertical posts may represent the remains of a bridge. Next to one of the posts, two Middle Bronze Age spearheads had been thrust point down into the mud (Cotton 2000, 16-17). At Cloncreen Bog in County Offaly, a series of anthropomorphic figurines were found, all close to trackways or platforms, most of which date to the Middle and Late Bronze Age (Figure 5.6; McDermott et al. 2003). The figures were carved from alder and comprised lengths of roundwood, worked to a blunt point at one end, and with a well-defined 'neck' and 'head' at the other; each also displayed a series of incised parallel notches across the body. The anthropomorphic figure found at Ballachulish, Highland, was found in 1880 overlooking a dangerous stretch of water where Lough Leven meets the sea on the west coast of Scotland (Christison 1881; Coles 1990, 320). Dating to the Earliest Iron Age, it too is made of alder, with quartzite pebbles for eyes. The pelvic area is deeply carved and appears to show that the figure is female; she is holding a phallic-shaped object in her hands. Placed at crossing points and other spaces of transition, anthropomorphic figures such as these indicate that travellers sought supernatural protection to face the perils of the journey;

Figure 5.6. Anthropomorphic figure from Cloncreen Bog, County Offaly (reproduced with permission of Conor McDermott and Michael Stanley, with slight alterations by Anne Leaver).

they also suggest that such locations were viewed as liminal places in which encounters with the other world could occur.

If travel was viewed as a dangerous and transformative process requiring ritual acts of various sorts, it is no surprise that boats themselves often appear to have been ritually decommissioned. The Dover boat (Figure 5.7), discovered in 1992 in the silts of a former channel of the River Dour in Kent, was partly dismantled and several of its structural elements were deliberately damaged to render it unusable (Champion 2004; Clark 2004, 12). The transoms of several of the eight logboats found in a palaeochannel at Must Farm in Cambridgeshire had been removed so that the vessels would sink (http://www.mustfarm.com/bronze-age-river/discoveries/); the logboats were not deposited at the same time, however, but span the Middle and Late Bronze Age. Fragments of a sewn-plank boat dating to the Late Bronze Age were deposited alongside other votive offerings including two bronze chapes, an amber bead, and the near complete skeleton of a dog in a river channel at Caldicot in Monmouthshire (Nayling and Caseldine 1997; Champion 2004; van de Noort 2009). As objects that had crossed boundaries, boats and their fragments were themselves powerful and potentially dangerous; this meant both that they needed to be disposed of with care at the end of their lives, and that fragments of boats could act as a means of marking out or drawing attention to liminal spaces.

Aspects of the materiality of the boats themselves also hint at the ritualization of travel. One of the Must Farm canoes is decorated with incised linear motifs (http://www.mustfarm.com/bronze-age-river/

Figure 5.7. The Dover boat during installation in Dover Museum (reproduced with permission of Canterbury Archaeological Trust).

discoveries/). Decoration can have a protective function, particularly in contexts where social boundaries are crossed (Braithwaite 1982), but it also draws attention to significant people, objects, and practices. Other Bronze Age canoes were very long: the Lurgan canoe from County Galway is over 14 metres in length (Cribbin et al. 1999)—far longer than required for fishing or fowling in inland waterways. It is possible that such vessels had a ceremonial role, for example as war canoes or in travels to exchange socially significant objects, and activities such as these may have formed a component of rites of passage (Helms 1988), for example initiation into adulthood. The symbolic meanings of the materials from which boats were constructed may also have been important (Helms 2009). The Dover boat, for example, is made of oak planks tied together with yew withies. In Celtic mythology and more recent folklore, oak and yew were considered to have had magical qualities: oak, for example, is long-lived, while yew is evergreen, so that both the symbolic potential and the technical properties of these woods may have been viewed as essential to the successful construction and use of this vessel.

Special places in the Middle and Late Bronze Age

It is evident from the foregoing discussion that travel by water was viewed as a dangerous, transformative activity. It has, of course, long been recognized that throughout the Bronze Age watery places such as bogs and rivers were considered sacred spaces in which aspects of the other world could be encountered. In the Middle and Late Bronze Age in particular, these were foci for the votive deposition of metalwork, including elaborate weaponry and ceremonial objects (e.g. Torbrügge 1971; Levy 1982; Bradley 1990; Fontijn 2002; Becker 2013). In the Netherlands, it has been argued that different categories of metal object were deposited in different parts of the landscape (Fontijn 2002). Small tools and simple ornaments have been found in and around Bronze Age settlements; items such as axes and spearheads were deposited in streams and marshes, while 'high-status' objects that may have spoken of supraregional identities, such as swords and elaborate ornaments, were consigned to rivers. Similar patterns can be seen in Britain and Ireland (Becker 2013). Large quantities of Bronze Age metalwork, particularly objects such as rapiers, swords, and spearheads, have been recovered from the Thames, for example (York 2002). The enormous deposit of Late Bronze Age metalwork found in a bog at Dowris, County Offaly (Eogan 1983, 117; Rosse 1984), included twenty-six horns, a cauldron, three buckets, and forty-eight crotals (rattle-pendants that may have functioned as musical instruments), as well as tools and weapons. These objects appear to have been originally deposited in open water, and it can be suggested that this was a location that saw repeated acts of deposition over a lengthy period of time.

Recently it has increasingly been recognized that metal objects were often deposited close to watery places as well in the waters themselves, for example on hillsides overlooking streams and rivers, or near springs (Yates and Bradley 2010). A hoard of socketed axes, bronze ornaments, amber beads, and two unique bronze cups from Glentanar in Aberdeenshire (Pearce 1971; 1977) was deposited on a hillside above a tributary of the River Dee, for example, while a collection of some fifty large spearheads and several other objects was deposited in a pit next to a spring at Broadward in Shropshire (Bradley et al. 2015). Deposition often focused on significant locations along these watercourses, including sources, confluences, and mouths: particular concentrations of metalwork, including rapiers and swords, have been found at fording points on the River Shannon, such as Keelogue, County Galway, and Athlone, County Westmeath (Bourke 2001), while a large hoard of tools and weapons was deposited in a pit overlooking the Great Stour where it cuts through the North Downs at Crundale, Kent (Yates and Bradley 2010, 62).

Inland waterways were not the only focus for such activities, and the deposition of objects also occurred on and near the coast. Two Late Bronze Age spearheads, discovered at different times, have been found on Thurlestone beach in Devon (Needham et al. 2013, 21), for example, while a dispersed scatter of finds from the foreshore of Swansea Bay includes a decorated Late Bronze Age spearhead, Middle Bronze Age rapiers, and a large Late Bronze Age pin (Gwilt et al. 2013). Some coastal finds are associated with dramatic and eye-catching locations: a scrap hoard was found in a cleft in the rock on the north-west slopes of St Michael's Mount in Cornwall, a striking rocky island connected to the mainland by a causeway only at low tide (Knight et al. 2015, 34, cat. no. 43). Other finds have good views of the sea: finds of Earliest Iron Age axes from Dorset, particularly those from Portland and Purbeck, were often deposited in locations overlooking the English Channel (Roberts et al. 2015, 384).

Away from the coast, wet places were not the only significant locations to be marked out through the votive deposition of metalwork and other objects. Like St Michael's Mount, some of these may have been considered special places (Cowie 2004; Jones 2012, 140). Finds from the cave at Heathery Burn in County Durham, for example, include bronze swords, spearheads, tools, chariot fittings, and a bucket; a gold bracelet and lock-ring; objects of bone, antler, jet, and amber; pottery; and human and animal bone (Greenwell 1894; Britton 1968). Caves may have been viewed as entries to the underworld, liminal locations between the world of the living and the world of the dead where rites of passage and other transformative processes could be carried out; this may explain the presence of metalworking debris, including a bronze mould, ingot fragment, and casting jet, at Heathery Burn (Britton 1968, GB.55, 10(6)).

However, metalwork was not only deposited in places associated with the underworld such as bogs and caves. Other locations may have been associated with the upper levels of a tripartite cosmological scheme. In 1692, for example, a gold bowl or hat of probable Late Bronze Age date was found in a bog on the Devil's Bit, County Tipperary (Eogan 1981, 348-9), a hill with a striking profile that features prominently in more recent local folklore; unfortunately this item is now lost. The assemblage of sword and spearhead fragments found close to a major gap in the Chiltern ridge at Ivinghoe in Buckinghamshire had been deliberately broken: the swords had been chopped into multiple pieces and one was badly bent (Dalwood 1987), perhaps as acts of ritualized destruction. The Roseberry Topping hoard from North Yorkshire contained a bronze mould and scrap, along with three socketed axes, a spearhead, gouge, chisel, and knife (Pearce 2006, 47-53). It was hidden in a rock cleft near a spring, halfway up a hill with an unusual and dramatic profile.

There is an interesting relationship between Late Bronze Age hoards and hillforts. A large hoard of horse-harness fittings was found at Parc-y-Meirch (Sheppard 1941), at the base of a crag beneath the ramparts on the west side of the hillfort at Dinorben, Clwyd. At Mooghaun, County Clare, labourers constructing the West Clare Railway in 1854 found over 150 Late Bronze Age gold ornaments including collars and bracelets (Eogan 1983, 69–73). These appear to have been deposited in a stone chamber at the edge of a lake at the foot of Mooghaun hillfort. The votive deposition of objects in or close to water below hillforts can be seen elsewhere. In County Armagh, one of a pair of hillforts, Haughey's Fort, was built during the Late Bronze Age (Mallory 1995). The Tamlaght hoard, found in a bog some 700 metres south-west of the site, comprised a bowl, cup, and ring imported from the Continent alongside a sword (Warner 2006), while just 200 metres to the north-east, an artificial pool known as the King's Stables produced clay mould fragments for the production of swords and part of a human skull (Figure 5.8; Lynn 1977). One kilometre to the east of Haughey's Fort lies Navan Fort, occupied from the Late Bronze Age onwards,

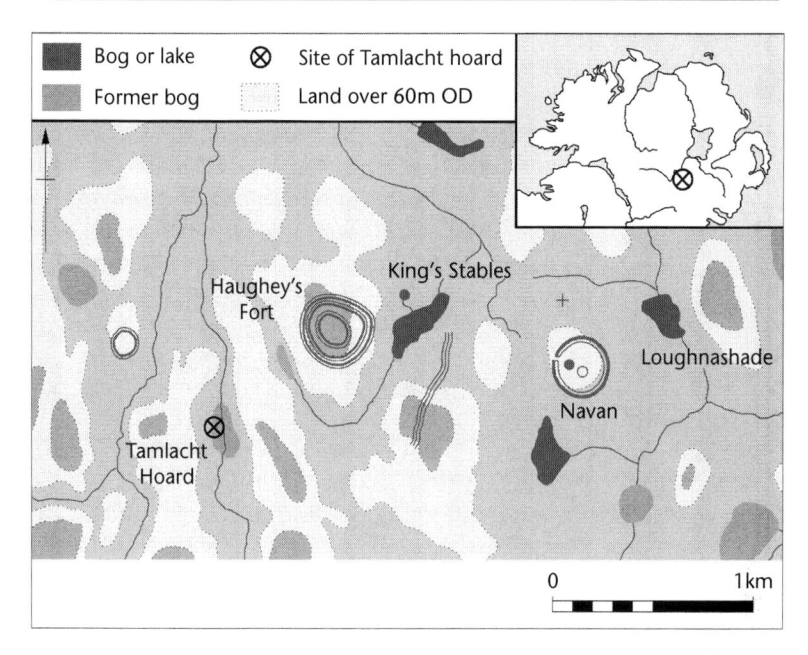

Figure 5.8. The relationship between hillforts, lakes, and votive deposits at Navan, County Armagh (reproduced with permission of Richard Warner, with slight alterations by Anne Leaver).

although the main *floruit* of activity there can be dated to 400–100 BC (Lynn 1997). Towards the end of that period, four Iron Age horns with elaborate La Tène decoration were deposited in the lake of Loughnashade some 300 metres to the east, suggesting an element of continuity in the symbolism attached to particular landscape features.

The association between hoards and hillforts can, of course, be interpreted as indicating that hillforts were high-status settlements whose occupants were able to amass quantities of wealth in the form of metal objects. Yet, as already noted in Chapter 4, excavations in the hillfort of Mooghaun itself produced very few finds (Grogan 2005), suggesting that it may be simplistic to apply such blanket interpretations to these sites. Large hoards, such as those from Mooghaun and Dinorben, may represent objects belonging to many people. Hillforts were frequently constructed in prominent and highly visible positions (Harding 2012, 15); the presence of earlier monuments such as round barrows in many hillforts suggests that these were locations where communities may have come together for a variety of social and ceremonial activities long before the construction of ramparts or ditches. It is possible to suggest that these were special places, and that the deposition of metalwork and the construction of hillforts were two different ways of marking their importance in the landscape.

The social and ritual significance of metalworking in the Bronze Age may explain why copper ores (like Neolithic axes before them) were sometimes sourced from striking places in the landscape, often in upland settings that may have been at a distance from contemporary settlement. Although the majority of Bronze Age copper mines identified in Britain have yielded dates around 1800–1700 BC, the extensive complex of shafts and galleries on the Great Orme near Llandudno in Conwy were in use throughout the Middle Bronze Age and into the Late Bronze Age (Dutton et al. 1994). These are in a particularly spectacular setting, located on a dramatic limestone headland that juts into the Irish Sea. The only known copper-smelting site in Britain has been found here too (Smith 2015; Williams 2013): copper-smelting slag and prills were recovered from in and around a small charcoal-rich pit of Late Bronze Age date located on a natural terrace part way down a series of sea cliffs on the east side of the peninsula. The selection of such a location for smelting activities is interesting, for it calls to mind the deliberate siting of Neolithic axe quarries in inaccessible but often dramatic places (Cooney 1998); indeed, the choice of such a liminal location for the transformative activity of smelting may be no coincidence.

Just as watery places, hilltops, and mountains were significant elements of Middle and Late Bronze Age cosmographies, so too there was a continued interest in the skies and celestial phenomena during this period, and this suggests elements of commonality with the belief systems reconstructed by Kaul (1998) for the Nordic Bronze Age. We have already seen in Chapter 4 that many roundhouses of the period were oriented east and south-east towards the rising sun. Although stone monuments were no longer constructed during the Middle and Late Bronze Age across most of lowland Britain, in Ireland and Scotland stone circles, stone rows, and small hengiform monuments continued to be built right through the period. At Ballymeanoch in mid-Argyll, cremated bone sealed in the socket of a stone that formed part of a stone row has been dated to c.1200 BC (Sheridan 2005), while charcoal from a stone hole in the short stone row at Ardnacross, northern Mull, has produced a similar date (Martlew and Ruggles 1996, 126). The cremated remains of an adolescent male were deposited at the centre of the recumbent stone circle at Drombeg, County Cork, and produced a Late Bronze Age radiocarbon date (Fahy 1959; O'Brien 1992, 33), while Late Bronze Age pottery was sealed beneath the bank surrounding the stone circle at Grange, County Limerick (Roche 2004).

As in the Neolithic, these monuments often indicate an interest in the movement of celestial bodies. The stone rows of northern Mull were oriented towards the southernmost rising and setting points of the moon at major standstill (Martlew and Ruggles 1996). At Glengorm, for example, the moon rises over Ben More, the highest mountain on Mull, at this point in the lunar cycle (Martlew and Ruggles 1996, 122–3). Drombeg, like the other recumbent stone circles of south-west Ireland, comprises stones that are carefully graduated in size, with the tallest pair creating an entranceway to the north-east (Fahy 1959). Opposite these and to the south-west lies the recumbent stone, over which the sun sets at midwinter. It should be noted that the dating of some of these monuments remains a matter of discussion, however. The cremation deposit at the centre of Drombeg, for example, may not be contemporary with the construction of the stone circle; the recumbent stone circles of north-east Scotland—which display interesting but possibly coincidental similarities to those of south-west Ireland—have been dated to the Late Neolithic and Early Bronze Age, but many of these monuments were reused, often as a focus for mortuary rites, during the Late Bronze Age (Welfare 2011). Likewise, the Ballymeanoch stone rows form part of a complex of ceremonial monuments, most of which can be dated to the late third and early second millennium BC (Scott 1991; Cook et al. 2010). Even if the evidence for later Bronze Age activities at such sites can be viewed as episodes of reuse, however, they indicate a continued interest in the movement of celestial bodies through the skies.

Field systems and land division in the Middle and Late Bronze Age

The preceding sections are important for two reasons. Firstly, the evident interest in watery places, caves, and hilltops suggests that the kind of tripartite cosmological structuring of the landscape into sky, earth, and underworld suggested for the Scandinavian Bronze Age may also be visible in Britain, not only during the early part of the period, but during the Middle and Late Bronze Age too. Secondly, it is clear that locations such as springs and mountaintops could be viewed as sacred places.

This has important implications for our models of human-landscape interaction during this period. Although it is widely accepted that metalwork from bogs and rivers can be interpreted as votive offerings, and hence that Bronze Age people's understanding of the world was very different to our own, this has had relatively little impact on how evidence for economic activities, particularly farming, is interpreted.

Perhaps the most significant restructuring of the Bronze Age landscape took place during the Middle Bronze Age (Barrett 1994; Brück 2000; Yates 2007). Prior to this, funerary and ceremonial monuments dominate the landscape, but from the middle of the second millennium BC, settlements and field systems provide the most extensive and visible evidence of human activity across much of Britain. These originate in the period 1800–1500 BC (English 2013, 149), though most date to the subsequent centuries. The ditched boundaries which form a series of rectilinear fields at Monkton Road, Minster, Kent are a particularly early example: dates on charred cereal remains indicate that these were built around 1900–1700 BC (Martin et al. 2012).

The form and structure of Bronze Age field systems vary. Curvilinear walls and banks forming small clusters of fields around individual settlements have been identified in many upland regions, for example in Derbyshire and on Dartmoor, although their dating remains unclear. Bradley (1978) coined the phrase aggregate field systems for these, arguing that they appear to have developed gradually (and in a fairly unplanned and organic way) over a period of time (Figure 5.9). At Gardom's Edge in Derbyshire, for instance, the stone banks defining individual plots varied significantly in height and width and followed a meandering course (Barnatt et al. 2017, 86–9). These features can best be interpreted as the result of protracted, episodic, and informal clearance activities: they developed gradually over a period of time, with the addition of stones from both sides contributing to changes in the direction and character of the boundaries.

In contrast, coaxial field systems appear to have been laid out in a systematic manner, often across large areas of the landscape (Figure 5.10). As the name suggests, these follow a dominant axis, with rectilinear fields creating a highly ordered landscape. The best-known coaxial field systems are found on Dartmoor, where extensive survey by Fleming (1988) has identified a series of field systems dating to the Middle Bronze Age around the lower margins of the moorland. The apparently planned layout of these, and their careful positioning relative to each other, have been taken to suggest that they were built in a single phase of expansion onto the moorland. This has been interpreted as indicating a drive to intensify agricultural production in order to generate a surplus for exchange and to feed a growing population (Barrett 1980a, 90; 1994, 148–9; Bradley 1984, 94). In turn, this has been linked to an increasing concern to control resources by defining and bounding separate landholdings. Similar coaxial field systems have now been identified in many other regions, notably in East Anglia and the Thames valley. In the latter region, they have been

Social landscapes

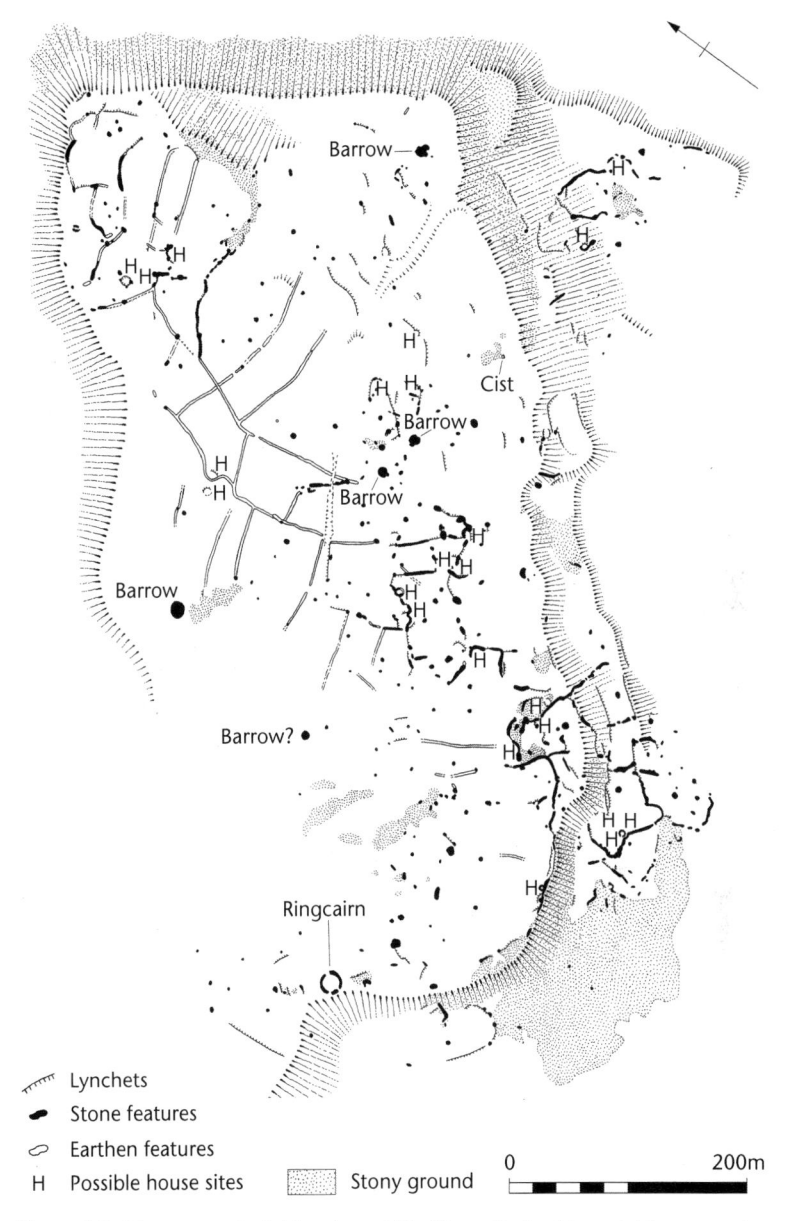

Figure 5.9. The aggregate field system at Big Moor, Derbyshire, which appears to have developed organically over a period of time (reproduced with permission of John Barnatt, Bill Bevan, and Mark Edmonds, with slight alterations by Anne Leaver; based on a survey undertaken by John Barnatt and Stewart Ainsworth for the Peak District National Park Authority and Royal Commission on the Historical Monuments of England).

Figure 5.10. Coaxial field system around Rippon Tor, Dartmoor, Devon (redrawn by Anne Leaver after Butler 1991b, map 5).

linked to the production of an agricultural surplus to support an emerging elite by providing for specialist craftsmen and obtaining prestige goods through exchange (Yates 2007, 122–6). Yet it is not always easy to sustain narratives of unilinear evolution: in parts of southern England, for example Brigmerston Down in Wiltshire (English 2013, 44), the extensive coaxial field systems of the Middle Bronze Age were replaced in the Late Bronze Age by smaller, aggregate systems. Elsewhere, for example in the Thames valley, coaxial field systems were built during both the Middle and Late Bronze Age, but they fell out of use during the Early Iron Age (Yates 2007, 36).

What is striking about many interpretations of coaxial field systems is that they impose a proto-capitalist rationalism onto the past. It is assumed that field boundaries were constructed in order to intensify production and to maximize economic output, and that the appearance of field systems indicates that land was viewed as an alienable commodity. This implies an exploitative relationship with landscape that is characteristic of post-Enlightenment Western society but may not be applicable in a Bronze Age context (Brück 2000). The discussion in the preceding sections suggests that Bronze Age landscapes were not viewed solely as an economic resource but were composed of a constellation of places that had cultural meaning and symbolic significance. Undoubtedly this affected how people engaged with the landscape, not only when they were depositing metalwork but also when they were tending crops or herding cattle. In other words, a model which sees Dartmoor's field systems as indicating colonization of the uplands and intensification of agricultural production does not sit easily with evidence such as the Dewerstone pot, described at the start of this chapter. The anthropologist Pálsson (1996) has usefully identified three key ways of interacting with landscape. Orientalism is a colonial regime, in which nature is seen as categorically different and set apart from human society; here, landscape becomes a passive object of exploitation. Paternalism similarly distinguishes between nature and culture, but views the natural world as requiring human protection. Communalism, on the other hand, draws no distinction between culture and nature, with things such as plants, animals, water, humans, and rocks each playing a role as agents in the social universe. Although the Dartmoor field systems have been interpreted in orientalist terms, the Dewerstone pot suggests a more mutualistic relationship with landscape in which humans gave gifts to spirits or ancestors associated with earth and stone.

Although it is frequently assumed that the construction of field systems indicates a drive to intensify agricultural production, it is far from clear if this was the case. Neither the fringes nor uplands of

Dartmoor, for example, appear to have been under significant pressure in the centuries preceding the building of coaxial field systems (Caseldine and Hatton 1996; Wickstead 2008, 60). During the Middle Bronze Age, land-use practices within the field systems themselves created extensive areas of improved, species-rich grassland, and there is little evidence for soil impoverishment through overexploitation of the land (Fyfe et al. 2008, 2259). Although the formation of colluvial deposits in valley bottoms in regions such as Sussex suggests increased levels of clearance and cultivation from the Early Bronze Age (Allen 2004), it would be unwise to interpret this as evidence for intensive agriculture. On Dartmoor, although some of the land within individual field systems is subdivided into small fields, much is not, suggesting that there may not always have been pressure to intensify production and that land scarcity was not a significant problem (Wickstead 2008, 59–61). Elsewhere, for example on the Marlborough Downs in Wiltshire (Gingell 1992, fig. 96), individual 'blocks' of coaxial fields can be discerned separated by extensive open areas. Ard marks have been identified on the floodplain of the Thames at Hopton Street and Lafone Street in Southwark, London (Bates 1996; Ridgeway 2000), but the evidence from both of these sites indicates just two or three ploughing events; here, at least, there is little evidence for intensive arable production. So too, the apparent shift in many parts of southern England from coaxial to aggregate field systems during the Late Bronze Age (English 2013) calls into question models of increasing intensification. The idea that the 'abandonment' of upland regions in the Late Bronze Age and Iron Age is a result of overexploitation of the landscape (Burgess 1985) is also problematic: although grazing intensity clearly decreases during this period in areas such as Dartmoor (Fyfe et al. 2008, 2260), the shift to cooler, wetter conditions (Amesbury et al. 2008) doubtless had a significant impact.

A second significant issue raised by the appearance of coaxial field systems is the extent to which these should be viewed as *imposed* on the landscape in a single planned phase of construction. This implies an orientalist mode of engagement in which the landscape is an object of control. It also suggests the existence of some form of centralized authority which could enforce an abstract and rationalized order on the world. In fact, there is evidence that coaxial field systems may not always have been laid out at once. At Bradley Fen in Cambridgeshire, the terminal ditch (the primary boundary or baseline from which multiple 'subsidiary' coaxial elements were laid out) runs along the edge of an island in the fens (Figure 5.11; Gibson and Knight 2006, 23). This was not dug as a single continuous feature, however. Instead, it 'existed as a

+ Spear
* Hoard
● Burnt mound

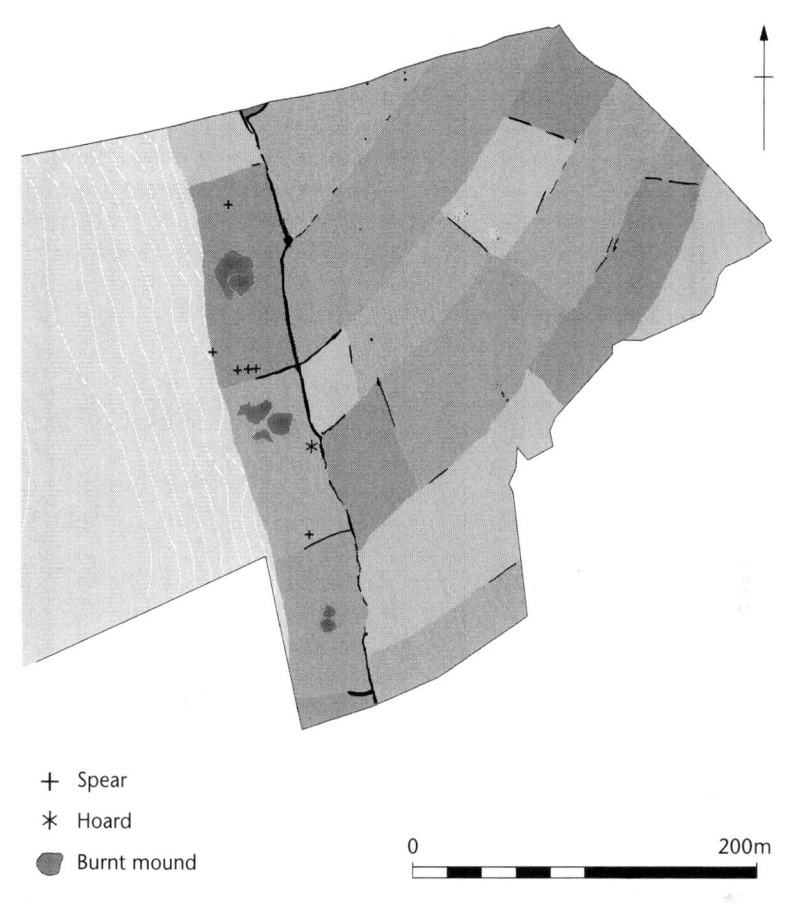

Figure 5.11. Landscape zoning at Bradley Fen, Cambridgeshire: field system on the higher ground to the east; burnt mounds and metalwork in the fen edge to the west (reproduced with permission of Cambridge Archaeological Unit, with slight alterations by Anne Leaver).

meandering boundary with gaps [and] pronounced diversions'. Many of the ditched boundaries that form part of this field system abut or stop short of one another at junctions, suggesting that they were not all cut at the same time but were instead constructed as part of an extended sequence. The boundaries projecting into the fen to the west of the terminal ditch were laid out on a slightly different orientation to those to the east, and this too may hint at a prolonged sequence of construction. At Game Farm, Brandon, Suffolk, the ditches of the coaxial field system were rarely straight but included curves and meanders suggesting a 'relatively organic process of development' (Gibson, C. 2004, 10), while the coaxial field system identified as 'farmstead 6' at Heathrow Terminal 5 appears to have been gradually extended from south to north (Leivers 2010, 176).

At Shovel Down on Dartmoor, topographical surveys suggest that the terminal boundary was the primary feature of this field system, and that it was employed as a baseline from which other significant boundaries were laid out roughly at right angles. However, on excavating one of the junctions between the terminal boundary and one of the 'secondary' elements, it became evident that the former was not constructed as a single uninterrupted length of drystone walling (Brück et al. 2003). Rather, a 'corner' comprising part of the terminal boundary and the drystone wall at right angles to this could be seen to have been constructed as a continuous run. The other part of the terminal boundary appears to have been added at a later point. This too was modified, for a cobbled entranceway had been laid in a secondary break through the wall; a piece of struck flint was found embedded in the entranceway, indicating that the entrance was created in prehistory. Fence-lines and ditches underlie some of the drystone walls on Dartmoor (Smith et al. 1981, 209–14; Gibson 1992), demonstrating that the latter were just one component in lengthy sequences of construction (Johnston 2005). Together, these examples suggest that coaxial and aggregate field systems may have more in common than one might initially think. Moreover, this has implications for our understanding of the process by which coaxial field systems were laid out. Fleming (1988, ch. 5) has argued that this may have involved communal decision-making and cooperative labour by relatively egalitarian groups rather than elite imposition. Certainly, if coaxial field systems were built, extended, subdivided, and reworked over relatively long periods of time, this indicates negotiation rather than imposition. Boundaries existed but they were not fixed and immutable, so that they created temporary and negotiable rather than stable identities (Johnston 2005).

Boundaries, landscape, and special places

One of the key reasons that coaxial field systems have been viewed as predominantly concerned with maximizing economic production is that they are often said to cut across the grain of the landscape in a way that is described as 'terrain oblivious' (Fleming 1988, 61; Yates 2007, 15). Yet this is not wholly true. On Dartmoor, each field system has a primary boundary or baseline (referred to by Fleming (1988) as the 'terminal reave'—reave being the local term for these drystone walls), with multiple 'subsidiary' coaxial boundaries laid out roughly perpendicular to this. These primary boundaries frequently follow the contours, so that the coaxial elements run from low ground to high ground, from river valleys towards the high moorland. Moreover, the drystone walls themselves often incorporate or are aligned on natural granite outcrops or tors—just as we saw for some of the barrows and cairns in the south-west during the preceding Early Bronze Age. Stone Tor on Shovel Down, for example, is situated on the line of the primary boundary from which other components of the field system were laid out, while nearby Thornworthy Tor lies along the course of a subsidiary reave (Butler 1991a, maps 36 and 37; unpublished RCHME survey). This suggests a sensitivity to 'natural' features that may have been regarded as special places imbued with ancestral significance: we have seen above that cairns were often built over tors in the south-west (see also Bender et al. 2007). Like the Dewerstone pot, field systems suggest that intimate, personalized relationships existed between people and landscape. Landscape was not an object of exploitation, but was part of the social universe, and a categorical distinction between nature and culture may not have been drawn.

Tors are not the only features to be incorporated into these boundaries, however. At Rippon Tor, a cairn was constructed over the tor itself, and there were two further cairns slightly downslope from this (Butler 1991b, map 5). Previous excavations of similar monuments on Dartmoor and elsewhere in south-west England indicate that these are likely to be Early Bronze Age in date and to predate the field systems. All three cairns were subsequently incorporated into coaxial boundaries (Figure 5.10). The two downslope from the tor both lie along the line of the same boundary, and it could be suggested that the spatial relationship between these two cairns generated the axis for the later field system. The relationship between field boundaries and stone rows (monuments that are generally considered to date to the Late Neolithic or Early Bronze Age in this region) is also interesting. Fleming (1978, 109) has observed that the 'terminal reaves' of individual field systems often run parallel and immediately adjacent to earlier stone rows. He suggests that stone rows may have played an important role in regulating pre-boundary land use—for example by dividing the lower-lying landholdings of individual communities from shared upland grazing. Although it seems likely that cairns and stone rows helped to create and maintain relationships between people and landscape, it is hard to view their role as solely territorial. Instead, we can suggest that features such as tors, cairns, and stone rows were sacred places that continued to be viewed as significant and meaningful elements of later landscapes (cf. Tilley 2004). Dartmoor therefore cannot be seen as some kind of colonial *tabula rasa* onto which the linear rationality of later field boundaries could be imposed according to solely functional imperatives. Rather, Middle Bronze Age field systems were worked into existing social landscapes—landscapes that were imbued with ancestral powers and with which communities already had intimate and long-term personal relationships (Fleming 1988, 103–5).

A recent study has also noted interesting relationships between Early Bronze Age barrows and Middle Bronze Age field systems in eastern England (Figure 5.12; Cooper 2016). In some places, the dominant alignment of field systems mirrored that of earlier linear barrow cemeteries. Field boundaries were often oriented on barrows, while elsewhere barrows were located immediately adjacent to boundaries. Some boundaries swerved to avoid earlier monuments, while in other locations one or more boundaries met at barrows. At Over/Barleycroft in Cambridgeshire, ring-ditch 1 was sandwiched between two parallel linear boundaries, while another boundary ditch was oriented on ring-ditch 4 (Evans and Knight 1998, 37). A further boundary ran immediately adjacent to ring-ditches 2 and 3, following the alignment created by this pair of monuments. Although the relationship between boundaries and barrows varies, it is evident that earlier mortuary monuments were frequently drawn into the politics of land tenure in subsequent centuries. Barrows gave material form to familial and community identities, and links with particular ancestors may have been important in establishing and maintaining tenurial relationships. Barrows acted as pivots, as points of articulation and division in the Middle Bronze Age landscape, just as the mortuary rites conducted at these monuments in previous centuries helped define and reshape interpersonal relationships.

Boundaries, personhood, and identity

It is often assumed that the appearance of field systems indicates new forms of social division, with acts of partition reflecting concerns over social boundaries, differentials in access, ownership, and belonging, and increasing social competition (e.g. Løvschal 2014; 2015). The construction of boundaries, it is argued, indicates a desire to express autonomy, individualism, and difference, with principles of symmetry and subdivision, for example, mirroring contemporary forms of social categorization. There is much to agree with here, particularly given the increasing construction of enclosed settlements, often with elaborate entrance features, described in the Chapter 4. There is a danger, however, that this model underplays the complexity of the evidence.

Social landscapes

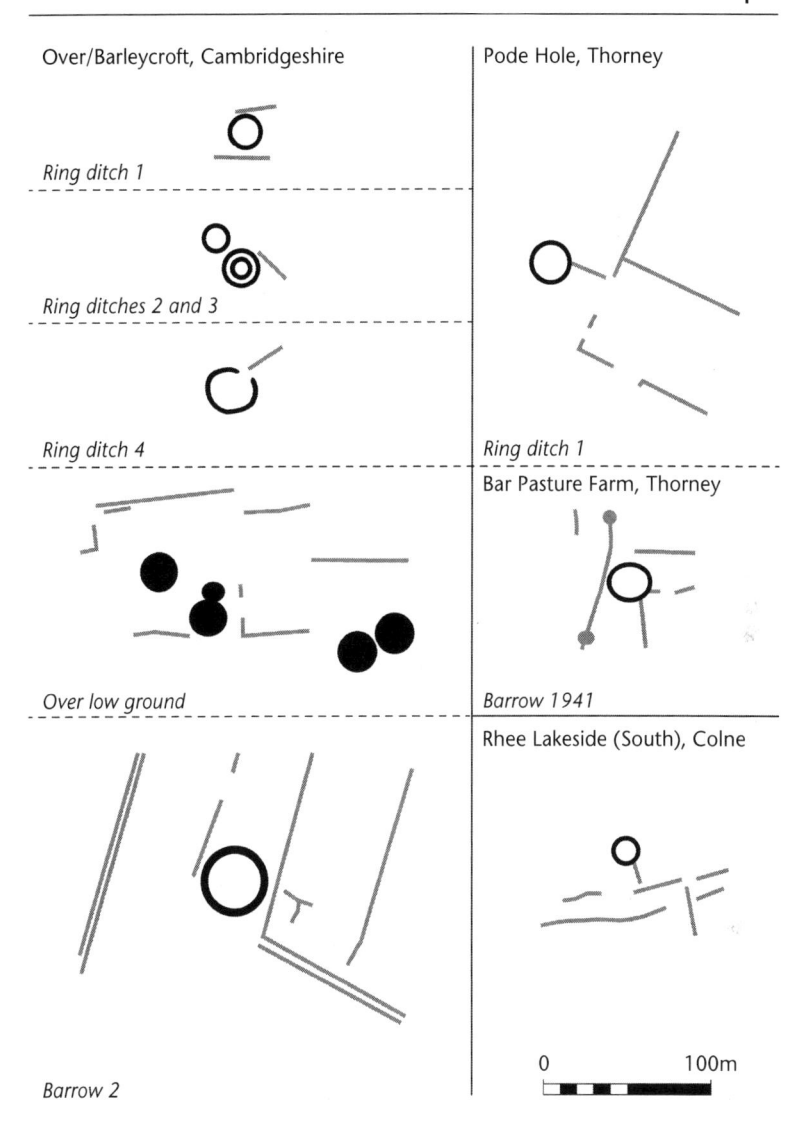

Figure 5.12. The relationship between Early Bronze Age barrows and Middle Bronze Age boundaries in the east of England (reproduced with permission of Anwen Cooper, with slight alterations by Anne Leaver).

To begin with, such a model implies the existence of a categorical distinction between self and other, something that much of the evidence reviewed both in this and previous chapters does not entirely uphold for the Middle or Late Bronze Age. The significance of features such as tors, for example, and the evident sensitivity to landscape suggested by the meanders and deviations visible in many boundaries indicate that landscape formed a core component of the self. Moreover, although boundaries may enact processes of division, they also connect and incorporate different elements of the social landscape. We have already seen how barrows may be located at junctions between boundaries in eastern England, and this is the case for other features too: on Dartmoor, for example, roundhouses were often incorporated into field boundaries or situated at junctions (Butler 1991b, map 5). Indeed, in this region roundhouses tend not to be evenly distributed across field systems but are clustered in particular areas (Fleming 1988, fig. 37), suggesting shared access rather than individual ownership. Walls presuppose agreement between those on either side, for they must be maintained: in this sense, walls are as much about relationships as difference.

Elsewhere in this volume, we have argued that the self was a composite entity that extended to enfold things outside of the body, and it has been suggested that partible concepts of personhood can also be seen in the coaxial field systems of the period. Wickstead (2008, 141) notes that on Dartmoor individual blocks of land are frequently subject to fractional subdivision, with fields of near identical width laid out along the terminal boundary. This is intriguing, for it echoes the splitting of objects such as sword blades into multiple fragments in Bronze Age hoards or the breaking of shale bracelets into halves and quarters at Potterne. The subdivision of land gave material form to nested and multiple sets of tenurial rights generated through interpersonal relationships. Relations were mapped onto the landscape through processes of spatial referencing and repetition that located people in a network of spatial and material links (Wickstead 2008); in this way, land embodied personhood, and tenurial rights were the outcome of bodily and other relations. The negotiation, maintenance, and reframing of those relationships were given material form in the upkeep, rebuilding, and removal of boundaries, in the creation and blocking of entrances, and in the rerouting of droveways: in Britain, as elsewhere in north-west Europe, lines of enclosure of various sorts appear to have embodied relatively labile and shifting interpersonal and inter-community relationships (Løvschal 2014).

Boundaries and cosmology

The link between people and landscape was not solely about land tenure, of course; instead, landscapes embodied cosmological principles in which belief systems intertwined with daily practice to legitimate social and political conditions. This is evident in the consistent orientation of field systems in some regions. In many parts of southern England, for example, north–south or north-east–south-west were the dominant alignments followed (English 2013, 134; McOmish et al. 2002, 54). On the one hand, this could be interpreted as indicating a lack of sensitivity to the underlying topography. On the other hand, it is widely accepted that the orientation of Middle and Late Bronze Age roundhouses towards the east or south-east embodied cosmological principles, incorporating concepts of light and fertility into roundhouse space through reference to the movement of the sun (Brück 1999b, 158). It is, of course, equally possible that the layout of field systems was governed by the symbolism ascribed to particular astronomical orientations—in this case perhaps referencing the midsummer sunrise and midwinter sunset. This may be one reason why Middle Bronze Age cremation burials are sometimes ranged in linear groupings that echo the orientation of contemporary field systems (Robinson 2007, 69–70): at Eye Quarry in Cambridgeshire, for example, a linear cemetery oriented north-east–south-west mirrored the alignment of the field system in which it was located (Cooper and Edmonds 2007, fig. 4.38). In this way belief systems, identity, and land tenure were woven together in the layout of the Middle Bronze Age landscape.

Field boundaries could also be a focus of ritual practice. At Kingsmead Quarry, Horton, Berkshire, a quoit-headed pin was recovered from the upper fill of a boundary ditch (https://www.wessexarch.co.uk/our-work/kingsmead-quarry-horton/). A saddle quern was placed in the terminal of one ditch at Eye Quarry in Cambridgeshire, while a spearhead was deposited in a pit cut into the end of another (Phillips and Mortimer 2012, 20–1). As we have already seen in Chapter 2, fragments of human bone and even complete bodies have also been found in Middle and Late Bronze Age field boundaries: at Gwithian in Cornwall, for example, four pits dug immediately adjacent to a drystone wall produced fragments of burnt human bone (Nowakowski et al. 2007, 29). Such finds speak to the ways in which land tenure, kinship, and social distinctions were intimately interconnected.

Field boundaries are not the only agricultural features to produce such finds. Human bone was recovered from one of three clearance cairns excavated at Dainton in Devon (Needham 1980, 179). Johnston (2001; 2008, 274–6) has noted comparable examples elsewhere and argues that similarities in architecture and depositional practice call into question archaeological attempts to differentiate clearance cairns from burial cairns; instead, the evidence suggests that the practical and the ritual were not distinguished in such categorical terms in the Bronze Age. Elsewhere, objects associated with agriculture form part of votive deposits. For example, a Late Bronze Age wooden ard share was deposited in the Thames at Dorney Lake, Buckinghamshire, close to a series of bridges of Middle Bronze Age to Iron Age date (https://ubp.buckscc.gov.uk/HBSMRGateway/AssocDocs/AssocDoc2115.pdf). Part of a wooden yoke found in Ballybeg Bog, County Offaly, has been dated to the Earliest Iron Age (Stanley et al. 2003); bogs were a focus for the votive deposition of a range of different artefacts throughout the Bronze Age, notably gold ornaments and ceremonial objects such as horns (Becker 2013), and it is possible to interpret the deposition of the yoke in a similar way. Such examples hint that agricultural productivity depended on reciprocal relationships between people and landscape.

We have suggested already that the Bronze Age cosmos may have been divided into an upper, middle, and lower world. We have seen that places such as hilltops and bogs were considered important locations during the Middle and Late Bronze Age, and field systems too seem to have been carefully positioned within this broader cosmological scheme. At Bradley Fen in Cambridgeshire, there is evidence for careful 'zoning' of the landscape (Figure 5.11; Gibson and Knight 2006). Here, a long ditch runs along the edge of a low-lying island in the fen, dividing the dryland from the wetland. As we have already seen above, the ditch forms the terminal boundary of a coaxial field system which extends onto the island. Beyond the terminal boundary, in the fen edge itself, were three burnt mounds, each accompanied by a waterhole, and a series of deposits of metalwork and human bone, including several isolated spearheads and a hoard of sword and spear fragments. A similar series of conceptual distinctions may be visible in other regions too. On the West Sussex coastal plain, for example, hoards and burnt mounds have been identified close to watercourses, while settlements appear to have been located at higher elevations nearby (Dunkin 2001, 262). Field systems and associated settlements, in other words, were assigned their own proper place in the Bronze Age cosmos—a place that was governed by belief systems which prescribed both practical and ritual action for the maintenance of human and agricultural fertility.

Human–animal relationships

We have discussed in some detail the significance of natural features such as mountaintops, rivers, and trees to Bronze Age communities, but we have yet to talk about animals despite their evident significance throughout the period. It has been suggested, for example, that the field systems of the Middle Bronze Age were constructed primarily to facilitate animal management rather than crop production (Pryor 1996), while the midden sites of the Late Bronze Age comprise large quantities of animal dung and stabling waste (Lawson 2000)—monumentalizing animals and their activities in the landscape. In this section, we will explore the changing relationships between animals and humans, from the inclusion of animal bodies in Early Bronze Age barrows to the deposition of animal-related artefacts in hoards of the Earliest Iron Age.

Human and animal bodies

The remains of animals were incorporated into Bronze Age mortuary contexts in a variety of interesting ways (Wilkin 2011). Sometimes, animal burials mimic human interments. At Down Farm, Dorset, two sheep and two cattle were buried in pits on the margins of an Early Bronze Age pond barrow (Figure 5.13; Green et al. 1991, fig. 4.8). The sheep burials were placed opposite each other just inside the northern and southern edges of the barrow, while the cattle were buried some 6 metres south-east and north-west of the monument respectively. The sheep were relatively poorly preserved but the cattle had been placed on their left-hand sides with their legs flexed. Human bodies—both crouched inhumations and cremation burials—were also deposited in and adjacent to the pond barrow. At Old Sarum Spur, Wiltshire, several Middle Bronze Age graves were identified close to an area of settlement. Three contained the inhumation burials of adult females and two contained the bodies of cows; one of the latter had a foetal sheep/goat between its ribcage and hind legs (Powell et al. 2005).

Complete and partial animal bodies were also deposited alongside human bodies in Chalcolithic and Early Bronze Age graves. Barrow 72 on Calais Wold, East Yorkshire, contained a crouched inhumation lying on its left side, with its head to the north-north-west (Mortimer 1905, 163). At the feet of this body were the remains of a young pig and two sheep or goats. All three animals were placed on their right sides, but, like the crouched inhumation, lay with their heads to the north-north-west. On the one hand, we can suggest that the animals were placed in the grave in a way that mirrors the human burial in the same context. On the other, it can be observed that they were deposited where objects such as pots were usually placed. This could be interpreted as suggesting that these animals were objectified. Against this, however, we have already noted that human cremation deposits could be placed

Personifying Prehistory

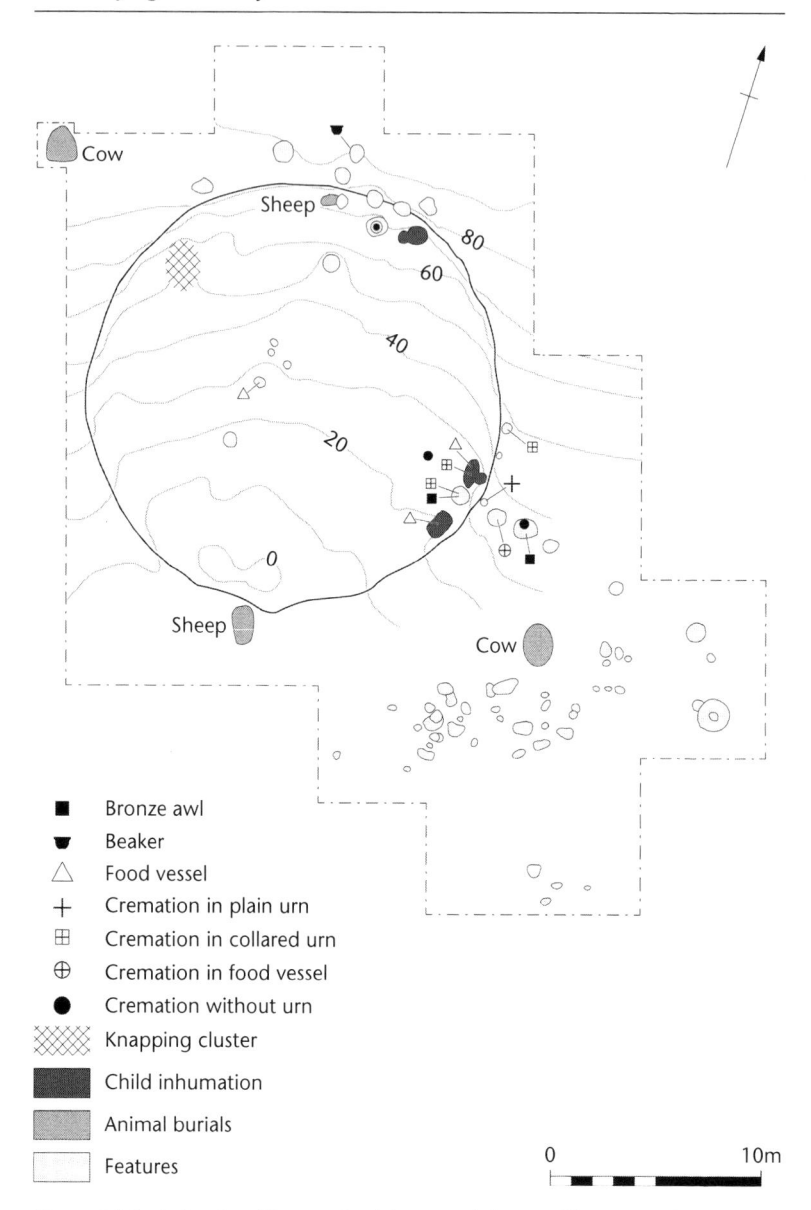

Figure 5.13. Animal and human burials around the pond barrow at Down Farm, Dorset (redrawn by Anne Leaver after Green et al. 1991, fig. 4.8).

in similar locations, and that the boundary between persons and objects was differently constituted—if it was recognized at all—during this period. Most animal remains from mortuary contexts belong to the Chalcolithic or Early Bronze Age, but occasional examples can be identified even in the later parts of the period, when funerary practices in many regions are archaeologically invisible. The Late Bronze Age mortuary deposits focused in and around a large pit at Cliffs End Farm in Kent produced a variety of interesting animal remains alongside the complete and partial human bodies we have already discussed in Chapter 2 (McKinley et al. 2014). A pair of foetal lambs had been laid together in the basal silts of this feature. The first of the human bodies to be deposited in the pit was that of an elderly female: another pair of neonatal lambs was placed over her pelvis. As we have already seen, it has been argued that she may have been a sacrificial victim; the presence of the lambs hints that she may have been killed in springtime as a component of fertility rites. This link between the bodies of humans and animals is seen in a second subadult female in the same feature whose head was laid on a cattle skull. Further deposits around the edge of the pit included a series of five cattle skulls.

Partial animal bodies in Bronze Age graves have often been interpreted as food offerings. At Aberdour Road, Dunfermline, Fife, the crouched inhumation of an adolescent female had been laid in a cist. At least four forelimbs from three different pigs (mostly comprising carpals, metacarpals, and phalanges) were placed at the knees of the body (Close-Brooks et al. 1972, 123, 132). A cist at Gairneybank, Kinross-shire, contained a crouched inhumation, probably a young adult male. This was accompanied by what can be interpreted as a joint of pork comprising part of the right humerus, the right radius, and right ulna of a pig (Cowie and Ritchie 1991, 98). By contrast, an articulated sheep or goat limb was deposited alongside the inhumation burial of an adult male at Perio, Northamptonshire (Hadnam 1973).

Rather different is the large assemblage of some 185 cattle skulls deposited on top of the mound of barrow 1, Irthlingborough, Northamptonshire (Davis 2007; Towers et al. 2010; Jones 2012, 129–31). These had probably originally been stacked the right way up in three or four layers. Most were young adults of prime meat-bearing age. A small number of other bones were present, and butchery marks on several cattle scapulae indicate that the animals had been eaten. Davis calculates that this number of cattle would have yielded enough meat to feed 500 people for more than two months. However, the paucity of postcranial bones and the under-representation of incisors and premolars (usually the first teeth to fall out once the flesh has decomposed) suggest that the skulls had been placed on the mound sometime after the animals were consumed. Radiocarbon dates on the skulls indicate that the cattle may not all have been butchered as part of the same event, and it is possible that some were curated and brought from elsewhere for final deposition on the barrow. The deposit may therefore reference multiple episodes of consumption over a period of time (and perhaps at various different locations), with only a portion of the bones representing the remains of a mortuary feast associated with the construction of the barrow itself. Strontium isotope analysis of the remains indicates that all but one of the cattle were from the local area, providing an interesting insight into the origins and affiliations of those who contributed to this unusual act of construction. As such, this deposit referenced the histories, origins, and relationships of individual herds and their owners (Jones 2012, 131).

Other finds cannot so easily be interpreted as food offerings or feasting remains, however. Grave 4969 at Barrow Hills in Oxfordshire contained the inhumation burial of a child lying in an alder coffin (Figure 5.14; Barclay 1999, 119–21). Six red-deer antlers had been carefully positioned along the sides of the coffin, four on one side and two on the other. Only one showed evidence of use as a pick, so these cannot simply be interpreted as tools discarded after digging the grave. Outside the coffin, and on either side of it, a cattle skull and a fragment of pig calcaneum had been placed directly opposite one another. The inhumation burial of an adult male from Gristhorpe, North Yorkshire, was accompanied by the metatarsal of a fox and several pine-marten phalanges (Sheridan et al. 2013, 159). These bones may have formed part of pelts, although detached animal paws may have functioned as amulets. A beaver's tooth and boar's tusk formed part of the equipment of the possible ritual specialist buried at Langton, North Yorkshire (Greenwell 1877, 138-9), and already described earlier in this chapter.

Animal bone has also been found as a component of Bronze Age cremation burials, indicating that, in cremation rites too, human and animal bodies could be treated in analogous ways. McKinley's study (1997) of approximately 130 British Bronze Age burials demonstrated that some 16 per cent of these contained small amounts of burnt animal bone, with sheep/goat and pig the most common animals found. At Glennan, Argyll and Bute, an urned cremation burial from a rock shelter comprised 1478.5 grams of human bone and 33.2 grams of animal bone, probably from a sheep or goat (Roberts 2003). The animal and human bone had been cleaned of pyre debris and were mixed throughout the urn, indicating that they had been cremated together on the same pyre. In many cases, the animal remains can be interpreted as food

Social landscapes

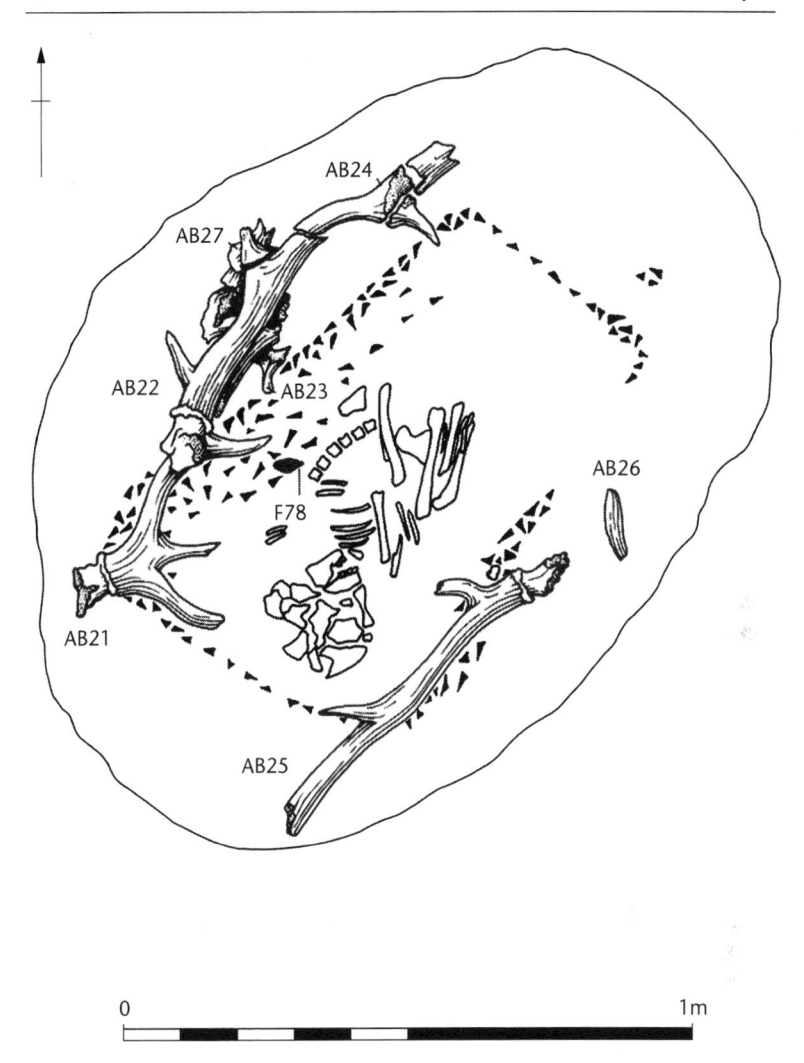

Figure 5.14. Grave 4969, Barrow Hills, Oxfordshire: AB21–5, red deer antlers; AB26, base and posterior of cattle skull; AB27, fragment of pig calcaneum; F78, flint piercer (after Barclay and Halpin 1999, fig. 4.62, with slight alterations by Anne Leaver; reproduced with permission of Oxford Archaeology).

offerings. Fragments of tibia shaft and innominate bone from cist 335 at Dunure Road, Ayrshire (Smith 2007), hint that the body may have been accompanied onto the pyre by the hind quarters of a sheep. By contrast, the burnt fragments of distal metapodial, probably belonging to a cow, from cist 178 would have produced relatively little meat, suggesting that in this case the meat-bearing elements had perhaps already been consumed by the mourners as part of the funerary feast.

Animal bone that cannot be interpreted as food for the afterlife or the remains of a funerary feast has also been found in Bronze Age cremation burials. At Seafield West, Highland, the cremated remains of a possible adult female were accompanied by three barbed and tanged arrowheads and a burnt fragment of mandible belonging to a dog or fox (Cressey and Sheridan 2003, 53), while the cremation burial of a child at Skilmafilly, Aberdeenshire, included a pair of burnt golden-eagle talons and a perforated bone or antler object (Johnson and Cameron 2012, 30); these items may have been worn together as part of a necklace. The burnt cervical vertebra of a possible polecat accompanied the cremated remains of a child at Lesmurdie Road, Elgin, Moray (Andrew Kitchener quoted in Sheridan et al. 2013, 160–1); the presence of this bone in particular makes it unlikely that we are looking at the remains of an animal pelt in this instance.

Animals were not only buried as complete and partial bodies during the Bronze Age; animal elements also occur as artefacts in the grave, particularly during the Chalcolithic and Early Bronze Age. Animal bone, for example, was used to make objects such as pins, awls, belt hooks, and tweezers (Woodward and Hunter 2015). Woodward (2000, 115) suggests that items such as awls and tweezers may have been used to prepare the body of the deceased or to mark the bodies of the mourners, for example through plucking the hair, tattooing, or scarification. Wilkin (2011, 67) too notes that bone artefacts often had a transformative function. Other animal products were probably also commonly used, although they rarely survive. Skins and pelts, for example, were employed to wrap both the bodies of the dead and their associated grave goods: the inhumation burial of a young adult female at Langwell Farm, Strath Oykel, Highland, had been wrapped in a brown cattle hide (Lelong 2014). As noted in Chapter 3, the process of wrapping may also have had a protective or transformative function, and it may be that this act imparted some of the qualities or symbolic attributes of that animal to the dead person (cf. Conneller 2004).

There is some evidence for use of selected species and/or skeletal elements in the production of bone artefacts. Bone points, for example, were often manufactured from the rear metapodials of sheep (Woodward and Hunter 2015, 102); the set of graduated bone points from Upton Lovell in Wiltshire, which are likely to have formed part of a costume rather than to have functioned as tools, were mostly from the left-hand side of the body. A significant number of bone dagger pommels were made from cetacean bone (Woodward and Hunter 2015, table 3.2.2): for example, the pommel from Forteviot, Perth and Kinross (Noble and Brophy 2011), is made from the tooth of a sperm whale. This is hard to explain in purely functional terms, for other types of bone would have been more readily available and equally easy to work. Instead, it seems likely that some of the characteristics or abilities of large marine mammals were considered desirable, or that these animals featured in Bronze Age myths; cetacean bone may therefore have been chosen for its symbolic properties.

Other animal objects show less evidence of working but may have formed elements of costumes. Boars' tusks, for example, show little use-wear and are more likely to have been items of adornment than tools (Woodward and Hunter 2015, 143). They often occur in pairs: two pairs of tusks accompanied the burial of the Amesbury Archer in Wiltshire, for example (Fitzpatrick 2011). Interestingly, tusks from the right side of the body were much more common than those from the left (Woodward and Hunter 2015, 141): all four of those from the grave of the Amesbury Archer were right tusks. Microscopic study of antlers from Chalcolithic and Early Bronze Age burials also show little evidence of use-wear (Woodward and Hunter 2015, 126–8), indicating that these were not merely tools for the digging of the grave. Instead, they display smooth surfaces that have been polished and worn from handling, and some have carefully shaped bases, perhaps to facilitate mounting as part of an item of headgear; indeed, some have been found positioned close to the head of the deceased in the grave. Here, too, items associated with particular animals may have given special powers to those who wore them (Wilkin 2011, 68–71).

Materials such as bone, skin, fur, and antler no doubt frequently formed part of composite objects, although few survive. The dagger from Rameldry, Fife, had a horn hilt and a sheath or scabbard of animal skin (Cameron 2003). The scabbard from Seafield West, near Inverness, Highland, was made of thin laths of oak covered with cattle hide (Cressey and Sheridan 2003, 62–3), while that from Lockington, Leicestershire, may have been lined with fur (Hughes 2000, 47). Often, an array of animal materials was brought together within an individual grave. For example, the inhumation burial of an adult male at Gristhorpe, North Yorkshire (Sheridan et al. 2013), had been wrapped in a cattle hide fastened with a bone pin made from the fibula of a pig. He was accompanied by a dagger with a whalebone pommel and—as we have already seen—the metatarsal of a fox and a number of pine-marten phalanges. Other items from this grave reference animal-related activities: microwear analysis of a planoconvex knife suggests this was used to cut or scrape hide, while examination of the lipid residues from a sewn-bark container indicate that this probably originally contained milk. Here, too, animal elements mapped the location of the deceased in a living landscape defined by complex and intimate human–animal relationships.

In summary, the evidence from Bronze Age mortuary contexts indicates that animal and human bodies could be treated in similar ways—inhumed as complete or partial burials or cremated on a pyre. Yet there were also differences, for example in the relative quantities of human and animal bone collected from the pyre, although the amount of cremated bone present need not directly relate to status. Animal bodies were sometimes placed relative to human burials in the grave, though, as we have discussed in Chapter 3, the positioning of different elements of mortuary assemblages (humans, animals, and artefacts) resulted in the creation of relational networks in which the distinction between subject and object was blurred. Animal parts—made into awls and tweezers or worn as amulets or as parts of special costumes—facilitated the transformation of the living and the dead, working to penetrate the boundary between this world and the next through the mediation of animal others, or perhaps even animal ancestors. Combined with other materials in composite objects and assemblages, they wrote the everyday and mythological landscape into the grave, bringing particular identities, relationships, and practices into focus.

The choice of specific animal elements, for example sperm-whale teeth, fox jaws, boar's tusks, or golden-eagle talons, suggests that such animals may have been esteemed for particular behavioural attributes, or perhaps symbolized certain ideals or values. Their remains may therefore have been employed to comment on the personal (or idealized) attributes of the deceased. Alternatively, they may have figured in significant origin myths or have been viewed as totems or symbols of family or group identity. The use of materials such as cetacean bone as elements of composite artefacts may therefore have imbued objects such as daggers with their own agency and spiritual power: as Woodward and colleagues put it, 'the employment of materials from the northern seas, and their icy depths, may have represented concepts of mystery and distance (in both space and depth), along with the powers of water and the ocean' (Woodward et al. 2015, 51). So too, items such as boars' tusks and materials such as antler may have spoken of qualities such as strength and courage, or the generative potential of seasonal regrowth (Wilkin 2011, 68–71).

The bones of animals such as cattle, pigs, and sheep, on the other hand, are more common, and can often be interpreted as the remains of the funerary feast, or as food offerings for the deceased. Yet, as the monumental assemblage of cattle skulls at Irthlingborough reminds us, this does not mean that these animals lacked social significance or were viewed solely as an economic resource, for feasting enacted social identities and relationships. As we have already seen, stable isotope analysis of Chalcolithic and Early Bronze Age inhumation burials indicates that people consumed a high level of animal protein during this period (Jay et al. 2012; Parker Pearson et al. 2016). Isotopic analysis and the presence of renal stones suggest that the man buried at Gristhorpe, North Yorkshire, had a high-protein diet; his stature (he was around 1.8 metres tall) and grave goods, which included a dagger with a whalebone pommel, have been read as indicating that he was a high-status individual (Melton et al. 2013). Yet it was not only men buried with 'high-status' grave goods who consumed abundant animal protein, for a similar diet is indicated by isotopic analysis of the remains of a woman buried at Langwell Farm, Strath Oykel, Highland (Lelong 2014). She was accompanied only by organic items of cloth and wood which, in traditional narratives, might be taken to indicate that she was an individual of relatively modest social standing. The evidence suggests, therefore, that pastoralism was probably a significant element of the Chalcolithic and Early Bronze Age economy. In societies where wealth in animals is a marker of status, accomplishment, family history, or adherence to moral values, people often have close relationships with their animals (Evans-Pritchard 1940; Comaroff and Comaroff 1991). The life histories of animals exchanged as part of significant events such as initiation rites or marriages may be viewed as intertwined with the biographies of their human owners, and it would be no surprise if the eventual consumption of these animals (perhaps even on the death of their owner) required the careful and ritualized disposal of their bodies.

This may be why the treatment of human and animal bodies is sometimes similar, and why the relationship between humans and animals—reflected, for example, in the placement of animal remains in the grave—appears to have been a matter of concern. This choreography of the body extends to the selection of particular anatomical elements—the head or the feet, for example, or bones from the left or right side of the body. It seems likely that different parts of the body were accorded different meanings and values (cf. Douglas 1970), and that these may have been chosen to define some aspect of the deceased's identity and position within the social and moral order. For example, the deposition of a cattle skull and fragment of pig calcaneum (a large bone in the foot) directly opposite one another on either side of the child's body in grave 4969 at Barrow Hills in Oxfordshire (Figure 5.14; Barclay 1999, 119–21, fig. 4.62) created dimensions of opposition or complementarity that could be used to express different types of relationship between the deceased and the living. One could suggest, for example, that beef and pork were considered appropriate food offerings from different categories of mourner, for instance from affinal and agnatic kinsfolk (cf. Battaglia 1990).

Animals in the settled landscape

Much of the evidence discussed above dates to the Chalcolithic and Early Bronze Age. From the beginning of the Middle Bronze Age, by contrast, animal bodies and animal elements are predominantly found not in barrows and graves but in contexts such as pits, ditches, and waterholes in and around settlements and more widely across the settled landscape. At Down Farm in Dorset, the skulls of five dogs and a cow were deposited in the south-east corner of the ditch that surrounded a Middle Bronze Age settlement (Green et al. 1991, 190). There is evidence to suggest that animal burials were sometimes made at significant points in the life of the settlement. At Cladh Hallan on the island of South Uist in the Outer Hebrides, two dogs were buried at the entrance to house 401 to mark the rebuilding of this structure (Figure 5.15; Marshall et al. 1998). Later, near complete antlers were placed in four

Figure 5.15. One of the dog burials from house 401, Cladh Hallan, South Uist; the head and hindquarters were lost due to later disturbance (reproduced with permission of Mike Parker Pearson).

of the postholes near the doorway after the posts had been removed, presumably as part of formalized abandonment rites.

Often it is evident that animal bodies were deposited with care and a degree of formality. Part of the skeleton of a horse was deposited in the lower fill of a pit on the north-eastern edge of the settlement at Runnymede in Surrey (Needham 1991, 110). Its forelimbs were articulated and had been arranged in the ground in a crossed formation. Above this lay a complete inverted hearth comprising a base of fired clay over a layer of charcoal and associated with part of a jar and burnished fineware bowl. The upper fill of the pit produced a fragment of antler cheekpiece, a fragment from a socketed bronze knife, a worked antler tine, unworked horn cores, a whetstone, a spindle whorl and two loom-weight fragments. Many of these items may relate to the production of horse harness equipment. At Westcroft Road, Carshalton, Surrey (Proctor 2002), a Late Bronze Age pit group produced a number of interesting finds. The skull of a horse had been laid on the base of pit 62. This was accompanied by several large quern fragments and a lump of carefully prepared potting clay moulded into a subsquare shape. Pit 77 contained a cluster of three large flint nodules, on top of which part of a bronze object (possibly an axe) had been placed. On either side of the flint nodules were two red-deer skulls (Figure 5.16). One of these was laid face down; both antlers were still attached, though they were broken. By contrast, only one of the antlers belonging to the second skull remained in place. The other had been shed, but was carefully deposited next to the pedicle to which it had originally been attached. Red deer shed their antlers in April or May, suggesting that this act of deposition may have taken place during late spring. Such animal deposits can be interpreted as offerings made at important points in the lifecycles of particular people or places, as sacrifices to ensure continued human, animal, and agricultural fertility, or to propitiate chthonic beings. The deposition of dogs, horses, and cattle hint that, in many cases, these may have been animals with whom people had close, personalized relationships, while the inclusion of other animal elements, such as antler, suggests that their symbolic potential could be drawn on to call to mind particular social values; as we shall see later in this chapter, some of these animals may have had mythological significance.

Animal elements also appear to have been employed as part of costumes and ceremonial regalia during this period. We have already seen in Chapter 4 that Late Bronze Age midden sites were locations where communities gathered for feasting, exchange, age-grade ceremonies, and activities relating to the breeding and management of livestock. The midden at Potterne in Wiltshire (Lawson 2000), for

Figure 5.16. The antlers deposited in pit 77, Westcroft Road, Surrey (© Pre-Construct Archaeology Ltd).

example, comprised enormous quantities of cattle dung and stabling waste but, as we have already discussed, it produced other animal elements too. These included the bones of fox, polecat, wildcat, and beaver—animals that may have been trapped for their pelts (Locker 2000). Perforated dog, horse, and deer teeth, a perforated fox mandible, and a perforated antler tine may have served as items of personal adornment. The presence of guillemot bones and the perforated claw of a white-tailed sea eagle hints that costumes may sometimes have incorporated elements from a distance, for Potterne is some 50 kilometres from the sea. The diversity of animal remains at this site hints that the groups that gathered here may each have had their own costumes: we can imagine that the dress and ceremonial regalia of different age grades, for example, or those from different regions or belonging to different kin groups may have been visually distinctive. The incorporation of animal elements into such costumes underscores their symbolic potency, for example as totems. Wearing such objects may have allowed the participants in particular ceremonies to take on animal qualities so that the boundary between human and animal dissolved (cf. Conneller

2004). Unusual animal remains have also been found at other midden sites, including a great white shark's tooth from Llanmaes (Gwilt and Lodwick 2009). The faunal assemblage from this site was interesting for other reasons too, for it was dominated by the right forequarters of pigs (Madgwick and Mulville 2015). Isotope analysis demonstrates considerable heterogeneity, indicating that these animals were raised in different areas and on a variety of diets. It is therefore possible to suggest that families or groups congregating at the site were each required to provide meat for feasting, and that the right forequarter was the prescribed contribution: this pattern of deliberate selection suggests that the symbolic attributes of pigs were considered significant.

Animal bone was, of course, also used to make a variety of artefacts during the Middle and Late Bronze Age, and these too are mostly found on settlements of the period. What is notable, however, is the significant increase in the number and variety of bone objects found at Late Bronze Age settlements and midden sites. The range of bone and antler tools from Potterne, for example, included rib knives, gouges, awls, needles, shuttle tips, weaving combs, and picks (Seager Smith 2000). The site also produced handles and mounts made from the same materials, as well as cheek pieces for the bridles of horses. Bone and antler ornaments included pins, rings, toggles, buttons, and beads. A small number of these objects (notably the bone and antler handles) were decorated with incised lines and ring and dot motifs not unlike the forms of decoration employed on Iron Age bone artefacts. This is important, for it indicates that, far from being viewed as common or low-status materials, bone and antler were employed to make objects of sufficient social significance to invite forms of elaboration designed to attract attention to those who wore or used these objects. Most of the artefacts were manufactured from the bones of sheep/goat, although horse, cattle, and pig bone were also used. Cloth production appears to have been one of the activities for which bone tools were used, and it is possible that sheep bone was viewed as a suitable material for this. Despite the obvious increase in the use of bone to make artefacts during the Late Bronze Age, however, there has been little research on this topic.

Animals and field systems

It has been argued that the field systems of the Middle and Late Bronze Age were predominantly built to contain and manage stock, with a relatively small arable component (Pryor 1996; 1998). Many fields have corner entranceways that would have helped to direct the movement of animals. Subdivided yards and drafting races to inspect and sort sheep have been identified at many sites, while droveways are also a common feature. At Bestwall Quarry in Dorset, for example, a Middle Bronze Age droveway and several drafting gates were found (Ladle and Woodward 2009, 85–7); a number of subrectangular settings of four postholes were also uncovered, which may be the remains of animal pens. At Hamilton in Leicestershire, a funnelled crowding alley and adjacent sheep race for controlling and sorting stock have been identified (Figure 5.17; Beamish and Shore 2008). Across many parts of southern and eastern England, waterholes are a common component of field systems: these often have ramped access to allow animals to drink. One of the waterholes at Bradley Fen in Cambridgeshire, for example, had a ramp with a metalled surface. Multiple hoofprints belonging to cattle, deer, and pig were concentrated around the edges of this feature (Gibson and Knight 2006, 53, fig. 20).

Given the economic and social significance of animals, it is little surprise that their remains form elements of votive deposits in boundary ditches and related features. South of Foxtrot Crossing near Warminster, Wiltshire, the near complete skeletons of a pregnant cow and two sheep were found on the base of a boundary ditch (Ellis and Powell 2008, 188). The feature had been widened to accommodate the body of the cow. A human skull was also found in the upper silts of the same ditch. At Corporation Farm in Oxfordshire, the junctions of field boundaries and enclosures were marked by the deposition of animal remains (Shand et al. 2003, 39, fig. 3.8). These included complete burials of sheep, cattle, and dog, as well as pig, cattle, and sheep mandibles. One of these contexts also produced a single fragment of human skull.

Complete and partial animal burials are also found in waterholes. The provision of water was, of course, an essential component of livestock management, particularly for cattle, and rituals involving the deposition of animal remains appear to have taken place both when these features were initially created and when they were backfilled and abandoned. At Eye Quarry in Cambridgeshire, for example, the skull of a cow was deposited on the bottom of a waterhole and surrounded by a ring of wooden stakes (Patten 2004, 24). By contrast, the primary fill of a waterhole at Clay Farm, Trumpington, Cambridgeshire, contained a sheep skeleton and the skull of a polecat (Phillips and Mortimer 2012, 24). It is interesting to note that it was not always the bones of domesticates that were deposited in these features: a fox skull and roe-deer jaw were placed on the base of a waterhole at Yarnton in Oxfordshire, for example (Hey et al. 2016, 585). As we have seen in other contexts dating to the Middle and especially the Late Bronze Age, human and animal bodies were often treated in similar ways: a waterhole at Bradley Fen in

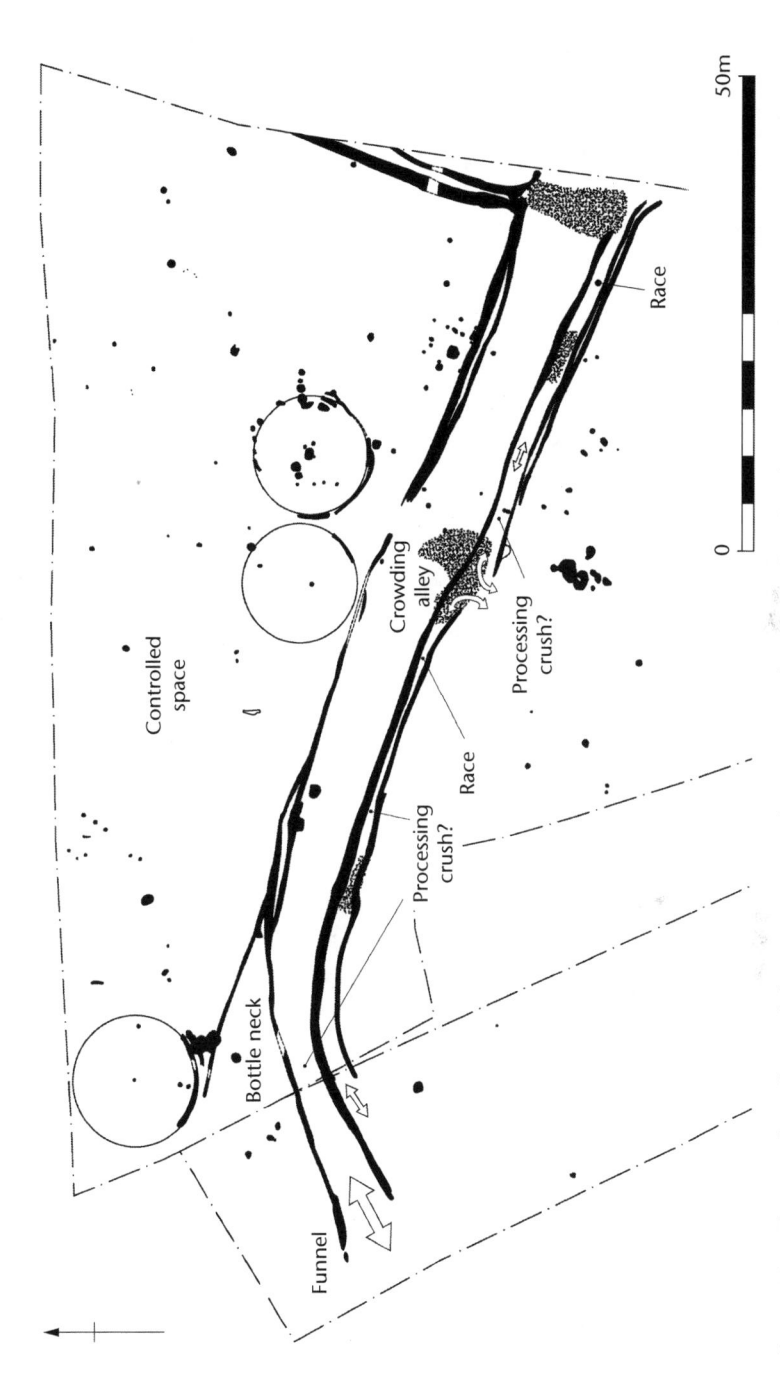

Figure 5.17. The crowding alley and sheep race at Hamilton, Leicestershire (reproduced with permission of Matt Beamish and University of Leicester Archaeological Services, with slight alterations by Anne Leaver).

Cambridgeshire, for example, produced the complete articulated bodies of an adult female and a dog (Gibson and Knight 2006, 35). These were deposited in the basal and uppermost fills respectively, as if bracketing the history of this feature.

Animal equipment and animal imagery

Specialist equipment relating to animal handling is very rare in the Bronze Age. The yoke from Loch Nell, Argyll, is an unusually early example, and has been dated to 1950–1525 cal BC (Sheridan 2002). The earliest wheel known in the British Isles was deposited immediately adjacent to the Flag Fen post alignment (Taylor 2001, 213–14; Pryor 2005, 153) and has been dated to *c.*1300 BC. Other examples have been identified in Late Bronze Age contexts, including a near complete wheel from the silts of a river channel at Must Farm, Cambridgeshire (http://www.mustfarm.com/progress/site-diary-19-discovering-britains-oldest-complete-wheel/), and part of a wheel from the base of a wooden trackway dated to 1206–970 cal BC at Edercloon, County Longford (Figure 5.18; Moore 2008, 8). Although the technology

Figure 5.18. Part of a wooden block-wheel from Edercloon, County Longford (reproduced with permission of John Sunderland and Cathy Moore, with slight alterations by Anne Leaver).

employed was relatively simple (these were not spoked wheels, but were constructed from blocks of wood), and it is likely that they were components of what we might refer to as 'carts' rather than 'chariots', it is evident that these were socially significant objects: all three of these wheels can be identified as votive deposits. It is not clear whether they were pulled by horses or cattle, although an articulated set of horse vertebrae was found close to the Must Farm example.

By the Late Bronze Age, specialist equipment for horse riding is known, although it is rare (e.g. Britnell 1976). Bone and antler cheek pieces formed parts of bridles and have been found at middens and timber platforms such as Potterne in Wiltshire (Seager Smith 2000) and Shinewater in East Sussex (https://historicengland.org.uk/listing/the-list/list-entry/1400780), indicating that it was considered important to render visible certain forms of human–animal relationship at sites where large numbers of people congregated to carry out ceremonial activities. Other horse equipment and vehicle fittings—for example nave bands, strap-distributors, and harness rings—were made of bronze (Cunliffe 1991, 411–15). Objects such as phalerae (bronze discs) and rattle pendants are thought to have formed decorative components of horse-gear (O'Connor 1975), as these have been found together with other types of horse equipment. Such items enhanced both the visual appearance and audibility of horses.

Often bridle fittings and other horse equipment formed part of special deposits of various sorts. At Eye Quarry in Cambridge, for example, a complete unused antler cheek was deposited in a pit along with pottery and animal bone, close to a series of roundhouses and other structures (Patten 2009, 38). The bronze hoard from Parc-y-Meirch at the foot of Dinorben hillfort, Clwyd, included objects interpreted as harness rings, jingles, phalerae, sliders, and strap ends (Sheppard 1941). The Isleham hoard contained horse equipment and vehicle fittings including cheek pieces, strap ends, phalerae, and axle caps, alongside weaponry and feasting equipment (Britton 1960; Malim et al. 2010, table 1), while nave bands and phalerae were amongst the diverse assemblage of artefacts found in the cave at Heathery Burn, County Durham (Britton 1968). Although horse equipment is a relatively rare component of Late Bronze Age hoards, it should be noted that animals could be incorporated into such assemblages in other ways: the hoard of Late Bronze Age spearheads and other weapons from Broadward in Shropshire, for example, was accompanied by horse and cattle bone (Burgess et al. 1972). A fragment of bugle-shaped fitting from the hoard may originally have formed part of a harness.

Personifying Prehistory

If animal equipment is rare, animal imagery is even more so. Two extraordinary examples are the Dunaverny flesh-hook and the Uffington white horse, both unique in their iconography in Ireland and Britain, although they can be related to similar imagery in a broader European context. The Dunaverny flesh-hook, dating to the late eleventh or tenth century BC, was found in a bog in 1829 and is decorated with miniature bronze models of two ravens and a family of swans (Figure 5.19; Bowman and Needham 2007). The Uffington white horse is a hill figure located high on an escarpment of the Berkshire Downs overlooking the Vale of the White Horse. It is some 110 metres long and was carved into the chalk so that it is visible from several kilometres away. OSL dating

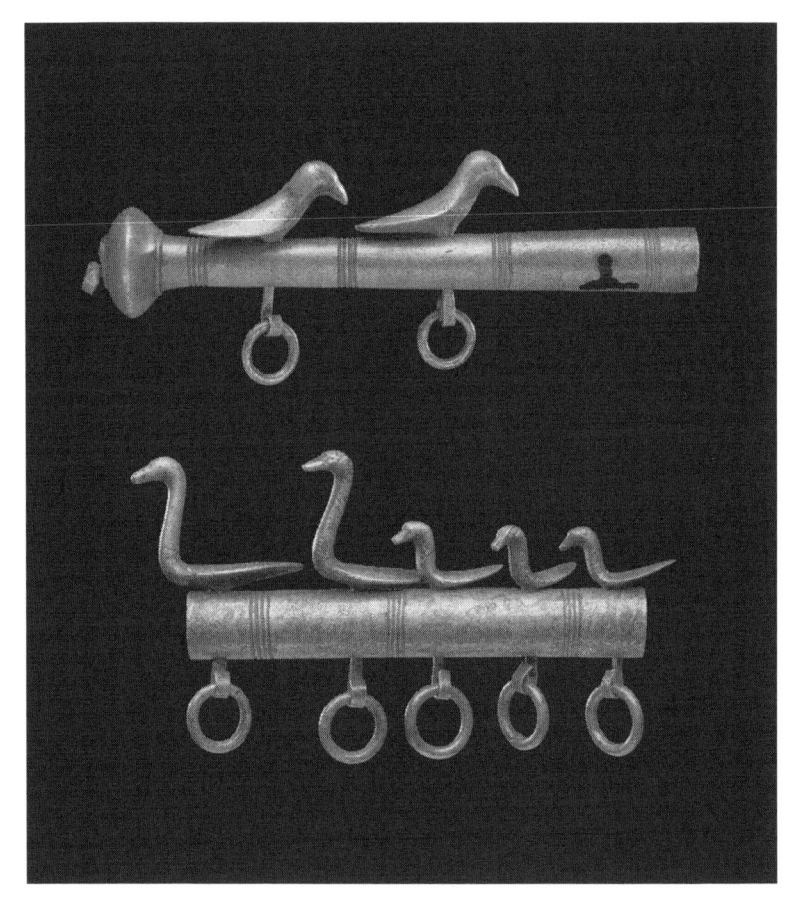

Figure 5.19. The ravens and waterbirds on the Dunaverny flesh-hook (© The Trustees of the British Museum).

indicates that it was created in the Late Bronze Age (Miles et al. 2003). Although parallels for the iconography of Dunaverny and Uffington are unknown in Britain or Ireland, depictions of horses and waterbirds frequently occur on the Late Bronze metalwork of central and northern Europe, notably on objects such as beaten bronze vessels and razors (Kaul 1998). These animals are often combined with imagery relating to the movement of the sun—drawn in a chariot through the sky by day and conveyed by boat at night through a watery underworld—most memorably in the famous Trundholm chariot. The Dunaverny and Uffington animals may therefore invoke common elements of northern European cosmologies (Pollard 2016): Pollard, for example, notes that the Uffington white horse is oriented towards the east and that the midwinter sun appears to rise from its back when observed from the springs at Woolstone Wells, the location where the best view of the horse is available.

Bowman and Needham (2007, 93), however, point out that the birds depicted on objects such as the buckets and amphorae of the central European Late Bronze Age are a different species (usually ducks) to those modelled on the Dunaverny flesh-hook, and they suggest instead geographically closer parallels in Irish mythology, first written down in the Middle Ages but with origins possibly in the Iron Age, if not earlier. Ravens and swans feature in many of these stories. These animals are often seen as having supernatural powers: ravens are associated with the goddesses of war and symbolize death and destruction, while swans were considered to have shape-shifting abilities and to be able to travel between the world of the living and the supernatural realm. As such, the juxtaposition of ravens and swans on the Dunaverny flesh-hook may have evoked the contrast between darkness and light, death and fertility (the swans are depicted with three cygnets), imparting symbolic potency (if not magical power) to this object and those who used it (Bowman and Needham 2007).

Horse harnesses, wheeled vehicles, and field boundaries can be viewed as technologies of domination, facilitating forms of control and manipulation that imply asymmetrical power relationships between people and animals by the end of the Bronze Age. The ability to command and restrain animal bodies may have enhanced the power and status of particular human individuals (Pare 1989). Yet this is to ignore the cosmogenic power of animals like the horse: those who could ride in a vehicle pulled by a horse may have shared some of that animal's supernatural potency. Argent (2016a; 2016b) has critiqued interpretations of Pazyryk Iron Age horse burials that view these animals as the property of powerful elites, arguing instead that they indicate relations of mutual trust, communication, and cooperation in the construction of shared lifeworlds. The evidence of depositional practice in Middle and Late Bronze Age settlements, field systems, and hoards indicates both the economic centrality and social significance of animals such as cattle, sheep, and horses. They may have been employed in important social transactions, such as marriage prestations, or have formed an element of sacrificial offerings during feasts and ceremonies. Ethnographic studies of societies where animals are a form of wealth indicate that people often form close emotional bonds with particular animal individuals (Evans-Pritchard 1940; Galaty 1989). In the Bronze Age, the treatment and deposition of animal and human bodies in similar ways—for example, the deposition of skull fragments in settlement contexts—suggest that there were symbolic as well as experiential and emotional links between people and animals, and it seems possible that people had special relationships with individual cattle, dogs, and horses. Yet it is evident that animals with a less clear economic role, such as polecats, foxes, guillemots, and swans, were also of interest and importance to Late Bronze Age communities, probably for the symbolic potential of the qualities they possessed, their role as totems, or their significance in Bronze Age mythology. The use of animal elements in Late Bronze Age costumes, for example, suggests that certain people may have been able to assume animal characteristics (even animal being) in ritual contexts, so that the boundary between human and animal bodies may sometimes have been viewed as relatively fluid.

Conclusion

It is evident from discussion in this chapter that Bronze Age landscapes cannot solely be viewed as objects of exploitation. Particular places and their constituent elements were bound up with personal and community identities. The selection of materials for the construction of Early Bronze Age barrows, for example, indicates that soil, stone, wood, and other 'natural' substances were meaningful components of the social world, evoking significant places and the people and practices associated with those locations. So too, the origin of grave goods such as stone battleaxes or amber beads conjured links with special places, while composite objects made of multiple materials—daggers with their wooden handles, bone pommels, leather sheaths, and moss wrappings, for example—mapped relationships with the non-human world. Of course, places and their constituent elements speak of particular cultural values, so that barrows can be viewed as structured assemblages of objects and materials that worked to recreate the cosmological order. This choreography of materials underlines the profoundly relational character of being.

Intimate, personalized relationships with landscape are visible in the Middle and Late Bronze Age too, for example in the deposition of special objects such as pots, axes, or gorgets under boulders, at springs, or in clefts in the rock. So too, it is often overly simplistic to claim that Bronze Age field boundaries were 'imposed' on the landscape, for detailed attention to individual boundaries—even in coaxial field systems—indicates that they were often the result of small-scale, gradual acts of addition and amendment. Although they may be rendered on maps as regular linear features, close examination on the ground shows that they frequently meander and change character over their length, and they are clearly attuned to the landscape itself, for they respond to pre-existing (and doubtless meaningful) features such as tors, cairns, and barrows. A mutualistic relationship with the landscape is surely indicated by the placing of votive deposits in contexts such as field boundaries, wells, and clearance cairns, and it is perhaps no coincidence that the components of such deposits—pots, querns, or animal bodies, for example—often speak of human, animal, and agricultural fertility. It is evident that Bronze Age people did not view the landscape as an object of exploitation but as an active subject which could be drawn into productive relationships through ritualized acts of gift exchange.

Moreover, there is much to suggest that Bronze Age cosmologies were mapped onto the landscape, so that landscape features were infused with cultural meaning. The deposition of metalwork and the siting of barrows indicate that prominent hilltops, for example, were often a particular focus of attention, and it is possible that these figured in origin myths or were viewed as locations where communication with celestial beings could take place. A tripartite division of the cosmos into sky, earth, and underworld is suggested also by the evident interest in features such as caves and dolines; the deposition of human bone in caves, for example, indicates that these may have been seen as hazardous, liminal spaces between the worlds of the living and the dead. Watery places such as bogs and rivers may have been viewed in similar terms: crossing bridges or trackways elicited acts of votive deposition, while the ritual decommissioning of boats suggests that travel was viewed as a dangerous transformative process. The world of the living was, of course, carefully located relative to the other world, and this can be seen in the structuring of landscape: at Bradley Fen, as we have seen, houses and field systems were located on the dryland, while the neighbouring fen was the setting for a range of transformative activities, indicated by the deposition of broken metalwork and human bone and the presence of burnt mounds (Figures 3.10 and 5.11; Gibson and Knight 2006). Although animal imagery is rare, the Uffington horse and the swans on the Dunaverny flesh-hook hint at shared elements with other northern European cosmographies, and it is possible that in Britain and Ireland too horses and waterbirds were thought to facilitate the cyclical passage of the sun through the sky and watery underworld. Aspects of such belief systems were incorporated into daily engagement with the landscape: the north-east–south-west orientation of many field systems, for example, indicates an interest in the diurnal and seasonal movements of the sun.

Yet this was not simply a case of mapping human culture onto landscape: the natural world was not a mere *tabula rasa* onto which cultural meanings could be layered. In fact, there is much to suggest that a distinct divide between culture and nature was not recognized during the Bronze Age. We have seen, for example, how Early Bronze Age barrows mimic landscape features such as low knolls, while cairns may incorporate tors and earthfast boulders. Fossils such as crinoids were employed as beads in assemblages that included visually similar artefacts made of jet and faience. Crinoids may have been understood as beads fashioned by the ancestors, although the distinction between 'natural' and made objects may not have been recognized or considered important (Brück and Jones 2018). Fossils were occasionally included in the burials of ritual specialists, while the juxtaposition of fossils and beads made from materials with unusual properties like amber and jet hints that such items were considered to possess curative or apotropaic powers; here, what we might identify as inert natural objects have agency. So too, the deposition of metalwork on hilltops suggests that these were considered powerful places; mountains in other cultural contexts are frequently worshipped as deities.

The existence of a nature–culture divide is also called into question by the significance of animals in the Bronze Age. Animal and human bodies were often treated in similar ways, from the incorporation of animal remains in Early Bronze Age burials to the deposition of human and animal skulls on Late Bronze Age settlements. The close relationship between people and animals and the evident economic significance of sheep and cattle hints that the biographies of humans and animals may have been interlinked. Cattle, for example, may have been prized as a form of wealth and exchanged in significant social transactions such as marriage prestations or on the birth of a child. The inclusion of other animal elements such as fox skulls or eagles' talons in burials and pit

Social landscapes

deposits may suggest a totemic relationship between humans and animals, so that animals were part of the social world. The selection of particular species or body parts for the manufacture of objects such as dagger pommels indicates that animal elements possessed cultural significance and that their qualities may have been used to ascribe value to particular categories of person. Yet animals were not merely ascribed symbolic meanings by human communities. Animal parts were used to wrap the bodies of the dead, they were employed as amulets and made into transformative objects such as awls, and it is likely that such items were themselves considered to possess agency and power. So too, the use of items such as tusks, teeth, skins, and feathers as elements of costume elided the distinction between humans and animals, allowing humans to take on animal characteristics and to penetrate the division between the world of the living and the realm of animal spirits and ancestors.

To return to the question posed at the beginning of this chapter—whether there was an increasingly exploitative relationship between humans and landscape during the later part of the Bronze Age—it is clear that this is too simplistic and reductionist a reading of the evidence. The landscape and its constituent elements (bogs, boar, sheep, trees, eagles, rocks, cattle, moss, etc.) were not viewed as objects that could be commodified, but as part of an animate cosmos. People entered meaningful social relationships with animals and other components of the landscape, and it is evident that these relationships were often construed in mutualistic terms. Mytho-cosmological belief systems infused the landscape with social and symbolic meaning. In such a context, it would not have been possible to *exploit* the natural world—for that implies the reduction of that world to the status of inanimate object.

6

Conclusion

The flow of life in Bronze Age Britain and Ireland

Self and substance

It is evident from the discussion in previous chapters that the projection into the past of dualistic conceptual frameworks that sharply distinguish subject from object, for example, or culture from nature, is problematic. Instead, the evidence suggests that the Bronze Age self was not constructed in opposition to an external 'other'. Things outside of the body, such as significant objects, formed inalienable components of the person, while parts of the human body circulated in the same exchange networks as objects. The self was constituted relationally, so that the social and political position of particular people depended on their connections with others. Special places, too, were sedimented into the self, forming an inextricable part of personal, family, and community histories. The Bronze Age person can therefore be viewed as a composite—an assemblage of substances and elements flowing in and out of the wider social landscape.

Indeed, it is interesting to note how ideas of substance may have changed from the Neolithic to the Bronze Age. Neolithic technologies—notably the grinding and polishing of stone axes—made evident the qualities of the material itself: polishing enhanced the colour, texture, and geological inclusions of such objects, rendering visible their very essence and origin (Whittle 1995; Cooney 2002). By contrast, bronze was made of a mixture of materials and its constituent elements were hidden. The production of composite objects also became more frequent during the Bronze Age (Jones 2002, 164–5), for example the

Conclusion

miniature halberd pendant made of gold, amber, and copper alloy from an Early Bronze Age grave at Wilsford G8 in Wiltshire (Needham et al. 2015a, 230). Sometimes particular components of such items were concealed: the conical pendant or button from Upton Lovell G2e in Wiltshire comprised a shale core covered with sheet gold (Needham et al. 2015a, 222–5). This need not indicate an attempt to deceive others into believing this item was made of solid gold, however, for shale was itself used to make decorative items and was evidently a valued material during this period.

Instead, we can suggest that the process of layering was considered an essential attribute of Early Bronze Age concepts of substance (Jones 2010). We have already discussed the wrapping of items such as daggers in layers of protective material and the deposition of cremated bone beneath inverted urns. Likewise, we have seen that many Early Bronze Age barrows comprise multiple distinct layers of mound material, so that the core components of these monuments were not always visible. Similar ideas may have extended to the living body also. Woodward (2000, 115), as we have seen, has suggested that the awls found in Early Bronze Age burials may have been used for tattooing, covering the skin in a protective layer; if so, it seems likely that similar motifs to those used to decorate pots (a second skin for the cremated body) might have been used. Together, this suggests that Neolithic and Bronze Age ideas about materiality and substance were quite different. In the Bronze Age, form and content were not always analogous. Instead, objects (and persons) were composed of assemblages of elements, not all of which were immediately visible.

Although this process of assembling the person can be seen from the beginning of the period, for example in the collections of objects placed in bags and boxes in Beaker graves, it seems possible that the introduction of metalworking had a profound effect on notions of self and substance. Unlike the production of stone objects, which involved revealing the intrinsic attributes of the material through subtractive processes such as flaking and polishing, metalworking required materials and objects to be brought together and amalgamated, particularly as recycling became more common, so that the histories and origins of individual artefacts were rendered invisible. Of course, this may not mean that the constituent components of a Bronze Age axe, for example, were unknown or insignificant, and we have argued that practices of deliberate fragmentation—central, of course, to the recycling of bronze objects—acted to create ancestral elements that possessed both meaning and power.

Destruction and exchange

The introduction of metalworking saw an increasing interest in the creative tension between death and reproduction (Helms 2012). As we have already discussed, the production of bronze objects required the recycling of old and broken artefacts. Fragmentation and transformation by fire were essential elements of other technological processes too, including pottery production, cremation, and cooking; for each of these, consumption is a prerequisite of reproduction. The negotiation of the tension between death and the renewal of life appears to have become a particular focus of interest during the period—addressed in metaphorical terms in productive technologies and assuming monumental form in the middens of the Late Bronze Age (Brück 2006b). We can suggest that this occurred in part because of the significance of exchange during the Bronze Age (Brück 2006a; 2015). It has long been recognized that the exchange of objects and materials over considerable distances was a key component of the Bronze Age economy (Childe 1930; Kristiansen and Earle 2015). As we have already seen, for example, copper from Ross Island in County Kerry was used to make the earliest metal objects across much of western and northern Britain (Northover 2004). Materials other than metals were also circulated both within the British Isles and over longer distances: the style and fabric of an Early Bronze Age urn from Monkton in Kent, for instance, indicate that it was made in Cornwall (Gibson et al. 1997, 438–41), while the origin of most amber objects is thought to lie even further afield in the Baltic region (Beck and Shennan 1991, 29–37). Similarities in artefact styles and burial practices on either side of the English Channel indicate intensive interaction between southern England, northern France, and the Low Countries at several points throughout the period, and it is possible that the primary social and political allegiances of these communities lay with those on the other side of the Channel rather than in their own immediate hinterlands (e.g. Glasbergen 1954; Needham et al. 2006). The changing character of regional and interregional interaction has long been a focus of study in the period, and our understanding of the waxing and waning of different axes of exchange continues to improve (e.g. O'Connor 1980; Rohl and Needham 1998; Needham et al. 2013).

Exchange, of course, fulfils a range of purposes beyond the simple acquisition of materials or objects that are not locally available. In most accounts of the Bronze Age, it is viewed primarily as a means of accumulating wealth or of acquiring exotic objects that can act as markers of status or as gifts to ensure the allegiance of followers (e.g. Kristiansen and Larsson 2005; Needham et al. 2006; Kristiansen and Suchowska-Ducke 2015). Yet exchange does more than this. Crucially, it plays a significant role in upholding the moral and social order (Bloch and Parry 1989; Hugh-Jones 1992). Exchange generates relationships between people and it is therefore often viewed as a moral imperative. By transforming strangers into kin, it acts as a means of incorporating and demystifying the 'other'. Yet, as Mauss (1990 [1954]) long ago demonstrated, the giving of gifts places people in asymmetrical relations of obligation and allows claims to be made over the resources of others. In this way, exchange encourages processes of comparison and distinction, differentiating the commensurable from the incommensurable and creating an order of value for both people and objects (Weiner 1992). The kinds of gifts given to a person allow others to estimate their social worth, for objects communicate identity, interpersonal relationships, and the economy of taste and value that structures the social universe. Exchange therefore functions as a means of negotiating mutual estimation and regard (Humphrey and Hugh-Jones 1992, 17). In such a context, gifts derive their significance not from some abstract measure of economic value but from the meanings ascribed to them and the way in which they are bound into personal and community histories.

Exchange is, however, an ambiguous process. On the one hand, it is crucial to the social, material, and biological reproduction of communities. Yet it also involves the transgression of social boundaries and exposes objects to 'tournaments of value' that may call into question the social categories they underpin (Appadurai 1986, 21). Gift-exchange and marriage transactions, for example, involve the loss of people and objects that form part of the self, but in return other objects and people are acquired (Valeri 1980; Weiner 1992). In the Bronze Age, there were clear structural similarities between exchange and technological processes such as metalworking, cooking, and cremation that required acts of destruction in order to facilitate new life; each involved processes of fragmentation, mixing, and amalgamation (Brück 2006a; 2006b). The duality of loss and gain was therefore one of the central motifs that ran through Bronze Age life, a contradiction that needed to be reconciled in order to maintain the continuity of society. An interest in cycles of growth, decay, and renewal is evident in other ways too, for example in the deposition of fragments of dead people and broken objects in the middens of the Late Bronze Age. Like working metals or dealing with the bodies of the dead, journeying for exchange was a dangerous and transformative process central to the reproduction of life, and this is doubtless why travel was ritualized during the period; in such circumstances, it is little surprise that boats, horses, or rivers should have assumed particular symbolic significance.

These points have interesting implications for the relationship between people and objects. Marriage, for example, involves the gifting of sons or daughters and the consequent loss of their reproductive potential. Yet, in return, a group may be repaid in objects that can be used to obtain new marriage partners for other members of the family. In this way, the flow of objects sustains the flow of life (Valeri 1980; Hoskins 1989; Battaglia 1990, 78–9, 171). However, it is not enough to say that objects come to stand for people because they circulate within exchange systems just like people do; the very act of exchange transforms people into objects and objects into people. This means that the objects given in exchange for the life force of a marriage partner must themselves have a life force (Battaglia 1990, 86–7). Objects have biographies because they stand in a structural relationship to people; each partakes in the qualities of the other (Hoskins 1998). The flow of objects in Bronze Age systems of exchange is therefore one reason why what we would view as inert artefacts were considered to possess power and agency in their own right (Brück 2015). Importantly, this indicates that, when people were exchanged as marriage partners, they were not viewed as 'objects' in the modern, Western sense of the term. Instead, the things and people that circulated as gifts played active roles in creating and maintaining intergroup relationships. Amongst other things, this has significant implications for how we view the role and status of women in the Bronze Age, for women are often figured as passive objects of exchange in accounts of the period (Jockenhövel 1991; Kristiansen 1998, 398).

Marriage transactions were, of course, not the only acts of exchange that facilitated the transformation of people into objects and vice versa. Death is often seen as the random and uncontrolled dispersal of valued substances (Bloch and Parry 1982; Battaglia 1990, 59). It is important not only that the vital energy of the deceased person should be released and recirculated at death but that this should be achieved in a controlled and socially productive way (Küchler 1987). Mortuary transactions are integral to this process, for they recreate the substance of the deceased in the form of objects (Forman 1980; Battaglia 1990, 163). The circulation of objects during funerary rites is a means of recompensing all those who contributed to the life of the deceased (Clamagirand 1980; Battaglia 1990, 171–9; Weiner 1992, 76, 92). For example, a woman's husband may be expected to give gifts to her descent group to repay them for the labour and resources they have invested in her during life. These gifts can be used to replace the woman they have lost and generate new life through new marriage alliances. Hence the deceased is turned into objects which are in turn converted into a living person (De Coppet 1981, 185–9; Strathern 1981; Battaglia 1990). By disaggregating the life force of the deceased and converting it into objects, new social relationships can be formed and the reproduction of the community (and community values) ensured. In this way, the giving of gifts at funerals allows kin groups to channel death into regeneration, ensuring the cyclical flow of substances and vitality.

Production and reproduction

In the Bronze Age, the retention of heirlooms, the disaggregation of items such as necklaces and daggers, and the circulation of human bone all hint at acts of exchange at the graveside: the circulation of ancestral fragments (such as pieces of human bone or parts of significant objects) in mortuary transactions allowed some of the life force or vitality of the deceased to be returned to the family group who originally gave that person in marriage (Brück 2006a; 2015). Such exchanges ensured the proper flow of vital substances and fertility within the wider community, so that no one kin group was depleted. Mortuary transactions formed part of an ongoing series of exchanges between families, exchanges that facilitated the regeneration of life and the harnessing of death for the good of society. As such, we can suggest that exchange, mortuary practices, and technological activities were considered structurally similar processes. In each case, they facilitated the production of the self and the reproduction of society through processes of fragmentation, disintegration, and loss.

It is interesting to note that as the recycling of bronze objects became more common, so too other new technologies, such as cremation, appeared. The development of the idea that social and material reproduction was achieved through cycles of burning, breaking, mixing, and reincorporation provided people with the conceptual tools necessary to develop new productive practices. At Gwithian in Cornwall, the active addition of manure to the fields can be discerned possibly from as early as 1800 BC (Nowakowski et al. 2007, 32), while burnt mounds—which appear to have been the focus for a range of heat-mediated transformative technologies—are the most common category of Bronze Age site in Ireland (Ó Néill 2009). Transformations mediated by heating and grinding were viewed as particularly powerful and productive, facilitating the regeneration of life through the harnessing of death. We have already discussed the production of pots and bronzes, but there are interesting similarities between the treatment of the dead and other activities too, for instance the processing of grain (Williams 2003). Like the dead, grain was parched to make it productive. It could then be ground and cooked or used in brewing. Seed corn was stored in ceramic vessels before planting, some of which were themselves placed in pits in the ground, just as the bodies of the dead were burnt, broken, and buried. Interestingly, although fragments of bone in British Bronze Age cremation burials tend to be relatively large, usually over 10 millimetres in length (McKinley 1994, 340), there is considerable variation in fragment size in Irish Bronze Age cremation burials, suggesting deliberate pounding or crushing of bone in specific instances (Lynch and O'Donnell 2007, 112): the burial of a young adult from Grange, County Limerick, for example, comprised 781 grams of burnt bone, 80 per cent of which was under 10 millimetres in length (Lynch and O'Donnell 2007, table 5.2).

These points have significant implications, for an understanding of transformative technologies such as pottery production, metalworking, and food preparation can each provide insights into concepts of the self (Brück 2006b). I would argue that production and reproduction were seen as fundamentally similar processes: the recycling of bronze and the tempering of ceramics with materials such as grog (fragments of broken pottery) and burnt flint (the by-product of cooking) suggest that the Bronze Age person was thought of as a fractal (Strathern 1988) and intensely historical entity. The self was made up of fragments—an amalgamation of elements brought together through such processes as marriage, exchange, and other interpersonal contacts. We can perhaps go as far as to suggest that the introduction of metallurgy provided new ways of thinking about the person. At some level, the process of making always involves the re-enactment of creation myths, for it embodies core beliefs about substance and temporality (Blier 1987; van der Laan 2016). It is therefore little surprise that the sorts of heat-mediated transformative activities that dominate the productive technologies of the British Bronze Age have elements in common with the cosmologies that have been reconstructed for other parts of northern Europe during the same period: Scandinavian Bronze Age iconography, for example, suggests an interest in the link between death and fertility, for the cyclical passage of the sun appears to have been of particular religious significance (Kaul 1998; see also Helms 2012).

Bronze Age technologies therefore provide insights into ideas of space and time: multiple elements of the social and material landscape, for example, were folded into objects such as bronze daggers. Metalworking embodies cyclical concepts of temporality, for it involves sequences of loss and regeneration. In a similar way, the use of grog

Conclusion

tempering in pottery indicates that change and continuity were viewed as interdependent processes; the projection of life into the future required attention to the past. So too, the human lifecycle may have been viewed as a series of stages mediated by rites of passage that facilitated the death of one social persona and the birth of another. The evident interest in refuse and decay and their place in the midst of life, particularly in the Late Bronze Age, hints that social practices such as the deposition of human bone in settlements or the creation of monumental middens helped people to conceptualize the passage of time and cope with the impact of social change. Concepts of temporality were not wholly cyclical, however: there is a sense of directional growth, for example, in the addition of layers to Early Bronze Age barrows or the sequential construction of a row of Middle Bronze Age roundhouses.

Exchange, commoditization, and social boundaries

Although exchange facilitates the construction and maintenance of interpersonal relationships, it also acts as a means of engaging with difference and distance (Sahlins 1972, ch. 5). Exchange defines and gives value to the 'other', but it also brings the distant and foreign into the social universe (Humphrey and Hugh-Jones 1992). As a social practice, it creates both similarities and differences; it allows boundaries to be identified but also to be crossed. In many societies, for example, affines are viewed as ambivalent beings: they may provide not only marriage partners, but assistance and resources, yet their demands also constitute a burden (Lévi-Strauss 1969). The integrity of the kin group is an ideal that cannot be realized in practice; marriage, like other forms of exchange, creates long-term relations of obligation that highlight both the benefits and the drawbacks of intergroup links. In such a context, the flow of objects plays a crucial role not only in mapping and making relationships, but also in defining and controlling the other (Bloch and Parry 1989; Weiner 1992).

This ambivalence about the transgression of social boundaries is particularly visible in the material practices of the later part of the Bronze Age. As we have seen, broken objects and fragments of human bone were deposited in locations such as boundaries and entrances; they were also recycled to make new objects and incorporated into midden material that was spread on the fields. This suggests that, on the one hand, processes of social and material transformation were viewed as dangerous and ambivalent but, on the other, were considered central to the regeneration of life. Acts of destruction symbolized death and its impact, but the circulation of significant fragments in networks of exchange and the amalgamation and mixing of such fragments in productive processes such as metalworking ensured the continuity of social relations.

These points have interesting implications for our understanding of the organization of Bronze Age exchange. There has been considerable debate over the past thirty years regarding the relative significance of gift and commodity exchange in the European Bronze Age. Classic anthropological formulations posit a categorical distinction between gift and commodity exchange (Polanyi 1968; Sahlins 1972; Gregory 1982). Commodity exchange is seen as fundamentally asocial, and money (its key vehicle) as dehumanizing, immoral, and impersonal (Taussig 1980). The reductive process of commodification makes the incommensurable commensurable, stripping away social qualities to reveal what can be quantified so that any object can be exchanged for any other (Gregory 1982, 71). In systems of commodity exchange, economic gain is prioritized. By contrast, the core purpose of gift exchange is social gain. Gifts forge stable social relationships that last beyond the moment of transaction, tying donor and recipient together in networks of mutual obligation (Mauss 1990 [1954]). The objects that are given as gifts are unique and socially meaningful: they embody the spirit of the donor and they are therefore inalienable. By contrast, commodities are alienable objects in which others have no residual interest and that can be disposed of as their owners desire. In this way, Gregory (1982, 42) argues, gift exchange establishes relationships between people, while commodity exchange establishes relationships between things.

Although gift exchange is generally considered to be the primary mechanism by which objects moved in the European Bronze Age, evidence for commodity transactions has also been identified. In central and southern Europe, for example, hoards of copper ingots have been taken to indicate the importance of commodity exchange (Sommerfeld 1994; Lenerz de Wilde 1995; Primas 1997; Wengrow 2008). In north-western Europe, such hoards are rare. Instead, scrap hoards are often viewed as evidence for the commoditization of bronze. Following Sahlins (1972), for example, Bradley (1985) has argued that commodity exchange tends to take place *between* groups rather than *within* groups, and he suggests that the hoards of broken bronzes found close to the coast of southern England are evidence for commodity transactions between different social groups on either side of the English Channel. 'Foreign' artefact types, he suggests, would not have retained their original cultural meanings outside their normal circulation zones, and

Conclusion

could therefore be broken and recycled into 'local' objects. By contrast, he notes that hoards away from the coast tend to comprise complete objects, with different artefact types (weapons and ornaments, for example) deposited separately, indicating that the meanings ascribed to these items continued to be significant.

This is an appealing model. We have argued elsewhere in this volume, however, that the process of fragmentation does not indicate that objects had lost their social significance; on the contrary, it was precisely because their histories and meanings continued to be important that people sought to obtain, curate, and deposit fragments of special objects. In other words, the act of breaking an object need not imply commodification (Brück 2015; 2016). Instead, relational identities were constructed via the circulation of meaningful fragments. In the contemporary Western world, the process of commodification is reliant on a categorical distinction between subject and object—a dichotomy that we have already argued was not always articulated in the Bronze Age. Commodification also presupposes a distinction between the economy and society. Yet this is a product of recent history (Carrier 1995) and should not be unthinkingly imposed on the past. During the eighteenth and nineteenth centuries, industrialization, secularization, and the emergence of the nation state resulted in the spatial and conceptual disjunction of the economic, ritual, political, and domestic spheres. The home, workplace, church, and other public spaces were distinguished and circumscribed, and this fulfilled particular political purposes, allowing the economic output of certain categories of worker to be controlled and appropriated while that of others (notably women working in the home) was concealed (e.g. Braun 1990; Digby 1992; Johnson, M. 1996). Where the economic and the social are not categorically distinguished, however, the process of commodification cannot occur because objects are inextricably intertwined with the personhood and social identities of those who make and use them.

In fact these points require us to call into question the distinction between gift exchange and commodity exchange and to ask if this is a helpful way of characterizing the circulation of objects in the Bronze Age (Brück 2015). It is possible to suggest that even market exchange in the contemporary Western world is socially embedded (Carrier 1995). Today, corporate directors strike deals on the golf course, while companies make employees into family through Christmas gifts. Money is sanctified with the moral authority of the state: the Queen's head appears on British currency, for example, while US dollars bear the motto 'in God we trust' (Hart 2005; Maurer 2006; Fontijn 2013). We disapprove of money that is used in the 'wrong' way, avoiding contact with 'dirty' money, for example, or deriding the nouveaux riches who spend their wealth in ways that the middle classes might identify as showy and tasteless. Indeed, the economic value of goods in the market economy is a mark of the cultural meanings and social values ascribed to them. Conversely, economic value can give objects—such as certain types of car—social cachet. It is therefore hardly surprising that shopping has itself become a highly ritualized and social activity bound up, for example, with certain types of age and gendered identity (Miller 1998); so too, activities on the trading floors of the New York or London stock exchanges in the 1980s were very much about the performance of a particular kind of masculine identity. Exchange, in other words, is always social, for it involves the reification of social categories and negotiation of cultural values. This means that the distinction between gift and commodity exchange is not helpful for understanding either the Bronze Age or the contemporary economy (Bloch and Parry 1989; Carrier 1995; Miller 2001b; Fontijn 2013). Gregory's argument (1982, 42) that gift exchange establishes relationships between people while commodity exchange establishes relationships between objects (a Mercedes is more expensive than a Ford, for example) is therefore an oversimplification, for objects stand for people and are inextricably bound up with social identities.

This is not to say, of course, that all objects are equal in the social roles they play. Weiner (1992) has argued that both alienable and inalienable objects can exist in any one society. This, she suggests, depends on how particular objects stand in relation to people; heirlooms, for example, may be considered inalienable because of the way they are bound up with family identity. This does not mean that alienable objects are devoid of social value, however. Instead, we can argue that certain categories of object are employed to maintain social boundaries, while others are used to mediate or even to transgress them. Exchange is fundamentally about defining, negotiating, and overcoming difference and distance (Humphrey and Hugh-Jones 1992). In the Bronze Age, it is evident that objects such as swords were treated differently to objects such as axes (e.g. Bradley 1990; Fontijn 2002; Becker 2013). Swords (usually deposited singly in water) may have been inalienable objects, while axes (often found in dryland hoards) may have been employed in marriage transactions and other intergroup exchanges. The deposition of fragments of objects, for example in scrap hoards, may have sanctioned the breaching of social categories (cf. Fontijn 2005; Becker 2013, 251–5), for instance by ritualizing metal recycling, but also it ensured the continuity of relational identities by allowing portions of socially significant artefacts to be incorporated into new objects. The deposition

Conclusion

of metalwork can therefore be seen to epitomize the paradox of creative consumption: for Bronze Age communities, death preceded rebirth just as both the maintenance and transgression of boundaries were integral to social reproduction. Thus the objects in bronze hoards were not commodities but powerful social agents whose fragmentation facilitated the regeneration of life (Brück 2006a). In the Bronze Age, the increasing concern over the mediation of difference and distance that resulted from the social significance of exchange can be seen in the creation of spatial boundaries and their marking through the deposition of bronzes, human bone, and other objects, both complete and fragmented.

Personhood and power

Although most researchers working on the period would agree that gift exchange was the primary mechanism by which objects circulated during the Bronze Age, in fact the ideology of competitive individualism so often conjured in accounts of the period is a particular feature of modern, Western capitalism (Brück and Fontijn 2013). If we accept that there is little evidence for commodity exchange during the period, this requires us to question existing models of the Bronze Age self. We have suggested that the Bronze Age person was not viewed as a static and homogeneous whole, but as fluid, fragmented, and composite. The flow of objects constituted the person not as an 'individual' but as relationally embedded and profoundly sociocentric. The non-human world was not objectified, but formed part of the self. The idea that people could own, manipulate, and dispose of objects or other things as they wished is therefore problematic, for the exploitative relations of capitalism are very different to the sorts of relationships in which Bronze Age persons were enmeshed. Objects with complex exchange histories, for example, could not be freely disposed of, for they were always subject to the claims of others.

This is not to deny that there were differentials of power. Certainly, objects such as bronze weapons allowed power to be performed and enacted on the bodies of others, and it is increasingly clear that these were not mere symbols of status but were often well used (Bridgford 1997; Molloy 2007). Yet there is little to suggest that conflict was anything other than small-scale and sporadic (Osgood 1998, 89–90); even male Beaker inhumation burials, so often identified as warrior graves because of the presence of archery equipment and daggers, rarely display osteological evidence for violence or trauma, while items such as the leaf-shaped spearheads of the Late Bronze Age may have been employed to define particular age grades rather than a political elite. Indeed, the ownership of weapons does not always map neatly on to political power: in the contemporary US, for example, it is often the disenfranchised and impoverished who are most attached to the idea of gun ownership. In Bronze Age Britain and Ireland, the evidence suggests that power was socially conferred and its limits contained. Moreover, the fluidity of composite forms of self hints that power relations are likely to have been contextually specific, so that those who held positions of power in certain settings may not have done so in others. It was not possible to exert complete control over another person, for the self was not a bounded entity but was constructed in spatially and temporally dispersed contexts. This requires us to challenge the static models of social hierarchy so often proposed for the period.

Social change and the end of the Bronze Age

Inevitably, the emergence of new concepts of temporality and substance had a significant impact on the direction of social and economic change. Each of the preceding chapters has attempted to provide some sense of changing social practices over the course of the Bronze Age, from dramatic differences in the organization of the landscape to new ways of treating the bodies of the dead. In general, there appears to have been an increasing interest in processes of subdivision across a range of different areas of social practice. Complete inhumation burials were more common in the first few centuries of the period, but by the end of the Bronze Age the bodies of the dead were represented by small deposits of cremated bone and occasional unburnt fragments. The deliberate fragmentation of objects was an element of ritual practice throughout the period, but by the Late Bronze Age this no longer occurred primarily in the intimate space of the grave, but took the form of highly visible communal action in the accumulation of monumental middens and the deposition of large numbers of broken bronzes in scrap hoards. We have described how Early Bronze Age barrows can be seen as composite models of the wider landscape. By contrast, the field systems of the Middle and Late Bronze Age suggest an interest in subdivision rather than assembly. The appearance of enclosed settlements during these later periods suggests, on the one hand, a concern to divide the inhabitants of these places from those beyond the boundaries and, on the other, a desire to maintain the integrity of the co-resident group in the face of increasing social fragmentation.

Conclusion

With the exception of Needham's important contribution (2007), there has been relatively little discussion of the end of the Bronze Age in recent years. It is possible that ironworking was occasionally carried out from relatively early in the Late Bronze Age. At Hartshill Copse, Upper Bucklebury, Berkshire, an otherwise unremarkable open settlement produced abundant iron hammer-scale, mostly from in and around a double-ring roundhouse (Collard et al. 2006). Radiocarbon dates suggest the site was occupied in the tenth century BC. Needham (2007, fig. 4) notes that the deposition of bronze reached a high point during the ninth century BC, after which the frequency of bronze objects decreases dramatically. This is not matched by a significant increase in iron objects, however. From the late ninth and early eighth centuries on, iron artefacts are sporadically found at settlements and other sites: a number of iron objects, including a possible punch and a possible awl, were found in contexts of this date at Potterne in Wiltshire (Cleal and Lawson 2000), while the eponymous Llyn Fawr hoard, found in a lake in the Cynon Valley, south Wales, produced an iron sword, spearhead, and sickle alongside a large number of bronze objects including two cauldrons, horse equipment, chisels, sickles, and axes (Crawford and Wheeler 1921; Fox and Hyde 1939). In general, however, iron objects are very rare in the Earliest Iron Age and indeed in the subsequent two centuries (Ehrenreich 1985; Needham 2007, 51–2): iron, it seems, did not immediately replace bronze as a common material for the production of everyday items, suggesting that neither its technical properties nor the widespread availability of iron ores can explain the demise of bronze. Indeed, there is some evidence to suggest that the aesthetic qualities of early iron objects were considered more important than their functional capacity: significant quantities of tin were added to some of the latest bronze axes, for example those from the hoard at Langton Matravers in Dorset, to give these objects a silvery colour, perhaps in imitation of iron (Roberts et al. 2015, 14).

Needham (2007, 54) suggests that the sudden decrease in the deposition of bronze from the eighth century BC on indicates that this material lost its economic and social value. He argues that the enormous hoards of the ninth-century Ewart Park period represent the mass dumping of a material that no longer played a key role in the maintenance of the social order. From this point on, he suggests, power and wealth were based on the control of agricultural production rather than on long-distance exchange (see also Thomas 1989; Barrett 1989a). Sites such as the monumental middens of southern Britain, whose main period of development appears to have been from the late ninth century on, indicate that access to animal products and control over animal reproduction became increasingly important at this time. New ways of engaging in intergroup competition and expressing social status developed, notably communal feasting and the use of decorated ceramics. A concern with agricultural fertility is expressed in the prevalence of roundhouses that face east (rather than south-east) from the eighth century on, while the increasing occurrence of dedicated storage facilities, such as large pits and raised granaries, indicates that wealth and status depended not on the accumulation of prestige goods but of an agricultural surplus (Needham 2007): for example, the majority of the group of nineteen four-post structures of probable Earliest Iron Age date at South Elmsall in East Yorkshire (Grassam 2010, 5) were arranged in a line, as if to be viewed while people moved through the landscape.

There is much to agree with in Needham's account of the transition, although there are points of divergence also. I would argue that the deposition of large bronze hoards, many of which—for example, the Carp's Tongue hoards of south-east England—included significant quantities of scrap metal, need not indicate the devaluation of bronze. Instead, I have suggested that such hoards were employed to mark and mediate processes of social and spatial transformation. This is true not only of the main phase of bronze deposition before 800 BC, but afterwards too. The enormous hoard of over 500 axes and axe fragments from Langton Matravers in Dorset is especially unusual, as it dates to the late seventh century (Roberts et al. 2015). These were not functional items, for they were high in tin and would therefore have been too brittle for use. Many retained their casting cores and were only partially finished; some were miscast, while others were broken. Their location close to the English Channel suggests that they may have performed a role as special-purpose items in specific social transactions, and their symbolic referencing of the transformative process of bronze-casting may be no coincidence. The final deposition of these items—probably relatively soon after they were made—is likely to have formed a core element of social practice, and cannot be read as indicating that these items were no longer considered valuable.

Moreover, many of the concerns of Earliest Iron Age societies identified by Needham have clear roots in previous centuries, not least the appearance of field systems in the Middle Bronze Age, with their monumentalization of agricultural practice and their evident concern to control animal and crop production (Barrett 1989b; 1994, ch. 6). Barrett has argued for the emergence of agrarian societies in the middle of the second millennium BC which were increasingly concerned with the link between death and fertility. We can therefore suggest that bronze technology sowed the seeds of its own demise. The production of bronze involved processes of fragmentation, mixing, and recycling; it also required the acquisition of materials and objects through the transgression of social boundaries. As such, bronzeworking made clear the link between death and regeneration—a link that fostered an increasing interest in fertility and the renewal of life throughout the Bronze Age. It seems possible that eventually these concerns made human, animal, and agricultural fertility a more logical (and more desirable) locus for the performance of acts of social reproduction and the negotiation of political power.

An ideology that invoked the productive purpose of fragmentation perhaps facilitated the subdivision of other things such as land or human bodies. It may have resulted also in a refocusing of interest on local identities—increasingly evident in the pottery repertoire—particularly given the ambivalent attitude to intergroup interaction and exchange that appears to have developed during the Late Bronze Age. These identities were not bounded and discrete, however: Brudenell (2012) has shown that the stylistic attributes of Late Bronze Age ceramics in East Anglia do not form neat bundles of spatially overlapping traits that might be mapped on to, for example, ethnicity but hint at the fluid and contextual realization of social identity through the strategic assembling of formal and decorative features. Nor, indeed, do we need to agree that an increasing interest in human, animal, and agricultural fertility indicates the replacement of one form of hierarchical society with another: the critique of concepts of competitive individualism set out in the previous section is equally relevant to models that invoke control over agricultural production as the key source of political power. The idea that Early Iron Age societies were chiefdoms has also been challenged (Hill 1989), and recent research has tended instead to focus on how community identities (rather than personal status) were created and negotiated in the first half of the first millennium BC (Sharples 2010, ch. 3; Davis 2015), for example through large-scale construction projects at hillforts.

Bronze Age legacies and representations

It has been argued that the idea of a Bronze Age is outmoded and unhelpful (Bradley 2001), and the appeal of this suggestion is easy to see. Certainly, as an archaeologist working on this period, it can be difficult to articulate its particular identity. When talking to members of the public in Britain, for example, it is much easier to conjure an image of the Neolithic (think of Stonehenge, for instance) or of Roman

Britain than to pithily encapsulate what it is that makes the Bronze Age interesting or unique. The situation is different in Ireland, however, for a dazzling collection of Bronze Age goldwork lies at the heart of the National Museum of Ireland's archaeology exhibits. Here, the Bronze Age is integral to the construction of narratives of national identity, and it is used to create a strong sense of the vigour, wealth, and independence of Irish society before the Norman Conquest. The period is drawn into contemporary discourse in other ways too, however. The extraordinary interest generated by the revelation that the Amesbury Archer may have grown up in central Europe, and the success of projects that use isotope analysis to track human mobility in attracting funding, can perhaps be linked to current concerns around immigration, although recent research drawing on aDNA, isotope, and archaeolinguistic analysis also conjures Beaker immigrants as 'our' ancestors, bringing Indo-European languages with them to Britain and Ireland (Cassidy et al. 2016; Olalde et al. 2018).

As such, the Bronze Age continues to feature in contemporary origin myths, though no longer, perhaps, as the start point of the modern economy. In some respects, the Bronze Age can be described as the original consumer society—but Bronze Age consumption was configured very differently to that intrinsic to the economics of modern capitalism. In Bronze Age Britain and Ireland, consumption was an inherently creative and productive act, although it involved a measure of ambivalence. As a period, the Bronze Age retains its own unique identity because of the centrality of activities—including metalworking and exchange—predicated on the indissoluble link between death and regeneration. This, as we have seen, set up the conditions for a range of significant changes to the economy and society over subsequent centuries, although these by no means generated a unilineal push towards modernity.

Finally, we can note that heuristic categories such as the Bronze Age continue to provide useful food for thought in and for the present—and some would argue that this, perhaps, is the primary role of archaeology as a discipline. It is evident, for example, that Bronze Age concepts of the self and ideas about the natural world were very different to our own. So too, although it is all too easy to project contemporary ideas about gendered identity or political power into the past, there is much to suggest that social relations in the Bronze Age were configured in quite different ways. The value of this, of course, is that it allows us to look afresh at our own cultural context and to ask just how 'natural' some of our own ideas about the world might be. In today's world, where essentializing notions—for example about the body, the value of consumer goods, or acceptable sources of energy—are increasingly being called into question, the concept of a Bronze Age continues to provide a location in which the possibility of alternative configurations of long-distance exchange, social identities, technological transformation, and agricultural change can be explored.

Bibliography

Note: Andy Jones (Cornwall Archaeological Unit) is listed below as A. Jones, while Andy Jones (University of Southampton) is listed as A. M. Jones. Mark Knight is listed as M. Knight, while Matt Knight is listed as M. G. Knight.

Alberti, B. and Bray, T. 2009. 'Animating archaeology: of subjects, objects and alternative ontologies', *Cambridge Archaeological Journal* 19(3), 337–43.

Allan, A. Rault, S., and Humble, J. 2007a. 'Barrow 3, built 2180–1930 cal BC (SS1.14)', in Harding, J. and Healy, F. *The Raunds Area Project. A Neolithic and Bronze Age landscape in Northamptonshire*, 148–53. London: English Heritage.

Allan, A. Rault, S., and Humble, J. 2007b. 'Barrow 4, built 2020–1600 cal BC (SS1.15)', in Harding, J. and Healy, F. *The Raunds Area Project. A Neolithic and Bronze Age landscape in Northamptonshire*, 165–6. London: English Heritage.

Allan, A. Rault, S., and Humble, J. 2007c. 'Barrow 5, built before 2140–1880 Cal BC (SS1.16)', in Harding, J. and Healy, F. *The Raunds Area Project. A Neolithic and Bronze Age landscape in Northamptonshire*, 141–7. London: English Heritage.

Allan, A. Rault, S., and Humble, J. 2007d. 'Barrow 1, built 2140–1800 Cal BC (SS1.12)', in Harding, J. and Healy, F. *The Raunds Area Project. A Neolithic and Bronze Age landscape in Northamptonshire*, 153–64. London: English Heritage.

Allan, G. and Crow, G. (eds) 1989. *Home and family*. London: Macmillan Press.

Allen, C. 2009. *Exchange and ritual at the riverside: Late Bronze Age life in the lower Witham valley at Washingborough, Lincolnshire*. Lincoln: Pre-Construct Archaeology.

Allen, C., Harman, M., and Wheeler, H. 1987. 'Bronze Age cremation cemeteries in the East Midlands', *Proceedings of the Prehistoric Society* 53, 187–221.

Allen, M. 1997. 'Environment and land-use: the economic development of the communities who built Stonehenge (an economy to support the stones)', in Cunliffe, B. and Renfrew, C. (eds) *Science and Stonehenge*, 115–44. Oxford: Oxford University Press.

Allen, M. 2004. 'Beaker occupation and development of the downland landscape at Ashcombe Bottom, near Lewes, East Sussex', *Sussex Archaeological Collections* 143, 7–33.

Allen, M., Leivers, M., and Ellis, C. 2008. 'Neolithic causewayed enclosures and later prehistoric farming: duality, imposition and the role of predecessors at Kingsborough, Isle of Sheppey, Kent, UK', *Proceedings of the Prehistoric Society* 74, 1–40.

Allen, T. 1999. 'Bogshole Lane, Broomfield, near Herne Bay', *Canterbury's Archaeology* 1998–1999, 12–13.

Bibliography

Amesbury, M., Charman, D., Fyfe, R., Langdon, P., and West, S. 2008. 'Bronze Age upland settlement decline in southwest England: testing the climate change hypothesis', *Journal of Archaeological Science* 35, 87–98.

Anderson, S. 2005. 'Cremated bone', in Holloway, B. and Spencer, P. *An archaeological excavation at Birch Pit northern extension, Maldon Road, Colchester, Essex, June–August 2003*. Colchester: Colchester Archaeological Trust Report 289 (available at http://cat.essex.ac.uk/reports/CAT-report-0289.pdf), 13–24.

Appadurai, A. 1986. 'Introduction: commodities and the politics of value', in Appadurai, A. (ed.) *The social life of things: commodities in cultural perspective*, 3–63. Cambridge: Cambridge University Press.

Appleby, J. 2013. 'Temporality and the transition to cremation in the late third millennium to mid second millennium BC in Britain', *Cambridge Archaeological Journal* 23(1), 83–97.

Argent, G. 2016a. 'Killing (constructed) horses: interspecies elders, empathy and emotion, and the Pazyryk horse sacrifices', in Broderick, L. (ed.) *People with animals: perspectives and studies in ethnozooarchaeology*, 19–32. Oxford: Oxbow.

Argent, G. 2016b. 'Horses, mourning: interspecies embodiment, belonging, and bereavement in the past and present', in DeMello, M. (ed.) *Mourning animals: rituals and practices surrounding animal death*, 21–30. East Lansing: Michigan State University Press.

Armit, I. 2012. *Headhunting and the body in Iron Age Europe*. Cambridge: Cambridge University Press.

Armit, I., Schulting, R., and Knüsel, C. 2011. 'Death, decapitation and display? The Bronze and Iron Age human remains from the Sculptor's Cave, Covesea, northeast Scotland', *Proceedings of the Prehistoric Society* 77, 251–78.

Armstrong, E. 1933. *Guide to the collection of Irish Antiquities. Catalogue of Irish gold ornaments in the collection of Royal Irish Academy*. Dublin: HMSO.

Ashbee, P. 1960. *The Bronze Age round barrow in Britain*. London: Phoenix House.

Ashbee, P. 1985. 'The excavation of Amesbury barrows 58, 61a, 61 and 72', *Wiltshire Archaeology and Natural History Magazine* 79, 39–91.

Atkins, R. 2011. 'Beaker pits and a probable mortuary enclosure on land off Stirling Way, near Witchford, Ely', *Proceedings of the Cambridge Antiquarian Society* 100, 47–65.

Atkinson, R. J. C. 1954. 'Excavations in Barrow Hills Field, Radley, Berks, 1944–45', *Oxoniensia* 17/18, 14–35.

Atkinson, R. J. C. 1972. 'Burial and population in the British Bronze Age', in Lynch, F. and Burgess, C. (eds) *Prehistoric man in Wales and the West*, 107–16. Bath: Adams and Dart.

Bailey, L., Green, M., and Smith, M. 2013. 'Keeping the family together. Canada Farm's Bronze Age burials', *Current Archaeology* 279, 20–6.

Baker, L., Sheridan, A., and Cowie, T. 2003. 'An Early Bronze Age 'dagger grave' from Rameldry Farm, near Kingskettle, Fife', *Proceedings of the Society of Antiquaries of Scotland* 133, 85–123.

Banks, I. 1995. 'The excavation of three cairns at Stoneyburn Farm, Crawford, Lanarkshire, 1991', *Proceedings of the Society of Antiquaries of Scotland* 125, 289–343.

Bibliography

Barclay, A. 1999. 'Final Neolithic/Early Bronze Age', in Barclay, A. and Halpin, C. *Excavations at Barrow Hills, Radley, Oxfordshire. Vol 1: the Neolithic and Bronze Age monument complex*, 35–148. Oxford: Oxbow.

Barclay, A. 2003. 'Fired clay', in Brossler, A. *Green Park (Reading Business Park). Phase 2 excavations 1995: Neolithic and Bronze Age sites*, 92–4. Oxford: Oxford Archaeological Unit.

Barclay, A. 2006a. 'Fired clay', in Cromarty, A., Barclay, A., Lambrick, G., and Robinson, M. *Late Bronze Age ritual and habitation on a Thames eyot at Whitecross Farm, Wallingford*, 102–3. Oxford: Oxford Archaeology, Thames Valley Landscapes monograph 22.

Barclay, A. 2006b. 'Late Bronze Age pottery', in Cromarty, A., Barclay, A., Lambrick, G., and Robinson, M. *Late Bronze Age ritual and habitation on a Thames eyot at Whitecross Farm, Wallingford*, 72–102. Oxford: Oxford Archaeology, Thames Valley Landscapes monograph 22.

Barclay, A., Boyle, A., and Keevill, G. 2001. 'A prehistoric enclosure at Eynsham Abbey', *Oxoniensia* 66, 105–62.

Barclay, A. and Doherty, C. 1998. 'A note on the analysis of white inlay in Beaker and Early Iron Age Pottery', *The Old Potter's Almanack* 6(6), 3–4.

Barclay, A. and Halpin, C. 1999. *Excavations at Barrow Hills, Radley, Oxfordshire. Vol 1: The Neolithic and Bronze Age Monument Complex*. Oxford: Oxbow.

Barfield, L. H. and Hodder, M. 1987. 'Burnt mounds as saunas, and the prehistory of bathing', *Antiquity* 61, 370–9.

Barley, N. 1997. *Dancing on the grave: encounters with death*. London: Abacus.

Barnatt, J., Bevan, B., and Edmonds, M. 2017. *An upland biography: landscape and prehistory on Gardom's Edge, Derbyshire*. Oxford: Oxbow.

Barnes, I., Boismier, W., Cleal, R., Fitzpatrick, A., and Roberts, M. 1995. *Early settlement in Berkshire*. Salisbury: Wessex Archaeology.

Barrett, J. 1980a. 'The evolution of Later Bronze Age settlement', in Barrett, J. and Bradley, R. (eds) *Settlement and society in the British Later Bronze Age*, 77–100. Oxford: British Archaeological Reports, British Series 83.

Barrett, J. 1980b. 'The pottery of the later Bronze Age in lowland England', *Proceedings of the Prehistoric Society* 46, 297–319.

Barrett, J. 1989a. 'Food, gender and metal: questions of social reproduction', in Thomas, R. and Sørensen, M. L. S.(eds) *The Bronze Age-Iron Age transition in Europe: aspects of continuity and change in European societies c. 1200 to 500 BC*, 304–20. Oxford: British Archaeological Reports, International Series S483.

Barrett, J. 1989b. 'Time and tradition: the rituals of everyday life', in Nordstrom, H.-A. and Knape, A. (eds) *Bronze Age studies*, 113–26, Stockholm: Statens Historiska Museum.

Barrett, J. 1990. 'The monumentality of death: the character of Early Bronze Age mortuary mounds in southern Britain, *World Archaeology* 22, 179–89.

Barrett, J. 1991. 'Early Bronze Age mortuary archaeology', in Barrett, J., Bradley, R., and Green, M. *Landscape, monuments and society: the prehistory of Cranborne Chase*, 120–8. Cambridge: Cambridge University Press.

Bibliography

Barrett, J. 1994. *Fragments from antiquity: an archaeology of social life in Britain, 2900–1200 BC*. Oxford: Blackwell.

Barrett, J. 2014. 'The material constitution of humanness', *Archaeological Dialogues* 21(1), 65–74.

Barrett, J. and Bradley, R. (eds) 1980. *Settlement and society in the British Later Bronze Age*. Oxford: British Archaeological Reports, British Series 83.

Barrett, J., Bradley, R. and Green, M. 1991. *Landscape, monuments and society: the prehistory of Cranborne Chase*. Cambridge: Cambridge University Press.

Barrett, J. and Needham, S. 1988. 'Production, circulation and exchange: problems in the interpretation of Bronze Age bronzework', in Barrett. J. and Kinnes, I. (eds.) *The archaeology of context in the Neolithic and Bronze Age: recent trends*, 127–40. Sheffield: Department of Archaeology and Prehistory, University of Sheffield.

Bates, J. 1996. *10–16 Lafone Street, London SE1, London Borough of Southwark: an archaeological evaluation*. London: Museum of London Archaeology, unpublished report.

Battaglia, D. 1990. *On the bones of the serpent: person, memory and mortality in Sabarl Island society*. Chicago: University of Chicago Press.

Bayliss, A. and Whittle, A. (eds) 2007. 'Histories of the dead: building chronologies for five southern British long barrows', *Cambridge Archaeological Journal* 17.1 (supplement).

Beadsmoore, E. 2007. *Feltwell Quarry, Feltwell, Norfolk: a strip, map. and record excavation*. Cambridge: Cambridge Archaeological Unit (available at: http://archaeologydataservice.ac.uk/archives/view/greylit/details.cfm?id=29337&det=y).

Beamish, M. 2005. 'Bronze Age settlement at Ridlington, Rutland', *Transactions of the Leicestershire Archaeological and Historical Society* 79, 1–26.

Beamish, M. and Shore, M. 2008. 'Taking stock in the Late Bronze Age to Early Iron Age transition: a crowding alley and settlement site at Hamilton, Leicester', *Transactions of the Leicestershire Archaeological and Historical Society* 82, 39–78.

Beck, C. and Shennan, S. 1991. *Amber in prehistoric Britain*. Oxford: Oxbow.

Becker, K. 2006. *Hoards and deposition of the Irish Bronze Age*. Dublin: University College Dublin, unpublished PhD thesis.

Becker, K. 2013. 'Transforming identities—new approaches to Bronze Age deposition in Ireland', *Proceedings of the Prehistoric Society* 79, 137–65.

Bell, M. 1990. *Brean Down: excavations 1983–1987*. London: English Heritage.

Bell, M., Richards, M., and Schulting, R. 2000. 'Skull deposition at Goldcliff and in the Severn Estuary', in Bell, M., Caseldine, A., and Neumann, H. (eds) *Prehistoric intertidal archaeology in the Welsh Severn Estuary*, 64–73. York: CBA Research Report 120.

Bellamy, P. 1991. 'The excavation of Fordington Farm round barrow', *Proceedings of the Dorset Natural History and Archaeological Society* 113, 107–32.

Bender, B., Hamilton, S., and Tilley, C. 2007. *Stone worlds: narrative and reflexivity in landscape archaeology*. Walnut Creek, CA: Left Coast Press.

Bibliography

Bender Jørgensen, L., Sofaer, J., and Sørensen, M. L. S. 2016. *Creativity in the European Bronze Age: textiles, metal and clay*. Cambridge: Cambridge University Press.

Benton, S. 1931. 'The excavations of the Sculptor's Cave, Covesea, Morayshire', *Proceedings of the Society of Antiquaries of Scotland* 65, 177–216.

Bergerbrandt, S. 2007. *Bronze Age identities: costume, conflict and contact in northern Europe 1600–1300 BC*. Stockholm: Bricoleur Press.

Birdwell-Pheasant, D. and Lawrence-Zuniga, D. (eds) 1999. *House life: space, place and family in Europe*. Oxford: Berg.

Bishop, B. and Boyer, P. 2014. 'A Late Bronze Age enclosed Settlement at the Oliver Close Estate, Leyton, London Borough of Waltham Forest', *Transactions of the London and Middlesex Archaeological Society* 65, 51–102.

Blier, S. P. 1987. *The anatomy of architecture: ontology and metaphor in Batammaliba architectural expression*. Cambridge: Cambridge University Press.

Bloch, M. and Parry, J. 1982. 'Introduction: death and the regeneration of life', in Bloch, M. and Parry, J. (eds) *Death and the regeneration of life*, 1–44. Cambridge: Cambridge University Press.

Bloch, M. and Parry, J. 1989. 'Introduction: money and the morality of exchange', in Parry, J. and Bloch, P. (eds) *Money and the morality of exchange*, 1–32. Cambridge: Cambridge University Press.

Boden, D. C., Rady, J., and Allison, E. 2006. *Ellington School, Pysons Road, Ramsgate, Kent. Archaeological excavation. Stratigraphic report*. Canterbury: Canterbury Archaeological Trust, unpublished report.

Boghi, F. 2007. 'Human remains', in Holloway, B. and Brooks, H. *An archaeological excavation at the Chelmsford Park and Ride phase II site, Sandon, Essex, June–July 2006*, 9–10. Colchester: Colchester Archaeological Trust Report 418 (available at http://cat.essex.ac.uk/reports/CAT-report-0418.pdf).

Bohannan, P. 1955. 'Some principles of exchange and investment among the Tiv', *American Anthropologist* 57(1), 60–70.

Boivin, N. 2010. *Material cultures, material minds: the impact of things on human thought, society, and evolution*. Cambridge: Cambridge University Press.

Bond, D. 1988. *Excavation at the North Ring, Mucking, Essex: a Late Bronze Age enclosure*. Chelmsford: East Anglian Archaeology monograph 43.

Booth, T., Chamberlain, A., and Parker Pearson, M. 2015. 'Mummification in Bronze Age Britain', *Antiquity* 89(347), 1155–73.

Boulden, K. 2011. 'Construction, colour and aesthetics of the Bronze Age barrows on Wyke Down, Cranborne Chase, Dorset', *Proceedings of the Dorset Natural History and Archaeological Society* 132, 111–19.

Bourgeois, J. and Talon, M. 2009. 'From Picardy to Flanders: Transmanche connections in the Bronze Age', in Clark, P. (ed.) *Bronze Age connections: cultural contact in prehistoric Europe*, 38–59. Oxford: Oxbow.

Bourke, L. 2001. *Crossing the Rubicon: Bronze Age metalwork from Irish rivers*. Galway: NUI Galway.

Bowman, S. and Needham, S. 2007. 'The Dunaverney and Little Thetford fleshhooks: history, technology and their position within the later Bronze Age Atlantic Zone feasting complex', *Antiquaries Journal* 87, 53–108.

Bibliography

Boyle, A. 2002. 'Human bone', in Brossler, A., Gocher, M., Laws, G., and Roberts, M. 'Shorncote Quarry: excavations of a late prehistoric landscape in the Upper Thames Valley, 1997 and 1998', *Transactions of the Bristol and Gloucestershire Archaeological Society* 120, 68–70.

Boyle, A. 2003. 'Worked bone assemblage', in Brossler, A., Early, R., and Allen, C. *Green Park (Reading Business Park). Phase 2 excavations 1995—Neolithic and Bronze Age sites*, 99–100. Oxford: Oxford Archaeology Thames Valley Landscapes Monograph 1.

Bradley, J. 2004. 'Moynagh Lough, Co. Meath, in the Late Bronze Age', in Roche, H., Grogan, E., Bradley, J., Coles, J., and Raftery, B. (eds) *From megaliths to metal: essays in honour of George Eogan*, 91–8. Oxford: Oxbow.

Bradley, P. 2007. 'The long barrow', in Harding, J. and Healy, F. *The Raunds Area Project. A Neolithic and Bronze Age landscape in Northamptonshire*, 166–9. London: English Heritage.

Bradley, R. 1978. 'Prehistoric field systems in Britain and north-west Europe: a review of some recent work', *World Archaeology* 9, 265–80.

Bradley, R. 1980. 'Subsistence, exchange and technology: a social framework for the Bronze Age in southern England c. 1400–700 BC', in Barrett, J. and Bradley, R. (eds) *Settlement and society in the British Later Bronze Age*, 57–75. Oxford: British Archaeological Reports, British Series 83.

Bradley, R. 1981. 'Various styles of urn: cemeteries and settlement in southern England c. 1400–1000 BC', in Chapman, R., Kinnes, I., and Randsborg, K. (eds), *The archaeology of death*, 93–104. Cambridge: Cambridge University Press.

Bradley, R. 1984. *The social foundations of prehistoric Britain: themes and variations in the archaeology of power*. Harlow: Longman.

Bradley, R. 1985. 'Exchange and social distance: the structure of bronze artefact distributions', *Man* 20(4), 692–704.

Bradley, R. 1990. *The passage of arms: an archaeological analysis of prehistoric hoards and votive deposits*. Cambridge: Cambridge University Press.

Bradley, R. 1998. *The significance of monuments: on the shaping of human experience in Neolithic and Bronze Age Europe*. London: Routledge.

Bradley, R. 2000a. *The good stones: a new investigation of the Clava cairns*. Edinburgh: Society of Antiquaries of Scotland.

Bradley, R. 2000b. *An archaeology of natural places*. London: Routledge.

Bradley, R. 2001. 'Afterword: back to the Bronze Age', in Brück, J. (ed.) *Bronze Age landscapes: tradition and transformation*, 229–31. Oxford: Oxbow.

Bradley, R. 2005a. *Ritual and domestic life in prehistoric Europe*. London: Routledge.

Bradley, R. 2005b. *The moon and the bonfire: an investigation of three stone circles in north-east Scotland*. Edinburgh: Society of Antiquaries of Scotland.

Bradley, R. 2006. 'Danish razors and Swedish rocks: cosmology and the Bronze Age landscape', *Antiquity* 80(308), 372–89.

Bradley, R. 2009. *Image and audience. Rethinking prehistoric art*. Oxford: Oxford University Press.

Bradley, R. 2011. *Stages and screens: an investigation of four henge monuments in northern and north-eastern Scotland*. Edinburgh: Society of Antiquaries of Scotland.

Bibliography

Bradley, R. 2012. *The idea of order. The circular archetype in prehistoric Europe.* Oxford: Oxford University Press.

Bradley, R. 2017. *A geography of offerings: deposits of valuables in the landscapes of ancient Europe.* Oxford: Oxbow.

Bradley, R. and Edmonds, M. 1993. *Interpreting the axe trade: production and exchange in Neolithic Britain.* Cambridge: Cambridge University Press.

Bradley, R., Entwistle, R., and Raymond, F. 1994. *Prehistoric land divisions on Salisbury Plain.* London: English Heritage.

Bradley, R. and Ford, D. 2004. 'A long distance connection in the Bronze Age: joining fragments from a Ewart Park swords from two sites in England', in Roche, H., Grogan, E., Bradley, J., Coles, J., and Raftery, B. (eds) *From megaliths to metal: essays in honour of George Eogan,* 174–7. Oxford: Oxbow.

Bradley, R. and Gordon, K. 1988. 'Human skulls from the river Thames, their dating and significance', *Antiquity* 62 (236), 503–9.

Bradley, R., Lewis, J., Mullin, D., and Branch, N. 2015. 'Where water wells up from the earth: excavations at the findspot of the Late Bronze Age Broadward hoard, Shropshire', *Antiquaries Journal* 95, 21–64.

Bradley, R., Lobb, S., Richards, J., and Robinson, R. 1980. 'Two Late Bronze Age settlements on the Kennet gravels: excavations at Aldermaston Wharf and Knight's Farm, Burghfield, Berkshire', *Proceedings of the Prehistoric Society* 46, 217–95.

Brady, K. 2006. *The prehistoric and Roman landscape at Beechbrook Wood, Westwell, Kent.* Channel Tunnel Rail Link Integrated Site Report Series (available at: http://archaeologydataservice.ac.uk/archiveDS/archiveDownload?t=arch-335-1/dissemination/pdf/PT1_Int_Site_Reps/21_Beechbrook_Wood/BBW_ISR_Text/BBW_ISR_text.pdf).

Braithwaite, M. 1982. 'Decoration as ritual symbol: a theoretical proposal and an ethnographic study in Southern Sudan', in Hodder, I. (ed.) *Symbolic and Structural Archaeology,* 80–8. Cambridge: Cambridge University Press.

Brandherm, D. 2014. *Book review. Claimed by the sea: Salcombe, Langdon Bay and other marine finds of the Bronze Age by Stuart Needham, Dave Parham and Catherine Frieman.* London: Prehistoric Society (available at: www.prehistoricsociety.org/files/reviews/Claimed_by_the_sea_Final_review.pdf).

Braun, R. 1990. *Industrialisation and everyday life.* Cambridge: Cambridge University Press.

Brennand, M. and Taylor, M. 2003. 'The survey and excavation of a Bronze Age timber circle at Holme-next-the-Sea, Norfolk, 1988–9', *Proceedings of the Prehistoric Society* 69, 1–84.

Bridgford, S. 1997. 'Mightier than the pen? an edgwise look at Irish Bronze Age swords', in Carman, J. (ed.) *Material harm: archaeological studies of war and violence,* 95–115. Glasgow: Cruithne Press.

Briggs, C. S. 1997. 'A Neolithic and early Bronze Age settlement and burial complex at Llanilar, Ceredigion', *Archaeologia Cambrensis* 146, 13–59.

Britnell, W. 1976. 'Antler cheekpieces of the British Late Bronze Age', *Antiquaries Journal* 56, 24–34.

Bibliography

Britnell, W. 1982. 'The excavation of two round barrows at Trelystan, Powys', *Proceedings of the Prehistoric Society* 48, 133–201.

Britnell, W., Silvester, R., Gibson, A., Caseldine, A., Hunter, K., Johnson, S., Hamilton-Dyer, S., and Vince, A. 1997. 'A middle Bronze Age round-house at Glanfeinion, near Llandinam, Powys', *Proceedings of the Prehistoric Society* 63, 179–97.

Brittain, M. 2004. '*Layers of life and death*: aspects of monumentality in the Early Bronze Age of Wales', in Cummings, V. and Fowler, C. (eds) *The Neolithic of the Irish Sea: materiality and traditions of practice*, 224–32. Oxford: Oxbow.

Britton, D. 1960. 'The Isleham hoard, Cambridgeshire', *Antiquity* 34(136), 279–82.

Britton, D. 1963. 'Traditions of metal-working in the later Neolithic and early Bronze Age of Britain: part 1', *Proceedings of the Prehistoric Society* 29, 258–325.

Britton, D. 1968. *Late Bronze Age finds in the Heathery Burn cave, Co. Durham*. London: Inventaria Archaeologica, Great Britain, 9th Set, GB 55.

Brophy, K. and Noble, G. 2009. *Forteviot, Perthshire, 2009: Excavations of a henge and cist burial. Data structure and interim report*. Glasgow: Strathearn Environs and Royal Forteviot Project (available at: www.gla.ac.uk/media/media_183910_en.pdf).

Brossler, A., Early, R., and Allen, C. 2003. *Green Park (Reading Business Park) Phase 2 Excavations 1995: Neolithic and Bronze Age Sites*. Oxford: Oxford Archaeology.

Brossler, A., Gocher, M., Laws, G., and Roberts, M. 2002. 'Shorncote Quarry: excavations of a late prehistoric landscape in the Upper Thames Valley, 1997 and 1998', *Transactions of the Bristol and Gloucestershire Archaeological Society* 120, 37–87.

Brown, A., Davis, S., Hatton, J., O'Brien, C., Reilly, F., Taylor, K., Dennehy, E., O'Donnell, L., Bermingham, N., Mighall, T., Timpany, S., Tetlow, E., Wheeler, J., and Wynne, S. 2016. 'The environmental context and function of burnt-mounds: new studies of Irish *fulachtaí fiadh*', *Proceedings of the Prehistoric Society* 82, 259–90.

Brown, G., Field, D., and McOmish, D. 1994. 'East Chisenbury midden complex, Wiltshire', in Fitzpatrick, A. and Morris, E. (eds) *The Iron Age in Wessex: recent work*, 46–9. Salisbury: Wessex Archaeology.

Brown, N. 1988. 'A Late Bronze Age enclosure at Lofts Farm, Essex', *Proceedings of the Prehistoric Society* 54, 249–302.

Brown, N. 1995. 'Ardleigh reconsidered: Deverel-Rimbury pottery in Essex', in Kinnes, I. and Varndell, G. (eds) *'Unbaked urns of rudely shape': essays on British and Irish pottery for Ian Longworth*, 123–44. Oxford: Oxbow.

Brown, N. and Medlycott, M. 2013. *The Neolithic and Bronze Age enclosures at Springfield Lyons, Essex*. Chelmsford: East Anglian Archaeology monograph 149.

Brück, J. 1995. 'A place for the dead: the role of human remains in Late Bronze Age Britain', *Proceedings of the Prehistoric Society* 61, 245–77.

Brück, J. 1999a. 'What's in a settlement? Domestic practice and residential mobility in Early Bronze Age southern England', in Brück, J. and Goodman, M. (eds.) *Making places in the prehistoric world: themes in settlement archaeology*, 53–75. London: UCL Press.

Bibliography

Brück, J. 1999b. 'Houses, lifecycles and deposition on Middle Bronze Age settlements in southern England', *Proceedings of the Prehistoric Society* 65, 245–77.

Brück, J. 1999c. 'Ritual and rationality: some problems of interpretation in European archaeology', *Journal of European Archaeology* 2:3, 313–44.

Brück, J. 2000. 'The Early-Middle Bronze Age transition in southern England', *Oxford Journal of Archaeology* 19(3), 273–300.

Brück, J. 2004a. 'Material metaphors: the relational construction of identity in Early Bronze Age burials in Ireland and Britain', *Journal of Social Archaeology* 4, 7–33.

Brück, J. 2004b. 'Early Bronze Age burial practices in Scotland and beyond: differences and similarities', in Shepherd, I. And Barclay, G. (eds) *Scotland in Ancient Europe*, 179–88. Edinburgh: Society of Antiquaries of Scotland.

Brück, J. 2006a. 'Death, exchange and reproduction in the British Bronze Age', *European Journal of Archaeology* 9(1), 73–101.

Brück, J. 2006b. 'Fragmentation, personhood and the social construction of technology in Middle and Late Bronze Age Britain', *Cambridge Archaeological Journal* 16(2), 297–315.

Brück, J. 2007. 'The character of Late Bronze Age settlement in southern Britain', in Haselgrove, C. and Pope, R. (eds) *The Earlier Iron Age in Britain and the near Continent*, 24–38. Oxford: Oxbow.

Brück, J. 2009. 'Women, death and social change in the British Bronze Age', *Norwegian Archaeological Review* 42(1), 1–23.

Brück, J. 2015. 'Gifts or commodities? Reconfiguring Bronze Age exchange in northwest Europe', in Suchowska-Ducke, P. and Vandkilde, H. (eds) *Forging identies: the mobility of culture in Bronze Age Europe*, 47–56. Oxford: British Archaeological Reports, International Series S2771.

Brück, J. 2016. 'Hoards, fragmentation and exchange in the European Bronze Age', in Hansen, S., Vachta, T., and Neumann, D. (eds) *Raum, Gabe, Erinnerung*, 75–92. Berlin: De Gruyter.

Brück, J. and Davies, A. 2018. 'The social role of non-metal "valuables" in Late Bronze Age Britain', *Cambridge Archaeological Journal* (https://doi.org/10.1017/S095977431800029X).

Brück, J. and Fontijn, D. 2013. 'The myth of the chief: prestige goods, power and personhood in the European Bronze Age', in Fokkens, H. and Harding, A. (eds). *Oxford handbook of Bronze Age Europe*, 197–215. Oxford: Oxford University Press.

Brück, J., Johnston, R., and Wickstead, H. 2003. 'Excavations of Bronze Age field systems on Shovel Down, Dartmoor, 2003', *PAST* 45, 11–12.

Brück, J. and Jones, A. M. 2018. 'Finding objects, making persons: fossils in British Early Bronze Age burials', in Harrison-Buck, E. and Hendon, J. (eds) *Relational identities and other-than-human agency in archaeology*, 237–62. Boulder: University Press of Colorado.

Brudenell, M. 2012. *Pots, practice and society: an investigation of pattern and variability in the post-Deverel Rimbury ceramic tradition of East Anglia*. York: University of York, unpublished PhD thesis.

251

Bibliography

Buckley, L. 1997. 'Skeletal report', in Mount, C. 'Adolf Mahr's excavations of an Early Bronze Age cemetery at Keenoge, County Meath', *Proceedings of the Royal Irish Academy* 97C, 44–57.

Burgess, C. 1968. 'The Later Bronze Age in the British Isles and north western France', *Archaeological Journal* 125, 1–45.

Burgess, C. 1985. 'Population, climate and upland settlement', in Spratt, D. and Burgess, C. (eds) *Upland settlement in Britain: the second millennium BC and after*, 195–230. Oxford: British Archaeological Report, British Series 143.

Burgess, C., Coombs, D. and Davies, D. 1972. *The Broadward complex and barbed spearheads*. Bath: Adams and Dart.

Burgess, C. and Shennan, S. 1976. 'The Beaker phenomenon: some suggestions', in Burgess, C. and Miket, R. (eds) *Settlement and economy in the third and second millennia BC*, 309–31. Oxford: British Archaeological Reports 33.

Burrow, A. and Mudd, A. 2008. *An Early Bronze Age pit, an Iron Age burial and Late Iron Age/Early Roman settlement at Bluntisham, Cambridgeshire. Excavations 2005*. Northampton: Northamptonshire Archaeology report 08/54 (available at: http://archaeologydataservice.ac.uk/archives/view/greylit/details.cfm?id=4206&det=y)

Busby, C. 1997. 'Permeable and partible persons: a comparative analysis of gender and body in South India and Melanesia', *Journal of the Royal Anthropological Institute* 3, 261–78.

Butler, J. 1991a. *Dartmoor atlas of antiquities. Vol. 2—the north*. Exeter: Devon Books.

Butler, J. 1991b. *Dartmoor atlas of antiquities. Vol. 1—the east*. Exeter: Devon Books.

Butler, J. 1997. *Dartmoor atlas of antiquities. Volume V: the second millennium*. Tiverton: Devon Books.

Cahill, M. 1995. 'Later Bronze Age goldwork from Ireland: form, function and formality', in Waddell, J. and Shee Twohig, E. (eds) *Ireland in the Bronze Age*, 63–72. Dublin: The Stationary Office.

Cahill, M. 2006. 'Roll your own lunula', in Condit, T. and Corlett, C. (eds) *Above and beyond: essays in memory of Leo Swan*, 53–62. Bray: Wordwell.

Cahill, M. 2015. 'Here comes the sun...', *Archaeology Ireland* 29(1), 26–33.

Cameron, E. 2003. 'The dagger: hilt and scabbard', in Baker, L., Sheridan, A., and Cowie, T. 'An Early Bronze Age "dagger grave" from Rameldry Farm, near Kingskettle, Fife', *Proceedings of the Society of Antiquaries of Scotland* 133, 99–101.

Carlin, N. 2011. 'Into the West: placing Beakers within their Irish contexts', in Jones, A. and Kirkham, G. (eds) *Beyond the core: reflections on regionality in prehistory*, 87–100. Oxford: Oxbow.

Carlin, N. and Brück, J. 2012. 'Searching for the Chalcolithic: continuity and change in the Irish Final Neolithic/Early Bronze Age', in Allen, M., Sheridan, A., and McOmish, D. (eds) *The British Chalcolithic: people, place and polity in the later third millennium*, 193–210. Oxford: Prehistoric Society/Oxbow.

Carr, G. and Knüsel, C. 1997. 'The ritual framework of excarnation by exposure as the mortuary practice of the early and middle Iron Ages of central southern

Bibliography

Britain', in Gwilt, A. and Haselgrove, C. (eds) *Reconstructing Iron Age societies*, 167–73. Oxford: Oxbow.

Carrier, J. 1995. *Gifts and commodities: exchange and Western Capitalism since 1700*. London: Routledge.

Carruthers, W. 2000. 'Mineralised plant remains', in Lawson, A. *Potterne 1982–5: animal husbandry in later prehistoric Wiltshire*, 72–84. Salisbury: Wessex Archaeology.

Carsten, J. 2012. *After kinship*. Cambridge: Cambridge University Press.

Carver, G. 2012. 'Pits and place-making: Neolithic habitation and deposition practices in East Yorkshire *c*. 4000–2500 BC', *Proceedings of the Prehistoric Society* 78, 111–34.

Case, H. 1966. 'Were Beaker-people the first metallurgists in Ireland?', *Palaeohistoria* 12, 141–77.

Caseldine, C. and Hatton, J. 1996. 'Vegetation history of Dartmoor—Holocene development and the impact of human activity', in Charman, D., Newnham, R., and Croot, D. (eds) *Devon and East Cornwall field guide*, 48–61. London: Quaternary Research Association.

Cassidy, L., Martiniano, R., Murphy, E., Teasdale, M., Mallory, J., Hartwell, B., and Bradley, D. 2016. 'Neolithic and Bronze Age migration to Ireland and establishment of the insular Atlantic genome.', *Proceedings of the National Academy of Sciences* 113(2), 368–73.

Caswell, E. and Roberts, B. 2018. 'Reassessing community cemeteries: cremation burials in Britain during the Middle Bronze Age (*c*. 1600–1150 BC)', *Proceedings of the Prehistoric Society*.

Chadwick, A. 2006. 'Bronze Age burials and settlement and an Anglo-Saxon settlement at Claypit Lane, Westhampnett, West Sussex', *Sussex Archaeological Collections* 144, 7–50.

Champion, T. 2004. 'The deposition of the boat', in Clark, P. (ed.) *The Dover Bronze Age boat*, 276–81. London: English Heritage.

Chapman, J. 2000. *Fragmentation in archaeology: people, places and broken objects in the prehistory of south eastern Europe*. London: Routledge.

Chapman, J. and Gaydarska, B. 2007. *Parts and wholes. Fragmentation in prehistoric context*. Oxford: Oxbow Books.

Chenery, C. and Evans, J. 2011. 'A summary of the strontium and oxygen isotope evidence for the origins of Bell Beaker individuals found near Stonehenge', in Fitzpatrick, A. *The Amesbury Archer and the Boscombe Bowmen. Bell beaker burials on Boscombe Down, Amesbury, Wiltshire*, 185–90. Salisbury: Wessex Archaeology.

Childe, V. G. 1925. *The dawn of European civilisation*. London: Kegan Paul.

Childe, V.G. 1930. *The Bronze Age*. Cambridge: Cambridge University Press.

Christison, R. 1881. 'On an ancient wooden image, found in November last at Ballachulish Peat-moss', *Proceedings of the Society of Antiquaries of Scotland* 15, 158–78.

Cipolla, C. 2018. 'Earth flows and lively stone: What differences does 'vibrant' matter make?', *Archaeological Dialogues* 25(1), 49–70.

Bibliography

Clamagirand, B. 1980. 'The social organisation of the Ema of Timor', in Fox, J. (ed.) *The flow of life: essays on eastern Indonesia*, 134–51. Cambridge, MA: Harvard University Press.

Clark, P. 2004. 'The Dover Boat ten years after its discovery', in Clark, P. (ed.) *The Dover Bronze Age boat in context: society and water transport in prehistoric Europe*, 1–12. Oxford: Oxbow.

Clarke, C. and Lavender, N. 2008. *An Early Neolithic ring-ditch and Middle Bronze Age cemetery: excavation and survey at Brightlingsea, Essex*. Chelmsford: East Anglian Archaeology 126.

Clarke, D. 1970. *Beaker pottery of Great Britain and Ireland*. Cambridge: Cambridge University Press.

Cleal, R. 2011. 'Pottery', in Fitzpatrick, A. *The Amesbury Archer and the Boscombe Bowmen. Bell beaker burials on Boscombe Down, Amesbury, Wiltshire*, 140–54. Salisbury: Wessex Archaeology.

Cleal, R. and Lawson, A. 2000. 'Iron objects', in Lawson, A. *Potterne 1982–5. Animal husbandry in later prehistoric Wiltshire*, 202–3. Salisbury: Wessex Archaeology.

Cleal, R. and Pollard, J. 2012. 'The revenge of the native: monuments, material culture, burial and other practices in the third quarter of the 3rd millennium BC in Wessex', in Allen, M., Gardiner, J. and Sheridan, A. (eds) *Is there a British Chalcolithic? People, place and polity in the later third millennium*, 318–32. Oxford: Prehistoric Society/Oxbow.

Cleal, R., Walker, K., and Montague, R. 1995. *Stonehenge in its landscape: twentieth century excavations*. London: English Heritage.

Cleary, K. 2005. 'Skeletons in the closet: the dead among the living on Irish Bronze Age settlements', *Journal of Irish Archaeology* 14, 23–42.

Cleary, K. 2015. *Archaeological networks: excavations on six gas pipelines in County Cork*. Cork: Collins Press.

Close-Brooks, J., Norgate, M., Ritchie, J., and Graham, N. 1972. 'A Bronze Age cemetery at Aberdour Road, Dunfermline, Fife', *Proceedings of the Society of Antiquaries of Scotland* 104, 121–36.

Coles, B. 1990. 'Anthropomorphic wooden figurines from Britain and Ireland', *Proceedings of the Prehistoric Society* 56, 315–33.

Coles, J. 1960. 'Scottish late Bronze Age metalwork: typology, distributions and chronology', *Proceedings of the Society of Antiquaries of Scotland*, 93, 16–134.

Coles, J. and Coles, B. 1986. *Sweet Track to Glastonbury: the Somerset Levels in prehistory*. London: Thames & Hudson.

Coles, J., Leach, P., Minnitt, S., Tabor, R., and Wilson, A. 1999. 'A later Bronze Age shield from South Cadbury, Somerset, England', *Antiquity* 73, 33–48.

Collard, M., Darvill, T., and Watts, M. 2006. 'Ironworking in the Bronze Age? Evidence from a 10th century BC settlement at Hartshill Copse, Upper Bucklebury, West Berkshire', *Proceedings* of Prehistoric Society 72, 367–421.

Comaroff, J. and Comaroff, J. L. 1991. 'How beasts lost their legs': cattle in Tswana economy and society', in Galaty, J. and Bonty, P. (eds) *Herders, warriors and traders: pastoralism in Africa*, 33–61. Boulder: Westview.

Bibliography

Conneller, C. 2004. 'Becoming deer. Corporeal transformations at Star Carr', *Archaeological Dialogues* 11(1), 37–56.

Cook, M. 2000. 'An Early Bronze Age multiple burial cist from Mill Road Industrial Estate, Linlithgow, West Lothian', *Proceedings of the Society of Antiquaries of Scotland* 130, 77–91.

Cook, M. 2006. 'Excavations of a Bronze Age roundhouse and associated palisade enclosure at Aird Quarry, Castle Kennedy, Dumfries and Galloway', *Transactions of the Dumfriesshire and Galloway Natural History and Antiquarian Society* 80, 9–27.

Cook, M., Ellis, C., and Sheridan, A. 2010. 'Excavations at Upper Largie Quarry, Argyll and Bute, Scotland: new light on the prehistoric ritual landscape of the Kilmartin Glen', *Proceedings of the Prehistoric Society* 76, 165–212.

Coombs, D., Northover, P. and Maskall, J. 2003. 'Tower Hill axe hoard', in Miles, D., Palmer, S., Lock, G., Gosden, C., and Cromarty, A. (eds) *Uffington White Horse and its landscape*, 203–25. Oxford: Oxford Archaeological Unit.

Coombs, D. and Thompson, F. 1979. 'Excavation of the hillfort of Mam Tor, Derbyshire', *Derbyshire Archaeological Journal* 99, 7–51.

Cooney, G. 1998. 'Breaking stones, making places: the social landscapes of axe production sites', in Gibson, A. and Simpson, D. D. A. (eds) *Prehistoric ritual and religion*, 108–19. Stroud: Sutton.

Cooney, G. 2002. 'So many shades of rock: colour symbolism and Irish stone axeheads', in Jones, A. M. and MacGregor, G. (eds) *Colouring the past: the significance of colour in archaeological research*, 93–107. Oxford: Berg.

Cooper, A. 2016. '"Held in place": round barrows in the later Bronze Age of lowland Britain', *Proceedings of the Prehistoric Society* 82, 291–322.

Cooper, A. and Edmonds, M. 2007. *Past and present: excavations at Broom, Bedfordshire 1996–2005*. Cambridge: Cambridge Archaeological Unit.

Coote, J. 1992. ' "Marvels of everyday vision": the anthropology of aesthetics and the cattle-keeping Nilotes', in Coote, J. and Shelton, A. (eds) *Anthropology, art and aesthetics*, 245–74. Oxford: Clarendon.

Copson, C. 1989. 'Fordington Farm round barro',. *Proceedings of the Dorset Natural History and Archaeological Society* 110, 144.

Costin, C. L. and Wright, R. (eds) 1998. *Craft and social identity*. Washington, DC: American Anthropological Association.

Cotton, J. 2000. 'Foragers and farmers: towards the development of a settled landscape in London, c. 4000–1200 BC', in Haynes, I., Hannigan, L. and Sheldon, H. (eds) *London under ground. The archaeology of a city*, 9–34. Oxford: Oxbow.

Cowell, M. and Middleton, A. 2011. 'Examination of the cushion stone', in Fitzpatrick, A. *The Amesbury Archer and the Boscombe Bowmen. Bell beaker burials on Boscombe Down, Amesbury, Wiltshire*, 117. Salisbury: Wessex Archaeology.

Cowie, T. 2004. 'Special places for special axes: Early Bronze Age metalwork from Scotland', in Shepherd, I. and Barclay, G. (eds) *Scotland in ancient Europe: the Neolithic and Early Bronze Age of Scotland in their European context*, 247–61. Edinburgh: Society of Antiquaries of Scotland.

Bibliography

Cowie, T., O'Connor, B. and Proudfoot, E. 1991. 'A Late Bronze Age hoard from St Andrews, Fife, Scotland: a preliminary report', in Chevillot, C. and Coffyn, A. (eds), *L'Age du Bronze Atlantique*, 49–58. Beynac: Musées du Sarladais.

Cowie, T. and Ritchie, G. 1991. 'Bronze Age burials at Gairneybank, Kinross-shire', *Proceedings of the Society of Antiquaries of Scotland* 121, 95–109.

Cox, P. and Hearne, G. 1991. *Redeemed from the heath: the archaeology of the Wytch Farm oilfield (1987–90)*. Dorchester: Dorset Natural History and Archaeology Society Monograph 9.

Crawford, O. G. S. and Wheeler, R. E. M. 1921. 'The Llyn Fawr and other hoards of the Bronze Age', *Archaeologia* 71, 133–40.

Cressey, M. and Sheridan, A. 2003. 'The excavation of a Bronze Age cemetery at Seafield West, near Inverness, Highland', *Proceedings of the Society of Antiquaries of Scotland* 133, 47–84.

Cribbin, G., Robinson, M., and Shimwell, D. 1999. 'Re-asssessing the logboat from Lurgan townland, Co. Galway, Ireland', *Antiquity*, 73(282), 903–8.

Cromarty, A. M., Barcaly, A., Lambrick, G., and Robinson, M. 2006. *Late Bronze Age ritual and habitation on a Thames eyot at Whitecross Farm, Wallingford. The archaeology of the Wallingford bypass 1986–92*. Oxford: Oxford Archaeology Thames Valley Landscapes Monograph 22.

Crummy, P. 1977. 'A Bronze Age cemetery at Chitts Hill, Colchester, Essex', *Essex Archaeology and History* 9, 1–16.

Cunliffe, B. 1970. 'A Bronze Age settlement at Chalton, Hants (Site 78)', *Antiquaries Journal* 50, 1–13.

Cunliffe, B. 1991. *Iron Age communities in Britain: an account of England, Scotland and Wales from the seventh century BC until the Roman conquest* (3rd edn). London: Routledge.

Cunningham, C. 1973. 'Order in the Atoni house', in Needham, R. (ed.) *Right and left: essays on dual symbolic classification*, 204–38. Chicago: University of Chicago Press.

Cunnington, M. E. 1907. 'Notes on the opening of a Bronze Age barrow at Manton, near Marlborough', *Wiltshire Archaeological and Natural History Magazine* 35, 1–20.

Dacre, M. and Ellison, A. 1981. 'A Bronze Age urn cemetery at Kimpton, Hampshire', *Proceedings of the Prehistoric Society* 47, 147–203.

Dalwood, H. 1987. 'An assemblage of Bronze Age artefacts from Ivinghoe, Buckinghamshire', *Oxford Journal of Archaeology* 6(1), 29–42.

Darvill, T. 2002. 'White on blonde: quartz pebbles and the use of quartz at Neolithic monuments in the Isle of Man and beyond', in Jones, A. M. and MacGregor, G. *Colouring the past: the significance of colour in archaeological research*, 73–91. Oxford: Berg.

Davis, O. 2015. 'From football stadium to Iron Age hillfort: creating a taxonomy of Wessex hillfort communities', *Archaeological Dialogues* 22(1), 45–64.

Davis, S. 2007. 'The Barrow 1 cattle bone deposit', in Harding, J. and Healy, F. 2007. *The Raunds Area Project. A Neolithic and Bronze Age landscape in Northamptonshire*, 258–63. London: English Heritage.

Bibliography

De Coppet, D. 1981. 'The life-giving death', in Humphreys, S. and King, H. (eds), *Mortality and immortality: the anthropology and archaeology of death*, 175–204. London: Academic Press.

Delanda, M. 2006. *A new philosophy of society: assemblage theory and social complexity*. London: Continuum.

Descola, P. 1994. *In the society of nature: a native ecology in Amazonia*. Cambridge: Cambridge University Press.

Descola, P. 2013. *Beyond nature and culture*. Chicago, IL: University of Chicago Press.

Dieterlen, G. 1957. 'The Mande creation myth', *Africa* 27(2), 124–38.

Digby, A. 1992. 'Victorian values and women in public and private', *Proceedings of the British Academy* 78, 195–215.

Dodwell, N. 1998. 'Human remains', in Evans, C. and Knight, M. *The Butcher's Rise ring-ditches: excavations at Barleycroft Farm, Cambridgeshire, 1996*, 50–60. Cambridge: Cambridge Archaeological Unit, unpublished report 283.

Dodwell, N. 2006. 'Human bone', in Gibson, D. and Knight, M. *Bradley Fen excavations, Whittlesey, Cambridgeshire, 2001–2004*, 110–5. Cambridge: Cambridge Archaeological Unit report 733 (available at http://archaeologydataservice.ac.uk/archives/view/greylit/details.cfm?id=25069).

Donaldson, P. 1977. 'The excavation of a multiple round barrow at Barnack, Cambridgeshire 1974–1976', *Antiquaries Journal* 57(2), 197–231.

Done, G. 1991. 'The animal bone', in Needham, S. *Excavation and Salvage at Runnymede Bridge, 1978: the Late Bronze Age Waterfront Site*, 327–42. London: British Museum Press.

Douglas, M. 1970. *Natural symbols: explorations in cosmology*. London: Barrie and Rockliff.

Downes, J. 1999. 'Cremation: a spectacle and a journey', in Downes, J. and Pollard, T. (eds) *The loved body's corruption. Archaeological contributions to the study of human mortality*, 19–29. Glasgow: Cruithne Press.

Doyle, I. 2005. 'Excavation of a prehistoric ring-barrow at Kilmahuddrick, Clondalkin, Dublin 22', *Journal of Irish Archaeology* 14, 43–75.

Drewett, P. 1975. 'The excavation of a turf barrow at Minstead, West Sussex, 1973', *Sussex Archaeological Collections* 113, 54–65.

Drewett, P. 1982. 'Later Bronze Age downland economy and excavations at Black Patch, East Sussex', *Proceedings of the Prehistoric Society* 48, 321–40.

Drewett, P. 1985. 'The excavation of Barrows V-IX at West Heath, Harting', *Sussex Archaeology Collections* 123, 35–60.

Duffy, P. 2007. 'Excavations at Dunure Road, Ayrshire: a Bronze Age cist cemetery and standing stone', *Proceedings of the Society of Antiquaries of Scotland* 137, 69–116.

Dunbar, L. 2007. 'Fluctuating settlement patterns in Bronze Age Sutherland: excavation of a roundhouse at Navidale, Helmsdale', *Proceedings of the Society of Antiquaries of Scotland* 137, 137–68.

Dunkin, D. 2001. 'Metalwork, burnt mounds and settlement on the West Sussex coastal plain: a contextual study', *Antiquity* 75, 261–2.

Bibliography

Dunlop, C. 2015. *Down the road: the archaeology of the A1 road schemes between Lisburn and Newry*. Belfast: Northern Archaeological Consultancy.

Dunne, L. and Doolin, A. 2001. 'Boat, trough or coffin—a prehistoric puzzle from County Kerry', *Archaeology Ireland* 15(3), 20–3.

Dunwell, A. 2007. *Cist burials and an Iron Age settlement at Dryburn Bridge, Innerwick, East Lothian*. Scottish Archaeological Internet Reports 24. Edinburgh: Society of Antiquaries of Scotland.

Dutton, A., Fasham, P., Jenkins, D., Caseldine, A., and Hamilton-Dyer, S. 1994. 'Prehistoric copper mining on the Great Orme, Llandudno, Gwynedd', *Proceedings of the Prehistoric Society* 60, 245–86.

Earle, T. 2002. *Bronze Age economics: the beginnings of political economies*. Oxford: Westview Press.

Edmonds, M. 1999. *Ancestral geographies of the Neolithic: landscapes, monuments and memory*. London: Routledge.

Ehrenreich, M. 1985. *Trade, technology, and the ironworking community in the Iron Age of southern Britain*. Oxford: British Archaeological Reports, British Series 144.

Elgee, H. W. and Elgee, F. 1949. 'An Early Bronze Age burial in a boat-shaped wooden coffin from north-east Yorkshire', *Proceedings of the Prehistoric Society* 15, 87–106.

Ellis, C. 2013. 'A Bronze Age corn-drying kiln from Argyll', *Past* 75, 3–4.

Ellis, C. and Powell, A. 2008. *An Iron Age settlement outside Battlesbury Hillfort, Warminster, and sites along the Southern Range Road*. Salisbury: Wessex Archaeology Report 22.

Ellis, P. 1989. 'Norton Fitzwarren hillfort: a report on the excavations by Nancy and Philip Langmaid between 1968 and 1971', *Somerset Archaeology and Natural History* 133, 1–74.

Ellis, P. 1993. *Beeston Castle, Cheshire: excavations by Laurence Keen and Peter Hough, 1968–85*. London: English Heritage.

Ellison, A. 1972. 'The Bronze Age pottery', in Holden, E. W. 'A Bronze Age cemetery-barrow on Itford Hill, Beddingham, Sussex', *Sussex Archaeological Collections* 110, 104–13.

Ellison, A. 1980. 'Deverel-Rimbury urn cemeteries: the evidence for social organisation', in Barrett, J. C. and Bradley, R. J. (eds) *Settlement and society in the British Later Bronze Age*, 115–26. Oxford: British Archaeological Reports, British Series 83.

Ellison, A. 1981. 'Towards a socioeconomic model for the Middle Bronze Age in southern England', in Hodder, I., Isaac, G. and Hammond, N. (eds) *Pattern of the past: studies in honour of David Clarke*, 413–38. Cambridge: Cambridge University Press.

Ellison, A. and Rahtz, P. 1987. 'Excavations at Hog Cliff Hill, Maiden Newton, Dorset', *Proceedings of the Prehistoric Society* 53, 223–69.

Elsden, N. 1996. *Cranford Lane, Harlington, London Borough of Hillingdon. Post Excavation Report*. London: Museum of London Archaeology, unpublished report.

English, J. 2013. *Pattern and progress: field systems of the second and early first millennia BC in southern Britain*. Oxford: British Archaeological Reports, British Series 587.

Bibliography

Eogan, G. 1966. 'A hoard of bronze objects from Booltiaghadine, Co. Clare', *North Munster Antiquarian Journal* 10(1), 67-9.

Eogan, G. 1981. 'The gold vessels of the Bronze Age in Ireland and beyond', *Proceedings of the Royal Irish Academy 81C*, 345-82.

Eogan, G. 1983. *The hoards of the Irish later Bronze Age.* Dublin: University College Dublin.

Evans, C. 2015. 'Wearing environment and making islands: Britain's Bronze Age inland north sea', *Antiquity* 89(347), 1110-24.

Evans, C., Appleby, G., and Lucy, S. 2015. *Lives in land—Mucking excavations.* Oxford: Oxbow.

Evans, C., Brudenell, M., Patten, R., and Regan, R. 2013. *Process and history: prehistoric communities at Colne Fen, Earith.* Cambridge: Cambridge Archaeological Unit.

Evans, C. and Knight, M. 1996. An Ouse-side longhouse—Barleycroft Farm, Cambridgeshire. *Past* 23, 1-2.

Evans, C. and Knight, M. 1998. 'The Butcher's Rise ring-ditches: excavations at Barleycroft Farm, Cambridgeshire, 1996', Cambridge: Cambridge Archaeological Unit, unpublished report 283.

Evans, C. and Patton, R. 2011. 'An inland Bronze Age: excavations at Striplands Farm, West Longstanton', *Proceedings of the Cambridge Antiquarian Society* 100, 7-45.

Evans, J. 1881. *The ancient bronze implements, weapons and ornaments of Great Britain and Ireland.* London: Longmans, Green and Co.

Evans-Pritchard, E. 1940. *The Nuer: a description of the modes of livelihood and political institutions of a Nilotic people.* Oxford: Oxford University Press.

Everton, R. 1981. 'The cremations', in Dacre, M. and Ellison, A. 'A Bronze Age cemetery at Kimpton, Hampshire', *Proceedings of the Prehistoric Society* 47, 185-9.

Fahy, E. 1959. 'A recumbent-stone circle at Drombeg, Co. Cork', *Journal of the Cork Historical and Archaeological Society* 64, 1-27.

Falkenstein, F. 1997. 'Eine Katastrophen-Theorie zum Beginn der Urnenfelderkultur', in Becker, C., Dunckelmann, M.-L., Metzner-Nebelsick, C., Peter-Röcher, H., Roeder, M., and Terzan. B. (eds) *Xonos*, 549-61. Espelkamp: Marie Leidorf.

Fitzpatrick, A. 1994. 'Outside in: the structure of an Early Iron Age House at Dunstan Park, Thatcham, Berkshire', in Fitzpatrick, A. and Morris, E. (eds) *The Iron Age in Wessex: recent work*, 68-72. Salisbury: Association Française d'Etude de l'Age du Fer/Wessex Archaeology, Salisbury.

Fitzpatrick, A. 2009. 'In his hands and in his head: the Amesbury archer as a metalworker', in Clarke, P. (ed.) *Bronze Age connections. Cultural contact in prehistoric Europe*, 176-88. Oxford: Oxbow.

Fitzpatrick, A. 2011. *The Amesbury Archer and the Boscombe Bowmen. Bell beaker burials on Boscombe Down, Amesbury, Wiltshire.* Salisbury: Wessex Archaeology.

Fleming, A. 1971. 'Territorial patterns in Bronze Age Wessex', *Proceedings of the Prehistoric Society* 37, 138-66.

Fleming, A. 1978. 'The prehistoric landscape of Dartmoor. Part I: south Dartmoor', *Proceedings of the Prehistoric Society* 44, 97-123.

Bibliography

Fleming, A. 1988. *The Dartmoor reaves: investigating prehistoric land divisions*. London: Batsford.

Fontijn, D. 2002. *Sacrificial landscapes: cultural biographies of persons, objects and 'natural' places in the Bronze Age of the Netherlands c. 2300–600 BC*. Leiden: Analecta Praehistorica Leidensia.

Fontijn, D. 2005. 'Giving up weapons', in Parker Pearson, M. and Thorpe, I. J. (eds) *Warfare, violence and slavery in prehistory*, 145–54. Oxford: British Archaeological Reports, International Series S1374.

Fontijn, D. 2012. 'Landscapes without boundaries? Some thoughts on Bronze Age deposition areas in north-west Europe', in Hansen, S., Neumann, D. and Vachta, T. (eds), *Hort und Raum. Aktuelle Forschungen zu bronzezeitlichen Deponierungen in Mitteleuropa*, 49–68. Berlin: De Gruyter.

Fontijn, D. 2013. 'Epilogue. Cultural biographies and itineraries of things: second thoughts', in Hahn, H. P. and Weiss, H. (eds) *Mobility, meaning and transformation of things: shifting contexts of material culture through time and space*, 183–96. Oxford: Oxbow.

Forman, S. 1980. 'Descent, alliance and exchange ideology among the Makassae of East Timor', in Fox, J. (ed.) *The flow of life: essays on eastern Indonesia*, 152–77. Cambridge, MA: Harvard University Press.

Foucault, M. 1970. *The order of things: an archaeology of the human sciences*. London: Tavistock.

Foucault, M. 1977. *Discipline and punish*. New York: Vantage.

Fowler, C. 2005. 'Identity politics: personhood, kinship, gender and power in Neolithic and Early Bronze Age Britain', in E. Casella and C. Fowler (eds), *The archaeology of plural and changing identities: beyond identification*, 109–34. New York: Plenum.

Fowler, C. 2013. *The emergent past: a relational realist archaeology of Early Bronze Age mortuary practices*. Oxford: Oxford University Press.

Fowler, C. 2017. 'Relational typologies, assemblage theory and Early Bronze Age burials', *Cambridge Archaeoological Journal* 27(1), 95–109.

Fox, C. 1932. *The personality of Britain: its influence on inhabitant and invader in prehistoric and early historic times*. Cardiff: National Museum of Wales.

Fox, C. and Hyde, H. 1939. 'A second cauldron and an iron sword from the Llyn Fawr hoard, Rhigos, Glamorganshire', *Antiquaries Journal* 19, 369–404.

Freeman, L. 2013. 'Separation, connection, and the ambiguous nature of emigré houses in rural highland Madagascar', *Home Cultures* 10(2), 93–110.

Frieman, C. 2012a. 'Going to pieces at the funeral: completeness and complexity in early Bronze Age jet "necklace" assemblages', *Journal of Social Archaeology* 12(3), 334–55.

Frieman, C. 2012b. 'Flint daggers, copper daggers and technological innovation in Late Neolithic Scandinavia', *European Journal of Archaeology* 15(3), 440–64.

Fyfe, R., Brück, J., Johnston, R., Lewis, H., Roland, T., and Wickstead, H. 2008. 'Historical context and chronology of land enclosure on Dartmoor, UK', *Journal of Archaeological Science* 35, 2250–61.

Galaty, P. 1989. 'Cattle and cognition: aspects of Maasai practical reasoning', in Clutton-Brock, J. (ed.) *The walking larder: patterns of domestication, pastoralism and predation*, 215–30. London: Unwin Hyman.

Gardiner, J. 1988. *The composition and distribution of Neolithic surface flint assemblages in central southern England*. Reading: University of Reading, unpublished PhD thesis.

Garrow, D., Lucy, S., and Gibson, D. 2006. *Excavations at Kilverstone, Norfolk: an episodic landscape history. Neolithic pits, later prehistoric, Roman and Anglo-Saxon occupation, and later activity*. Norwich: East Anglian Archaeology 113.

Garrow, D., Meadows, J., Evans, C., and Tabor, J. 2014. 'Dating the dead: a high-resolution radiocarbon chronology of burial within an Early Bronze Age barrow cemetery at Over, Cambridgeshire', *Proceedings of the Prehistoric Society* 80, 1–30.

Garwood, P. 1991. 'Ritual tradition and the reconstitution of society', in Garwood, P., Jennings, D., Skeates, R. and Toms, J. (eds) *Sacred and profane: Proceedings of a Conference on Archaeology, Ritual and Religion, Oxford, 1989*, 10–32. Oxford: Oxford University Committee for Archaeology.

Garwood, P. 2007. 'Before the hills in order stood: chronology, time and history in the interpretation of Early Bronze Age round barrows', in Last, J. (ed.) *Beyond the grave: new perspectives on round barrows*, 30–52. Oxford: Oxbow.

Garwood, P. 2012. 'The present dead: the making of past and future landscapes in the British Chalcolithic', in Allen, M., Gardiner, J. and Sheridan, A. (eds) *Is there a British Chalcolithic? People, place and polity in the later third millennium*, 298–316. Oxford: Prehistoric Society/Oxbow.

Gates, T. 2009. 'Excavation of a late second/early first millennium BC unenclosed roundhouse at Halls Hill, near East Woodburn, Northumberland', *Archaeologia Aeliana* 38, 43–85.

Geber, J. 2009. 'The human remains', in McQuade, M., Molloy, B., and Moriarty, C. 2009. *In the shadow of the Galtees: archaeological excavations along the N8 Cashel to Mitchelstown Road Scheme*, 209–40. Bray: National Roads Authority/Wordwell.

Gell, A. 1998. *Art and agency: an anthropological theory*. Oxford: Clarendon Press.

Gelling, H. and Davidson, P. 1969. *The chariot of the sun and other rites and symbols of the Northern Bronze Age*. London: J. M. Dent and Sons.

Gent, H. 1983. 'Centralised storage in later prehistoric Britain', *Proceedings of the Prehistoric Society* 49, 243–67.

Gerloff, S. 2010. *Atlantic cauldrons and buckets of the Late Bronze and Early Iron Ages in western Europe*. Stuttgart: Franz Steiner Verlag.

Gibson, A. 1992. 'Excavation of an Iron Age settlement at Gold Park, Dartmoor', *Proceedings of the Devon Archaeological Society* 50, 19–46.

Gibson, A. 2004. 'Burials and Beakers: seeing beneath the veneer in late Neolithic Britain', in Czebrezuk, J. (ed.), *Similar but different: Bell Beakers in Europe*, 173–92. Poznan: Adam Mickiewicz University.

Gibson, A., MacPherson-Grant, N., and Stewart, I. 1997. 'A Cornish vessel from farthest Kent', *Antiquity* 71, 438–41.

Bibliography

Gibson, C. 2004. *Lines in the sand: Middle to Late Bronze Age settlement at Game Farm, Downham Way, Brandon.* Norwich: East Anglian Archaeology Occasional Paper 19.

Gibson, D. and Knight, M. 2006. *Bradley Fen excavations 2001–2004, Whittlesey, Cambridgeshire. An assessment report.* Cambridge: Cambridge Archaeological Unit, report 733 (available at http://archaeologydataservice.ac.uk/archives/view/greylit/details.cfm?id=25069).

Gingell, C. 1992. *The Marlborough Downs: a Later Bronze Age landscape and its origins.* Devizes: Wiltshire Natural History and Archaeological Society.

Ginn, V. and Rathbone, S. 2011. *Corrstown: a coastal community. Excavations of a Bronze Age village in Northern Ireland.* Oxford: Oxbow.

Glasbergen, W. 1954. 'Barrow excavations in the Eight Beatitudes. The Bronze Age cemetery between Toterfout and Halve Mijl, North Brabant II: the implications', *Palaeohistoria* 3, 1–204.

Goldhahn, J. 2012. 'On war and memory and the memory of war: the Middle Bronze Age burial from Hvidegarden on Zealand in Denmark revisited', in Berge, R., Jasinski, M., and Sognes, K. (eds) *N-TAG ten: Proceedings of the 10th Nordic TAG conference at Stiklestad, Norway 2009*, 237–50. Oxford: British Archaeological Reports, International Series S2399.

Goldhahn, J. and Østigård, T. 2007. *Dödens hand—en essä om brons- och hällsmed.* Gothenburg: Göteborgs Universitet.

González-Ruibal, A., Hernando, A., and Politis, G. 2011. 'Ontology of the self and material culture: arrow-making among the Awá hunter-gatherers (Brazil)', *Journal of Anthropological Archaeology* 30(1), 1–16.

Gosden, C. and Lock, G. 1998. 'Prehistoric histories', *World Archaeology* 31(1), 2–12.

Goves, C. 2003. 'Dendrochronology', in Brennand, M., and Taylor, M. 'The survey and excavation of a Bronze Age timber circle at Holme-next-the-Sea, Norfolk, 1988–9', *Proceedings of the Prehistoric Society* 69, 31–6.

Grassam, A. 2010. *Excavations on land between Field Lane and Doncaster Road, South Elmsall, West Yorkshire.* Leeds: Archaeological Services WYAS, unpublished report 2030.

Greatorex, C. 2005. 'Later prehistoric settlement on the Hoo Peninsula: excavations at Kingsmead Park, Allhallows, Kent', *Archaeologia Cantiana* 125, 67–81.

Green, M., Bradley, R., and Barrett, J. 1991. 'The excavations: Down Farm enclosure and cemetery', in Barrett, J., Bradley, R., and Green, M. *Landscape, monuments and society: the prehistory of Cranborne Chase*, 183–200. Cambridge: Cambridge University Press.

Greenwell, W. 1877. *British barrows: a record of the examination of sepulchral mounds in various parts of England.* Oxford: Clarendon Press.

Greenwell, W. 1894. 'On the antiquities of the Bronze Age found in the Heathery Burn Cave, County Durham', *Archaeologia* 54, 87–114.

Gregory, C. 1982. *Gifts and commodities.* London: Academic Press.

Gregory, N. 2005. 'Analysis of artefact 97E158:265:1', in Gowan, M., Ó Néill, J., and Phillips, M. (eds) *The Lisheen Mine archaeological project 1996–8*, 311–28. Bray: Wordwell.

Bibliography

Greig, J. and Colledge, S. 1988. *The prehistoric and early medieval waterlogged plant remains from multiperiod Beckford sites HWCM 5006 and 5007 (Worcestershire), and what they show of the surroundings then*. London: English Heritage Ancient Monuments Laboratory Report 54/88.

Grimes, W. 1938. 'A barrow on Breach Farm, Llanbleddian, Glamorgan', *Proceedings of the Prehistoric Society* 4, 107–21.

Grinsell, L. 1941. 'The Bronze Age round barrows of Wessex', *Proceedings of the Prehistoric Society* 7, 73–113.

Grogan, E. 1990. 'Bronze Age cemetery at Carrig, Co Wicklow', *Archaeology Ireland* 4(4), 12–14.

Grogan, E. 1999. *The Late Bronze Age hill fort at Mooghaun South*. Dublin: Discovery Programme.

Grogan, E. 2004. 'Middle Bronze Age burial traditions in Ireland', in Roche, H., Grogan, E., Bradley, J., Coles, J. and Raftery, B. (eds) *From Megaliths to metals: essays in honour of George Eogan*. 63–71. Oxford: Oxbow.

Grogan, E. 2005. *The North Munster Project. Vol. 1: the later prehistoric landscape of County Clare*. Dublin: Discovery Programme.

Guilbert, G. 1981. 'Double-ring roundhouses, probable and possible, in prehistoric Britain', *Proceedings of the Prehistoric Society* 47, 299–317.

Guilbert, G. 1982. 'Post-ring symmetry in roundhouses at Moel y Gaer and some other sites in prehistoric Britain', in Drury, P. (ed.) *Structural reconstruction: approaches to the interpretation of the excavated remains of buildings*, 67–86. Oxford: British Archaeological Reports, British series 110.

Guttmann, E., Last, J., Gale, R., Harrison, E., McDonald, T., Macphail, R., Scaife, R., and Waldron, T. 2000. 'A Late Bronze Age landscape at South Hornchuch, Essex', *Proceedings of the Prehistoric Society* 66, 319–59.

Gwilt, A., Kucharski, K., and Silvester, R. 2005. 'A Late Bronze Age hoard from Trevalyn Farm, Rossett, Wrexham', *Studia Celtica* 39, 27–61.

Gwilt, A. and Lodwick, M. 2009. 'The "champion's portion"? Prehistoric feasting at Llanmaes', *Current Archaeology* 233, 29–35.

Gwilt, A., Lodwick, M., and Worrell, S. 2013. 'Reporting finds, sharing treasures: Bronze Age metalwork discoveries from Wales', *PAST* 75, 10–12.

Haaland, R. 2004. 'Technology, transformation and symbolism: ethnographic perspectives on European iron working', *Norwegian Archaeological Review* 37, 1–19.

Hadnam, J. 1973. 'An early Bronze Age burial at Perio', *Durobrivae* 1, 24.

Hall, K. 2000. 'Fired clay objects', in Lawson, A. *Potterne 1982–5: animal husbandry in later prehistoric Wiltshire*, 179–83. Salisbury: Wessex Archaeology.

Halstead, P. and Cameron, E. 1992. 'Bone remains from Flag Fen platform and Fengate power station post alignment', *Antiquity* 66(251), 499–501.

Hamilton, S. and Manley, J. 1997. 'Points of view: prominent enclosures in 1st millennium BC Sussex', *Sussex Archaeological Collections* 135, 93–112.

Hamilton, S. and Manley, J. 2001. 'Hillforts, monumentality and place: a chronological and topographic review of first millennium BC hillforts in south-east England', *European Journal of Archaeology* 4(1), 7–42.

Bibliography

Hansen, S. 1994. *Studien zu den Metalldeponierungen während der älteren Urnenfelderzeit zwischen Rhônetal und Karpatenbecken*. Bonn: Universitätsforschungen zur Prähistorischen Archäologie Band 21.

Hansen, S. 1996–1998. 'Migration und Kommunikation während der späten Bronzezeit. Die Depots als Quelle für ihren Nachweis', *Dacia* 40(2), 5–28.

Hansen, S. 2016. 'A short history of fragments in hoards of the Bronze Age', in Baitinger, H. (ed.) *Material culture and identity between the Mediterranean and central Europe*, 185–208. Mainz: Römisch-Germanischen Zentralmuseum.

Haraway, D. 1991. *Simians, cyborgs and women: the reinvention of nature*. London: Routledge.

Harbison, P. 1969. *The axes of the Early Bronze Age in Ireland*. Munich: Prähistorische Bronzefunde IX, 1.

Harding, D. 2012. *Iron Age hillforts in Britain and beyond*. Oxford: Oxford University Press.

Harding, J. and Healy, F. 2007. *The Raunds Area Project. A Neolithic and Bronze Age landscape in Northamptonshire*. London: English Heritage.

Harding, J., Healy, F. and Boyle, A. 2007. 'The treatment of the body', in Harding, J. and Healy, F. *The Raunds Area Project. A Neolithic and Bronze Age landscape in Northamptonshire*, 224–38. London: English Heritage.

Harding, P. 2011. 'Flint', in Fitzpatrick, A. *The Amesbury Archer and the Boscombe Bowmen. Bell beaker burials on Boscombe Down, Amesbury, Wiltshire*, 88–103. Salisbury: Wessex Archaeology.

Harley, B. 2009. 'Maps, knowledge and power', in Cosgrove, D. and Daniel, S. (eds) *The iconography of landscape*, 277–312. Cambridge: Cambridge University Press.

Hart, K. 2005. 'Money: one anthropologist's view', in Carrier, J. (ed.) *A handbook of economic anthropology*, 160–75. Cheltenham: Edward Elgar.

Heal, V. 1986. 'Comment on the form of the central grave coffin', in Lawson, A. *Barrow excavations in Norfolk, 1950–82*, 45–7. Gressenhall: Norfolk Archaeological Unit.

Heard, K. 2013. *Late Bronze Age settlement at Bloodmoor Hill, Carlton Colville, Suffolk*. Bury St Edmonds: Suffolk County Council Archaeological Service (available at: http://archaeologydataservice.ac.uk/archives/view/greylit/details.cfm?id=23671).

Helm, R. 2001. 'Bogshole Lane, Broomfield', *Canterbury's Archaeology* 2000–2001, 23–4.

Helms, M. 1988. *Ulysses' sail: an ethnographic odyssey of power, knowledge, and geographical distance*. Princeton: Princeton University Press.

Helms, M. 2009. 'The master(y) of hard materials: thoughts on technology, materiality and ideology occasioned by the Dover boat', in Clark, P. (ed.) *Bronze Age connections; cultural contact in prehistoric Europe*, 149–58. Oxford: Oxbow.

Helms, M. 2012. 'Nourishing a structured world with living metal in Bronze Age Europe', *Journal of World Art* 2(1), 105–18.

Hencken, H. 1942. 'Ballinderry crannóg no 2', *Proceedings of the Royal Irish Academy* 47C, 1–76.

Henshall, A. 1950. 'Textiles and weaving appliances in prehistoric Britain', *Proceedings of the Prehistoric Society* 16, 130–62.

Bibliography

Herbert, E., 1993. *Iron, gender and power: rituals of transformation in African Societies*. Bloomington: Indiana University Press.

Hey, G., Bell, C., Dennis, C., and Robinson, M. 2016. *Yarnton: Neolithic and Bronze Age settlement and landscape. Results of excavations 1990–98*. Oxford: Oxford Archaeology Thames Valley Monographs 39.

Hill, J. D. 1989. 'Rethinking the Iron Age', *Scottish Archaeological Review* 6, 16–24.

Hingley, R. 1997. 'Iron, ironworking and regeneration: a study of the symbolic meaning of metalworking in Iron Age Britain', in Gwilt, A. and Haselgrove, C. (eds) *Reconstructing Iron Age societies*, 9–18. Oxford: Oxbow.

Hinman, M. and Malim, T. 1999. 'Ritual activity at the foot of the Gog Magog Hills, Cambridge', *Past* 31, 1–3.

Hirsch, E. and O'Hanlon, M. 1995. *The anthropology of landscape: perspectives on place and space*. Oxford: Clarendon Press.

Hodder, I. 2012. *Entangled: an archaeology of the relationships between humans and things*. Oxford: Wiley-Blackwell.

Holbraad, M. 2006. 'The power of powder: multiplicity and motion in the divinatory cosmology of Cuban Ifa (or mana, again)', in Henare, A., Holbraad, M., and Wastell, S. (eds) *Thinking through things: theorising artefacts ethnographically*, 189–225. London: Routledge.

Hølleland, H. 2010. 'Spells of history: Childe's contribution to the European identity discourse', *Bulletin of the History of Archaeology* 21(1), 30–7.

Holmes, P. and Molloy, B. 2006. 'The Charlesland (Wicklow) pipes', in Hickmann, E., Both, A. and Eichmann, R. (eds) *Music archaeology in contexts*, 15–40. Rahden: Marie Leidorf.

Hoskins, J. 1989. 'Why do ladies sing the blues? Indigo dyeing, cloth production and gender symbolism in Kodi', in Weiner, A. and Schneider, J. (eds) *Cloth and human experience*, 141–73. Washington, DC: Smithsonian Institution Press.

Hoskins, J. 1998. *Biographical objects: how things tell the stories of people's lives*. London: Routledge.

Hughes, G. 2000. *The Lockington gold hoard: an Early Bronze Age barrow cemetery at Lockington, Leicestershire*. Oxford: Oxbow.

Hughes, S. 2009. *A Bronze Age roundhouse at Bellever Tor, Dartmoor Forest, Devon*. Exeter: AC Archaeology Ltd (available at: http://archaeologydataservice.ac.uk/archives/view/greylit/details.cfm?id=12254&det=y).

Hugh-Jones, S. 1992. 'Yesterday's luxuries, tomorrow's necessities: business and barter in northwest Amazonia', in Hugh-Jones, S. and Humphrey, C. (eds) *Barter, exchange and value: an anthropological approach*, 42–74. Cambridge: Cambridge University Press.

Hull, G. 2015. *Gas pipeline to Great Island, site 34–2&3, Greatisland, Co. Wexford, 12E0396. Final archaeological excavation report for Bord Gáis Networks*. Crisheen: TVAS, unpublished report.

Hull, G., Johnston, P. and O'Donnell, L. 2006. 'Excavation of a Bronze Age Round-House at Knockdomny, Co. Westmeath', *Journal of Irish Archaeology* 15, 1–14.

Humble, J. and Healy, F. 2008. 'Three of the artefacts from the primary burial in Barrow 1 (SS3.7.1)', in Harding, J. and Healy, F. *The Raunds Area Project*.

Bibliography

A Neolithic and Bronze Age landscape in Northamptonshire, 252–3. London: English Heritage.

Humphrey, C. 1974. 'Inside a Mongolian tent', *New Society* 31, 273–5.

Humphrey, C. and Hugh-Jones, S. 1992. 'Introduction: barter, exchange and value', in Hugh-Jones, S. and Humphrey, C. (eds) *Barter, exchange and value: an anthropological approach*, 1–20. Cambridge: Cambridge University Press.

Huth, C. 1997. *Westeuropäische Horte der Spätbronzezeit. Fundbild und Funktion*, Regensburg: Universitätsverlag Regensburg.

Ingold, T. 1996. 'The optimal forager and economic man', in Descola, P. and Pálsson, G. (eds) *Nature and society: anthropological perspectives*, 12–24. London: Routledge.

Ingold, T. 2011. *Being alive: essays in movement, knowledge and description*. London: Routledge.

Jackson, R. 2015. *Huntsman's Quarry, Kemerton: a Late Bronze Age settlement and landscape in Worcestershire*. Oxford: Oxbow.

Jackson, R. and Napthan, M. 2015. 'The Late Bronze Age activity', in Jackson, R. *Huntsman's Quarry, Kemerton: a Late Bronze Age settlement and landscape in Worcestershire*, 20–47. Oxford: Oxbow.

Jahoda, G. 1999. *Images of savages: ancient roots of modern prejudice in western culture*. Hove: Routledge.

Jay, M., Parker Pearson, M., Richards, M., Nehlich, O., Montgomery, J., Chamberlain, A., and Sheridan, A. 2012. 'The Beaker People Project: an interim report on the progress of the isotopic analysis of the organic skeletal material', in Allen, M., Gardiner, J. and Sheridan, A. (eds) *Is there a British Chalcolithic? People, place and polity in the later 3rd millennium*, 226–36. Oxford: Prehistoric Society Research Paper 4/Oxbow.

Jockenhövel, A. 1991. 'Räumliche Mobilität von Personen in der mittleren Bronzezeit des westlichen Mitteleuropa', *Germania* 69, 49–62.

Johnson, M. 1996. *The archaeology of Capitalism*. Oxford: Wiley.

Johnson, M. and Cameron, K. 2012. *An Early Bronze Age unenclosed cremation cemetery and Mesolithic pit at Skilmafilly, near Maud, Aberdeenshire*. Scottish Archaeological Internet Reports 53. Edinburgh: Society of Antiquaries of Scotland.

Johnson, N. 2015. *From Malvern to the Irish Sea: Early Bronze Age barrows in a border landscape*. Worcester: University of Worcester, unpublished PhD thesis.

Johnston, D. 1978. 'The excavation of a bell-barrow at Sutton Veny, Wiltshire', *Wiltshire Archaeological and Natural History Magazine* 72/73, 29–50.

Johnston, P., Kiely, J., and Tierney, J. 2008. *Near the bend in the river: the archaeology of the N25 Kilmacthomas Realignment*. Bray: NRA monographs/Wordwell.

Johnston, R. 2001. *Land and society: the Bronze Age cairnfields and field systems of Britain*. Newcastle: Newcastle University, unpublished PhD thesis.

Johnston, R. 2005. 'Pattern without a plan. Rethinking the Bronze Age coaxial field systems on Dartmoor, southwest England', *Oxford Journal of Archaeology*, 24, 1–21

Johnston, R. 2008. 'Later prehistoric landscapes and inhabitation', in Pollard, J. (ed.) *Prehistoric Britain*, 268–87. Oxford: Blackwell.

Bibliography

Jones, A. 1998. 'The excavation of a Later Bronze Age structure at Callestick', *Cornish Archaeology* 37, 5–55.

Jones, A. 2005. *Cornish Bronze Age ceremonial landscapes c.2500–1500 BC*. Oxford: British Archaeological Reports, British Series 394.

Jones, A. 2015. 'Ritual, rubbish or everyday life? Evidence from a Middle Bronze Age settlement in mid-Cornwall', *Archaeological Journal* 172(1), 30–51.

Jones, A. 2016. *Preserved in the peat: an extraordinary Bronze Age burial on Whitehorse Hill, Dartmoor, and its wider context*. Oxford: Oxbow.

Jones, A., Gossip, J., and Quinnell, H. 2015. *Settlement and metalworking in the Middle Bronze Age and beyond: new evidence from Tremough, Cornwall*. Leiden: Sidestone Press.

Jones, A., Taylor, S., and Sturgess, J. 2012. 'A Beaker structure and other discoveries along the Sennen to Porthcurno South West Water pipeline', *Cornish Archaeology* 51, 1–69.

Jones, A. M. 2001. 'Drawn from memory: the archaeology of aesthetics and the aesthetics of archaeology in Earlier Bronze Age Britain and the present', *World Archaeology* 33(2), 334–56.

Jones, A. M. 2002. 'A biography of colour: colour, material histories and personhood in the Early Bronze Age of Britain and Ireland', in Jones, A. and MacGregor, G. (eds) *Colouring the past: the significance of colour in archaeological research*, 159–74. Oxford: Berg.

Jones, A. M. 2010. 'Layers of meaning: concealment, memory and secrecy in the British Early Bronze Age', in Borić, D. (ed.) *Archaeology and memory*, 105–20. Oxford: Oxbow.

Jones, A. M. 2012. *Prehistoric materialities: becoming material in prehistoric Britain and Ireland*. Oxford: Oxford University Press.

Jordanova, L. 1980. 'Natural facts: a historical perspective on science and sexuality', in MacCormack, C. and Strathern, M.(eds) *Nature, culture and gender*, 42–69. Cambridge: Cambridge University Press.

Joy, J. 2014. ' "Fire burn and cauldron bubble": Iron Age and Early Roman Cauldrons of Britain and Ireland', *Proceedings of the Prehistoric Society* 80, 327–62.

Jupp, P. and Walter, T. 1999. 'The healthy society, 1918–1998', in Jupp, P. and Gittings, C. *Death in England: an illustrated history*, 256–82. Manchester: Manchester University Press.

Kaul, F. 1998. *Ships on bronzes. A study in Bronze Age religion and iconography*. Copenhagen: National Museum of Denmark.

Kiely, J. and Sutton, B. 2007. 'The new face of Bronze Age pottery', in Stanley, M. and O'Sullivan, J. (eds) *New routes to the past*, 25–34. Dublin: National Roads Authority monograph series 4.

Kilbride-Jones, H. 1935. 'An account of the excavation of the stone circle at Loanhead of Daviot, and of the standing stones of Cullerlie, Echt, both in Aberdeenshire, on behalf of HM office of Works', *Proceedings of the Society of Antiquaries of Scotland* 69, 169–214.

Kilbride-Jones, H. 1936. 'A Late Bronze Age cemetery: being an account of the excavations of 1935 at Loanhead of Daviot, Aberdeenshire, on behalf of HM

Bibliography

office of works', *Proceedings of the Society of Antiquaries of Scotland* 70, 278–310.

Knappett, C. 2014. *An archaeology of interaction: network perspectives on material culture and society*. Oxford: Oxford University Press.

Kneisel, J., Kirleis, W., Dal Corso, M., Taylor, N., and Tiedtke, V. (eds) 2012. *Collapse of continuity? Environment and development of Bronze Age human landscapes*. Kiel: Universitätsforschungen zue prähistorischen Archäologie Band 205.

Knight, M. 2007. 'Prehistoric pottery', in Beadsmoore, E. *Feltwell Quarry, Feltwell, Norfolk: a strip, map and record excavation*, 10–12. Cambridge: Cambridge Archaeological Unit (available at: http://archaeologydataservice.ac.uk/archives/view/greylit/details.cfm?id=29337&det=y).

Knight, M., Harris, S., and Appleby, G. 2016. 'Must Farm: an extraordinary tale of the everyday', *Current Archaeology* 319, 12–19.

Knight, M. G. 2016. 'A Late Bronze Age hoard from Long Bredy, Dorset (blog posting available at: https://alifeinfragments.wordpress.com/2016/03/25/a-late-bronze-age-hoard-from-long-bredy-dorset/).

Knight, M. 2018. The intentional destruction and deposition of Bronze Age metalwork in south west England. PhD thesis, University of Exeter.

Knight, M. G. In press. 'Putting 'out-of- time' metalwork in its place: commemorating and forgetting traditions through the Bronze Age metalwork of southern Britain', in Gibson, C., Pyzel, J. and Brown, D. (eds) *Making and Unmaking Memories. Mundane Mnemonics, Artificial Amnesia and Transformed Traditions*. Oxford: Archaeopress.

Knight, M. G., Ormrod, T., and Pearce, S. 2015. *The Bronze Age metalwork of southwestern Britain*. Oxford: British Archaeological Reports, British Series 610.

Kristiansen, K. 1998. *Europe before history*. Cambridge: Cambridge University Press.

Kristiansen, K. and Earle, T. 2015. 'Neolithic versus Bronze Age social formations: a political economy approach', in Kristiansen, K., Šmelda, L. and Turek, J. (eds) *Paradigm found. Archaeological theory: past, present and future*, 234–47. Oxford: Oxbow.

Kristiansen, K. and Larsson, T. 2005. *The rise of Bronze Age society: travels, transmissions and transformations*. Cambridge: Cambridge University Press.

Kristiansen, K. and Suchowska-Ducke, P. 2015. 'Connected histories: the dynamics of Bronze Age interaction and trade 1500–1100 BC', *Proceedings of the Prehistoric Society* 81, 361–92.

Kubach-Richter, I. and Kubach, W. 1989. 'Bronzezeitliche Hügelgräberkultur zwischen Rhein und Mosel', in Pautreau, J.-P. (ed.) *Dynamique du Bronze moyen occidentale. Actes du 113ème Congrès National des Sociétés Savantes, Strasbourg 1988*, 79–98. Paris: Éditions du CTHS.

Küchler, S. 1987. 'Malangan: art and memory in a Melanesian society', *Man* 22(2), 238–55.

Kuijpers, M. 2008. *Bronze Age metalworking in the Netherlands: a research into the preservation of metallurgy related artefacts and the social position of the smith*. Leiden: Sidestone Press.

Ladle, L. and Woodward, A. 2009. *Excavations at Bestwall Quarry. Wareham 1992–2005. Vol. 1: the prehistoric landscape*. Dorchester: Dorset Natural History and Archaeological Society.

Bibliography

Lamdin-Whymark, H., Brady, K., and Smith, A. 2009. 'Excavation of a Neolithic to Roman landscape at Horcott Pit near Fairford, Gloucestershire, in 2002 and 2003', *Transactions of the Bristol and Gloucestershire Archaeological Society* 127, 45–129.

Last, J. 1998. 'Books of life: biography and memory in a Bronze Age barrow', *Oxford Journal of Archaeology* 17(1), 43–54.

Latour, B. 1999. *Pandora's hope: essays on the reality of science studies*. Cambridge, MA: Harvard University Press.

Lawson, A. 2000. *Potterne 1982–5. Animal husbandry in later prehistoric Wiltshire*. Salisbury: Wessex Archaeology.

Leivers, M. 2010. 'The emergence of the agricultural landscape and its development (2nd and 1st millennia BC)', in Lewis, J., Leivers, M., Brown, L., Smith, A., Cramp, K., Mepham, L., and Phillpotts, C. *Landscape evolution in the middle Thames Valley: Heathrow Terminal 5 excavations volume 2*, 135–242. Oxford/ Salisbury: Framework Archaeology.

Lelong, O. 2014. 'Wrappings of power: a woman's burial in cattle hide at Langwell Farm, Strath Oykel', *Proceedings of the Society of Antiquaries of Scotland* 144, 65–131.

Lenerz-de Wilde, M. 1995. 'Prämonetäre Zahlungsmittel in der Kupfer- und Bronzezeit Mitteleuropas', *Fundberichte aus Baden-Wiirttemberg* 20, 229–327.

Lévi-Strauss, C. 1969. *The elementary structures of kinship*. Boston: Beacon Press.

Levy, J. 1982. *Social and religious organization in Bronze Age Denmark: an analysis of ritual hoard finds*. Oxford: British Archaeological Reports, International Series S124.

Lewis, J. 2007. 'The creation of round barrows in the Mendip Hills, Somerset', in Last, J. (ed.) *Beyond the grave: new perspectives on barrows*, 72–82. Oxford: Oxbow.

Lobb, S. and Rose, P. 1996. *Archaeological survey of the Lower Kennet Valley, Berkshire*. Salisbury: Wessex Archaeology report 9.

Locker, A. 2000. 'Animal bone', in Lawson, A. *Potterne 1982–5. Animal husbandry in later prehistoric Wiltshire*, 101–19. Salisbury: Wessex Archaeology.

Lodwick, M. and Gwilt, A. 2004. 'Cauldrons and consumption: Llanmaes and LLyn Fawr', *Archaeology in Wales* 44, 77–81.

Løvschal, M. 2014. 'Emerging boundaries: social embedment of landscape and settlement divisions in northwestern Europe during the first millennium BC', *Current Anthropology* 55(6), 725–50.

Løvschal, M. 2015. 'Lines of landscape organisation: Skovbjerg Moraine (Denmark) in the first millennium BC', *Oxford Journal of Archaeology* 34(3), 259–78.

Lucas, G. 1996. 'Of death and debt: a history of the body in Neolithic and Early Bronze Age Yorkshire', *Journal of European Archaeology* 4, 99–118.

Lynch, F. 1971. 'Report on the re-excavation of two Bronze Age cairns in Anglesey: Bedd Branwen and Treiorwerth', *Archaeologia Cambrensis* 120, 11–83.

Lynch, L. and O'Donnell, L. 2007. 'Cremation in the Bronze Age: practice, process and belief', in Grogan, E., O'Donnell, L. and Johnston, P. (eds) *The Bronze Age landscapes of the pipeline to the west: an integrated archaeological and environmental assessment*, 105–14. Bray: Wordwell.

Bibliography

Lynn, C. 1977. 'Trial excavation at the King's Stables, Tray townland, County Armagh', *Ulster Journal of Archaeology* 40, 42–62.

Lynn, C. 1997. *Excavations at Navan Fort 1961–71*. Belfast: Northern Irish Archaeological Monographs.

McClintock, A. 1995. *Imperial leather: race, gender and sexuality in the colonial contest*. London: Routledge.

McDermott, C., Moore, C., Murray, C., and Stanley, M. 2003. 'Bog standard?', *Archaeology Ireland* 17(4), 20–3.

McKinley, J. 1993. 'Bone fragment size and weights of bone from modern British cremations and the implications for the interpretation of archaeological cremations', *International Journal of Osteoarchaeology* 3(4), 283–7.

McKinley, J. 1994. 'Bone fragment size in British cremation burials and its implications for pyre technology and ritual', *Journal of Archaeological Science* 21, 339–42.

McKinley, J. 1997. 'Bronze Age "barrows" and funerary rites and rituals of cremation', *Proceedings of the Prehistoric Society* 63, 129–45.

McKinley, J. 2000. 'Human bone', in Lawson, A. *Potterne 1982–5. Animal husbandry in later prehistoric Wiltshire*, 95–101. Salisbury: Wessex Archaeology.

McKinley, J. 2003. 'The cremated human bone', in Cressey, M. and Sheridan, A. 'The excavation of a Bronze Age cemetery at Seafield West, near Inverness, Highland', *Proceedings of the Society of Antiquaries of Scotland* 133, 69–72.

McKinley, J. 2006. 'Human bone', in Chadwick, A. 'Bronze Age burials and settlement and an Anglo-Saxon settlement at Claypit Lane, Westhampnett, West Sussex', *Sussex Archaeological Collections* 144, 33–6.

McKinley, J. 2008. 'Human bone', in Ellis, C. and Powell, A. 2008. *An Iron Age settlement outside Battlesbury Hillfort, Warminster, and sites along the Southern Range Road*, 176–80. Salisbury: Wessex Archaeology Report 22 (available at: http://www.wessexarch.co.uk/publications/iron-age-settlement-battlesbury-hillfort).

McKinley, J. 2011. 'Human remains', in Fitzpatrick, A. *The Amesbury archer and the Boscombe bowmen. Bell Beaker burials at Boscombe Down, Amesbury, Wiltshire*, 18–32. Salisbury: Wessex Archaeology Report 27.

McKinley, J., Leivers, M., Schuster, J., Marshall, P., Barclay, A., and Stoodley, N. 2014. *Cliffs End Farm, Isle of Thanet, Kent: a mortuary and ritual site of the Bronze Age, Iron Age and Anglo-Saxon period with evidence for long-distance maritime mobility*. Salisbury: Wessex Archaeology Reports 31.

McOmish, D. 1996. 'East Chisenbury: ritual and rubbish at the British Bronze Age-Iron Age transition', *Antiquity* 70, 68–76.

McOmish, D., Field, D., and Brown, G. 2002. *The field archaeology of the Salisbury Plain Training Area*. London: English Heritage.

McOmish, D., Field, D. and Brown, G. 2010. 'The Bronze Age and Early Iron Age midden site at East Chisenbury, Wiltshire', *Wiltshire Archaeological and Natural History Magazine* 104, 35–101.

Macpherson-Grant, N. 1994. 'The pottery', in Perkins, D., Macpherson-Grant, N., and Healey, E. 'Monkton Court Farm evaluation, 1992'. *Archaeologia Cantiana* 114, 248–88.

Bibliography

McQuade, M., Molloy, B., and Moriarty, C. 2009. *In the shadow of the Galtees: archaeological excavations along the N8 Cashel to Mitchelstown Road Scheme*. Bray: National Roads Authority/Wordwell.

Madgwick, R. and Mulville, J. 2015. 'Feasting on fore-limbs: conspicuous consumption and identity in later prehistoric Britain', *Antiquity* 89 (345), 629–44.

Malim, T., Boreham, S., Knight, D., Nash, G., Preece, R., and Schwenninger, J.-L. 2010. 'The environmental and social context of the Isleham hoard', *Antiquaries Journal* 90, 73–130.

Mallory, J. 1995. 'Haughey's Fort and the Navan complex in the Late Bronze Age', in Waddell, J. and Shee Twohig, E. (eds) *Ireland in the Bronze Age*, 73–86. Dublin: The Stationary Office.

Manby, T. G. 1995. 'Skeuomorphism: some reflections of leather, wood and basketry in Early Bronze Age pottery', in Kinnes, I. and Varndell, G. (eds), *'Unbaked urns of rudely shape': essays on British and Irish pottery for Ian Longworth*, 81–8. Oxford: Oxbow.

Maraszek, R. 2000. 'Late Bronze Age axe hoards in western and northern Europe', in Pare C. (ed.) *Metals make the world go round. The supply and circulation of metals in Bronze Age Europe*, 208–24. Oxford: Oxbow.

Marcigny, C. and Talon, M. 2009. 'Sur les rives de la Manche. Qu'en est-il du passage de l'Âge du Bronze à l'Âge du Fer à partir des découvertes récentes?', in Lambert-Roulière, M.-J., Daubigney, A., Milcent, P.-Y., Talon, M. et Vitaléd, J. (eds) *De l'Âge du Bronze à l'Âge du Fer (X-VIIème siècle av. J.-C.) Actes du colloque international APRAB-AFEAF de St Romain-en Gall 2005*, 385–403. Dijon: APRAB-AFEAF.

Marshall, A. 2004a. *Interpretation of an Early Bronze Age round barrow: excavation of the monument at Guiting Power 3, Glos. (UK)*. Guiting Power: Guiting Power Amenity Trust.

Marshall, A. 2004b. *Analysis of an Early Bronze Age round barrow: a case study at Guiting Power 1,Glos. (UK)*. Guiting Power: Guiting Power Amenity Trust.

Marshall, P., Mulville, J., Parker Pearson, M., and Gidlow, J. 1998. 'Cladh Hallan (South Uist parish), Late Bronze Age-Early Iron Age settlement', *Discovery and Excavation in Scotland*, 103.

Martin, E. and Denston, C. 1976. 'The excavation of two tumuli on Waterhall Farm, Chippenham, Cambridgeshire, 1973', *Proceedings of the Cambridge Antiquarian Society* 66, 1–22.

Martin, J., Schuster, J., and Barclay, A. 2012. 'Evidence of an Early Bronze Age field system and spelt wheat growing together with an Anglo-Saxon sunken featured building, at Monkton Road, Minster in Thanet', *Archaeologia Cantiana* 132, 43–52.

Martlew, R. and Ruggles, C. 1996. 'Ritual and landscape on the west coast of Scotland: an investigation of the stone rows of northern Mull', *Proceedings of the Prehistoric Society* 62, 117–31.

Mason, P. 2011. *Excavation of a Middle Bronze Age round barrow and associated features at Watton, Norfolk: assessment report and updated project design*. Northampton: Northamptonshire Archaeology report 11/70 (available at http://archaeologydataservice.ac.uk/archives/view/greylit/details.cfm?id=31435).

Bibliography

Maurer, W. 2006. 'The anthropology of money', *Annual Review of Anthropology* 35, 15–36.

Mauss, M. 1985. 'A category of the human mind. The notion of the person; the notion of the self', in Carrithers, M., Collins, S., and Lukes, S. (eds) *The category of the person. Anthropology, philosophy, history*, 1–25. Cambridge: Cambridge University Press.

Mauss, M. 1990 (1954). *The gift: the form and reason for exchange in archaic societies.* London: Routledge.

Mays, S. 2007. 'Cremations from Barrows 1, 3, 4 and 5', in Harding, J. and Healy, F. *The Raunds Area Project. A Neolithic and Bronze Age landscape in Northamptonshire*, 709–15. London: English Heritage.

Medina-Pettersson, C. 2013. *Bronze Age urned cremation burials of mainland Scotland: mortuary ritual and cremation technology.* Edinburgh: University of Edinburgh: unpublished PhD thesis.

Melton, N., Knüsel, C., and Montgomery, J. (eds) 2013. *Gristhorpe man: a life and death in the Bronze Age.* Oxford: Oxbow.

Melton, N., Montgomery, J., Roberts, B., Cook, G., and Harris, S. 2016. 'On the curious date of the Rylstone log-coffin burial', *Proceedings of the Prehistoric Society* 82, 383–92.

Metcalf, P. 1978. 'Death be not strange: as anthropologists learn to see other peoples' ways as natural, customs closer to home begin to seem exotic', *Natural History* 87(6), 6–8.

Metcalf, P. and Huntingdon, R. 1991. *Celebrations of death: the anthropology of mortuary ritual.* Cambridge: Cambridge University Press.

Middleton, A. 1987. 'Technological investigation of the coatings on some 'haematite-coated' pottery from southern England', *Archaeometry* 29, 250–61.

Miket, R. 1985. 'Ritual enclosures at Whitton Hill, Northumberland', *Proceedings of the Prehistoric Society* 51, 137–48.

Miles, D., Palmer, S., Lock, G., Gosden, C., and Cromarty, A. 2003. *Uffington White Horse Hill and its landscape: investigations at White Horse Hill, Uffington, 1989–95 and Tower Hill, Ashbury, 1993–4, Oxfordshire.* Oxford: Oxford Archaeology.

Miller, D. 1998. *A theory of shopping.* Cambridge: Polity.

Miller, D. (ed.) 2001a. *Home possessions: material culture behind closed doors.* Oxford: Berg.

Miller, D. 2001b. 'Alienable gifts and inalienable commodities', in Myers, F. (ed.) *The empire of things: regimes of value and material culture*, 91–115. Santa Fe, AZ: School for Advanced Research Press.

Millett, M. and Schadla-Hall, T. 1991. 'Rescue excavations on a Bronze Age and Romano-British site at Daneshill, Basingstoke, 1980–81', *Proceedings of the Hampshire Field Club and Archaeological Society* 47, 83–105.

Mitford, J. 1996. *The American way of death revisited.* London: Penguin Random House.

Mizoguchi, K. 1992. 'A historiography of a linear barrow cemetery: a structurationist's point of view', *Archaeological Review from Cambridge* 11, 39–49.

Bibliography

Mizoguchi, K. 1993. 'Time in the reproduction of mortuary practices', *World Archaeology* 25, 223–35.

Molloy, B. 2007. 'What's the bloody point? Bronze Age swordsmanship in Britain and Ireland', in Molloy, B. (ed.) *The cutting edge: studies in ancient and Medieval combat*, 90–111. Stroud: Tempus.

Molloy, B. 2009. 'Killemly, Co. Tipperary, Late Bronze Age occupation, site 203.3', in McQuade, M., Molly, B., and Moriarty, C. *In the shadow of the Galtees: archaeological excavations along the N8 Cashel to Mitchelstown road scheme*, 65–8. Bray: National Roads Authority/Wordwell.

Monaghan, J. 1994. 'An unenclosed Bronze Age house site at Lookout Plantation, Northumberland', *Archaeologia Aeliana* 22, 29–41.

Moody, G., McPherson-Grant, N., and Anderson, T. 2010. 'Later Bronze Age cremation at West Cliff, Ramsgate', *Archaeologia Cantiana* 130, 147–72.

Moore, C. 2008. 'Old routes to new research: the Edercloon wetland excavations in County Longford', in O'Sullivan, J. and Stanley, M. (eds) *Roads rediscovery and research: proceedings of a public seminar on archaeological discoveries on national road schemes, August 2007*, 1–12. Dublin: National Roads Authority.

Moore, J. and Jennings, D. 1992. *Reading Business Park: a Bronze Age landscape*. Oxford: Oxford Archaeological Unit.

Morris, B. 1991. *Western conceptions of the individual*. Oxford: Berg.

Morris, B. 1994. *Anthropology of the self: the individual in cultural perspective*. London: Pluto Press.

Morris, E. 2000. 'Fabrics', in Lawson, A. *Potterne 1982–5. Animal husbandry in later prehistoric Wiltshire*, 140–9. Salisbury: Wessex Archaeology.

Morris, M. 1992. 'The rise and fall of Bronze Age studies in England 1840–1960', *Antiquity* 66(251), 419–42.

Mortimer, J. R. 1905. *Forty years' researches in British and Saxon burial mounds of East Yorkshire*. London: A. Brown and Sons.

Mörtz, T. 2010. 'Spätbronzezeitliche Waffendeponierungen Großbritanniens.', *Archäologische Informationen* 33(1), 153–7.

Mörtz, T. 2014. *Late Bronze Age weapon depositions—the case of the Tattershall hoard* (blog posting available at https://www.thecollectionmuseum.com/?/blog/view/late-bronze-age-weapon-depositions-the-case-of-the-tattershall-hoard).

Mount, C. 1997a. 'Early Bronze Age burial in south-east Ireland in the light of recent research', *Proceedings of the Royal Irish Academy* 97C(3), 101–93.

Mount, C. 1997b. 'Adolf Mahr's excavations of an Early Bronze Age cemetery at Keenoge, County Meath', *Proceedings of the Royal Irish Academy* 97C(1), 1–68.

Mount, C. and Hartnett, P. 1993. 'Early Bronze Age cemetery at Edmondstown, County Dublin', *Proceedings of the Royal Irish Academy* 93C(2), 21–79.

Mullin, D. 2001. 'Remembering, forgetting and the invention of tradition: burial and natural places in the English Early Bronze Age', *Antiquity* 75 (289), 533–7.

Murphy, P. 1988. 'Plant macrofossils', in Brown, N. 'A Late Bronze Age enclosure at Lofts Farm, Essex', *Proceedings of the Prehistoric Society* 54, 281–93.

Bibliography

Murphy, P. 1994. 'The molluscs', in French, C. *Excavation of the Deeping St Nicholas barrow complex, south Lincolnshire*, 79–81. Sleaford: Lincolnshire Heritage.

Musson, C. 1991. *The Breiddin hillfort: a later prehistoric settlement in the Welsh Marches*. London: CBA Research Report 76.

Nayling, N. and Caseldine, A. 1997. *Excavations at Caldicot, Gwent: Bronze Age palaeochannels in the Lower Nedern Valley*. York: Council for British Archaeology Research Report 108.

Nebelsick, L. 2000. 'Rent asunder: ritual violence in Late Bronze Age hoards', in Pare, C. (ed.) *Metals make the world go round. The supply and circulation of metals in Bronze Age Europe*, 160–75. Oxford: Oxbow.

Needham, S. 1980. 'An assemblage of Late Bronze Age metalworking debris from Dainton, Devon', *Proceedings of the Prehistoric Society* 46, 177–215.

Needham, S. 1988. 'Selective deposition in the British Early Bronze Age', *World Archaeology* 20(2), 229–48.

Needham, S. 1989. 'The clay mould assemblage', in Ellis, P. 'Norton Fitzwarren hillfort: a report on the excavations by Nancy and Philip Langmaid between 1968 and 1971', *Somerset Archaeology and Natural History* 133, 1989, 24–9.

Needham, S. 1991. *Excavation and salvage at Runnymede Bridge, 1978: the Late Bronze Age waterfront site*. London: British Museum Press.

Needham, S. 1992. 'The structure of settlement and ritual in the Late Bronze Age of south-east Britain', in Mordant, C. and Richard, A. (eds.), *L'habitat et l'occupation du sol à l'âge du bronze en Europe*, 49–69. Paris: Editions du Comité des Travaux historiques et scientifiques.

Needham, S. 1996. 'Chronology and periodisation in the British Bronze Age', in K. Randsborg (ed.) 'Absolute chronology: archaeological Europe 2500–500 BC', *Acta Archaeologica* 67, 121–40.

Needham, S. 2000a. 'Power pulses across a cultural divide: cosmologically driven acquisition between Armorica and Wessex', *Proceedings of the Prehistoric Society* 66, 151–207.

Needham, S. 2000b. 'The gold and copper metalwork', in Hughes, G. *The Lockington hoard: an Early Bronze Age barrow cemetery at Lockington, Leicestershire*, 23–47. Oxford: Oxbow.

Needham, S. 2007. '800 BC: the great divide', in Haselgrove, C. and Pope, R. (eds) *The Earlier Iron Age in Britain and the near continent*, 39–63. Oxford: Oxbow.

Needham, S. 2011a. 'Cushion' stone', in Fitzpatrick, A. *The Amesbury Archer and the Boscombe Bowmen. Bell beaker burials on Boscombe Down, Amesbury, Wiltshire*, 113–17. Salisbury: Wessex Archaeology.

Needham, S. 2011b. 'Gold basket-shaped ornaments from graves 1291 (Amesbury archer) and 1236', in Fitzpatrick, A. *The Amesbury Archer and the Boscombe Bowmen. Bell beaker burials on Boscombe Down, Amesbury, Wiltshire*, 129–38. Salisbury: Wessex Archaeology.

Needham, S. 2011c. 'Copper dagger and knives', in Fitzpatrick, A. *The Amesbury Archer and the Boscombe Bowmen. Bell beaker burials on Boscombe Down, Amesbury, Wiltshire*, 120–7. Salisbury: Wessex Archaeology.

Bibliography

Needham, S. 2012. 'Case and place for the British Chalcolithic', in Allen, M., Gardiner, J. and Sheridan, A. (eds) *Is there a British Chalcolithic? People, place and polity in the later third millennium*, 1–26. Oxford: Prehistoric Society/Oxbow.

Needham, S. 2014. 'Thanet: fulcrum of the north-western seaways', in McKinley, J., Leivers, M., Schuster, J., Marshall, P., Barclay, A., and Stoodley, N. 2014. *Cliffs End Farm, Isle of Thanet, Kent: a mortuary and ritual site of the Bronze Age, Iron Age and Anglo-Saxon period with evidence for long-distance maritime mobility*, 219–21. Salisbury: Wessex Archaeology Reports 31.

Needham, S. and Bimson, M. 1988. 'Late Bronze Age Egyptian blue at Runnymede', *Antiquaries Journal* 68, 314–15.

Needham, S., Lawson, A., and Woodward, A. 2010. '"A noble group of barrows": Bush Barrow and the Normanton Down Early Bronze Age cemetery two centuries on', *Antiquaries Journal* 90, 1–39.

Needham, S., Northover, P. Uckelmann, M., and Tabor, R. 2012. 'South Cadbury: the last of the bronze shields?', *Archäologisches Korrespondenzblatt* 42, 473–92.

Needham, S., Parfitt, K. and Varndell, G. (eds) 2006. *The Ringlemere cup: precious cups and the beginning of the Channel Bronze Age*. London: British Museum.

Needham, S., Parham, D., and Frieman, C. 2013. *Claimed by the sea: Salcombe, Langdon Bay and other marine finds of the Bronze Age*. York: Council for British Archaeology.

Needham, S. and Spence, A. 1996. *Refuse and disposal at Area 16 East, Runnymede*. London: British Museum.

Needham, S., Woodward, A., and Hunter, J. 2015a. 'Gold objects', in Woodward, A. and Hunter, J. *Ritual in Early Bronze Age grave goods: an examination of ritual and dress equipment from Chalcolithic and Early Bronze Age graves in England*, 209–34. Oxford: Oxbow.

Needham, S., Woodward, A., and Hunter, J. 2015b. 'The regalia from Wilsford G5, Wiltshire (Bush Barrow)', in Woodward, A. and Hunter, J. *Ritual in Early Bronze Age grave goods: an examination of ritual and dress equipment from Chalcolithic and Early Bronze Age graves in England*, 235–54. Oxford: Oxbow.

Netting, R., Wilk, R., and Arnould, E. (eds) 1984. *Households. Comparative and historical studies of the domestic group*. Berkeley: University of California Press.

Newman, T. and Miket, R. 1973. 'A dagger-grave at Allerwash, Newbrough, Northumberland, *Archaeologia Aeliana* (5th series) 1, 87–95.

Noble, G. and Brophy, K. 2011. 'Ritual and remembrance at a prehistoric ceremonial complex in central Scotland: excavations at Forteviot, Perth and Kinross', *Antiquity* 85(329), 787–804.

Northover, J. P. 1982. 'The exploration of long distance movement of bronze in Bronze and Early Iron Age Europe', *Bulletin of the Institute of Archaeology* 19, 45–71.

Northover, J. 1999. 'The earliest metalworking in southern Britain', in Hauptmann, A., Pernicka, E., Rehren, T., and Yalçin, Ü. (eds) *The beginnings of metallurgy*, 211–26. Bochum: Deutsches Bergbau-Museum.

Northover, J. 2004. 'Ross Island and the physical metallurgy of the earliest Irish copper', in O'Brien, W. (ed.) *Ross Island. Mining, metal and society in early Ireland*, 525–38. Galway: National University of Ireland.

Bibliography

Northover, J. P. 2013. 'Metal analyses', in Needham, S., Parham, D., and Frieman, C. *Claimed by the sea: Salcombe, Langdon Bay and other marine finds of the Bronze Age*, 101–11. York: Council for British Archaeology.

Nowakowski, J. 1991. 'Trethellan Farm, Newquay: excavation of a lowland Bronze Age settlement and Iron Age cemetery', *Cornish Archaeology* 30, 5–242.

Nowakowski, J. 2001. 'Leaving home in the Cornish Bronze Age: insights into planned abandonment processes', in Brück, J. (ed) *Bronze Age landscapes: tradition and transformation*, 139–48. Oxford: Oxbow.

Nowakowski, J., Quinnell, H., Sturgess, J., Thomas, C., and Thorpe, C. 2007. 'Return to Gwithian: shifting the sands of time', *Cornish Archaeology* 46, 13–76.

O'Brien, W. 1992. 'Boulder-burials: a later Bronze Age megalith tradition in south-west Ireland', *Journal of the Cork Historical and Archaeological Society* 9, 11–35.

O'Brien, W. 1994. *Mount Gabriel: Bronze Age copper mining in Ireland*. Galway: National University of Ireland, Galway.

O'Brien, W. 2004. *Ross Island. Mining, metal and society in early Ireland*. Galway: National University of Ireland, Galway.

O'Brien, W. 2012. 'The Chalcolithic in Ireland: a chronological and cultural framework', in Allen, M., Gardiner, J., and Sheridan, A. (eds) *Is there a British Chalcolithic? People, place and polity in the later third millennium*, 211–25. Oxford: Prehistoric Society/Oxbow.

O'Connor, B. 1975. 'Six prehistoric phalerae in the London Museum and a discussion of other phalerae from the British Isles', *Antiquaries Journal* 55, 215–26.

O'Connor, B. 1980. *Cross-channel relations in the Later Bronze Age*. Oxford: British Archaeological Reports, International Series S91.

O'Connor, S. 2015. 'Discussion on cetacean bone', in Woodward, A. and Hunter, J. *Ritual in Early Bronze Age grave goods: an examination of ritual and dress equipment from Chalcolithic and Early Bronze Age graves in England*, 53. Oxford: Oxbow.

Ó Donnabháin, B. 1988. 'Report on the bone remains from sites on the Mitchelstown-Limerick and Bruff-Mallow gas pipelines', in Gowen, M. *Three Irish gas pipelines: new archaeological evidence in Munster*, 192–5. Dublin: Wordwell.

O'Donnell, L. 2016. 'The power of the pyre—a holistic study of cremation focusing on charcoal remains', *Journal of Archaeological Science* 65, 161–71.

Olalde, I., Brace, S., Allentoft, M., Armit, I., Kristiansen, K., Rohland, N., Mallick, S., Booth, T., Szécsényi-Nagy, A., Mittnik, A., Altena, E., Lipson, M., Lazaridis, I., Patterson, N., Broomandkhoshbacht, N., Diekmann, Y., Faltyskova, Z., Fernandes, D., Ferry, M., Harney, E., de Knijff, P., Michel, M., Oppenheimer, J., Stewardson, K., Barclay, A., Alt, K., Avilés Fernández, A., Bánffy, E., Bernabò-Brea, M., Billoin, D., Blasco, C., Bonsall, C., Bonsall, L., Allen, T., Büster, L., Carver, S., Castells Navarro, L., Craig, O., Cook, G., Cunliffe, B., Denaire, A., Dodwell, N., Ernée, M., Evans, C., Kuchařík, M., Farré, J., Fokkens, H., Fowler, C., Gazenbeek, M., Garrido Pena, R., Haber-Uriarte, M., Haduch,

Bibliography

E., Hey, G., Jowett, N., Knowles, T., Massy, K., Pfrengle, S., Lefranc, P., Lemercier, O., Lefebvre, A., Lomba Maurand, J., Majó, T., McKinley, J., McSweeney, K., Mende, B., Modi, A., Kulcsár, G., Kiss, V., Czene, A., Patay, R., Endrődi, A., Köhler, K., Hajdu, T., Cardoso, J., Liesau, C., Parker Pearson, M., Włodarczak, P., Price, T. D., Prieto, P., Rey, P.-J., Ríos, P., Risch, R., Rojo Guerra, M., Schmitt, A., Serralongue, J., Silva, A. M., Smrčka, V., Vergnaud, L., Zilhão, J., Caramelli, D., Higham, T., Heyd, V., Sheridan, A., Thomas, M., Sjögren, K.-G., Stockhammer, P., Pinhasi, R., Krause, J., Haak, W., Barnes, I., Lalueza-Fox, C., and Reich, D. 2018. 'The Beaker Phenomenon and the Genomic Transformation of Northwest Europe', *Nature* 555, March 2018, 190–6.

Olsen, B. 2010. *In defense of things. Archaeology and the ontology of objects*. Lanham: Altamira Press.

Olwig, K. 2002. *Landscape, nature, and the body politic: from Britain's Renaissance to America's New World*. Madison, WI: University of Wisconsin Press.

Ó Néill, J. 2009. *Burnt mounds in northern and western Europe: a study of prehistoric technology and society*. Saarbrücken: Verlag Dr Müller.

Ó Nualláin, S. 1975. 'The stone circle complex of Cork and Kerry', *Journal of the Royal Society of Antiquaries of Ireland* 105, 83–131.

Osgood, R. 1998. *Warfare in the Late Bronze Age of north Europe*. Oxford: British Archaeological Reports, International Series 694.

Osgood, R., Monks, S., and Toms, J. 2000. *Bronze Age warfare*. Stroud: Sutton.

O'Sullivan, J. 1998. 'The architecture of prehistoric settlement at Lairg', in McCullagh, R. and Tipping, R. (eds) *The Lairg project 1988–1996: the evolution of an archaeological landscape in northern Scotland*, 102–12. Edinburgh: Scottish Trust for Archaeological Research.

O'Sullivan, M. 2005. *Duma na nGiall, Tara: the Mound of the Hostages*. Bray: Wordwell.

Owoc, M.-A. 2002. 'Munselling the mound: the use of soil colour as metaphor in British Bronze Age funerary ritual', in Jones, A. M. and MacGregor, G. (eds) *Colouring the past: the significance of colour in archaeological research*, 127–40. Oxford: Berg.

Owoc, M.-A. 2004. 'A phenomenology of the buried landscape: soil as material culture in the Bronze Age of southwestern Britain', in Boivin, N. and Owoc, M.-A. (eds) *Soils, stones and symbols: cultural perceptions of the mineral world*, 107–22. London: UCL Press.

Pálsson, G. 1996. 'Human-environmental relations: orientalism, paternalism and communalism', in Descola, P. and Pálsson, G. (eds) *Nature and society: anthropological perspectives*, 63–81. London: Routledge.

Pare, C. 1989. 'From Dupljaja to Delphi: the ceremonial use of the wagon in later prehistory', *Antiquity* 63, 80–100.

Parker Pearson, M. 1996. 'Food, fertility and front doors in the first millennium BC', in Champion, T. and Collis, J. (eds) *The Iron Age in Britain and Ireland: recent trends*, 117–32. Sheffield: J. R. Collis Publications.

Parker Pearson, M. 1999. *The archaeology of death and burial*. Stroud: Sutton.

Parker Pearson, M., Chamberlain, A., Collins, M., Craig, O., Marshall, P., Mulville, J., Smith, H., Chenery, C., Cook, G., Craig, G., Evans, J., Hiller, J., Montgomery,

Bibliography

J., Schwenninger, J.-L., Taylor, G., and Wess, T. 2005. 'Evidence for mummification in Bronze Age Britain', *Antiquity* 79, 529–46.

Parker Pearson, M., Chamberlain, A., Jay, M., Richards, M., Sheridan, A., Curtis, N., Evans, J., Gibson, A., Hutchison, M., Mahoney, P., Marshall, P., Montgomery, J., Needham, S., O'Mahoney, S., Pellegrini, P., and Wilkin, N. 2016. 'Beaker people in Britain: migration, mobility and diet', *Antiquity* 90 (351), 620–37.

Parker Pearson, M., Marshall, P., Pollard, J., Richards, C., Thomas, J., and Welham, K. 2013. 'Stonehenge', in Fokkens, H. and Harding, A. (eds) *The Oxford handbook of the European Bronze Age*, 159–78. Oxford: Oxford University Press.

Parker Pearson, M. and Richards, C. 1994. 'Architecture and order: spatial representation and archaeology', in Parker Pearson, M. and Richards, C. (eds) *Architecture and order: approaches to social space*, 38–72. London: Routledge.

Parker Pearson, M., Sharples, N. and Symonds, J. 2004. *South Uist: Archaeology and history of a Hebridean Island*. Tempus: Stroud.

Parrington, M. 1978. *The excavation of an Iron Age settlement, Bronze Age ring-ditches and Roman features at Ashville Trading Estate, Abingdon (Oxfordshire) 1974–76*. London: Council for British Archaeology.

Patten, R. 2004. *Bronze Age and Romano-British activity at Eye Quarry, Peterborough. Phase 3*. Cambridge: Cambridge Archaeological Unit report 633 (available at http://archaeologydataservice.ac.uk/archives/view/greylit/details.cfm?id=26007).

Patten, R. 2009. *Excavations at Eye Quarry: the southern extension*. Cambridge: Cambridge Archaeological Unit report no. 869.

Pearce, I. 2006. *Roseberry Topping: geology, landscape, history, heritage*. Great Ayton: Great Ayton Community Archaeology Project.

Pearce, S. 1971. 'A Late Bronze Age hoard from Glentanar, Aberdeenshire', *Proceedings of the Society of Antiquaries of Scotland* 103, 57–64.

Pearce, S. 1977. 'Amber beads from the Late Bronze-Age hoards from Glentanar, Aberdeenshire', *Proceedings of the Society of Antiquaries of Scotland* 108, 124–9.

Pearce, S. 1983. *The Bronze Age metalwork of south western Britain*. Oxford: British Archaeological Reports, British Series 120.

Perkins, D. n.d. *An assessment/research design: South Dumpton Down, Broadstairs*. Canterbury: Trust for Thanet Archaeology, unpublished report.

Perkins, D. 2010. 'The distribution patterns of Bronze Age round barrows in north-east Kent', *Archaeologia Cantiana* 130, 277–314.

Perkins, D. and Gibson, A. 1990. 'A Beaker burial from Manston, near Ramsgate', *Archaeologia Cantiana* 108, 11–27.

Petersen, F., Shepherd, I. and Tuckwell, A. 1975. A short cist at Horsbrugh Castle Farm, Peebleshire. *Proceedings of the Society of Antiquaries of Scotland* 105, 40–62.

Petersen, P. F. 1972. 'Traditions of multiple burial in Later Neolithic and Early Bronze Age Britain', *Archaeological Journal* 129, 22–55.

Petersen, P. F. 1981. *The excavation of a Bronze Age cemetery on Knighton Heath, Dorset*. Oxford: British Archaeological Reports, British Series 98.

Pettit, P. 1974. *Prehistoric Dartmoor*. Newton Abbot: David & Charles.

Phillips, R. 1997. *Mapping men and empire: a geography of adventure*. London: Routledge.

Phillips, T. and Mortimer, R. 2012. *Clay Farm, Trumpington, Cambridgeshire: post-excavation assessment*. Oxford: Oxford Archaeology East report 1294.

Pickles, J. 2003. *A history of spaces: cartographic reason, mapping, and the geo-coded world*. London: Taylor & Francis.

Pierpoint, S. 1980. *Social patterns in Yorkshire prehistory 3500–750 BC*. Oxford: British Archaeological Reports, British Series 74.

Piggott, C. M. 1938. 'A Middle Bronze Age Barrow and Deverel-Rimbury Urnfield, at Latch Farm, Christchurch, Hampshire', *Proceedings of the Prehistoric Society* 4, 169–87.

Piggott, C. M. 1943. 'Excavation of fifteen barrows in the New Forest', *Proceedings of the Prehistoric Society* 9, 1–27.

Piggott, P. 1940. 'Timber circles: a re-examination', *Archaeological Journal* 96, 192–222.

Piggott, S. and Piggott, C. M. 1944. 'Excavations of barrows on Crichel and Launceston Down, Dorset', *Archaeologia* 90, 47–80.

Plumwood, V. 1993. *Feminism and the mastery of nature*. London: Routledge.

Polanyi, K. 1968. 'The economy as instituted process', in Dalton, G. (ed.) *Primitive, archaic and modern economies: essays of Karl Polanyi*, 139–74. Boston: Anchor Books.

Pollard, J. 1999. '"These places have their moments": thoughts on settlement practices in the British Neolithic', in Brück, J. and Goodman, M. (eds) *Making places in the prehistoric world: themes in settlement archaeology*, 76–93. London: UCL Press.

Pollard, J. 2016. 'The Uffington White Horse geoglyph as sun-horse', *Antiquity* 91(356), 406–20.

Pollard, S. and Russell, P. 1969. 'Excavation of round barrow 248b, Upton Pyne, Exeter', *Proceedings of the Devon Archaeological Society* 27, 49–78.

Pope, R. 2015. 'Bronze Age architectural traditions: dates and landscapes', in Hunter, F. and Ralston, I. (eds) *Scotland in later prehistoric Europe*, 159–84. Oxford: Oxbow.

Powell, A. 2007. 'The first settlers: prehistoric activity', in Timby, J., Brown, R., Biddulph, E., Hardy, A., and Powell, A. *A slice of rural Essex. Archaeological discoveries from the A120 between Stansted Airport and Braintree*, 13–80. Oxford: Oxford Wessex Archaeology Monograph 1.

Powell, A., Allen, M., Chapman, J., Every, R., Gale, R., Harding, P., Knight, S., McKinley, J., and Stephens, C. 2005. 'Excavations along the Old Sarum water pipeline, north of Salisbury', *Wiltshire Archaeological and Natural History Magazine* 98, 250–80.

Power, C. 2008. 'Human remains', in Doody M. *The Ballyhoura Hills Project*, 131. Bray: Wordwell.

Primas, M. 1997. 'Bronze Age economy and ideology: central Europe in focus', *Journal of European Archaeology* 5(1), 115–30.

Bibliography

Proctor, J. 2002. 'Late Bronze Age/Early Iron Age placed deposits from Westcroft Road, Carshalton: their meaning and interpretation', *Surrey Archaeological Collections* 89, 65–103.

Pryor, F. 1978. *Excavation at Fengate, Peterborough, England: the second report*. Toronto: Royal Ontario Museum.

Pryor, F. 1996. 'Sheep, stockyards and field systems: Bronze Age livestock populations in the Fenlands of eastern England', *Antiquity* 70(268), 313–24.

Pryor, F. 1998. *Farmers in prehistoric Britain*. Stroud: Tempus.

Pryor, F. 2001. *The Flag Fen Basin: archaeology and environment in a fenland landscape*, 167–228. London: English Heritage.

Pryor, F. 2005. *Flag Fen: life and death of a prehistoric landscape*. Stroud: Tempus.

Quinn, B. and Moore, D. 2008. 'Brewing and *fulachta fiadh*', *Archaeology Ireland* 22(1), 47–8.

Raftery, B. 1976. 'Rathgall and Irish hillfort problems', in Harding, D. (ed.) *Hillforts. Later prehistoric earthworks in Britain and Ireland*, 339–57. London: Academic Press.

Raftery, B. 2004. 'Pit 119: Rathgall, Co. Wicklow', in Roche, H., Grogan, E., Bradley, J., Coles, J. and Raftery, B. (eds) *From megaliths to metals: essays in honour of George Eogan*, 83–90. Oxford: Oxbow.

Raftery, B. and Becker, K. In press. *The excavations at Rathgall, Co.Wicklow*. Bray: Wordwell.

Raftery, J. 1967. 'The Gorteenreagh hoard', in Rynne, E. (ed.) *North Munster studies: essays in memory of Monsignor Michael Moloney*, 61–71. Limerick: Thomond Archaeological Society.

Rahtz, P. 1970. 'Excavations on Knighton Hill, Broad Chalke, 1959', *Wiltshire Archaeological and Natural History Magazine* 65, 74–88.

Ralston, I. 1996. 'Four short cists from north-east Scotland and Easter Ross', *Proceedings of the Society of Antiquaries of Scotland*, 126, 121–55.

Rees, T. 1997. 'The excavation of Cairn well ring-cairn, Portlethen, Aberdeenshire', *Proceedings of the Society of Antiquaries of Scotland* 127, 255–79.

Renfrew, A. C. 1974. 'Beyond a subsistence economy: the evolution of prehistoric Europe', in Moore, C. B. (ed.) *Reconstructing complex societies*, 69–95. Cambridge, MA: Bulletin of the American Schools of Oriental Research 20.

Ride, D. 2001 'The excavation of a cremation cemetery of the Bronze Age and a flint cairn at Easton Down, Allington, Wiltshire, 1983–1995', *Wiltshire Archaeological and Natural History Magazine* 94, 161–76.

Ridgeway, V. 2000 'Prehistoric finds at Hopton Street in Southwark', *London Archaeologist* 9(3), 72–6.

Ripper, S. and Beamish, M. 2012. 'Bogs, bodies and burnt mounds: visits to the Soar wetlands in the Neolithic and Bronze Age', *Proceedings of the Prehistoric Society* 78, 173–206.

Robb, J. and Harris, O. (eds) 2013. *The body in history. Europe from the Palaeolithic to the future*. Cambridge: Cambridge University Press.

Roberts, B. 2007. 'Adorning the living but not the dead: a reassessment of Middle Bronze Age ornaments in Britain', *Proceedings of the Prehistoric Society* 73, 135–67.

Bibliography

Roberts, B. 2009. 'Production networks and consumer choice in the earliest metal of western Europe', *Journal of World Prehistory* 22, 461–81.

Roberts, B., Boughton, D., Dinwiddy, M., Doshi, N., Hook, D., Meeks, N., Mongiatti, A. Woodward, A., Woodward, P., and Fitzpatrick, A. 2015. 'Collapsing commodities or lavish offerings? Understanding large scale Late Bronze Age metal deposition at Langton Matravers, Dorset', *Oxford Journal of Archaeology* 34(4), 365–95.

Roberts, B. and Frieman, C. 2012. 'Drawing boundaries and building models: investigating the concept of the 'Chalcolithic frontier' in north-west Europe', in Allen, M., Gardiner, M., and Sheridan, A. (eds) *Is there a British Chalcolithic? People, place and polity in the later third millennium*, 27–39. Oxford: Prehistoric Society/Oxbow.

Roberts, J. 2003. 'The human and animal bones from the urn', in MacGregor, G. *Excavation of an urned cremation burial of the Bronze Age, Glennan, Argyll and Bute*, 9–10. Scottish Archaeology Internet Report 8. Edinburgh: Society of Antiquaries of Scotland.

Robertson, D. 2016. 'A second timber circle, trackways and coppicing at Holme-next-the-Sea beach, Norfolk: use of salt- and freshwater marshes in the Bronze Age', *Proceedings of the Prehistoric Society* 82, 227–58.

Robinson, I. 2007. 'Middle Bronze Age cremation practice in East Anglia: continuity and change in cemetery form and development', Cambridge: University of Cambridge, MPhil thesis (available at: https://www.academia.edu/6980998/Middle_Bronze_Age_cremation_practice_in_East_Anglia_Continuity_and_change_in_cemetery_form_and_development).

Robinson. M. 2006. 'Macroscopic plant and invertebrate remains', in Cromarty, A., Barclay, A., Lambrick, G., and Robinson, M. *Late Bronze Age ritual and habitation on a Thames eyot at Whitecross Farm, Wallingford*, 110–41. Oxford: Oxford Archaeology, Thames Valley Landscapes monograph 22.

Roche, H. 2004. 'The dating of the embanked stone circle at Grange, Co. Limerick', in Roche, H., Grogan, E., Bradley, J., Coles, J., and Raftery, B. (eds) *From megaliths to metals: essay in honour of George Eogan*, 109–16. Oxford: Oxbow.

Roe, F. 2011. 'Bracers', in Fitzpatrick, A. *The Amesbury Archer and the Boscombe Bowmen. Bell beaker burials on Boscombe Down, Amesbury, Wiltshire*, 103–12. Salisbury: Wessex Archaeology.

Roe, F. and Barclay, A. 2006. 'Worked and burnt stone', in Cromarty, A., Barclay, A., Lambrick, G., and Robinson, M. *Late Bronze Age ritual and habitation on a Thames eyot at Whitecross Farm, Wallingford*, 71–2. Oxford: Oxford Archaeology, Thames Valley Landscapes monograph 22.

Rogers, A. 2013. *Female burial traditions of the Chalcolithic and Early Bronze Age. A pilot study based on modern excavations*. Oxford: British Archaeological Reports, International Series S581.

Rohl, B. and Needham, S. 1998. *The circulation of metal in the British Bronze Age: the application of lead isotope analysis*. London: British Museum Press.

Ross, A. 1986. 'Lindow man and the Celtic tradition', in Stead, I., Bourke, J., and Brothwell, D. (eds) *Lindow man: the body in the bog*, 162–9. London: British Museum.

Bibliography

Rosse, A. 1984. 'The Dowris hoard', *Éile. The Journal of the Roscrea Heritage Society* 2, 57–66.

Rowlands, M. 1980. 'Kinship, alliance and exchange in the European Bronze Age', in Barrett, J. and Bradley, R. (eds) *Settlement and society in the British Later Bronze Age*, 59–72. Oxford: British Archaeological Reports, British Series 83.

Rowlands, M. 1986. 'Modernist fantasies in prehistory?', *Man* 21/4, 745–8.

Russel, A. 1990. 'Two Beaker burials from Chilbolton, Hampshire', *Proceedings of the Prehistoric Society* 56, 153–72.

Russell, M. 1996. 'Problems of phasing: a reconsideration of the Black Patch Middle Bronze Age "nucleated village"', *Oxford Journal of Archaeology* 15(1), 33–8.

Rynne, E. 1963. 'Notes on some antiquities in Co. Kildare', *Journal of the Kildare Archaeological Society* 13, 458–62.

Sahlins, M. 1972. *Stone Age economics*. Chicago, IL: Aldine.

Samson, A. 2006. 'Offshore finds from the Bronze Age in north-west Europe: the shipwreck scenario revisited', *Oxford Journal of Archaeology* 25(4), 371–88.

Santos Granero, F. 2009. *The occult life of things: native Amazonian theories of materiality and personhood*. Tucson, AZ: University of Arizona Press.

Saunders, N. 2002. 'The colours of light: materiality and chromatic cultures of the Americas', in Jones, A. M. and MacGregor, G. (eds) *Colouring the past: the significance of colour in archaeological research*, 209–26. Oxford: Berg.

Schmidt, P. and Burgess, C. 1981. *The axes of Scotland and northern England*. Munich: Prähistorische Bronzefunde IX, 7.

Schneider, J. and Weiner, A. 1989. 'Introduction', in Weiner, A. and Schneider, J. (eds) *Cloth and human experience*, 1–29. Washington: Smithsonian Institution Press.

Schulting, R. and Bradley, R. 2013. '"Of human remains and weapons in the neighbourhood of London": new AMS 14C dates on Thames "river skulls" and their European context', *Archaeological Journal* 170, 30–77.

Scott, J. 1991. 'The stone circles at Temple Wood, Kilmartin, Argyll', *Glasgow Archaeological Journal 15*, 53–124.

Seager Smith, R. 2000. 'Worked bone and antler', in Lawson, A. *Potterne 1982–5. Animal husbandry in later prehistoric Wiltshire*, 222–40. Salisbury: Wessex Archaeology.

Seager Thomas, M. 1999. 'Stone finds in context', *Sussex Archaeological Collections* 137, 39–48.

Serjeantson, D., Bagust, J., and Jenkins, C. 2010. 'Animal bone', in McOmish, D., Field, D., and Brown, G. 'The Bronze Age and Early Iron Age midden site at East Chisenbury, Wiltshire', *Wiltshire Archaeological and Natural History Magazine* 104, 62–5.

Shand, P., Henderson, E. and R., and Barclay, A., 2003. 'Corporation Farm, Wilsham Road, Abingdon: a summary of the Neolithic and Bronze Age excavations, 1971–4', in Barclay, A., Lambrick, G., Moore, J., and Robins, M. *Lines in the landscape. Cursus monuments in the Upper Thames Valley*, 31–40. Oxford: Oxford Archaeology.

Bibliography

Sharples, N. 2010. *Social relations in later prehistory: Wessex in the first millennium BC*. Oxford: Oxford University Press.

Shennan, S. 1982. 'Ideology, change and the European Early Bronze Age', in Hodder, I. (ed.) *Symbolic and structural archaeology*, 155–61. Cambridge: Cambridge University Press.

Shennan, S. 1999. 'Cost, benefit and value in the organization of early European copper production', *Antiquity* 73, 352–63.

Shepherd, A. 2012. 'Stepping out together: men, women, and their Beakers in time and space', in Allen, M., Gardiner, J. and Sheridan, A. (eds) *Is there a British Chalcolithic? People, place and polity in the later third millennium*, 257–80. Oxford: Prehistoric Society/Oxbow.

Shepherd, I. 1982. 'Comparative background: the assemblage', in Watkins, T. 'The excavation of an Early Bronze Age cemetery at Barns Farm, Dalgety, Fife', *Proceedings of the Society of Antiquaries of Scotland* 112, 129–32.

Shepherd, I. 2007. ' "An awesome place". The Late Bronze Age use of the Sculptor's Cave, Covesea, Moray', in Burgess, C., Topping, P., and Lynch, F. (eds) *Beyond Stonehenge: essays on the Bronze Age in honour of Colin Burgess*, 194–203. Oxford: Oxbow.

Sheppard, T. 1941. 'Parc-y-meirch hoard, St George parish, Denbighshire', *Archaeologia Cambrensis* 96, 1–10.

Sheridan, A. 2002. 'The radiocarbon dating programmes of the National Museums of Scotland', *Antiquity* 76(293), 794–6.

Sheridan, A. 2005. 'The National Museums of Scotland radiocarbon dating programmes: results obtained during 2004/5', *Discovery and Excavation in Scotland* 6, 182–3.

Sheridan, A. 2012. 'A Rumsfeld reality check: what we know, what we don't know and what we don't know we don't know about the Chalcolithic in Britain and Ireland', in M. Allen, J. Gardiner, and A. Sheridan (eds) *Is there a British Chalcolithic? People, place and polity in the later third millennium*, 40–55. Oxford: Prehistoric Society/Oxbow.

Sheridan, A. 2015. 'Discussion of disc bead and spacer plate necklaces of jet and jet-like materials', in Woodward, A. and Hunter, J. *Ritual in Early Bronze Age grave goods: an examination of ritual and dress equipment from Chalcolithic and Early Bronze Age graves in England*, 341–62. Oxford: Oxbow.

Sheridan, A. and Davis, M. 1998. 'The Welsh "jet set" in prehistory: a case of keeping up with the Joneses?', in Gibson, A. and Simpson, D. (eds) *Prehistoric ritual and religion*, 148–63. Stroud: Sutton Publishing.

Sheridan, A. and Davis, M. 2002. 'Investigating jet and jet-like artefacts from prehistoric Scotland: the National Museums of Scotland project', *Antiquity* 76, 812–25.

Sheridan, A., Needham, S., O'Connor, S., Melton, N., Janaway, R., Cameron, E., and Evans, A. 2013. 'The Gristhorpe coffin and its contents', in Melton, N., Knüsel, C., and Montgomery, J. (eds) *Gristhorpe man: a life and death in the Bronze Age*, 148–65. Oxford: Oxbow.

Sheridan, A. and Shortland, A. 2003. 'Supernatural power-dressing', *British Archaeology* 30, 18–23.

Bibliography

Sheridan, A., Woodward, A., and Hunter, J. 2015. 'Spacer plate necklaces of jet and jet-like materials', in Woodward, A. and Hunter, J. *Ritual in Early Bronze Age grave goods: an examination of ritual and dress equipment from Chalcolithic and Early Bronze Age graves in England*, 286–340. Oxford: Oxbow.

Simmonds, A., Anderson-Whymark, H., and Norton, A. 2011. 'Excavations at Tubney Wood Quarry, Oxfordshire, 2001–9', *Oxoniensia* 76, 105–72.

Simpson, D., Gregory, R. and Murphy, E. 2003. 'Excavation at Manish Strand, Ensay, Western Isles', *Proceedings of the Society of Antiquaries of Scotland* 133, 173–89.

Simpson, D., Murphy, E., and Gregory, R. 2006. *Excavations at Northton, Isle of Harris*. Oxford: British Archaeological Reports, British Series 408.

Simpson, I., Dockrill, S., Bull, I., and Evershed, R. 1998. 'Early anthropogenic soil formation at Tofts Ness, Sanday, Orkney', *Journal of Archaeological Science* 25, 729–46.

Smith, C. 2007. 'The animal remains', in Duffy, P. 2006. 'Excavations at Dunure Road, Ayrshire: a Bronze Age cist cemetery and standing stone', *Proceedings of the Society of Antiquaries of Scotland* 137, 94.

Smith, G. 1987. 'A Beaker (?) burial monument and a Late Bronze Age assemblage from East Northdown, Margate', *Archaeologia Cantiana* 104, 237–89.

Smith, G. 2015. 'Rescue excavation at the Bronze Age copper smelting site at Pentrwyn, Great Orme, Llandudno, Conwy, 2011', *Archaeology in Wales* 54, 53–71.

Smith, G., Caseldine, A., Griffiths, C., Peck, I., Nayling, N., and Jenkins, D. 2017. 'An Early Bronze Age burnt mound trough and boat fragment with accompanying palaeobotanical and pollen analysis at Nant Farm, Porth Neigwl, Llŷn Peninsula, Gwynedd', *Studia Celtica* 51/1, 1–63.

Smith, I. 1965. 'Excavation of a bell barrow, Avebury G55', *Wiltshire Archaeological and Natural History Magazine* 60, 24–46.

Smith, I. and Simpson, D. 1966. 'Excavation of a round barrow on Overton Hill, North Wiltshire, England', *Proceedings of the Prehistoric Society* 32, 122–55.

Smith, K., Coppen, J., Wainwright, G., and Beckett, S. 1981. 'The Shaugh Moor Project: third report—settlement and environmental investigations', *Proceedings of the Prehistoric Society* 47, 205–73.

Smith, M. 1959. 'Some Somerset hoards and their place in the Bronze Age of Southern Britain', *Proceedings of the Prehistoric Society* 25, 144–87.

Smith, M., Allen, M., Delbarre, G., Booth, T., Cheetham, P., Bailey, L., O'Malley, F., Parker Pearson, M., and Green, M. 2016. 'Holding on to the past: southern British evidence for mummification and retention of the dead in the Chalcolithic and Bronze Age', *Journal of Archaeological Science: Reports* 10, 744–56.

Smith, R., Healy, F., Allen, M., Morris, E., Barnes, I., and Woodward, P. 1997. *Excavations along the route of the Dorchester by-pass, Dorset, 1986–8*. Salisbury: Wessex Archaeology.

Sofaer, J. 2006. *The body as material culture: a theoretical osteoarchaeology*. Cambridge: Cambridge University Press.

Bibliography

Sofaer Derevenski, J. 2002. 'Engendering context. Context as gendered practice in the early Bronze Age of the Upper Thames Valley, UK', *European Journal of Archaeology* 5(2), 191–211.

Sommerfeld, C. 1994. *Gerätegeld Sichel. Studien zur montären Struktur bronzezeitlicher Horte im nördlichen Mitteleuropa*. Berlin: De Gruyter.

Sørensen, M. L. S. 1991. 'The construction of gender through appearance', in Walde, D. and Willows, N. (eds) *The archaeology of gender. Proceedings of the 22nd Annual Chacmool Conference*, 121–9. Calgary: University of Calgary Archaeological Association.

Sørensen, M. L. S. 1997. 'Reading dress: the construction of social categories and identities in Bronze Age Europe', *Journal of European Archaeology* 5(1), 93–114.

Sørensen, T. 2013. 'We have never been Latourian. Archaeological ethics and the posthuman condition', *Norwegian Archaeological Review* 46, 1–18.

Spain, D. 1992. *Gendered spaces*. Chapel Hill: University of North Carolina Press.

Stanford, S. C. 1982. 'Bromfield, Shropshire—Neolithic, Beaker and Bronze Age sites, 1966–79', *Proceedings of the Prehistoric Society* 48, 279–320.

Stanley, M., McDermott, C., Moore, C., and Murray, C. 2003. 'Throwing off the yoke', *Archaeology Ireland* 17(2), 6–8.

Start, M. 2003. 'Cremated remains', in Pine, J. 'Excavation of a Medieval settlement, Late Saxon features and a Bronze Age cremation cemetery at Loughton, Milton Keynes', *Records of Buckinghamshire* 43, 96–8.

Stevens, C. and Fuller, D. 2012. 'Did Neolithic farming fail? The case for a Bronze Age agricultural revolution in the British Isles', *Antiquity* 86(333), 707–22.

Stevenson, S. 1995. 'The excavation of a kerbed cairn at Beech Hill House, Coupar Angus, Perthshire', *Proceedings of the Society of Antiquaries of Scotland* 125, 197–235.

Strachan, R., Ralston, I., and Finlayson, B. 1998. 'Neolithic and later prehistoric structures, and early medieval metal-working, at Blairhall Burn, Amisfield, Dumfriesshire', *Proceedings of the Society of Antiquaries of Scotland* 128, 55–94.

Strathern, A. 1981. 'Death as exchange: two Melanesian cases', in Humphreys, S. and King, H. (eds) *Mortality and immortality: the anthropology and archaeology of death*, 205–23. London: Academic Press.

Strathern, M. 1988. *The Gender of the Gift*. Berkeley, CA: University of California Press.

Suchowska-Ducke, P., Scott Reiter, S., and Vandkilde, H. 2015. *Forging identities. The mobility of culture in Bronze Age Europe*. Oxford: British Archaeological Reports, International Series S2771 and 2772.

Tarlow, S. 1992. 'Each slow dusk a drawing down of blinds', *Archaeological Review from Cambridge* 11(1), 125–40.

Taussig, M. 1980. *The devil and commodity fetishism in South America*. Chapel Hill, NC: University of North Carolina Press.

Taussig, M. 2009. *What colour is the sacred?* Chicago, IL: University of Chicago Press.

Taylor, H. 1951. 'The Tynings barrow group, third report', *Proceedings of the University of Bristol Spelaeological Society* 8(2), 111–73.

Bibliography

Taylor, J. 1999. 'Gold reflections', in Harding, A. (ed.) *Experiment and design: archaeological studies in honour of John Coles*, 108–15. Oxford: Oxbow.

Taylor, K. 2004. 'Inchagreenoge fulachta fiadh, ritual deposit of a human skull, wooden artifacts, post-Medieval trackway', in Bennett, I. (ed.) *Excavations 2002*, 322–4. Bray: Wordwell.

Taylor, M. 2001. 'The wood', in Pryor, F. *The Flag Fen Basin: archaeology and environment in a fenland landscape*, 167–228. London: English Heritage.

Thomas, J. 1991. 'Reading the body: Beaker funerary practice in Britain', in Garwood, P., Jennings, D., Skeates, R., and Toms, J. (eds) *Sacred and profane: proceedings of a conference on archaeology, ritual and religion, Oxford, 1989*, 33–42. Oxford: Oxford University Committee for Archaeology Monograph 32.

Thomas, J. 1999. *Understanding the Neolithic*. London: Routledge.

Thomas, N. 2005. *Snail Down: the Bronze Age barrow cemetery and related earthworks, in the parishes of Collingbourne Ducis and Collingbourne Kingston. Excavations 1953, 1955 and 1957*. Devizes: Wiltshire Archaeology and Natural History Society Monograph 3.

Thomas, R. 1984. 'Bronze Age metalwork from the Thames at Wallingford', *Oxoniensia* 49, 9–18.

Thomas, R. 1989. 'The Bronze Age-Iron Age transition in southern England', in Thomas, R. and Sørensen, M. L. S. (eds) *The Bronze Age-Iron Age transition in Europe: aspects of continuity and change in European societies c. 1200 to 500 BC*, 263–86. Oxford: British Archaeological Reports, International Series S483.

Thomas, R., Robinson, M., Barrett, J., and Wilson, B. 1986. 'A Late Bronze Age riverside settlement at Wallingford, Oxfordshire', *Archaeological Journal* 143, 174–200.

Thorpe, N. and Richards, C. 1984. 'The decline of ritual authority and the introduction of Beakers into Britain', in Bradley, R. and Gardiner, J. (eds) *Neolithic studies: a review of some recent work*, 67–84. Oxford: British Archaeological Reports, British Series 133.

Tilley, C. 1999. *Metaphor and material culture*. Oxford: Wiley-Blackwell.

Tilley, C. 2004. *The materiality of stone: explorations in landscape phenomenology*. London: Bloomsbury.

Tolan-Smith, C. 2005. 'A cairn on Birkside Fell: excavations in 1996 and 1997', *Archaeologia Aeliana* 34 (5th series), 55–65.

Torbrügge, W. 1971. 'Vor- und frühgeschichtliche Flussfunde. Zur Ordnung und Bestimmung einer Denkmälergruppe,' *Berichte der Römisch-Germanischen Kommission* 51/52, 1–146.

Towers, J., Montgomery, J., Evans, J., Jay, M., and Parker-Pearson, M. 2010. 'An investigation of the origins of cattle and aurochs deposited in the Early Bronze Age barrows at Gayhurst and Irthlingborough', *Journal of Archaeological Science* 17, 508–13.

Turner, L. 2010. *A re-interpretation of the Later Bronze Age metalwork hoards of Essex and Kent*. Oxford: British Archaeological Reports, British Series 507.

Turner, V. 1967. *The forest of symbols*. Ithaca: Cornell University Press.

Tylecote, R. 1987. *The early history of metallurgy in Europe*. London: Longman.

Bibliography

Tyson, N. 1995. 'Excavation of a Bronze Age cremation cemetery', *Manchester Archaeological Bulletin* 9, 5–22.

Valeri, V. 1980. 'Notes on the meaning of marriage prestations among the Huaulu of Seram', in Fox, J. (ed.) *The flow of life: essays on eastern Indonesia*, 178–92. Cambridge, MA: Harvard University Press.

van de Noort, R. 2009. 'Exploring the ritual of travel in prehistoric Europe: the Bronze Age sewn-plank boats in context', in Clark, P. (ed.) *Bronze Age connections: cultural contact in prehistoric Europe*, 159–75. Oxford: Oxbow.

van der Laan, J. 2016. *Narratives of technology*. New York: Palgrave Macmillan.

Van Dyke, R. 2015. 'Materiality in practice: an introduction', in Van Dyke, R. (ed.) *Practicing materiality*, 1–32.Tucson, University of Arizona Press.

Waddington, C. 2002. 'An Early Neolithic settlement and Late Bronze Age burial cairn near Bolam Lake, Northumberland: fieldwalking, excavation and reconstruction', *Archaeologia Aeliana* 30, 1–47.

Waddington, K. 2008. 'Topographies of accumulation at Late Bronze Age Potterne', in Davis, O., Sharples, N. and Waddington, K. (eds) *Changing perspectives on the first millennium BC*, 161–84. Oxford: Oxbow.

Waddington, K. 2010. 'The politics of the everyday: exploring 'midden' space in Late Bronze Age Wiltshire', in Maltby, M. and Morris, J. (eds) *Integrating social environmental archaeologies: reconsidering deposition*, 103–18. Oxford: British Archaeological Reports, International Series S2077.

Waddington, K. 2013. *Settlements of northwest Wales from the Late Bronze Age to the Early Medieval period*. Cardiff: University of Wales Press.

Wainwright, G. and Smith, K. 1980. 'The Shaugh Moor Project: second report—the enclosure', *Proceedings of the Prehistoric Society* 46, 65–122.

Walsh, F. 2014. 'Excavation and conjecture of a Late Bronze Age farmstead at Tober, Co. Offaly', *Journal of the Royal Society of Antiquaries Ireland* 141, 9–31.

Warner, R. 2006. 'The Tamlaght hoard and the Creeveroe axe: two new finds of Late Bronze Age date from near Navan, Co. Armagh', *Emania* 20, 20–8.

Waterman, D. 1951. 'A food-vessel barrow in Yorkshire', *Antiquaries Journal* 31, 1–24.

Waterson, R. 1990. *The living house: an anthropology of architecture in south-east Asia*. Oxford: Oxford University Press.

Watkins, T. 1982. 'The excavation of an Early Bronze Age cemetery at Barns Farm, Dalgety, Fife', *Proceedings of the Society of Antiquaries of Scotland* 112, 48–141.

Watts, S. 2014. *The life and death of querns*. Southampton: Highfield Press.

Webley, L. 2004. *Bronze Age, Iron Age and Romano-British settlement at Baston Quarry, Langtoft, Lincolnshire: areas B to E*. Cambridge: Cambridge Archaeological Unit (available at: http://archaeologydataservice.ac.uk/archives/view/greylit/details.cfm?id=16733).

Webley, L., Adams, S., and Brück, J. 2020. *The social context of technology: Non-ferrous metalworking in later prehistoric Britain and Ireland*. London: Prehistoric Society.

Weiner, A. 1983. '"A world of made is not a world of born": doing kula in Kiriwina', in Leach, J. and Leach, E. (eds) *The kula: new perspectives on Massim exchange*, 147–70. Cambridge: Cambridge University Press.

Bibliography

Weiner, A. 1992. *Inalienable possessions: the paradox of keeping-while-giving*. Berkeley: University of California Press.

Weiner, A. and Schneider, J. (eds) 1989. *Cloth and human experience*. Washington: Smithsonian Institution Press.

Welfare, A. 2011. *Great crowns of stone: the recumbent stone circles of Scotland*. Edinburgh: Royal Commission on the Ancient and Historical Monuments of Scotland.

Wells, C. 1977. 'The human bones', in Donaldson, P. 'The excavation of a multiple round barrow at Barnack, Cambridgeshire 1974–1976', *Antiquaries Journal* 57(2), 216–25.

Wells, C. and Hodgkinson, D. 2001. 'A Late Bronze Age human skull and associated worked wood from a Lancashire wetland', *Proceedings of the Prehistoric Society* 67, 163–74.

Wengrow, D. 2008. 'Prehistories of commodity branding', *Current Anthropology* 49(1), 7–34.

Whittle, A. 1995. 'Gifts from the earth: symbolic dimensions of the use and production of Neolithic flint and stone axes', *Archaeologia Polona* 33, 247–59.

Whittle, A., Atkinson, R., Chambers, R., Thomas, N. Harman, M., Northover, P., and Robinson, M. 1992. 'Excavations in the Neolithic and Bronze Age complex at Dorchester-on-Thames, Oxfordshire, 1947–1952 and 1981', *Proceedings of the Prehistoric Society* 58, 143–201.

Wickstead, H. 2008. *Theorising tenure: land division and identity on later prehistoric Dartmoor*. Oxford: British Archaeological Reports, British Series 465.

Wilkin, N. 2011. 'Animal remains from Late Neolithic and Early Bronze Age funerary contexts in Wiltshire, Dorset and Oxfordshire', *Archaeological Journal* 168, 64–95.

Wilkin, N. 2017. 'Combination, composition and context: readdressing British Middle Bronze Age ornament hoards (c. 1400–1100 cal BC)', in Martin, T. and Weetch, R. (eds) *Dress and society: contributions from archaeology*, 14–47. Oxford: Oxbow Books.

Wilkinson, T. and Murphy, P. 1995. *The archaeology of the Essex coast, volume 1: the Hullbridge survey*. Norwich: East Anglian Archaeology 71.

Williams, A. 2013. 'Linking Bronze Age copper smelting slags from Pentrwyn on the Great Orme to ore and metal', *Historical Metallurgy* 47(1), 93–110.

Williams, H. 2004. 'Death warmed up. The agency of bodies and bones in early Anglo-Saxon cremation rites', *Journal of Material Culture* 9(3), 263–91.

Williams, M. 2003. 'Growing metaphors: the agricultural cycle as metaphor in the later prehistoric period of Britain and north-western Europe', *Journal of Social Archaeology* 3, 223–55.

Witmore, C. 2007. 'Symmetrical archaeology: excerpts of a manifesto', *World Archaeology* 39, 546–62.

Woodward, A. 2000. *British barrows: a matter of life and death*. Stroud: Tempus.

Woodward A. 2002a. 'Beads and Beakers: heirlooms and relics in the British Early Bronze Age', *Antiquity* 76, 1040–7.

Bibliography

Woodward, A. 2002b. 'Inclusions, impressions and interpretation', in Woodward, A. and Hill, J. D. (eds) *Prehistoric Britain: the ceramic basis*, 106–18. Oxford: Oxbow.

Woodward, A. and Hunter, J. 2011. *An examination of prehistoric stone bracers from Britain*. Oxford: Oxbow.

Woodward, A. and Hunter, J. 2015. *Ritual in Early Bronze Age grave goods: an examination of ritual and dress equipment from Chalcolithic and Early Bronze Age graves in England*. Oxford: Oxbow.

Woodward, A., Hunter, J., and Bukach, D. 2015. 'Age and sex', in Woodward, A. and Hunter, J. *Ritual in Early Bronze Age grave goods: an examination of ritual and dress equipment from Chalcolithic and Early Bronze Age graves in England*, 517–27. Oxford: Oxbow.

Woodward, A., Hunter, J., Needham, S., and O'Connor, S. 2015. 'Pommels', in Woodward, A. and Hunter, J. *Ritual in Early Bronze Age grave goods: an examination of ritual and dress equipment from Chalcolithic and Early Bronze Age graves in England*, 45–53. Oxford: Oxbow.

Woodward, A. and Jackson, R. 2015. 'Prehistoric pottery', in Jackson, R. *Huntsman's Quarry, Kemerton: a Late Bronze Age settlement and landscape in Worcestershire*, 47–63. Oxford: Oxbow.

Woodward, A. and Needham, S. 2012. 'Diversity and distinction: characterising the individual buried at Wilsford G58, Wiltshire', in Jones, A. M., Pollard, J., Allen, M., and Gardiner, J. (eds) *Image, memory and monumentality: archaeological engagements with the material world*, 116–26. Oxford: Prehistoric Society/ Oxbow.

Woodward, P. 1991. *The South Dorset Ridgeway Project: survey and excavations 1977–84*. Dorchester: Dorset Natural History and Archaeological Society monograph 8.

Yates, D. 2007. *Land, power and prestige: Bronze Age field systems in southern England*. Oxford: Oxbow.

Yates, D. and Bradley, R. 2010. 'The siting of metalwork hoards in the Bronze Age of south-east England', *Antiquaries Journal* 90, 41–72.

York, J. 2002. 'The lifecycle of Bronze Age metalwork from the Thames', *Oxford Journal of Archaeology* 21(1), 77–92.

Index

Please note: "f" following a locator indicators a *figure*.

abandonment, rituals of 147, 211
Aberdeen 170
Aberdeenshire 45, 56, 183, 206
Aberdour Road 203
Abingdon 40
accumulation, aggrandizement, and display, strategies of 4
activities, gendering of 159–60
agrarian societies, emergence of 238
agricultural practice 114
agriculture, intensification of 6
Aird Quarry, roundhouse at 51
Aldro 19
Allerwash 27
Allington 39, 76
amber 76, 81, 89, 167–70
  considered to possess curative or apotropaic powers 222
  curated as heirlooms 89
  may have been viewed as magical substance 89
  objects, origin of 226
  ornaments 91
  other-worldly character of 89
Amesbury 79–81, 170
Amesbury Archer, The 16, 83, 84(f), 87, 120, 207, 240
Amisfield 146
amphibolite 167
ancestors, venerated 67
ancestral burial grounds 34
ancestral relic, -s 32, 38, 62, 92
ancestry, ideal of 106
Anglesey 166–7
animal bodies; *see* bodies, animal
animal equipment and animal imagery 216–20
animal handling 216–18
animal imagery 222
animal management 201

animal protein, people consumed high level of 209
animal reproduction 238
animal skins employed to wrap bodies and associated grave goods 206
animal spirits and ancestors, realm of 223
animals
  and field systems 213–16
  and humans, relationship between 209, 219, 223
  economic centrality and social significance of 220
  in the settled landscape 210–13
  may have been esteemed for particular behavioural attributes 208
  ritualized disposal of bodies 209
  seen as having supernatural powers 219
animate objects in the Early Bronze Age 88–91
anthropomorphic figurines 180
Appleby, Jo 29, 36–9
architecture, domestic 11–15, 46, 108, 116, 125–59, 162–4; *see also* houses
Argyll 186, 204, 216
Armagh, County 98, 184
Arran, island of 177
arrowheads 16, 43(f), 77, 79, 80(f), 81, 83, 85–6, 119–20, 206
artefacts 107, 141
  assemblages, diverse 111
  broken, deposition facilitated reformulation of relational identities 95
  buried with the dead 70
  selection, patterns of 94
Ashbury 96
Ashville Trading Estate 40
assembling and fragmenting the person in Early Bronze Age burials 73–6
Athlone 183

Index

authority, centralized 192
Avebury 3, 39
Avon, River 152
axes 9, 13, 32, 35, 55, 70–1, 81, 88–9, 107–8, 112, 147, 157–8, 211, 220–6, 234–8
  broken 94
  bronze 9, 32, 70, 127, 157
  deposited in the graves of men 107
  deposited singly or as components of hoards 71
  Neolithic axe quarries 167, 186
  stone 147, 224
Ayrshire 33, 56–7, 74, 169, 177, 205

Babraham Road 25–7
Ballachulish 180
Ballinderry 158
Ballintaggart 43, 44(f)
Ballybeg Bog 200
Ballylegan 125, 127(f), 131–2
Ballymeanoch 186–7
Ballynora 51
Balnuaran of Clava 169
Baltic, the 168, 226
Banc Gorddwr 174
Barleycroft Farm 133, 196
Barnack 20, 75
Barns Farm 37, 71, 178
Barrett, J. 14, 32, 65
Barrow Hills 40, 79, 80(f), 81, 82(f), 204, 205(f), 209
Barrow, Wilsford 30
barrow, -s
  and ancient routeways, relationship between 175
  and boundaries in the east of England 197(f)
  and field systems, relationship between 196
  and sinkholes, concentration of, possible link between 172
  and special places 171–5
  and temporality of landscape 168–9
  barrow-making, process of 169
  bell 27, 31
  bowl 34
  cemeteries 20, 23, 36, 44(f), 46–7, 171–7, 196
  construction 204
  cosmographies 165–78
  grave material, reuse of 23
  landscape context of 177
  likely to have been focal points for gatherings 46

linear 175
located at junctions between boundaries 198
location in river valleys 174
long 28
mapped the deceased and their relationships with places and people 171
points of articulation and division in the landscape 196
turf-mound 24
Basingstoke 43
Baston Quarry 121, 123
Bath 175
Battlesbury 42, 56
Beaker burials 17, 20–4, 83, 120, 235
Beaker folk 3
Beaker immigrants 240
Beaker pits 30
Beaker pottery 13, 17, 77–9, 83–5, 118, 121
Beaulieu Heath II, mortuary house at 30
Bedd Branwen 166
Beech Hill House 75
Beeston Castle 157
belief systems 199, 200, 222–3
Bellever Tor 131
Ben More 187
Berewan 66
Berkshire 40, 50, 57, 103, 108, 136, 139, 145, 178, 199, 237
Berkshire Downs 218
Bestwall Quarry 131, 147–9, 214
Biconical Urn 121
Big Moor, Derbyshire 189(f)
Birkside Fell 34
Black Patch 141, 145
Blackmoor hoard 92
Blackwater, River 180
Blairhall Burn 146
Bloodmoor Hill 134
Bloody Pool 92, 93(f)
Bluntisham 30
bodies, animal
  burials mimic human interments 201
  deposited alongside human bodies 201
  elements occur as artefacts in the grave 206
  partial, in graves, interpreted as food offerings 203
  placed relative to human burials in the grave 208
  remains from mortuary contexts 203
  ritualized disposal of 209
bodies, human and animal 201–10
  boundary between 220

292

Index

treatment and deposition of 220
treatment is sometimes similar 209
bodily boundaries, permeable nature of 64
bodily disaggregation, processes of 25
bodily integrity and genealogical position,
   link between 38
bodily integrity, ideology of 63
bodily relations 19–24
Bodmin Moor 171
body, -ies, human
   and liminality 52–6
   and objects, treatment of 112
   and other materials, boundary between
      the 50
   certain persons kept complete while
      others were fragmented 65
   deliberate preservation of 58
   deposited both complete and
      incomplete 61
   different elements ascribed specific
      cultural meanings 81
   different understanding of the integrity
      of 64
   disarticulated and employed to create
      relational forms of identity 63
   fragmentation and commingling of 62–3
   fragmentation of 62
   integrity of 65
   manipulating 68
   patterning in the location of objects
      around 81
   processing the 32
   transformative processes brought to
      bear on 64
   treated with care 47
   treatment on death 102
   unburnt body in the Chalcolithic and
      Early Bronze Age, the 17–32
bog, -s 10, 185(f), 218, 221, 223
   decorated objects deposited in 90
   deposition of metalwork in 92, 177, 182,
      184, 187
   human bone found in 65
   may have been viewed as dangerous or
      liminal location 101, 182, 200
   relationship between boundaries and 10
   skulls frequently recovered from 52
   social and cultural significance 164,
      182, 200
   temporary deposition in 58
Bogshole Lane 96
Bolam Lake 50
bone, -s, human
   curated or disinterred and redeposited 61
   deliberate pounding or crushing of 230

demineralization of 58
deposited at boundaries and entrances 65
deposition in settlements 231
deposition in wells 98
deposition of 235
disarticulated 54
discovered in domestic context 51
fleshed, cremation of 51
found in liminal locations 52, 65, 68
heirloom 61
manipulation of 59
may be considered source of animacy 89
may have been distributed among
   mourners 48
may have been viewed as dangerous
   material 55
objects made of 66
possibly brought from Scandinavia or
   Mediterranean before deposition 61
post-mortem manipulation of 57
routine deposition in settlement
   contexts 66
seen as potent substance 89
symbolic significance of 56
symbolized hazards of encounters
   between different worlds 65
treatment of cremated 63
unburnt 51, 57
used to make objects 62–3
used to mark out significant points in
   settlement space 63
Booltiaghadine hoard 94
Booth, T. 29
Borneo 66
Boscombe Bowmen, the 17, 18(f)
boundaries
   and cosmology 198–200
   and features, relationship between 10
   as socially sensitive spaces 65
   between people and the material world 7
   between self and other, permeable 64
   bogs, and rivers 101
   concern with 65
   creation of 161
   crossing of 101
   field 5, 10, 42, 43(f), 96, 108, 190(f), 191,
      195–9, 214, 219, 221
   landscape, and special places 194–6
   personhood, and identity 196–8
   social 227, 234
   transgression of social 227
Bradeham Dale 167
Bradley Fen 50, 52, 96, 97(f), 192, 193(f),
   200, 214
Bradley, R. 14, 95, 188

293

Index

Brandon 51, 193
Breach Farm 89
Breiddin 155, 156(f), 157
Brightlingsea 44
Brighton 120
Brigmerston Down 191
Broad Chalke 40
Broadward 183, 217
Brockagh axe 90, 91(f)
broken vessels 122
Bromfield 47, 49, 50, 63, 175, 176(f)
Bronkham Hill 172
bronze
  axes 9, 32, 70, 127, 157
  broken bronzes 93–4, 99, 101, 236
  commoditization of 232
  gendered dimension to the production of 106
  hoards, interpretation of 91
  linked with transformative powers 89
  ornaments 108, 183
  spearheads and ferrules 92
  sword, -s 96–8, 114, 155
  tools and weapons 91
Bronze Age Ireland and Britain, 2500–600 BC 12–15
Bronze Age legacies and representations 239–41
Bronze Age, from the Early to the Late 178–82
Broomfield 96
Buckinghamshire 47, 92, 184, 200
Burdale 167
burial, -s
  Beaker 120, 235
  Chalcolithic 65, 88
  communal 24
  evidence for the careful placement of 47
  gendered dimension between inhumation and cremation 38
  Iron Age horse 219
  lines of 47
  male and female 88
  multiple, practices of 19–20, 49
  orientation of 23
  rarely accompanied by objects other than pots 47
  relationship between people and things in 71–91
  reopened and bodies disassembled and rearranged in the grave 62
  spatial arrangement of 46
  traditions of single 4
  urned 34
  virtually unknown in Late Bronze Age 50

  well-furnished 88
burial, -s, cremation 19, 32–4, 40, 42–4, 88
  accompanied by a Food Vessel 39
  analysis of Scottish 35
  and bronzeworking 114
  and deposition 40, 48
  and inhumation 36–9
  and inhumation burial, gendered dimension to the distinction between 38
  arranged in an arc 47
  became increasingly common 62
  deposited in bags, boxes, and pots 64
  deposited in urns 72
  deposits 46
  frequent recovery of incomplete ceramic vessels from 101
  identification of partial or 'token' 33
  inserted into a ring-cairn 56
  mortuary rites prior to 35
  multiple 36
  of fleshed bone 51
  often deposited on south side of earlier barrows 66
  practices of 32–3
  prevalence of 113
  rites involved complex and highly structured practices 47
  technological similarities with metalworking and pottery production 102
  traditions of 51
  urned, study of Scottish 33
  weight of bone found in 48
burial, -s, inhumation 17–20, 24–5, 29, 31, 34, 39, 42, 50, 67, 163, 170, 204–9
  Beaker 120
  gendered dimension 38
  particular points of the body were emphasized 81
  placed in coffins and mortuary houses 64
  reopened and bones manipulated and rearranged 65
  secondary 30
  traditions of 65
burning, breaking, combination, and regeneration, cycles of 102
burning, mixing, fragmenting, layering, and (un)veiling 64
Bush Barrow 89, 90(f)
Butcher's Rise 44–6, 49

cairn, -s 17, 33–5, 39, 43–5, 50, 56, 72, 115, 146, 160, 165–72, 173(f), 189(f), 190(f), 195, 199, 221–2

Index

Cairnwell 45
Calais Wold 167, 201
Caldicot 181
Callestick 115
Cambridge 25, 217
Cambridgeshire 23, 27, 30, 36, 42–52, 75, 96, 116, 121, 133, 169, 174, 181, 192, 196–200, 214–16
Canada Farm 29, 42
capitalism
  origins of 6
  social and economic conditions of 66
Carlton Colville 134
Carp's Tongue hoards 94, 238
Carrig 33, 39
Carshalton 211
Castle Kennedy 51
categories, social 89
categorization
  and difference 108–111
  processes of 71
  tyranny of 9–12
cattle
  buildings used to house 139
  burial of 201
  cattle bone 30, 208, 213, 217
  deposition of 211
  dung 152, 212
  economic significance of 222
  grazing of 145, 177
  herding 191
  hide 206–7
  hoofprints 214
  livestock management of 214
  major source of meat 151
  may have been considered significant form of wealth 152
  possibly used for pulling carts 217
  skull, -s 59, 203–4, 205(f), 209, 210, 214
  social significance of 220
Cavan, County 90
cave, -s
  and cosmological structuring of the landscape 187, 221
  casting of bronze objects in 55
  finds from 183, 217
  human bone was also deposited in 54, 65, 68
  may have been viewed as entries to the underworld 184
Cefn Panagored 172
Celtic mythology 182
ceramics
  Beaker 13, 118, 121
  bone-tempered 101

ceramic forms of Earliest Iron Age 110(f)
  coarseware 139
  decorated, use of 238
  deposition of 159
  deposits of 40, 53(f), 59(f)
  domestic 30
  fineware 137–9, 151
  Food Vessel 72, 121–3
  Late Bronze Age 57, 109, 186
  Late Bronze Age, stylistic attributes of 239
  may have been deliberately removed & retained from mortuary context 101
  Middle Bronze Age 109
  plainware 136, 157
  technology and production 101–2, 230
  Urns, Biconical 121
  Urns, Collared 34, 39, 75, 121
  Urns, Cordoned 39, 170
  Urns, Encrusted 77
  variety of new forms 109
cereal production 164
Chalton 137
Chancellorsland 52
Charlesland 179
Chelmsford Park 50
Cheshire 157
Chetwynd 51
Chichester 120
Chilbolton 29
Childe, Vere Gordon 2–3
Chitts Hill 47–9
chronological schemes 14
chthonic beings 211
Church Farm 107
circulating the dead in the Late Bronze Age 59–61
circulation and exchange, processes of 113
Cladh Hallan 10, 29, 57, 58(f), 63, 67, 132, 210
Clare, County 93–4, 158, 184
Clava cairns 169
Clay Farm 42, 214
Cliffs End Farm 57–60, 67, 203
Cloghabreedy 121, 122(f), 126–8, 129(f), 134
Cloncreen Bog 180
cloth
  associated with ideas of fertility and regeneration 105
  dyes for 104
  gendered dimension to the production of 106
  may have been woven on handheld looms 104
  production 69, 102–6
  weaving of 102

295

Index

Clwyd 94, 172, 184, 217
Clyde, Firth of 177
coffin, oak-log 50
coffins, boat-shaped 177-8
Colchester 47-9
Collared Urns 34, 39, 75, 121
collections and containment 76-9
Colne Brook 152
colour symbolism 89, 109
commensality, intergenerational 148-9
commodification, process of 231-3
communal burials 24
communal decision-making 194
communal feasting 238
communities, fragmentation of 115
community gathering-places in the Late Bronze Age 149-54
community organization and integration 141
comparison and distinction, processes of 227
conceptual structures and systems of value 7
Coneygre Farm 48
connection and division, tension between processes of 113
consumer society, Bronze Age as the original 240
containers, frequency of various sorts in burials 64
continuity and connection, concepts of 107
continuity, cyclical 149
Conwy 186
cooperative labour 194
copper and gold, appearance of 89
copper mines 12, 186
copper objects, analysis of 12, 85
copper-smelting 186
Corcreeghy 118, 119(f)
Cordoned Urn 39, 170
Cork, County 1, 51, 55, 186
Cornwall 63, 115, 118, 146, 166, 167, 171-2, 183, 199
Corrstown 99, 139, 145-8
Corve, River 175
cosmographies, northern European 222
cosmological concerns 132
cosmological order 221
cosmological principles 198-9
cosmologies, northern European 219
cosmos, tripartite division of 221
Coupar Angus 75
Covesea 54
cowrie shell 81, 170
Cranborne Chase 120

Cranford Lane 98
creation myths 113
cremation; *see* burial, -s, cremation
crop production 201
Crossdoney 90
Crouch estuary 54
Crow's Buttress 163
Crundale 183
cultural categories, transgression of 101
cultural values 4
culture and nature, distinction between 164-5
Cumbria 167
curating the dead 27-32
curation and temporality in cremation burials 34-6
Cynon Valley 237

dagger, -s 31, 72-5, 79, 81-3, 92
Dainton 199
Dalgety 178
Daneshill 43
Dartmoor 77, 131, 146, 163, 168, 188, 191-9
Davis, S. 203
dead, the
 circulating in the Late Bronze Age 59-61
 curating 27-32
 familiar, interest in engaging with 68
 potent means of symbolizing transformative processes 65
death
 and fertility, link between 230
 and travel by water, symbolic connection between 177
 harnessing of, for the good of society 229
 means of symbolically marking 94
 ontological significance and social impact of 87
decommissioning, ritual 93
decoration, increased use of 109
Dee
 River 183
 Valley 171
Denbighshire 171
deposition
 and cremation, possible spatial and temporal disjunctions between 48
 decommissioning items prior to 93
 possible selection of particular body parts for 48
 practice 48
depositional context of metalworking residues in the Middle and Late Bronze Age, the 96-100

Index

deposits
  floor 132
  marked important points in space 148
  votive 161, 200
Derbyshire 73, 149, 157, 188
destruction and exchange 226–9
destruction, acts of 227
  emotive power of 149
  symbolized death 232
detritus of daily activities, people's relationship with 160
Devil's Bit 184
Devon 92, 99, 128, 131, 149, 163–8, 183, 199
Dewerstone pot, the 191, 195
diet, high-protein 163, 209
Dinorben 184, 217
domestic architecture of the Middle and Late Bronze Age, the 125–59
domestic architecture, monumental 164
domestic space
  key context in which social identities were constructed 117
  use of, ethnographic analysis of 144
Dorchester 145
Dorney Lake 200
Dorset 29, 42, 64, 94, 120, 124, 128, 131, 145–9, 165, 172, 201, 210, 214, 237–8
Dorset Ridgeway 175
Dour, River 99, 181
Dover boat, the 181–2
Down Farm 147, 201, 202(f), 210
Down, County 43, 118
Dowris 182
Drewett, P. 141–2
Drombeg 55–6, 186
Dryburn Bridge 25, 26(f)
dryland contexts 93–4
dualisms 9
Dublin, County 51, 123, 170
Duggleby 167
Dumfries 51
Dumfriesshire 146
Dunaverny flesh-hook, the 218–22
Dunfermline 203
Dunure Road 33, 56–7, 74, 169, 177, 205
Durham, County 54, 183, 217

eagle talons 206–8, 222
East Anglia 47, 171, 188, 239
East Chisenbury 151–3
East Lothian 25, 29
East Northdown 57
East Sussex 76, 99, 107, 141
East Woodburn 126, 146–8

East Yorkshire 19–23, 39, 69, 88, 166–7, 175, 201, 238
Easton Down 39, 76–7
Edercloon 216
Edmondstown 170
egalitarian groups 194
Elgin 206
Ellison, A. 139, 142
Encrusted Urns 77
England, France, and the Low Countries, intensive interaction between 100, 226
Ensay, island of 50, 123
Essex 44–54, 137–9, 143, 148, 155
Europe, continental, main source of bronze in British Isles 99
European ideology and identity 2
European Union 2
event-marking deposits and the social life of the house 145–9
evolutionist narratives 6
Ewart Park 94, 157, 237
excarnation 56–7, 62–4
exchange, -s
  and technological processes, structural similarities between 227
  anthropological studies of 105
  between families, series of 229
  exchange, commoditization, and social boundaries 231–5
  facilitated regeneration of life 229
  facilitates construction and maintenance of interpersonal relationships 231
  functions as means of negotiating mutual estimation 227
  intergroup 234
  relative significance of gifts and commodities 232
  social significance of 235
  systems of 228
Eye Quarry 47, 199, 214, 217

faience 69, 76–7, 81, 89, 170, 222
family and community identities 74
feasting 10, 67, 104, 111, 124, 147, 151–4, 158–60, 204, 209–13, 217, 238
Feltwell Quarries 121–3
female gendered identity, markers of 77
fertility
  agricultural 238
  and death, link between 230
  and regeneration, idioms of 169
  and regeneration, linked concepts of 101
  human and agricultural 200
  ideas of growth and 149
  stores of 67

Index

field boundaries 5, 10, 42, 43(f), 96, 108, 190(f), 191, 195–9, 214, 219, 221
field systems 12, 188, 220
  aggregate 188, 189(f), 192–4
  alignment of 47
  and barrows, relationship between 196
  and land division in the Middle and Late Bronze Age 187–200
  appearance of 6
  boundaries 98
  coaxial 133, 188, 190(f), 191–5, 198, 200, 221
  creation of 108
  land-use practices within 192
  suggest personalized relationships between people and landscape 195
field-walking surveys 119
Fife 37, 72, 108, 178, 203, 207
fineware 137–9, 151
Flag Fen 54, 216
flat inhumation graves 36
Fleming, A. 188
flow of life in Bronze Age Britain and Ireland, the 224–41
folklore 182
Fontijn, D. 95
food
  consumption key arena for the performance of social difference 109
  consumption, rituals of 117
  offerings 204–8
  preparation 230
  production 101
Food Vessel ceramics 72, 121–3
Fordington Farm 64, 124
Forteviot 170, 207
fossils, inclusion in Early Bronze Age graves 77, 170
Fox, Cyril 13
Foxtrot Crossing 214
fragmentation
  cycles of 112
  deliberate, of objects 74
  facilitated relationships between the living and the dead 76
  linked concepts of fertility and regeneration 100–2
  mixing, and recycling, processes of 239
  of unburnt bodies 62
  particular categories of person may have been more subject 65
  practices of deliberate 76, 101
  process of 62
  productive purpose of 239
  sequences of 64
  social 236
  speaks of moments of profound transformation 66
fragmenting and combining the Middle Bronze Age body 47–50
fragmenting the body 15–68
fragments, meaningful, circulation of 233
France 12–13, 85, 99–100
funeral rite 78, 83, 166, 174, 228
funerary and ceremonial monuments 163, 188
funerary cairns 115
funerary feast 206–8
funerary prestations 104

Gairneybank 203
Galloway 51
Galway, County 182–3
Game Farm 51, 193
Gardiner, J. 120
Gardom's Edge 149, 188
Garton Slack 69, 70(f), 71
Garwood, P. 65
Gell, Alfred 8
gender
  gender, space, and social models of the Bronze Age household 141–5
  gender, status, and personhood 87–8
  gendered dimension to distinction between inhumation & cremation burial 38
  gendered identities 116, 144, 149, 234
  gendering of activities 159–60
  gendering of settlement space 143
  gendering of space 142–3
  groups 108, 149
  relationships 116–17
  understanding of 87
genealogical position and bodily integrity, link between 38
genealogical succession, ideals of 23
geographies of the body 79–83
gift and commodity exchange, significance of 232
gift exchange 4, 221, 232
Ginn, V. 140
Glamorgan 89
Glanfeinion 148
Glengorm 187
Gleninsheen 94
Glennan 204
Glentanar 183
Gloucestershire 40, 51, 103
gold
  and copper, appearance of 89

Index

beads 158
bowl or hat 184
bracelets 94, 125, 150(f), 153, 162, 184
consumption of 67
destruction of gold objects 92
gold-studded stone bracer 75
goldwork, -ing 83, 86, 240
gorgets 10, 93, 96
objects 93–4, 153
ornaments 16, 83, 86, 105, 184, 200
particular properties of 113
pendant 225
ring 158
sun disc, -s 72–3, 89, 107
transformative powers of 89
Goldcliff 180
Golf Crossing 42, 43(f)
goods, prestige 87
Gorteenreagh 93
Gradoge, River 1
grain, processing of 230
Grange, stone circle at 186
grave as *mappa mundi*, the 167–8
grave goods 4–5, 30, 49, 60, 63, 77, 87, 169, 209
    constituted in relational terms 112
    destruction of 92
    difference between male and female inhumation burials 87
    do not solely function to indicate wealth and status 88
    gender differences 88
    may have been given as gifts by the mourners 81
    may not always have been owned by the deceased 81
    quantity not necessarily a reflection of wealth and status 87
    rarely deposited with the dead in the Middle or Late Bronze Age 70
    significant percentage of Early Bronze Age burials produce none 87
grave, narratives of the social world in the 168
Great Langdale 167
Great Orme 186
Great Ouse, River 175
Greatisland 178
Green Park 57, 136, 178–9
Grindlow 73
Gristhorpe 204–9
growth, death, and renewal, cycles of 161
Guiting Power 40
Gwent 180
Gwithian 199
Gwynedd 178

Halls Hill 146–8
Hamilton 214, 215(f)
Hampshire 29–30, 43, 46, 48, 92, 137, 179
Harding, Jan 23, 172
Harlington 98
Harris, island of 118
Harting 168
Hartshill Copse 237
Haughey's Fort 184
headhunting and display of trophy heads, evidence for 68
Healy, F. 172
Heathery Burn 54–5, 183–4, 217
Heathrow 194
heirloom, -s 13, 17, 61, 66, 72–5, 78, 85, 89, 96, 229, 234
Herefordshire 175
hierarchization, increasing 109
Highland 35
hillforts 5, 155, 158
    early 157
    frequently constructed in prominent and highly visible positions 184
    gathering places for dispersed communities 157
    intercommunity gatherings 162
    Irish 158
hoard, -s 69, 92–6, 106, 184, 200, 217, 220, 233, 237–8
    and broken objects 91–6
    bronze 96, 235
    composition of dryland 94
    copper and bronze axes were deposited in 70
    deposited at significant locations 71
    may have been the product of marriage prestations 108
    mixed 94
    of damaged weapons deposited at junction of field system 52
    patterns of artefact selection 94
    scrap 95–8, 232, 236
    wetland 92
Hog Cliff Hill 128
Holme-next-the-Sea 172, 174(f), 175
home, the
    monumentalization of 117
    significance of 115
Hopton Street 192
Horcott Pit 103
Horsbrugh Castle Farm 25–7
horse riding 217

299

Index

Horton 108, 199
household space
  inter-site variability in the use of 162
  subdivision of 133
household
  lifecycle of 145
  productivity of 149
houses
  and people, lifecycles of 161
  and people, symbolic link between 146
  architecture, domestic 11–15, 46, 108, 116, 125–59, 162–4
  Bronze Age, lifecycles of 117
  little to suggest marked social differences between 141
  monumentalized 146
  organization of space within 132
Huggate Wold 172, 175
human and animal bodies; *see* bodies, human and animal
human–animal relationships 200–20, 223
human–environment relations 6
Hunter, John 30, 81
Huntingdon, Richard 24
Huntsman's Quarry 146–7

Iberia 85
Icknield Way 175
iconography 177, 230
identity
  and alterity in Bronze Age Britain and Ireland 1–15
  concepts of personhood and 69
  deconstruction of particular 95
  family and community 74
  gendered 144, 234
  not static or homogeneous 112
  personal and community 169
  reformulation of relational 95
  relational 63, 96, 161, 233–4
  sociocentric character of 96
  symbols of family or group 208
ideological purposes 62
Imber 172
immigration, current concerns around 240
incense cup 89
Inchagreenoge 179
individual, idea of the 5
individualism 196, 235
Indo-European languages 240
Indonesia 105
inheritance 65, 88, 108
inhumation; *see* burial, -s, inhumation
initiation rites 209
intercommunity relationships 65

intermarriage 92
interpersonal and familial relationships, significance of 20
interpersonal interaction 92
interpersonal links, creation and transformation of 92
interpersonal relationships 46, 81, 124, 196
  aspects of 88
  indices of 92
  made on a local scale 162
  maintenance and regeneration of 113
  specific types of 65
Inverness 35, 177, 207
Ireland 51, 170, 187, 240
Irish mythology 219
Irthlingborough Island 28, 72–7, 78(f), 174, 203, 209
Isleham hoard, the 217
isotope analysis 3, 34, 68, 83, 120, 163, 204, 209, 213, 240
Ivinghoe 184

jet 71–7, 89, 96, 114, 152, 167–70, 184, 222
  considered to possess curative or apotropaic powers 222
  curated as heirlooms 89
  may have been viewed as magical substances 89
  necklaces 74
  objects 168

Keelogue 183
Keenoge 27, 32–3, 38
Kemerton 103, 109, 146–7
Kent 20, 24, 29, 43, 57–8, 67, 96, 99, 107, 181–3, 188, 203, 226
Kerry, County 12, 179, 226
Kildare, County 90
Kilgobbin 123
Killoran 178
Kilmahuddrick 51
Kilmartin Glen 124
Kimpton 48
kin group, integrity of 231
King's Stables, the 98, 184
Kingsmead Quarry 108, 199
Kinrossshire 203
kinship 65, 88, 107, 114
Knight, Matt 92
Knighton Hill 40
knives, copper 16, 38, 83–7
Knobley Brook 175
Knook 74
Kodi 105
Kuijpers, M. 85

Index

La Tène decoration 184
labour, gendered division of 106
Ladywell 172
Lafone Street 192
Lairg 132
Lanarkshire 33
Lancashire 52, 72
landscape, -s
   and cosmology in the Early Bronze Age 175–8
   engagement with 169
   genealogy of 160
   had cultural meaning and symbolic significance 191
   link between people and 198
   monumental 163
   mutualistic relationship with 221
   overexploitation of 192
   part of the social universe 195
   relationships between people and 195
   tripartite cosmological structuring of 187
   zoning of 200
Langdale tuff 167
Langdon Bay, shipwreck sites at 99, 100(f)
Langtoft 121
Langton 170, 204
Langton Matravers, hoard at 237–8
Langwell Farm 206, 209
Lansdown 175
Latch Farm 46
Lehenaghmore 51
Leicestershire 53, 207, 214
Lesmurdie Road 206
Lewes 107
Leyton 135
life and death, symbolism of 169
life, regeneration of 114, 232, 235
lifecycle rites 160
lifecycle, -s 211, 231
Limerick, County 48, 179, 186
liminal location, -s 65, 101, 181, 184, 186
Lincolnshire 98, 121
linen 103–4
links, intergroup, benefits and the drawbacks of 231
Linlithgow 25
living and the dead, familiarity and intimacy between 67
living house, the 115–62
Llanblethian 89
Llandudno 186
Llanmaes 151, 213
Loanhead of Daviot 56
Loch Nell 216
Lockington 207

Lofts Farm 139
logboats 181
London 98, 135, 180, 192
Londonderry, County 99, 139, 145–8
Long Bredy 94
Longford, County 216
Lookout Plantation 147
loom weights, evidence for 104
Loose Howe 178
Lough Leven 180
Loughnashade 184
Loughton 47
Low Countries 12
lunulae 90
Lurgan canoe, the 182

Madgwick, R. 151
magical materials 71
Mains of Scotstown 170
Mam Tor 157
manipulating the body 24–7
Manish Strand 50, 123
Manston 24
Margate 57
Marlborough Downs 192
marriage 38, 92, 101–8, 145, 209, 220–2, 227–31, 234
   alliances 229
   form of exchange 231
   prestations 222
   transactions 228, 234
materiality and substance, ideas about 225
materiality of Early Bronze Age cremation burials, The 39–42
materials
   choreography of 221
   deposition of 171
McKinley, J. 204
McOmish, D. 154
Meath, County 27, 32–8, 154
Medina-Pettersson, Cecilia 33–4
Mediterranean 61
metal recycling, ritualizing 234
metals and the sun, links sometimes drawn between 89
metalwork
   deposition of 92, 152, 186
   played significant role in transformation of social identity 95
   votive deposition of 182
metalworking 69, 230
   as transformative process 113
   depositional context of residues in Middle and Late Bronze Age, the 96–100

301

Index

metalworking (*cont.*)
  embodies cyclical concepts of temporality 230
  ensured continuity of social relations 232
  evidence of, recovered from liminal contexts 98
  introduction of 226
  involved new concepts of materiality and substance 113
  linked colour and luminosity of materials with transformative powers 89
  may have been viewed as sources of life and vitality 89
  often viewed as hazardous and transformative process 55
  residues, deposition in liminal contexts 99
  residues, depositional context of 96
  social and ritual significance of 186
  technological similarities with pottery production & cremation practices 102
  transformative act of 86
  transformative potential of 98
  waste 94
Metcalf, Peter 24
micropolitics of power 8
midden, -s
  appear to have been locations where people congregated 153
  creation of 124
  diverse range of finds from 158
  intercommunity gatherings 162
  material spread on fields as manure 144
  monumental, creation of 231
  sites 211–13
  surface 123
Middle Barn Farm 36, 37(f)
Middle Farm 145
Mill Road 25
Mill Road Industrial Estate 29
Milsom's Corner 93, 96, 114
Milton Keynes 47
Minstead 169
Minster 188
mistletoe, significance of 30
Mitchelstown 1, 9, 13
Mitchelstowndown 48
Mizoguchi, Koji 23
mobility
  and the domestic domain in the Chalcolithic and Early Bronze Age 118–24
  human 240
  residential 161–3
Moel Tŷ-Uchaf 171

Monkton, Kent 226
Monkton Road 188
Monmouthshire 181
monumental domestic architecture 164
monumental landscapes 163
monuments
  ceremonial and funerary 56, 163
  circular 134
  funerary and ceremonial 163, 188
Mooghaun 158, 184
Moray 206
Moray Firth 54, 55(f)
Mortimer, John and Richard 69, 167
mortuary assemblages 168, 208
mortuary contexts
  animal remains from 203
  remains of animals incorporated into 201
mortuary evidence, complexity and variability of 61
mortuary feasts 204
mortuary practice, -s
  and identity 42
  and identity in the Middle Bronze Age 42–50
  and idioms of fertility and regeneration 169
  importance of interpersonal relationships in 63
mortuary remains, curation and redeposition of 48
mortuary rite,-s and rituals 16–17, 27, 35, 39, 67, 74, 78, 81, 85–8, 92, 187, 196
mortuary structure 29
mortuary transactions 229
Mound of the Hostages 36
Mount Caburn 76
Moynagh Lough 158
Mucking North Ring 143–5, 155
Mull 187
multielement analysis 178
Mulville, J. 151
mummification 10, 29, 58, 63, 67
music 32, 179
Must Farm 51, 104, 116, 181, 216–17
myths 207, 223

Nant Farm 178
National Museum of Ireland 240
nature and culture in Early Bronze Age barrows 169–71
nature–culture divide, existence of 222
Navan 98, 185(f)
Navidale 128, 130(f), 131
Neat's Court 29
necklace, -s 73–7, 88–9, 92, 206, 229

Index

Needham, Stuart 14, 237–8
Nene, River 174
Neolithic 2
Neolithic technologies 224
Nigeria 141
Norfolk 43, 121, 172, 175
Norman Conquest, the 240
North Downs 183
North Hampshire Downs 120
North Yorkshire 50, 165, 170, 184, 204, 207, 209
Northamptonshire 28, 34, 36, 72, 75, 77, 78(f), 172, 174, 203
Northton 118
Northumberland 27, 34, 49–50, 126, 146–8
Norton Fitzwarren, hilltop enclosure at 98
Nottinghamshire 48

oak
    considered to have magical qualities 182
    timber of choice for construction of roundhouses 146
object, -s
    act of breaking 233
    agency of 113–14
    amber, origin of 226
    and bodies, treatment of 112
    biographies 69–114
    broken metal 93
    broken, cannot simply be seen as 'rubbish' 92
    broken, social role of 113
    bronze, iconography engraved on 177
    burning and breaking of 112
    circulation of, during funerary rites 228
    complex exchange histories 235
    composite, dissolution of 92
    composite, production of 224
    considered to have lifecycles 102
    core component of the self 112
    decommissioning of 95
    decoration of 90
    deliberate fragmentation of 74, 236
    deliberately decommissioning prior to deposition 93
    deposition embodies complex network of relationships 83
    deposition sometimes used to mark out social boundaries 108
    destruction and reassembly of 113
    destruction facilitated transformation of social identities 96
    destruction of bronze and gold 92
    destruction of, significant element of social and ritual practice 112
    exchange, mixing, and deposition of fragments of 101
    facilitated social categorization 113
    form, dissolution of 101
    gendered associations 107
    had their own life force 89
    helped articulate interconnections & define distinctions 79
    important, often deposited at the entrances to roundhouses 128
    in dryland contexts, fragmentation of 95
    juxtaposition of, allowed the performance of cosmologies 111
    markers of identity 113
    may have been considered to possess agency 90
    may sometimes have been thought of as animate 88
    people and 69, 71, 88, 146, 228
    powerful social agents 235
    process of assembling or 'bundling' 78
    ritual decommissioning of 93
    ritualized transformation of 100
    socially significant 96
    special, deposition of 148
    special, thrown into water during intercommunity gatherings 153
    symbolic properties of 86
    symbolized collective identities of family or lineage groups 96
    transformation of people into 228
    viewed as fluid, composite entities 102
    votive deposition in or close to water below hillforts 184
obligation, relations of 231
obsolescence, dirt, and decay, contemporary ideas around 66
Ockham, hoard 106–7
Offaly, County 128, 132, 135, 158, 180–2, 200
Old Sarum Spur 201
Oliver Close Estate 135, 155
opium-poppy seeds 153
opposition and complementarity, ideas of 89
Orkney 66
Outer Hebrides 210
Over 24, 36, 174, 196
Overton Hill 10, 124
Oxfordshire 30, 40, 72, 79, 81, 96, 103, 151, 204, 209, 214
Oxteddle Bottom 76

Painsthorpe Wold 166
palaeoenvironmental analysis 178

303

Index

Pálsson, G. 191
Parc-y-Meirch 184, 217
Parker Pearson, M. 143–4
pastoralism 164, 209
paternalism 191
Peak District 88, 157
Peeblesshire 25, 35
people and houses, symbolic link between 146
people and objects; *see* object, -s
people and things, relationship between 6–9, 71–91
people into, transformation of 228
Perio 203
person
  viewed as comprising multiple components 112
  viewed as fluid, fragmented, and composite 235
personhood
  and power 235–6
  changes to concepts of 113
  concepts of 108, 198
  essential attributes of 96
  relational character of 63
  transient concepts of 95
  varying concepts of 88
Perth and Kinross 75, 170, 207
pits, scatters, and place-making 120–4
places, special, in the Middle and Late Bronze Age 182–7
plainwares 136
plant fibres 104
pond barrows 24
Porth Neigwl 178
Portland 183
Portlethen 45
post-Enlightenment rationalism 11
post-humanist perspectives 7
post-mortem manipulation, practices of 56–61
pots and people, metaphorical link between 71
Potterne 57, 104, 111, 150(f), 151–4, 198, 211–13, 217, 237
pottery; *see* ceramics
Poulton-le-Fylde 52
Powys 10, 148, 174–5
processing the body in Early Bronze Age cremation burials 32–42
production
  and reproduction 229–31
  changing patterns of 88
  fragmentation, and exchange in the Middle and Late Bronze Age 91–111

Purbeck 183
pyre, -s
  careful tending of 47
  debris 39–40, 49, 63
  objects accompanied the body onto the 75

quartz pebbles 41, 63, 69, 75, 115, 118, 169–71, 180
Quernhow 165
quernstones 57, 63, 66, 101–2, 117, 125, 139, 142, 148–9, 154, 158, 160, 164
  deliberate burning and breaking of 149
  deposition of 149, 160

Radley 40
Rameldry 207
Ramsgate 43
Rathbone, S. 140
Rathgall 158
rationalism, post-Enlightenment 11
Raunds 36, 172
Reading Business Park 50, 103, 136–9, 145, 148
Rectory Road 30
recycling, practice of 106
red steatite 81, 170
Redlands Farm 28
referencing, process of 77
refuse
  does not appear to have had solely negative connotations 66–7
  valued as a material which spoke of identity and memory 160
regalia, ceremonial 90
relational identity in the grave of the Amesbury Archer 83–7
relationality, sense of 76
relationship between people and things, the 6–9
  in Early Bronze Age burials, the 71–91
relationships
  interpersonal 46, 196
  intimate 161
relics, ancestral 62
remains, human
  cremation, further processing of 48
  curation of 29
  deposited at ceremonial monuments 55
  deposition in ditches surrounding settlements 117
  linked with concepts of light, life, fertility, and rebirth 66
  often deposited in boundaries 52
  practices involving intimate engagement with 67

Index

Renfrew, Colin 19
residential mobility 161
Richards, C. 143–4
Ride 50
Ridlington 126(f), 131
Riggs 20, 22(f)
ring-cairns 171
ringworks 13
  creation of 155
  settings for significant communal acts of food consumption 155
Ripple 107
Rippon Tor 190(f), 195
rites
  abandonment 211
  funerary 166
  life-cycle 160
  of passage 95, 161, 231
ritual activities 153, 160
ritual acts 102, 147
  of commensality 148
  of destruction 93, 96, 184
  of gift exchange 221
ritual potency 90
ritual practice 92, 236
rivers, lakes and bogs
  and ritual practice 92
  social and cultural significance 164
rock art 177
Roseberry Topping hoard 184
Ross Island 12, 226
Rossett 94
Rough Tor 171
roundhouses
  architectural elaboration of entranceways 128
  architecture of 162
  entrances often marked by deliberate deposition of important objects 128
  may have been conceptually divided into left-hand and right-hand side 131
  may have been viewed as living things with their own spirit 161
  oriented towards the rising sun 186, 238
  stone, converted into cairns 146
Runnymede 134, 148, 151–2, 211
Russell, P. 142
Rutland 131
Rylstone 50

sacred spaces 182
sacrifice, human 59
sacrifices 211
Salcombe 99–100
Salisbury Plain 174

Scandinavia 61, 175
Scarcewater 146
Scotland 23, 34, 56, 126, 170, 187
Scottish urned cremation burials, study of 33
Sculptor's Cave 54, 55(f)
Seafield West 35, 177, 206–7
Seager Thomas, M. 142
self
  and substance 224–6
  concepts of 5, 62–3, 69, 88, 116, 230
  relational construction of 112
  self-worth, emotional security, and social position, cultivation of 115
Sennen 118
Seram 105
settlement contexts 93
settlement space
  gendering of 143
  use of 117
  values ascribed to helped to define gendered identities 144
settlements
  and status in the Late Bronze Age 155–9
  enclosed, appearance of 236
  Middle and Late Bronze Age 134–41
Severn
  Estuary 180
  Valley 157
shale 16, 70–2, 76, 83, 103, 108, 111, 125, 137–9, 148, 150(f), 152–3, 157–8, 162, 168–70, 198, 225
Shannon, River 183
Shaugh Moor 128, 149
Shepherd 23
Sheridan, Alison 73
shield, -s 10, 92–6, 114
Shinewater 99, 217
Shorncote Quarry 51
Shovel Down 194–5
Shropshire 47–50, 63, 175, 183, 217
Sidbury 52
skeuomorphs in Early Bronze Age burials, deposition of 77
Skilmafilly 206
skull, -s 18(f), 19, 25–9, 33–5, 42, 48, 52–4, 57, 60–1, 67–8, 97(f), 98, 153, 179–80, 184, 214, 220
  badger 118
  cattle 59, 203–4, 205(f), 209, 210, 214
  deposition in the Thames 152
  dog 210
  fox 214
  frequently recovered from rivers, lakes, and bogs 52

305

Index

skull, -s (*cont.*)
  horse 211
  human and animal skulls, deposition of 222
  human, found in peat 52
  human, in midden deposit 51, 116
  human, unburnt 40, 51
  polecat 214
  red-deer 211
smelting, transformative activity of 186
Snail Down 10, 35, 39–40, 41(f), 44, 75, 124, 169
Soar, River 53
social and political allegiances 226
social and political change 115
social and political conditions 199
social and political identities, construction of 62
social and ritual practice 16
social and sacred geography 157
social and spatial boundaries, transgressing 99
social and spatial transformation, processes of 238
social and spatial transition, significant points of 113
social boundaries 227, 231–4
social categories 113, 196
  and cultural values 89
  definition of 65
social change and the end of the Bronze Age 236–9
social cohesion 111
social complexity, increasing 109
social difference and division 117
social distinction 111, 155
social hierarchy 236
social identity 117, 154
  aspects of 65
  transformation of 95
social landscapes 163–223
social relations, symbols of significant 74
social relationships 7, 117, 133
social reproduction, acts of 239
social roles and relationships 133
social status 238
social transactions 104–8, 222
socially sensitive spaces 128
society as increasingly hierarchical 16
Somerset 34, 93, 96–8, 106, 175
South Cadbury 93
South Dorset Ridgeway Project 119
South Dumpton Down 20, 21(f)
South Elmsall 238
South Glamorgan 151

South Hornchurch 52, 53(f), 137, 138(f), 148, 155
South Lodge Camp 148
South Uist 10, 57, 67, 132, 210
Southwark 192
space, gendering of 142–3
spaces, socially sensitive 128
spearheads 14, 53, 92, 95–6, 99, 108, 114, 157–8, 180–4, 199–200, 217, 235–7
special places in the Middle and Late Bronze Age 182–7
Springfield Lyons 155
springs 119, 166, 174, 179, 183–4, 187, 219, 221
St Andrews 108
St Michael's Mount 183
Staffordshire 95
status, marker of 112, 209
status, means of expressing 111
Stirling Way 121
stone
  axe 147, 224
  bracer, -s 16, 75
  burnt stone 121, 146, 151, 178
  cairn 146
  circle, -s 45, 55–6, 186–7
  cist 36
  coloured, use of 169
  cushion stone 83–6
  fossiliferous 90
  monuments 186
  mould, -s 98–9, 141
  objects, production of 225
  renal stones 209
  rubbing stones 115, 128
  standing stone 56
  stone-built structures 118, 126, 131–2, 146
  stone-lined hearth 131
  tools 70, 157
  wristguard 83
Stone Hall 50
Stone Tor 195
Stonehenge 3, 16, 124, 239
Stoneyburn Farm 33
Strath Oykel 206, 209
Striplands Farm 51
structures, orientation of 132
subdivision, processes of 236
substances
  changing concepts of 114
  potent 89
  significant may be considered sources of animacy 89
Suffolk 51, 134, 193
Sumba 105

306

Index

Summergil Brook 175
sun, the
   and metals, links sometimes drawn between 89
   cyclical passage of 230
   properties of 89
sunburst motif 89
sun-discs of the Chalcolithic 89
Surrey 106, 134, 211
Sussex 142, 192
Sussex High Weald 120
Sussex loops 107
Sussex, East 217
Sutherland 128, 131–2
Sutton Veny 27, 28(f), 64
sword moulds, deposits of 155
sword, -s 92–4
   agency of 114
   as 'high-status' object 182
   as votive offerings 92
   damaged 52
   deliberately broken 184
   deliberately destroyed prior to deposition 92
   deposited as isolated finds on hilltops 95
   deposited singly or as components of hoards 52, 70–1, 94, 96
   deposition of 53
   found at fording points on River Shannon 183
   found on seabed 99
   found in cave at Heathery Burn 183–4
   indicate improvement in martial functionality 6
   iron 237
   production of 98, 158, 184
   sword and spear fragments, hoard of 200
   sword blades, splitting of 198
   treated differently to objects such as axes 234

talons, eagle 206–8, 222
Tamlaght hoard 184
Taplow Mills 92
technological activities 229
technologies, new 69, 108
Teme, River 175
Templenoe 47–9
temporality
   change, and loss, conceptions of 112
   concepts of 116
   cyclical concepts of 230
Testwood Lakes 179–80
textiles, manufacture of 104
Thames, River 52, 92, 103, 114, 152
   deposition of fine metalwork and human skulls in 152
   floodplain of the 192
Thames Valley 188, 191
Thomsen, Christian Jürgensen 2
Thornworthy Tor 195
three-age system 2
Thurlestone 183
timber-platform sites 159
Tipperary, County 47–9, 52, 121, 125–8, 131–4, 178, 184
Tober 128, 131, 135
Tomies East 179
Tone, River 107
tools 70, 79, 83–5, 91, 94, 104, 108–14, 125, 132, 139, 154, 157–8, 182–4, 204–7, 213, 229
totems 208
Tower Hill 96
Towthorpe 167
transformations, heat-mediated 101
transformative powers 89
transformative processes 64–5, 114
transformative technologies, understanding of 230
transition, places and moments of 65
travel, ritualized 227
Treen Common 172
Tregarrick Tor 172, 173(f)
Treiorwerth 167
Trelystan 10
Trent, River 95
Trumpington 42, 214
Trundholm chariot, the 219
Tubney Wood 72
Turner, L. 94
Tynings South 34

Uffington white horse, the 218–19, 222
unburnt body in the Chalcolithic and Early Bronze Age, The 17–32
underworld, springs as entrances to 174
Upper Bucklebury 237
Upton Lovell 206, 225
Upton Pyne 165, 166(f)
urned burials 34
Urns, Biconical 121
Urns, Collared 34, 39, 75, 121
Urns, Cordoned 39, 170
Urns, Encrusted 77

Vale of the White Horse 218
value, -s
   cultural 89
   systems of 7

307

Index

Vauxhall 180
vessels, broken 122
votive deposition 54, 184
votive deposits 161, 200, 217, 221
votive offerings 92, 181, 187

Wales 126, 167, 237
Wallingford 103, 151–3
Walton Basin 175
Wareham 147
Warminster 36, 42, 56, 214
Washingborough 98
water
   and cosmological structuring of the landscape 187
   and ritual decommissioning of items 54, 92, 98, 153, 158, 177, 183–4, 221
   as medium of transformation 175
   associated with the underworld 177, 219, 222
   consigning bodies to 54, 98
   for the processing of wool or flax 103
   Metalwork deposited in 177, 183
   Swords deposited in 234
water, travel, and transformation from Early to Late Bronze Age 178–82
Waterhall Farm 27, 169
Watton 43
wealth, means of expressing 111
weapons 6, 91–4, 108, 158, 164, 182–3, 217, 233, 235–6
weaving
   and cloth production 102–5
   as a metaphor for human relationships 105
   evidence for 102
Weir Bank Stud Farm 145
Weird Law 35
wells, deposition of human bone in 98
Wessex 12, 88
West Buckland 106
West Clare Railway 184
West Cliff 43
West Cotton 34
West Heath 35, 39, 168
West Lothian 25
West Sussex 35, 39, 46–9, 168–9, 200
Westcroft Road 211, 212(f)
Western Isles 50, 118, 123
Westhampnett 46–9
Westmeath, County 183
wetlands 54, 92, 99, 158, 190(f), 200
Wexford, County 178
wheel, -s
   earliest known in the British Isles 216
   identified as votive deposits 217
Whitehorse Hill 77, 168
Whitelow Cairn 72
Whitton Hill 49
Wicklow, County 33, 39, 158, 179
Wickstead, H. 198
Wilburton phase 92
Willingdon Levels 99
Wilsford barrow 30, 31(f)
Wiltshire 10, 16, 27, 30, 35–6, 39–44, 52, 56–7, 64, 74–6, 79, 81–3, 89, 104, 111, 120, 124, 151, 170–2, 191–2, 201, 206–7, 211, 214, 217, 225, 237
Witchford 121
Witham, River 98
Woodburn 147
Woodward, Ann 30, 77, 81, 89, 206–8, 225
Worcestershire 103, 109, 146–7
Wrexham 94
Wyke Down 165

Yarnton 30, 214
York, J. 92
Yorkshire 178
Yorkshire coast 168
Yorkshire Wolds 23, 120, 172
Yorkshire, East 19–23, 39, 69, 88, 166–7, 175, 201, 238
Yorkshire, North 50, 165, 170, 184, 204, 207, 209

308

The manufacturer's authorised representative in the EU for product safety is Oxford University Press España S.A. of El Parque Empresarial San Fernando de Henares, Avenida de Castilla, 2 - 28830 Madrid (www.oup.es/en or product.safety@oup.com). OUP España S.A. also acts as importer into Spain of products made by the manufacturer.

Printed and bound by CPI Group (UK) Ltd, Croydon, CR0 4YY